THE CAREER MAKERS

THE
CAREER
MAKERS

*America's Top 150
Executive Recruiters*

Revised and Expanded

JOHN SIBBALD

HarperBusiness
A Division of HarperCollins*Publishers*

HarperCollins books may be purchased for educational, business, or sales promotional use. For information, please call or write: Special Markets Department, HarperCollins Publishers, Inc., 10 East 53rd Street, New York, NY 10022. Telephone: (212) 207-7528; Fax: (212) 207-7222.

FIRST EDITION

Library of Congress Cataloging-in-Publication Data

Sibbald, John (John R.)
    The career makers : America's top 150 executive recruiters / John Sibbald. – Rev. and exp.
        p.   cm.
    Includes index.
    ISBN 0-88730-550-4
    1. Executives—United States—Recruiting—Directories. I. Title.
HD38.25.U6S53   1992
658.4'07111'02573—dc20   91-47692

92 93 94 95 96 PS / HC 10 9 8 7 6 5 4 3 2 1

CONTENTS

Talent, in whatever form or degree,
still begs its diviner and sponsor.
—JOHN SIBBALD

ACKNOWLEDGMENTS

This book might not have been necessary without the culpability of the last two Administrations.

This book would not have been possible without the exceptional cooperation of the heads or principal contacts of 362 retainer-type executive search firms and the chief executive officers or senior personnel executives of almost 800 client organizations of all types. The questionnaires that both groups completed form the core of the project. Thanks are also due the 150 recruiters who were nominated by both clients and peers and who completed the individual survey forms used to rank them among their peers. Every recruiter who qualified as one of North America's 150 most accomplished recruiters is included in this book.

A very special thanks is due those ten top recruiters who were so kind as to contribute "war stories" of their own to the book, specifically, Lynn Tendler Bignell, Otis Bowden, Robert Dingman, Leon Farley, Pendleton James, John Johnson, John Lucht, Barbara Provus, Gerard Roche, and Fred Wackerle. Without their willingness to share some of their recruiting vicissitudes, there would not have been a fun chapter in the book.

There also might not have been the 11 top recruiters identified and profiled from Canada and Mexico without the counsel and suggestions of George Enns and Anne Fawcett, two of Canada's most accomplished recruiters, and Horacio McCoy, a similar recruiting luminary from Mexico. The venerable and irrepressible "conscience of the consultants," James H. Kennedy, publisher of *Executive Recruiter News*, has also made a most important contribution in convincing me to restructure the weighting system used in ranking the top recruiters. Jim Kennedy and I usually view things in the field of executive recruiting in about the same manner that Siskel and Ebert review movies: respectfully but often divergently (on second thought, *usually* divergently).

The Career Makers: America's Top 150 Executive Recruiters owes its title and very existence to Virginia Smith, my executive editor at HarperBusiness. I called her "oh-so-patient" in my writing of the first edition. This second edition has put her in line for sainthood or martyrdom—distinctions I'm sure she would rather defer until a later point in life. May her anxiety levels eventually descend to normal—if that is possible when one has to work with a headhunter author who is also still trying to make a living hunting heads.

INTRODUCTION

The notion of selecting the best professionals in any field of endeavor and then ranking them against each other is audacious by anyone's measure. But that is exactly what the first edition of *The Career Makers: America's Top 100 Executive Recruiters* set out to do in 1990. It may be only fitting, then, that *The Career Makers* made its debut about equidistant in time between the published works of two other imperiled authors: Salman Rushdie and Kitty Kelley.

"BRING ME THE HEAD OF JOHN SIBBALD," trumpeted the headline of *BusinessWeek* in the first review of *The Career Makers*. Other critics were kind enough to stop short of decapitation. Said one recruiter who didn't qualify for the first edition, "Anyone who does not include me in the book is an ass." His chances would have been considerably better if he had returned his own firm's nomination form and had received more than a solitary client or fellow-recruiter recommendation. (Upon reflection, I am particularly offended by his denunciation because I don't believe that even Nancy Reagan called Kitty Kelley an ass— at least publicly.)

Another recruiter—one who actually ranked in the top ten— proclaimed that "this book will mean nothing to my clients." I was further chastised for omitting mention of the highly visible cofounder of the world's largest executive search firm. There was reason for that, too. *The Career Makers* identifies the top *practicing* recruiters—not those who essentially oversee the work of other recruiters. In addition, the celebrated recruiter who was omitted was just then on a leave of absence from his firm, finishing up a stint at the United Nations. What a bloody shame and how untimely. The UN could certainly make use of some bona fide headhunters today, especially in the neighborhood of Iraq.

The flurry of comments from critics did cause me momentarily to contemplate fleeing into exile myself. But at the time there was no room at the inn: Scotland Yard was quite occupied with Mr. Rushdie, and our own Feds had their hands full with Manuel Noriega. Alas, this "brash" book—as one critic called it—would have to make it on its own. The passage of time suggests that it has.

The Career Makers resides today as a much-consulted reference in thousands of corporate offices, is a well-worn directory in most outplacement firms, and has already been a handy guide by which thousands of job seekers have gone about finding employment in very hard times. Their protestations notwithstanding, headhunters themselves snapped up over 3000 copies of the book before it ever reached bookstore shelves. And in many parts of the country throughout the summer of 1990, *The Career Makers* stood in the top ten among nonfiction bestsellers.

So it is against that backdrop of controversy I venture forth audaciously again. This second edition of *The Career Makers* is completely revised, somewhat enlarged (there are now 150 recruiters profiled compared to 100 in the first edition), some formats changed, and several important new features added.

The book remains, however, what it was intended to be from its inception:

- A handy reference for professionals in every line of work who either need a job *now,* or aspire to a better one
- An equally handy guide for employers of all types who spend countless hours and dollars trying to find the right professionals to employ

The heros and heroines of the book are executive recruiters, those shadowy figures whose telephone calls can start the adrenaline flowing in anyone who toils in the workplace. But as virtually everyone knows, most recruiters shun the limelight. *The Career Makers* thrusts the very best of them into a most unaccustomed—and perhaps to some, uncomfortable—position of personal visibility. For what comfort it may bring to those who find their new prominence unnerving, there is the old Chinese proverb: "Better to be celebrated victim than unseen in Peking."

Being unseen is standard visibility for executive recruiters, who also answer to a variety of other titles: search consultants, searchers, and headhunters—a name they used to cower at but increasingly accept. But whatever they are called, they all stand for the same thing. For the job seeker lucky enough to be known by them, these are the true Good Samaritans of the job market. They can grease the skids to the perfect job for you now. But, alas, they are an elusive group and terribly whimsical. When they want you, you may not want them; and when you need them most, they are nowhere to be found.

Even in recessionary times, executive recruiters are the keepers of the key to many of North America's best opportunities in every field of endeavor. Because of the significance of the top management positions they fill, the business press increasingly labels them as "kingmakers." Yet you will find recruiters filling, by many thousands, more positions in the middle management ranks. That's why the title for this book, *The Career Makers,* seems so apt—because in the final analysis that's really what they do. Very few of us will emerge in top management, but in one form or another we all have careers.

In the minds of most of us, executive recruiters do their work in the corporate jungle. And most of it is done there. They're the people we spot behind the potted palm in the Union League Club, sleuthing out the next chairman of Intercosmic Express or the Vice President—Technology for Real Water Ltd. Yet there is a large and growing number of recruiters who have an eye especially calibrated only for university presidents, hospital administrators, school superintendents, physicians, lawyers, association executives, municipal and government officials, and many other non-business-sector types. In fact, the headhunter lurking behind that potted palm in the Union League Club just might be sizing up the club manager and not assessing a giant of industry.

Although executive recruiters may be directly engaged with only about one-fourth of all managerial and executive hiring done today, the positions they are asked to fill represent a disproportionate number of the highest-paying and most prestigious jobs in the United States and abroad. Thus, for an executive in any line of work, or the manager who aspires to the executive level, and for every young professional on the way up, it is prudent to know one or more executive recruiters, *especially those recruiters who specialize in searches in one's particular line of work.*

The latter point is worth special emphasis. Although the business press may highlight the chief executive officer placements of such New York-based heavy hitters as Gerry Roche of Heidrick & Struggles and Tom Neff of SpencerStuart, most top management searches represent only the tip of the executive recruiting iceberg. The 90 percent that is below the surface is where the bulk of the search work goes on in the executive employment marketplace. It is this vastly larger part of the job market that makes it *imperative* for job-seeking professionals to identify and cultivate those specific individual recruiters who concentrate their recruiting activities in fields of mutual interest. *The Career Makers* is the only guide that can help you do that.

Up to now, we've been speaking about the value of knowing a search consultant from the employee's or job seeker's aspect. It is every bit as important for employers to know individual recruiters—the right recruiter for the specific need they're out to fill. Sometimes the choice is easy because the organization has used the recruiter for a similar successful search in the past. But what if that search did not go well? Or what if the job to be filled is a new one or in a field where the recruiter customarily used has never worked? Although many of the most accomplished headhunters profess to be generalists able to recruit for any position in any field, the truth is that virtually all of them have certain functional areas, industries, or professions in which they are considerably more proficient and up-to-date. An employer who ignores this modern fact of executive recruiting is, in effect, entrusting a general medical practitioner to perform a lobotomy.

So where does the savvy employer turn to locate the best individual executive recruiter in America to help fill the highly specialized and supercritical job that can make or break the entire organization? For starters, the employer can make some phone calls to friends. (But is it safe to let others know about how crucial this need is, or to reveal that the employer is planning to replace the incumbent in the job?) Fortunately, there are a number of reference guides to executive search firms. One in particular stands out as the most timely, comprehensive, and trustworthy year after year: *The Directory of Executive Recruiters* (Kennedy & Kennedy, Templeton Road, Fitzwilliam, NH 03447) contains listings of almost all executive search firms, and it also cross-indexes the firms by areas of particular expertise and geographic location.

Useful as this guide is, however, it provides no way to pinpoint those few individual recruiters best equipped to handle the employer's all-important search. Thus, the process of finding the most effective recruiter to help the employer fill a specific need comes down to the time-consuming and risky process of calling each of the search firms listed under the directory heading of particular interest and trusting those called to be candid about their expertise in recruiting in a particular field. I do not intend to impugn the integrity of any executive search firm, but I have found that the margin of distortion in firms' statements of apparent qualifications or preeminence can range from complete truth to downright fiction.

Complicating the situation further for both the professional seeking a new opportunity and the employer scouring the universe for an employee who walks on water is this cruel fact: there are recruiters and there are recruiters. This is not a book about those who hunt heads for a bounty. Recruiters who work on a contingency basis are paid when and if they are successful in bagging the right body for the right job opening. Such recruiters serve a worthwhile purpose in satisfying many organizations' recruitment needs, but they are most effective in filling lower-level jobs.

Those headhunters who are not contingency recruiters are called *retained recruiters* and belong to retainer-type executive scarch firms. The most ethical of these firms do not do any search work on a contingency basis—even in the grip of the recession we hope we're now recovering from. Retainer firms pride themselves on standards of ethical conduct and performance that they believe reflect well on the caliber of clients they serve and the candidates they place. They get paid whether they're successful in the search or not, with the first one-third of their ultimate fee usually coming as their retainer at the time they start the search.

The Career Makers: America's Top 150 Executive Recruiters is a book about a very select few of the 10,000 (some say double that) men and women employed with retainer-type executive search firms. This is not a book about the search firms themselves because in my 22 years in the search business, both as partner in the large consulting organization of Booz, Allen & Hamilton and in the firm I now run, I've never known a recruiting organization to make a placement. Individual recruiters, not recruiting firms, make placements.

The first edition of this book broke new ground and spotlighted for the first time the individual recruiters most worth knowing; the most effective and reputable recruiters in the United States. The industry's crème de la crème were identified, categorized by area of competence, and profiled so that professionals looking for work or advancement, and employers searching for just the right headhunter, had a precise way to reach them.

This new edition progresses several steps further. The original roster of 100 recruiters who were individually profiled has grown to 150. And they are no longer only those from the United States. Eleven of the most talented recruiters from Canada and Mexico have been identified for the first time and profiled so that job seekers and employers can find the very best headhunters in these increasingly important countries.

The Career Makers you are reading has one other new dimension. For the first time anywhere, America's most accomplished companies in the *science of developing management talent* have been identified, categorized, and ranked. We have called these "academy companies" because over the passage of many years, they have established themselves as particularly adept at producing stand-out alumni—not unlike some of our premier undergraduate and graduate schools. So why would one find such information in a book about executive recruiters? The answer is a simple one: these special companies are career makers in their own rights.

Experience has shown that time spent in an academy company can be a catapult in one's own career development and advancement. All job seekers, recent graduates included, stand to benefit from knowing which are the academy companies in their own fields of interest. Employers of all types have a selfish interest in knowing which of their competitors have done the best job of developing management talent. And, of course, headhunters who make their living by knowing the right employers to probe for candidates, and who consequently represent the best possible sources of academy company information, need to know. Indeed, one might aptly call academy companies the headhunters' personal trout pools.

The book is divided into two parts for ease in use. Part I, "Working with the Top Executive Recruiters," contains four chapters. The first of these describes how the Top 150 recruiters were selected and lists the characteristics they share. It also discusses how the academy companies were identified and ranked. Chapter 2 is intended primarily for job seekers and those who contemplate changing employers or careers at some time in the future. Employing organizations of all types will find Chapter 3 helpful to them in pointing out how to work most effectively with executive recruiters. Chapter 4 is for your easy reading pleasure. Yet there are important messages for job seekers and employers alike in the real-life war stories in this chapter, each one contributed from the diary of one of America's top headhunters.

In Part II of this book, the most accomplished 1 percent of all of North America's executive recruiters are individually profiled (perhaps a better term is "exposed"). For once, the headhunters have had the tables turned on them. The phantoms of the employment world have stepped out of their closets for the first time—and even shown their faces.

Part II also contains the important chapter entitled "Areas of Recruiter Specialization." This chapter ranks the recruiters who qualified for this book in the order of their expertise as seen through the eyes of clients and fellow recruiters alike. Chapter 7 identifies and ranks the academy companies of the United States, by both industry and function.

There are also some things this book is not intended to be. An employer will not find information here on how to negotiate a compensation package or conduct the ultimate interview. Likewise, an individual will not discover how to compose the perfect resume or launch the most successful job search in history. Bookshelves are sagging with these types of guides now. Astute users of this book—whether they are job seekers or employers— will find that their days of shotgunning the marketplace in search of the right recruiters to help them have ended. Now, too, executive recruiters themselves have the first market-developed guide to the best-stocked trout pools in America in which to cast for candidates. *The Career Makers: America's Top 150 Executive Recruiters* gives its readers—be they job seekers, employers, or headhunters—the chance to use the accuracy of a rifle to take clear aim at their respective targets for the very first time.

THE CAREER MAKERS

PART I

WORKING WITH THE TOP
EXECUTIVE RECRUITERS

1

THE TOP 150 RECRUITERS: THEIR SELECTION AND CHARACTERISTICS

Your Monday morning did not start out well at all. When you arose at 5:30 A.M. in Glencoe, the thermometer read −12 degrees. In the children's room Rachel was coughing even worse than she had all night. She would have to stay home from school, and you'd have to call Mrs. Nawrocki to see if she could take Rachel for the day.

You have a major client presentation to make today at the agency, so you've already picked out the right outfit to wear. Then it's a fast cup of coffee, your boots and coat on, Rachel bundled up, and out to start the car. Fortunately, after those prayerful moments of nothing but grinding, the engine turns over. You get Rachel over to Mrs. Nawrocki's and arrive in the parking lot just in time to make your 7:00 A.M. train into Chicago. The partners' meeting is always at 9:00 A.M. sharp on Monday morning. It's a command performance.

You've barely settled into your seat with the newspaper when the train grinds to a halt. Twenty minutes later the conductor finally comes through your car to announce that a switch down the line is frozen. You sit and fume.

Two hours later, you rush into your offices on the eighty-third floor of the Sears Tower. The receptionist's "good morning, Amanda" sounds sarcastic to you. Your secretary's first words to you are "Amanda, where have you been? The partners' meeting is already over." You utter something profane barely under your breath and plop yourself, coat, boots, and all, into your chair.

Just then your secretary buzzes you. "There's a call on. He says it's personal and important, but he won't give me his name."

Oh God, you think, is it Rachel? You snatch up the receiver.

"Top o' the mornin' to you, and it's a crisp one, isn't it?" pipes a voice you've never heard before. "Is it Agatha, Samantha, or Amanda?" he asks but does not wait for an answer. "My source wasn't sure of your first name, but aren't you the account exec on the Deep Fried Pizza account? My client has really been impressed with what you've done with that line." By this time you've sensed where the call is coming from. It's not the emergency room at Evanston Hospital but somewhere along the corridors of the United concourse at O'Hare airport.

You muster all the civility you can and say, "Mister, I don't know who you are, but why are you bothering me?"

"Because *we* want you! Just call me Seeker Swift—the world's fastest headhunter. In fact, I just got this search this weekend on the ninth hole at Medinah Golf Club. My client is the top dog at Fudd's Frosted Bagels. He needs a new VP—Marketing; the last one didn't know bread dough from granola. You've got to. It's a big, big job, Samantha, one that's got a real future. My client is going to take Fudd's public. He'll need a successor because he just bought himself an 87-footer and he wants to sail the Caribbean. The dollars are right, too. Trust me."

You finally cut in. "Look, Mr. Swift, or whatever your name is, you're not as swift as you think. You've got the wrong account exec at the wrong agency. I think you want Chanda Wall over at J. Walter Katz. Good luck and goodbye." Click.

Now that was a headhunter. A *schlock headhunter*. Fortunately, not the headhunters this book is all about. There are thousands of headhunters very different from Seeker Swift. With few exceptions, these individuals conduct themselves professionally, discreetly, and in a manner fully appreciative of the unique trust their candidates and clients invest in them. They are trained in the business, belong to respected recruiting firms of all sizes and types, and subscribe to acceptable industry practices and ethics. These recruiters might be with either contingency types of recruiting organizations or retainer firms. However, this book is concerned only with recruiters with the latter. Among the thousands of retainer recruiters are a few especially talented individuals who stand apart from their colleagues in the minds of both their fellow headhunters and clients. The pages that follow are about them.

For individuals to be selected as among the 150 best search consultants in North America is a high honor. It means that he or she stands in the top 1 percent of all his or her recruiting peers. This recognition is especially noteworthy in a personal services business seemingly unable to establish for itself any type of individual certification of competency.

In the absence of any industry certification of recruiter proficiency, it was difficult to decide how to begin to identify the Top 150. Executive recruiters' skills are on display to only three groups: the clients they serve, their peers in the business, and the candidates with whom they deal. This third group was rejected as a survey category because of the transitory nature of candidate contacts with recruiters, their consequential lack of perspective or objectivity, and the logistical difficulties of locating them to solicit their responses. Accordingly, the focus of the selection process was on surveying clients and peers of recruiters, both competitors and those employed in the same search firms. The career makers featured in this book have been identified by what the marketplace thinks of them and not by the arbitrary and subjective judgments of a few self-styled industry experts and the largest search firms' public relations agencies.

Because the book was intended from its inception to be of value to the widest possible range of professionals—not just those in business—questionnaires were sent to the chief executive officers, or their equivalents, of America's:

- 1000 largest public corporations, from the *Fortune 500* lists of industrial and service companies
- 500 largest privately held companies from *Forbes* magazine and the *Macmillan Directory of Leading Private Companies*
- 97 prominent venture capital firms
- 150 largest hospitals and health care providers
- 200 leading public and private colleges and universities
- 130 largest professional societies and trade associations
- 125 major hospitality organizations, including hotel and restaurant chains, private clubs, and resorts

- 12 governmental and quasi-governmental agencies known to have used search firms

These chief executives (or more immediately involved senior officers) were asked, "In your own opinion, who are the most effective *individual recruiters* (by name and firm) who have served your organization in the last several years?" The respondents were asked to list no more than five recruiters and not necessarily in order of preference. The list of recruiter nominees was further refined by this question: "If you were personally responsible—*to such an extent that your own job was on the line*—for recruiting the next chief executive officer of your organization, to which *individual recruiter* would you entrust that search?"

To balance the employer or client side of the picture, a similar inquiry was made to key contacts or managing principals at 412 retainer executive search firms based in the United States, Canada, and Mexico. For firms with more than one office or key contact, the mailing was made to the principal headquarters listed. One question asked of these recruiters was, "In your opinion, who are the most effective *individual recruiters* within your *entire organization* (including those in other offices), working with North American-based clients, who actually handle client searches directly—not those who act as managers or overseers of more junior consultants who actually do the majority of the work?"

As with the clients, the heads of the search firms were requested to limit their nominees to no more than six from their own organizations. Again, in order to establish the most capable individual of those they listed, the addressees were asked, "If the entire reputation and future of your firm rested on the success of one exceptionally significant search, to which of those you nominated would you entrust that search?" The last question asked of the recruiter group was to provide the names of up to six of the most effective headhunters from executive search firms *other than their own*. Survey forms came back from 362 of the 412 search firms queried, an outstanding response rate of approximately 88 percent.

The combined survey responses from both client organizations and executive search firms resulted in a total of 877 individual executive recruiters who received at least one nomination for excellence. All of those individuals were then invited to submit the names and addresses of six client executives they had recently served. This new dimension to the nomination process was added to provide fair consideration for those recruiters who work at levels below chief executive officers, with small companies and subsidiaries, in Canada or Mexico, or in such seldom-surveyed fields as venture capital. A letter with nominating questionnaire was sent to each client listed by that recruiter—*but without any indication of the recruiter who had submitted their name.* (A fair number of the recruiters would have been dismayed to discover that the clients they thought would nominate them did not.)

Adding this new feature to the client nomination part of the survey resulted in an overall client response of 35 percent, a statistically significant response rate.

The Weighting System Used to Select and Rank Nominees

Recruiter nominations have been valued somewhat differently in this edition than in its predecessor. The cogent observations of Jim Kennedy, publisher of *Executive Recruiter News,* have persuaded me to reverse the value of points awarded for competitor nominations and those from one's own firm. Accordingly, a nomination from a competitive search firm has been awarded three points—in contrast to one point in the first edition. The value of a nomination from one's own firm has been reduced from five points to two, although to be judged as the very best recruiter in one's own firm is worth an additional point. Nominations from clients are worth two points each, with an additional two points being awarded if the client considered the recruiter to be the very best of those listed.

There will likely be those who quibble with this weighting formula and the point allocations, or even with the selection of executives with client organizations to whom the original questionnaires were sent. Nevertheless, we could find no other system that was as fair and objective for recruiters with both large and small search firms and for those who specialize or work at levels lower than top management.

The profiles of the Top 150 are arranged in the book alphabetically, just as in the first edition. However, a significant change

has been made in the chapter titled "Areas of Recruiter Specialization." As in the first edition, the recruiters are ranked on
a frequency-of-mention basis—but this time *no more than the top
10 in each category are ranked.* All others who ranked among the
top 40 in that category are listed in alphabetical order. There
is one important exception. In the highly significant functional
area of General Management, the top 20 recruiters are ranked,
with the following 80 most highly rated headhunters listed
alphabetically.

To create the areas of recruiter specialization, each of the
Top 150 recruiters was asked to select up to ten *functional* areas
of recruiting competence and up to ten *organizational* specialties.
Choices were listed in descending order of the recruiter's own
preference and experience.

A weighting formula was also applied in arriving at the actual
rankings of recruiters within each category. Although a few of
the old guard may differ with me, it is my conviction that no
recruiter can be equally competent in every choice of functional
or organizational expertise. Thus a sequential reduction of 10
percent of the recruiter's total nomination points was made for
each selection below a first choice. As an example, recruiters who
accumulated an overall point total of 85 received full value for
their first choice in both the functional area and organizational
preferences. But their point totals—and thus their place in the
rankings—for their fifth choices would be 51, a reduction of 40
percent of their point total. Their tenth-place choices, if they
selected that many, would give them a point total of 10 percent
of their overall total, or 8.5 points.

Search consultants who work almost exclusively in specific
fields such as health care, hospitality, and legal are ranked only
in the organizational categories in which they concentrate. Their
choices of functional competencies, however, are treated in the
same way as the choices of those who do not specialize. With this
in mind, the user of this book should consult the rankings of
both functional preferences *and* organizational specialization in
selecting recruiters to contact. Failure to cross-reference by either
an employer or individual seeking a general manager's position
in industry could result in the mutually wasteful consideration of
approaching a recruiter who is experienced only in health care
searches—simply because the health care recruiter ranked rela-

tively high in the functional area of general management, yet does no recruiting at all in industry.

The top recruiters from Canada and Mexico are listed separately on page 395 and are ranked only on a total nominations basis. They are not included in the specialization rankings in this first edition including them. It is worth noting that many of these highly accomplished recruiters work on assignments for U.S. clients as well as those in their respective countries.

Characteristics of the Top 150

The Top 150 are as diverse a group of individuals as the candidates they seek out for their clients. Who, for instance, can visualize a top headhunter, stuffy as they are perceived to be, playing tuba in a dixieland band? Or collecting Don Quixote memorabilia and toy trains? Saltwater bird carving is the special interest of another. Then there is the real-life counterpart of Indiana Jones in pursuit of Mexican archaeology, if not the lost ark.

Geographically, North America's top headhunters hail from all over the United States—and 11 now call Canada and Mexico home. Most have found their professional bases in major cities. As one might expect, the New York metropolitan area is the home office for the greatest number (51), with Chicago living up to its reputation as second city. California has 24 of the best but the rest of the West, the Mountain and Plains states, and the Middle Atlantic region have sparse representation.

Of the 100 who qualified and were profiled in the first edition of *The Career Makers,* 79 are repeaters in this edition. Of those who stood in the top ten in that edition in the highly significant functional area of General Management, six made this especially select group again. Robert Lamalie, who came in third in the original book, now has fully retired.

The Top 150 are also well seasoned. There are none of the young hotshots Wall Street and the investment community brag about—or at least used to. The average age of North America's most accomplished recruiters is an AARP-qualifying 54. The youngest is 39, as of this writing, and the oldest is 80. Perhaps even more impressive is that the group averages nearly 21 years each of executive recruiting experience. It clearly takes many years to build up the relationships, credibility, and reputation to make it into the top 1 percent. Once there, though, few step down at 65. With apologies to Douglas MacArthur, it might be said that old headhunters never die; they just dial away.

Discussions over the years among the recruiters themselves have often focused on what type of work background is most likely to lead to success in the search business. Many have claimed that a strong grounding in the personnel, or human resources, function is preferable and gives a search consultant with that heritage a considerable advantage. A review of the backgrounds of the Top 150 shows that over 40 percent of the top recruiters do come from personnel, but the majority have their work backgrounds in other functions. General management is the functional career path of one in five, the same ratio for those with marketing and sales backgrounds. Nineteen grew up in the financial function.

The Top 150 are perhaps most distinctively different from their colleagues in such other personal services vocations as medicine, teaching, law, public accounting, banking, the ministry, and the like, in that none of them probably ever visualized a career for themselves in executive recruiting before they got into it. If serendipity was how they found their way into the career they are now so good at, not one that I have talked with would ever think of leaving it.

As noted in the original *Career Makers,* the survey reveals that with the exception of a few search consultants who concentrate their work in a single area of specialization, *no one of the Top 150 who recruit essentially in industry enjoys anything close to preeminence in the minds of those who engage recruiters in client organizations.*

Yet there are, of course, those who stand out even among the crème de la crème. Gerry Roche of Heidrick & Struggles leads in 8 categories and has retained his position as North America's most accomplished recruiter of top management. Tom Neff of SpencerStuart, a rapidly closing-in number two, personally leads 6 categories, and is tied with Roche in ranking in the top 10 in 11 categories. Yet it is worth noting that both of these sure-fire inductees into a future Headhunters' Hall of Fame (Tombstone, Arizona, would make a most apt spot for the Hall, especially adjacent to the OK Corral) achieved their high standings with a relatively small number of client nominations. What propelled them, and most others in the top 20 in the General Management category, to the top were the abundant nominations they received from competitors.

Although growth continues for large firms, many with their own international arms or affiliates, executive recruiting is still a business of individuals. Recruiters may band together in large, medium-sized, and small firms, but what counts most is how well they perform as individuals. Both clients and the recruiters themselves strongly agree on this point. Almost 99 percent of all client organizations surveyed said that it was the individual recruiter, not the recruiter's firm, that made the difference in whom they selected to serve them. And 98 percent of the recruiters agreed. This response underscores the need for growing specialization on the part of individual recruiters, if not firms themselves. Most executive search firms are already acknowledging this development.

North America's executive recruiters have been very hard hit by the recession, which still lingers in the white collar employment area. Some have gone out of business entirely, and others have reached out for mergers and affiliations both in the United States and abroad. Firms of all sizes have embarked on diversification efforts yet to be demonstrated as compatible with their expertise and nature. Compounding these difficulties further is the fact that almost 70 percent of the clients who responded to the survey reported that they consider search firm fees in general to be too high for the service rendered—a percentage increase of some 20 points compared to the same question asked in 1989.

Notwithstanding the current hard times, the business of executive recruiting will survive and even prosper beyond its healthy heritage. Just over the horizon is the greatest boon of all for the headhunters of North America. Manpower forecasts from numerous sources project a skilled labor shortage the likes of which North America has never witnessed. But the needs of our society will be for increasingly specialized employee skills, so recruiters themselves must be prepared to meet and adapt to a more refined and sophisticated marketplace. Market niches will be as sought after among the headhunters as they are today by health and beauty aids marketers. The jack-of-all-trades recruiter, politely known in the past as a "generalist," will follow the old-time medicine man into professional obsolescence.

Academy Companies: The Other Career Makers

Just as the top executive recruiters are career makers for working professionals worldwide, so, too, are companies—the ones with the right stuff, that is. With very few exceptions, every industry and every organizational function has a small cadre of employers that over the years have developed a particular knack or expertise in developing talented performers. These companies have earned reputations of being the top boot camps for aspiring professionals in everything from aerospace to packaged goods marketing. They have a leg up on even the best graduate business schools. No case studies here, no ivory tower theorists—this is the real world. These are what we call the academy companies.

There have been books published in the past about the best companies to work for, those that offer the best employee benefits, working conditions, promotion policies, location, and other nice-to-have goodies. Academy companies, on the other hand, are usually not *nice* companies to work for. They have a mission, and working for them is more like serving in the Marine Corps than just keeping your nose clean and retiring with security from a public utility. They heap on responsibility early, and when they find someone who can handle it they just keep pouring it on.

The Career Makers represents the first time that America's academy companies have been systematically identified and ranked according to their organizational and functional areas of management development prowess. To accomplish this task, what better panel of experts exists than the subjects of this book? Decade after decade, headhunters have made their livings and created the $4 billion a year business they preside over by probing the right corporate corridors and consuming all the press and gossip they can about talent.

Thus, for every experienced professional who aspires to a better job and for every recent graduate who has the brass ring in his or her eye, it pays big dividends to gain employment with an academy company. *Academy companies multiply your visibility to the outside world and its opportunities even as they create and sharpen your occupational skills.* Academy companies are where competitive companies turn when they are out to recruit their own new superstars. Academy companies are where every astute headhunter starts a search. And as a logical consequence of these factors, academy companies usually pay a better-than-competitive dollar to retain their high achievers.

Work hard to work for an academy company—the earlier in your career, the better. But it's essential that you choose the right academy company for your particular field of interest. If your chosen field is corporate finance, buy a Ford now. If it's the transportation industry that you're interested in, fly as fast as you can to American Airlines. But be alert. If you're interested in health care marketing, Merck stands as number one among all drug *industry* employers but can't hold a Bunsen burner to Baxter International when it comes to the *functional* area of health care marketing. To maximize your opportunities to develop your management skills and to reap your ultimate rewards, you have to be employed with the right functional *and* industry leader.

For the list and rankings of the academy companies found in Chapter 7, every executive recruiter who was nominated for this book was asked to select four areas of his or her own recruiting specialization. Two of the areas were to be functional specialties and the other two industry or organizational competencies. The recruiters were then requested to select and rank the three employers in each area that in their experience had been the most fertile organizations for finding talent in that particular specialty. The total points and rankings that appear in Chapter 7 were derived from 356 recruiter responses, with three points awarded for a first-place nomination, two for a second, and one for a third.

Will the recruiters like where they stand in this second edition of *The Career Makers*? Probably about as much as they liked where they stood—or did not stand—in the first edition. From my years as an executive recruiter, I am comforted by the awareness that even those recruiter colleagues of mine whose feelings are wounded in one way or another are still blessed with egos sufficient to sustain them until the next edition of this audacious volume, should there ever be one.

And how will the academy companies like being singled out and ranked? Who knows? But the chances are good that, as with the recruiters two years ago, there will be a tiny tempest or two. All I can say for sure is that like the rest of the headhunters in this book—and for every professional who yearns to get approached by one—we pray that these particularly fecund companies never get around to disconnecting their telephones.

2

GAINING THE HELP OF THE RIGHT RECRUITERS

Sally Skimfast has the worst job in an executive search firm. She has to review the 50 to 200 unsolicited resumés from managerial and executive job seekers that pour in every morning to the offices of Clouseau & Cousteau Associates, a small but up-and-coming executive search firm. To the considerable surprise of the headhunter fraternity, one of CCA's recruiters actually qualified for *The Career Makers*. (Frankly, it was a bit of an embarrassment in CCA itself because neither of the celebrated founders of the firm made the book. But then they have already gained their fortunes and fame.)

Today it is the same old story for Sally. Resumé after resumé comes addressed to one of the firm's founders, and with slight variation all 101 cover letters start like this:

Dear Mr. Clouseau:

Enclosed for your review and consideration against your firm's current roster of executive search assignments is my resume reflecting 25 years of progressively more responsible assignments and accomplishments with three of America's most respected beauty aid companies. As you will note, I have risen through a wide range of consumer marketing positions to where I most recently have been responsible for a division with sales of $200 million.

The cover letter, of course, goes on for several more paragraphs but by this time sore-eyed Sally has either dumped it into her wastebasket or doomed it for life to the "miscellaneous write-in" file. If the sender had done even minimal research he or she would have discovered that Clouseau & Cousteau do virtually no work in the health and beauty aids field or in consumer marketing. Ninety-nine other resumes, all products of the same nonselective mailing lists, are pitched soon after into oblivion. What a waste!

But voilà! What's this?

Dear Mr. Verne:

I'm taking the liberty of writing you because I need your help and you may need mine. I've recently read about you in a book about North America's top executive recruiters. My research from the book tells me that while your firm, Clouseau & Cousteau works in several fields, you personally specialize in searches in extraterrestrial investigation, especially the waterworld. That's my thing too. I'm presently the Chief Bullion Cleaner for Galleons Discovered, and I'm looking for a more challenging position.

Sally Skimfast can hardly move fast enough to get this letter to Jules Verne, IV. She may not know for sure whether Recruiter Verne has quite the right opportunity for the job seeker but she does know he will want to review this resume very carefully.

Only that one resume out of the entire batch received by CCA that day was on target. It was directed to the *right individual recruiter* –the one who specializes in filling positions in the job seeker's precise area of interest. Executive recruiting has been around since 1926, over 65 years. Yet only a small fraction of job seekers have yet learned that it is totally ineffective as well as personally discouraging to shotgun their resumes to long, indiscriminating lists of recruiters and recruiting firms. This is as sensible as believing that any lawyer can handle any legal issue, that all physicians can treat all ailments, and that every preacher serves every faith.

So, you ask, how does one go about getting one's resume into the hands of the right recruiters? That's precisely why *The Career Makers* was written. This is the first reference that identifies not only who the top recruiters are in North America but the industries and functions in which they specialize. Then it tells you how to maximize your opportunities to interest them in you and how to cultivate them as career-long collaborators in your own career progress.

Many of you are reading this book because you have recently embarked on an active job search. In too many instances you've been forced into the job market because you've become one more no-fault victim of the tidal wave of restructurings, megamergers, cutbacks, consolidations, closings, and call it anything else you wish, that are the aftershocks of the trickle-down theory of economics. In short, you've been dumped on.

Perhaps you've been wise or fortunate in the past in having developed some kind of work relationship with a headhunter, or, better yet, several of them. If you have, you've got a leg up on your search. There is great truth to the old maxim that the best time to start looking for a job is *before* you have to. This includes the development of some prior positive contacts with headhunters. The more the merrier, and the earlier in your career you can do this, the better.

Once your earnings are at the $50,000-a-year level, you've stepped into the hunting grounds of North America's retained recruiters: the women and men this book is all about. In your job search, anywhere from one in five to one in three of your new opportunities will involve an executive recruiter. If you are looking for a position in the $125,000 level and above, you can increase that to something like one in two. At some very senior levels, and for certain jobs where committees are the selection bodies, a top recruiter will be a party in almost every situation. Accordingly, you cannot afford to take on a proper job search without tapping into the unique resource that executive recruiters comprise.

Initiating a Relationship with the Right Recruiters

Except for those fortunate few who are approached regularly by the *right* headhunters, most of us have to be the initiators of the relationships we establish with recruiters—and that is what it is, a relationship. To think that any recruiter is going to jump through hoops for you just because you believe that your resume paints the picture of an exceptional talent is naive. Not only do search consultants get many resumes every day "over the transom," but most of these resumes never are seen by the recruiters they're addressed to. Search firms, except for the smallest, have research departments, and these unsolicited resumes are first screened by researchers like Sally Skimfast. Only if a background appears to meet the specific needs of a current search is the resume passed along to the recruiter handling that search. Without getting your resume to precisely the right recruiters, the chances of your unsolicited resume fitting an ongoing search, even in one of the largest search firms, is probably less than one in a hundred. The odds are worse in smaller firms.

Some recruiters never consider an unsolicited resume. They always generate their own candidates, or so they say. Consider this type of headhunter to be about as smart as the prospector panning for gold who throws away the nugget that gets wedged between his toes because he didn't find it in the bottom of his pan. Don't be discouraged by such claims. The recruiters good enough to be listed in this book are savvy enough to accept any favor, including those that come unexpectedly over the transom.

Even directing your resume to the right recruiters is no guarantee of success in initiating that all-important relationship. There are some ways to dramatically improve your chances, however. It comes down to basic marketing. If you think of yourself as a new product—a very good new product—that you're launching, then your resume represents that new product. Your resume reflects what your product is made of, what it has been able to do in the past, and what its potential is for the future.

But an appealing new product by itself is not enough in today's job market. Your consumer—in this case a headhunter—must want to pick your new product off a shelf that's already glutted with both old and other new products. What your new product needs is what we call a "handle"—a special attractor that positions your new product (consider it packaging) and causes your consumer to reach out and select it from all the others on the shelf. The handle we're talking about is best presented in the cover letter that accompanies your resume. The cover letter should not take up more than three to five paragraphs and never exceed a page in length. But most important is what the cover letter says and to whom.

Virtually all resumes that reach our top recruiters are accompanied by cover letters. Yet as we've seen at the beginning of this chapter, not one cover letter in a hundred contains an effective handle. This deficiency is even more pronounced with the standardized cover letters (to say nothing about resumes) pouring out of guide books on how to write "the perfect" resume and spilling from the boiler-plate files of the less reputable outplacement firms. *Finding the handle that makes your resume stand out to the right executive recruiters is the single most important objective for smart job seekers today.*

This book gives you more opportunities for coming up with handles that sell than have ever been available before. You should start your search for these handles by first identifying the recruiters who will be the targets of your new product marketing effort. Let's say that your background and future interests happen to be in the high-tech, electronics, and office machinery industries. A quick turn to Chapter 6, Areas of Recruiter Specialization, and the subheading of Organizational or Industry Specialization will give you a list of those individual search consultants most heavily involved in these industries.

Your interests then should be further refined to include your functional areas of competence. Let's say that they are in general management and industrial marketing. Under the other sub-heading in Chapter 6, Functional Specialization, you can find recruiters with significant recruiting experience and clients in these two functional areas. Look for the overlap of those who have proficiency in both the *organization and industry* areas of interest and the *functional* areas you prefer. It should make no difference to you whether the recruiters you select are in the top ten or twenty, or ranked alphabetically. The list of recruiters you generate from this cross-referencing will become your own personal target list of executive recruiters.

The recruiters listed in your organization and industry selection should always take precedence over those listed under your functional specialty. The optimum choices are those recruiters you find listed in both the organization list *and* the functional list. The higher they stand on both lists, the higher on your target list they should rank. As you can expect, the more specialized and esoteric your interests, the fewer the number of headhunters who will appear on your target list. Opening up your criteria somewhat will give you a larger number of headhunters to contact. For example, the merchandising manager interested in making a radical career switch into television broadcasting should include recruiters with strengths in the functional area of advertising/promotion, in addition to recruiters listed with organization and industry specialties of communications and radio/television broadcasting.

Armed now with your target list of names of recruiters, it's time to get personal. Chapter 5 contains the profiles in alphabetical order of North America's 150 top recruiters. As will be shown, there are many opportunities to find handles for those with profiles. Incidentally, do not concern yourself too much with where the recruiters in this book are based. Virtually all serve clients throughout North America, and, in some instances, they serve international clients as well.

Study the profiles of the recruiters from the Top 150 who make your list. In addition to the obvious handle you already have—that they recruit in your areas of functional and organizational interest—there are many other opportunities to find additional handles on which to capitalize. Your goal is to find as many common threads of interest, contacts, or coattails as you can.

The possibilities are limited only by one's resourcefulness and luck. I remember when one of America's largest search firms would interview almost anybody who graduated from Yale. (And not coincidentally, many of their original staff hailed from that esteemed Ivy League institution.) Another senior recruiter was an avid supporter of Ducks Unlimited. He was never blind (pardon the pun) to meeting with those who shared his waterfowl hunting interest. The old school tie has great appeal for many recruiters, as does the locale where they grew up. If you can establish a link to either and communicate that effectively, your chances of meeting that headhunter face-to-face soar. Belonging to the same private club or association, or knowing someone influential who does, can also increase your chances appreciably.

Each of the top recruiters has been asked to describe *in their own words* what they look for in a candidate. The adroit professional who picks up on what a recruiter says about candidates who have "the right stuff" and draws a convincing parallel, or offers a sharp rebuttal, may well be rewarded with some form of dialogue with that recruiter. Headhunters, even busy ones, are natural philosophers and generalizers. They enjoy stimulating communication.

There are two other major areas of opportunity for finding a handle in each profile. The first of these is in the recruiter's employment history. Perhaps you were toiling in the textile stretch department of Jockey International at the same time your target recruiter was over in marketing warming up Jim Palmer for his classic underwear ads. Reference to a former employer held in common works even better when you were higher up in the organization than the recruiter—unless, of course, you were part of the reason the recruiter left, in which case it may be more astute for you to skip to the next individual on your target list. (Search consultants have long memories for setbacks.)

Another highly effective area of opportunity for creating a handle is the recruiter's list of "significant and representative placements." Perhaps you know one of the five that most of the Top 150 have named, or you might know a senior executive who works in a placement's organization. Few handles are as likely to capture a headhunter's attention as a specific reference to a past or current client. Although you can certainly refer to the individual you know either in your cover letter or in a telephone contact, by far the most successful way of exploiting this handle is to have your friend in the client organization make the connection for you. It's astonishing how accessible headhunters are when a client is doing your bidding for you.

By this time you have the picture: the way to get the initial attention of top recruiters is to employ a handle that plays to their background and special interests or makes clear that you know someone who has the current or potential clout to either help or hurt that recruiter. You don't need many handles with each recruiter on your target list. One will do nicely, more if you have them, but don't force them on the headhunters you wish to contact. The handle or handles you come up with belong in your cover letter. Getting past a headhunter's secretary via the telephone is about as easy as reaching the IRS with a question at tax return time.

Some job seekers may not be able to identify any handles at all for certain search consultants on their target list. Among them may be the ones highest on their list. What then? Well, you're reasonably fortunate already because you know precisely which recruiters you need—to establish relationships with—the ones in your fields of particular interest. These same recruiters also have interest in getting to know you because you have experience in the fields in which they do much of their work. Their research departments or secretaries may have instructions to forward such resumes to them with or without handles, just like Sally Skimfast did.

Or you can be audacious and solicit the help of a gadfly or two. Every industry and every profession seems to have a few of them. They can be both a curse and salvation for an executive recruiter. A gadfly is that unusual person who seems to know everything going on in a given industry or occupation and all the right people to influence. Gadflies get their name because they are endowed with a special antenna for picking up scuttlebutt and then passing it along with about as much discretion as your local barber or hairdresser.

Executive recruiters enjoy a love/hate relationship with gadflies: on the one hand they appreciate the industry information and names that gadflies volunteer so readily; but on the other, gadflies have no qualms about breaking a confidence—which, for many searches, can spell disaster. Enlisting the aid of a gadfly can help you make a connection with a recruiter. Gadflies know the recruiters who work in their fields, and whether the recruiters like it or not, they are to some extent dependent upon referrals from these individuals. So take a gadfly to lunch—at least once. It can work wonders for you in opening recruiters' doors.

Gadflies usually work in organizations other than your own. Yet there may well be individuals within your own organization—supervisors, peers, or subordinates—who are in a position to help you make contact with those on your target list. Then there are all of the former alumni of your old employer. They may be scattered to the winds but some of them will know the recruiters on your target list. A few may even have been placed by the very recruiters you also need to meet.

What to do When the Headhunter Calls

Whether you used resumes with smart cover letters or the intercessions of contacts, sooner or later your efforts will be rewarded with a call or letter from some of those on your target list. When this happens, you can consider yourself to be on the brink of being in the recruiter's system. You want that more than anything. Most often the first communication from the headhunters you're trying to cultivate will come in the form of a telephone call. How you handle the contact determines your chances of becoming a prospect, and perhaps later a candidate, to that recruiter.

The best recruiters do not make idle telephone calls. When one calls you, you can be sure that the recruiter is doing one or more of these three things: (1) sounding you out as a possible candidate, (2) determining whether you might be a source—in other words, whether you can suggest a candidate or two for one of the searches the recruiter is handling, or (3) repaying a favor to a client, former client, prospective client, a prior placement, a fellow recruiter, a current candidate, or a gadfly. Regardless of the recruiter's motives for calling you, do something on your end of the line to cause that recruiter to have good reason to either arrange a personal visit or make a mental note to keep in touch with you. In brief, don't squander the opportunity to make yourself memorable to that headhunter.

Ah, but you *are* fortunate this time. Jules Verne IV, Sally Skimfast's recruiter colleague, has got a real live possibility for you. He's called you after reading your resume because he's working on a search to find the new Vice President—Undersea Exploration for an unnamed client. It seems that the former incumbent did not resurface after Jaws was seen in the neighborhood. Recruiter Verne passes along some other general background on the opportunity and it all sounds interesting to you. You know you want a personal interview but you also know that you do not want to sound overly eager.

Be savvy but not coy. You don't have to go through the normal ritual of determining whether Mr. Verne is reputable. He's got to be or he wouldn't be one of those profiled in this book. In fact, he's one of the top 1 percent in the business. After his first description of the job to you, Jules Verne will have some reasonably probing questions to ask you over the telephone. He needs to be as sure as he can be that he doesn't waste his time or his client's dollars on a very costly face-to-face interview.

Be prepared to respond to questions that attempt to fix the current scope of your responsibilities and the structure and nature of your current or past employer. If you've listened well when the recruiter first described his need to you, you'll pick up on some of the key background and personal experience factors the recruiter must find in your background in order to qualify you as a viable candidate. Headhunters are working from what they call a specification, or candidate profile, an outline which highlights the must-have and desirable-to-have features in a prospect's background.

Further along in the conversation Jules Verne is going to inquire about your willingness to relocate, whether there are children and a working spouse involved, and at least some idea of what your compensation requirements are going to be. Make no mistake about it—recruiter Verne is still just sizing you up against his job specifications. He'll also ask you such delicate-to-deal-with questions as why you're looking for a new position and, if you're currently out of work, the names of your most recent superior and others who know your work and circumstances. Obviously, it's wise that what you give as the reason you are between jobs— or "on the beach," as the recruiters put it—jibes with what your boss says. And you can be quite sure that recruiter Verne is going to run a reference check on you with your last superior before having you visit him for a personal interview.

As noted in the introduction to *The Career Makers*, this is not a book about interviewing techniques. Hundreds of paperbacks on this subject fill the "careers" section of your local bookstores. Unfortunately, most have been written for entry-level job seekers or individuals who will forever wear short-sleeve shirts or polyester bend-overs to work. The best book that I know of on interviewing techniques and most other aspects of job changing for middle managers and above is a hardcover volume by John Lucht. The author knows what he's talking about because he's also one of the top recruiters profiled in these pages. His book is entitled *Rites of Passage at $100,000+* (Viceroy Press, $24.95).

I hope you win your interview, and I wish you good luck with it. There is one tip I might offer: if your interview happens to be with one of the top recruiters profiled here, it would be smart for you to review the recruiter's profile before you make your visit. That way you might avoid the rather awkward moment that I experienced not too long ago with a job seeker who wanted to leave me with a nice personal touch. The interview happened to be in the fall, during football season, and he smiled broadly at me as he was exiting my office. Then he suddenly thrust out a big hand and chanted, "GO BIG RED!" I was momentarily stunned. Then it dawned on me. I had graduated many years ago from the University of Nevada. He had apparently misread my school somewhere as the University of Nebraska. Oh well; it was a nice try. Both schools do start with "Ne."

Cultivating a Long-Term Relationship with Recruiters

As I said earlier in this chapter, the best time to start looking for a job is before you have to. So perhaps you're one of the very fortunate who still has a job, but you're not happy or fulfilled in it. Or maybe you're still hanging on as a middle manager in some organization that has not quite flattened its organizational structure enough yet to compress you into escape velocity. But you can see it coming and you want to prepare for the worst.

It's never too soon to start building that all-important relationship with North America's top headhunters. Once again, you must start with the identification of the right executive recruiters—those whose recruiting interests coincide with your own employment interests. It's a matter of creating your personal target list of recruiters to cultivate, as outlined earlier in this chapter. Then comes the ongoing process of becoming known to the right recruiters and helping them create a file on you that causes them to call you on every search they do that is in your field of interest and aspirations.

The first step, of course, is getting your well-crafted resume into the hands of the right recruiters. Your cover letter with a compelling handle helps you accomplish this critical step. Maybe the first call-back from a headhunter will be right on target. But chances are better that it will be about a job for which you neither fit nor would be interested in. Let's say your call is from the recruiter we read about earlier, Jules Verne IV. He's still looking for his Vice President–Undersea Exploration. Do you just say, "No, Mr. Verne, I'm not interested," and hang up? No; instead, you put your mind in gear to help that headhunter with a suggestion. The light bulb goes on in your memory bank of seldom-used but hopefully useful facts, and out comes a response like this: "I'm sorry I'm not quite right for your search, but I do have a suggestion of a possible candidate for you. He and I were in the Navy together. The last I heard he was working with a group to raise the Titanic. Would you like to know more about him?" Of course your recruiter friend would.

Or maybe your response is along these lines: "Try as I might, I don't have a single individual to suggest to you as a candidate, but I can give you the names of a couple of terrific sources. They own their own exploration businesses, so they aren't recruitable, but they know everybody who ever went treasure hunting or trained dolphins to carry out military espionage." In addition to gems like these, you might know of a journal on diving or an association concerned with undersea exploration. Whatever you do, leave that recruiter whom you have worked so hard to cultivate with food for thought—and a nice warm feeling that you are a very worthwhile contact. Your name and phone number will go into the recruiter's workbook as a good source, someone for him to call again.

Then, as fate would have it, a week later you see in the *Navy Journal* that your old pal, Christopher Columbo, is retiring from active duty. You remember that he was big in exploration, particularly in the Caribbean. You promptly follow up with your recruiter friend by phone or with a copy of the news clipping. By this time most of the top 150 recruiters in this book will very likely have started a file on you even if you have not yet become a candidate on any of their searches.

Now it's a matter of gently but regularly stuffing the file folder with your name on it in that headhunter's office. You're in no immediate hurry to make a change, but you do want to know when an exceptional opportunity opens up. Jules Verne IV will not only add items to your file, but he will also store key elements from your background in a computer. This data will be available for years to come not only to Recruiter Verne, but to all other search consultants in his firm and those in branch offices.

Don't be concerned if no acknowledgments come from your recruiter. Keep adding to his file on you. Some always-helpful items are company news releases or house organs that talk about your department or division, or clippings from a trade journal that has an article referring to you or a new product you've launched. If you happen to be with a government agency, school system, college or university, hospital, hotel, or association, the same logic holds. Take advantage of articles and stories that talk about you and what you are responsible for. Please do not send complete curricula that you've worked on for your high school, a copy of the Federal Budget for the United States of America with a paperclip on the page which refers to your department in a footnote, or the membership directory for the University Club—copies of each of which I received in the past.

Annual reports can be good or bad. Unless you are president, chairman, or the vice president of communications responsible for its production, do not send the full report. Select a summary page from the financials or those pages from the president's letter or from the report somewhere that refer to you and your department. Annual reports pollute headhunter's offices and take up valuable space in the circular files and recycling bins already overflowing with the monsoons of ill-directed resumes raining down upon America's recruiters.

Periodically, it's wise to update your resume and be sure you get one in the hands of not only Recruiter Verne, but every other executive recruiter you've been able to build a relationship with. Try attaching a short note to it that says something along these lines: "Just thought you'd like to add this most recent resume of mine to your file. My current compensation is a base of $75,000 with a bonus paid last February of $15,000. I remain keenly interested in an officer-level position in undersea exploration."

Now what's this we hear? You've won election to your local school board. Or you've been selected for the board of the Marine Salvage Council of America. That is major news for your file, so send it in. Membership, but especially leadership, in your association is one of the most important credentials you can add to your attributes in furthering your relationship with those on your target list. One of the most well-worn directories in any recruiter's office is the *Encyclopedia of Associations*. Few searches neglect contacting the leadership of trade associations or professional societies. The fact that your peers think enough of you to elect you to a leadership role in your field of work is one of the very strongest credentials any professional can have. Broadcast it.

In the final analysis, what every smart professional is really after is *visibility* with those on your target list. Very few of us become renowned in our own field. We can dream about writing an article or a book or making a scientific discovery of great merit that catches everyone's attention. But most of what goes into our file with our headhunter friends will be a steady accumulation of little things that eventually add up to a significant record of achievement. Never forget that visibility also can be acquired by what Daniel Patrick Moynihan has called "creeping gradualism." It may not be as exciting as achieving instant fame, but it often proves far more enduring.

As one might expect, some things will go into your file that you have not provided or even knew that your recruiter contact had. The headhunter you're out to win over will have made a note and put it in your file if you were abusive, devious, or pushy with his secretary. Or maybe he noticed that you wore short socks to your interview with him or that you bathed in so much fragrance that he got a headache from your cologne and couldn't work the rest of the day. Like many firms, my own has a form in which we evaluate every person we meet on such subjective factors as presence, energy level, listening ability, language facility, and many other personal factors. This too goes into your file although you will never see it. So will copies of the reference reports the recruiter does on you, including verification of your college degree—the single biggest item of candidate fabrication today, and yet one of the easiest things for employers to check.

Perhaps you "forgot" in your resume to add a former employer you had for less than a year; a recruiter from your target list may discover this and add the information to your file. Or you might have made a "simple error" in calculation and overstated your earnings by 30 to 40 percent. When the recruiter uncovers that tidbit, another entry goes into your file. A cardinal rule for every headhunter is *"no surprises for a client."* Your headhunter's entire reputation as a top professional rests on thoroughness. The best sniff out every fabrication. You can count on that from every one of the Top 150 in this book.

It is hard for me to confess this, but even these top search consultants have an endemic weakness. They are not very forgiving when a job seeker takes advantage of them. It is difficult for headhunters to build a relationship with a client and then win a search from that client. Recruiters do not take it kindly when a job seeker let them down in such a way that it jeopardizes the relationship between consultant and client—or, worst of all, ends it. Two of the most common embarrassments that recruiters suffer through are (1) when a candidate's spouse or family will not move after the breadwinner has proceeded all the way to the altar and received an offer, and (2) when a candidate has received an offer from a new employer and then used that to extract a counteroffer from the old employer. Although black balls tend to take up too much file space, Avery Label makes a nice flat black dot that applies very neatly to an individual's file folder. Only the most foolish would risk that censure with any of the Top 150. Many a professional who has taken advantage of a recruiter has discovered that even elephants don't survive as long as the memory of a headhunter wronged.

Fortunately, nothing like this is going to happen to you. You are out to develop the most positive possible relationship with the headhunters in your future. It might be interesting for you to scan the representative placements made by the Top 150. Impressive, aren't they? Remember too that these represent only a small fraction of that recruiter's work over the years. Those placements at one time were nothing more than a name on a recruiter's long list of initial possibilities on that search. Somehow they prevailed over all the others. Each of them had a file started on them in that recruiter's office, probably years before they were placed. They very likely had files in other recruiters' offices too. Some had been placed by headhunter after headhunter throughout their rises to the top.

Many of America's top executives in every field of work have never really had to look for a job, even though they've had a number of different employers. The opportunities always came to them. In the majority of instances, the bearers of glad tidings were the headhunters they had met and cultivated along the way. Wouldn't it be nice to have the feeling that even while you have your head down working away at your current grindstone, someone out there is constantly sensitive to you and your aspirations? Your recruiter friends would be minding your career for you.

Even after you've succeeded in taking a new position with the help of a recruiter, don't just close the door on a relationship that took a long time to build and to pay off. A good recruiter will stay in touch with you, but that recruiter is more interested in hearing from you periodically. There may even come a time when you can reward your friend by passing along a search yourself. Just because you've been placed doesn't mean that your file goes into storage. Although no reputable recruiter is ever going to recruit you away from the client organization where you were placed, the world of employment takes strange turns. Who knows when you may need your hard-earned friend again? Make that *friends*—you will want to keep in touch with all of those on your target list.

Cultivating the right headhunters can be the wisest investment you'll ever make—one that pays dividends for a working lifetime—and costs you nothing more than postage.

3

AN EMPLOYER'S GUIDE
TO WORKING WITH
THE TOP RECRUITERS

As an employer—and thank goodness some of you still hire people—there are four good reasons for you to be reading this chapter:

1. You need to hire a talented professional right now.
2. You anticipate hiring a talented professional or a number of them in the near future.
3. You want to be informed and realize that it is savvy to know who the best recruiters are and what fields they specialize in when a boss, fellow working associate, close friend, or family member asks you.
4. You possess the vision to realize that virtually all jobs today are subject to someone else's call. Today's employer is tomorrow's job seeker. You are wise enough to know that you may need help from America's best headhunters in a more intimate way—personally.

For whatever reason an employer initiates contact with a headhunter, the single most important decision is the choice of the right recruiter to serve you. Large search firms claim to provide expertise and resources to an employer that are unmatchable by smaller firms, and the small firms counter by emphasizing the personalized services they can offer and their access to a wider range of organizations that they are free to probe for candidates. Both clients and recruiters agree, however, that *the success of a search rests essentially with the skills and motivation of the individual recruiter handling the assignment.*

Ironically, however, the most revealing piece of information derived from the comprehensive survey of several thousand client organizations and 362 executive search firms that forms the backbone of this project is that, notwithstanding the prominence in the business press of a few New York-based headhunters, *no single executive recruiter is preeminent in the minds of corporate clients.* As noted in an earlier chapter, some recruiters well down on the lists of rankings actually received more nominations from client organizations than those standing in the top 20. Is it any wonder that employers of all types are frequently confused about whom to call when a need occurs either in their organization or for themselves personally?

Selecting the Recruiters to Get to Know

If you could persuade a headhunter to be completely open with you, and if you asked this individual to tell you exactly which functions and types of industries or organizations he or she felt most competent and up-to-speed in, you would get the candid, marketplace-tested, first-of-its-kind information you will discover later in this book. Unfortunately, at least for employers, organizations often approach recruiters with a question like this: "Mort, old friend, we're going to be looking for a new Senior Vice President of Information Services for our publishing division. Have you ever done a search like that?"

Mort, as eager as any other recruiter to book a search at a salary level well over $100,000, and not being totally dishonest— after all, he did a search five years ago for a Director of Programming for a commercial printer—responds with, "Well, yes, I have." Without further probing from the employer, one more search consultant who lacks the know-how and feel for the marketplace has just been qualified by an employer to perform a search that he is not nearly as well equipped to carry out as others would be.

Can you blame the recruiter? Probably not. Ask a similar question of professionals in other fields of competitive endeavor and you're likely to receive just as suspect an answer. Too many employers, whether they are in business or whether they serve other types of organizations, are naive when it comes to selecting the right search consultants to serve them. They make three basic mistakes. The first of these is trusting good ol' Mort, who has recruited faithfully for them for years, to do all of their search work, regardless of the functional area or business involved. The second occurs when an employer attempts to screen several recruiters for their competencies and makes the mistake of inquiring about their experience with no great diligence. The third mistake takes place when an employer calls a friend or contact who knows little regarding the exact need and inquires about which recruiter the friend has used in the past.

All three of these mistakes cost employers dearly. Not only should you as an employer wonder about the comprehensiveness of the universe for candidates ostensibly explored by a less qualified recruiter, but you must also be concerned with the overall caliber of your placement—if, in fact, you achieved one. In addition, the reality is that a major part of the fee you paid that recruiter went to educate him or her about your industry or the function in which the search was conducted.

Those same dollars spent with the right executive recruiter go toward a precisely directed, decidedly more discriminating, and less time-consuming search. This usually leads to a considerably more successful ultimate placement. Until now, however, employers had few ways to identify the best-qualified recruiters to help them with each specific search. And major employers who hire many executives and other professionals every year often find themselves in a recruiting rut. They turn again and again to the same individual or individuals simply because they don't know better-qualified alternatives. Just as these organizations bring in fresh talent from the outside, they should periodically engage *well-qualified recruiters who are new to them.*

So you might ask, "How do I know whether I've been using the right recruiters to help me?" You've raised the right question. It's time to take advantage of the information in Chapter 6, Areas of Recruiter Specialization. Just as professionals looking for a new job were encouraged to do in the preceding chapter, you should turn to the section entitled Organizational or Industry Specialization. If you have a recruitment need in the academic, association, health care, hospitality, or consulting areas, your recruiter choices are usually confined to those specialties alone. The same holds true for many industry areas of specialization. On the other hand, a number of industry classifications might warrant your inclusion of several different categories for recruiter consideration. For example, if your main business is in food products, the recruiters able to help you also could be listed in several other consumer product areas or possibly even under the holding company category. For the same reason, an employer whose principal business is in nonelectrical machinery may find it advantageous to consider recruiters listed under the fabricated metal products and electromechanical equipment categories.

In doing this initial sorting out of recruiters, you are beginning to create your own target list of the right recruiters for you to become familiar with and possibly to use in the future. You are likely to come up with a rather lengthy list of recruiters from this first screening, so it will be important to fine-tune your list further. You can do this by referring next to the section entitled Functional Areas of Specialization, which lists those recruiters reporting expertise in specific functional areas.

Some functions, like finance, planning, public relations, and human resources, can appear to be transferable to virtually any kind of industry or organization. Even so, there are subtle or not-so-subtle differences in the types of industries or organizations in which they operate. Whether you acknowledge this or not, your goal is to create a target list of recruiters whose names appear in your areas of choice in both the industry or organizational rankings *and* those for functional specialization.

When you have reduced your target list to a half-dozen or so finalists, you're ready to make your first direct contacts with the recruiters themselves. Note that I say "recruiters themselves"— not their firms. Keep in mind that, in using the information in this book, you are now able to do your own search, in effect, for the best individual recruiters to serve you or your organization. You have the right names and telephone numbers to use. Under no circumstances do you want to get passed along to some junior recruiter who is a less experienced member of the same search firm. And unless your need is for an executive at the highest level of your organization, that's exactly what is likely to happen.

Accordingly, when you make your initial telephone calls to the finalists on your target list, ask who will actually handle your search. A number of other questions are equally important; all of these qualifying or screening questions should be asked of the recruiters on your list themselves—not an associate, the administrative partner, the new business department, or even the recruiter's executive secretary. If you can't talk directly to the recruiter you're interested in doing business with, scratch that individual from the list of those to consider.

Let's turn now to those key qualifying questions that you should ask over the telephone. It is appropriate for you to identify yourself and your organization to the recruiter, *but don't tip your hand yet about the specific need you have in mind.* After identifying yourself, your flow of screening questions might go like this:

1. **In what industries and types of organizations do you personally do most of your work?** (How closely does this jibe with what your research from this book shows?)
2. **Are there functional areas in which you feel especially competent and current?** (Does this parallel your research findings?)
3. **How do you determine whether you personally handle the work or delegate it to another individual?** (This is a very important question, so listen carefully to the recruiter's response. Is the determination based on salary level, organization level, current search load, or what? Would your search qualify for the recruiter's personal handling or not?)
4. **Who does the research on the search, and is the researcher involved directly with the client?** (Optimally, the recruiter will handle personally the most important research. A recruiter who is fed all candidate information from a researcher is seldom as up-to-speed on a given industry as one who personally conducts research. One of the fringe benefits of a good search assignment is the industry scuttlebutt passed along by a recruiter. This type of super-timely market research can often be of competitive value to you.)

5. **Who makes the initial contact with a possible candidate—you, a junior recruiter, or a researcher?** (This is another very important question. Would you trust a junior recruiter, maybe someone who has never met you or sensed your organization's culture, to initiate that critical first contact on your behalf? Can a junior person represent your opportunity properly and at the same time maintain the confidentiality of your search? How well have you responded when junior recruiters or researchers called you?)

6. **When do you start reference checking, who conducts the references, and what kind of references do you ultimately provide a client?** (Are references checked before or after a client's first visit with the candidate? Does the recruiter or a less involved individual conduct them? Are references submitted in narrative form, attributable to those individuals offering specific comments, or simply summarized?)

7. **Approximately how long after you start the search will you, as the client, begin to meet candidates face-to-face?** (Is it the recruiter's practice to offer up a few "trial balloon" candidates within a few weeks of starting, or to reserve candidate presentations until most of the research is completed?)

8. **How do you price your work?** (Is it a percentage of starting base salary only, or a percentage of first-year compensation? Will the recruiter work on a fixed fee basis? What happens if you call off the search a few weeks into it? How are out-of-pocket expenses handled?)

9. **What kind of guarantee do you offer if a placement leaves or doesn't work out?** (Most will replace at no additional professional fee, charging out-of-pocket expenses only, if the placement does not last a year.)

10. **What is your client block policy—that is, how long will you abstain from approaching any person in our organization after your last search with us?** (Most will refrain for two years, and a few longer than that, but it is also important to determine whether all of your divisions, subsidiaries, and plants are off limits—including those located outside your own country.)

These ten questions should give you enough information about your recruiter to help you decide whether you want to reveal more and possibly set up a direct visit, or politely close out the conversation and save both of you a considerable amount of time and later grief. Let's say, however, that the recruiter's answers seem satisfactory to you. Only then is it appropriate to be more specific about your staffing need. You should start by giving the recruiter a capsule description of the search you envision. It is essential that you tell the recruiter the title and scope of the job, who the position reports to, how soon you need it filled, and whether it is newly created or a replacement (and if the latter, why). The recruiter also should be told a bit about the expectations of the position and whether the search is a confidential one. After providing this background, you are ready to ask the recruiter a few final questions:

1. **Would you be personally interested in handling this search on the basis of what I've told you?** (A good straightforward question deserves a similar response. If it is "No" or something like "I'd be pleased to oversee the work of one of our best associates," close the conversation with a comment to the effect that you will call the recruiter again sometime and place a quick call to the next one on your target list.)
2. **Have you done a comparable or near-comparable search to this one? How recently?** (Again, listen carefully to the recruiter's answer. Does it sound credible? Has the work been done within the last year or so, or is it older than that?)
3. **May I ask you who your client was on that search? Are there some others for whom you've done similar searches?** (Many of the top recruiters will be able to give you specific names of clients they have served, just as most of them have been willing to do in their profiles in this book. Others, however, may work for firms with more circumspect policies regarding the confidentiality of client information. Some client information is understandably off-limits, but not all client information should be. Don't ever let a recruiter or recruiting firm hide behind a veil of total confidentiality. Why engage a recruiter who must be counted on to reference-check candidates but who is unwilling to provide you with references on his or her own past performance?)
4. **What companies or organizations that might be good places to find candidates for my job will be off limits to you because**

of your firm's previous work with them? (This is one of the most important but most infrequently asked questions of recruiters. Be especially sensitive to "Academy Companies" [see Chapter 7] that are off limits to the recruiter. If two or three of the most likely target firms are blocked to this recruiter, you may be better off working with another one from your target list who is less restricted.)

5. **With your sense of the job market for the kind of person I'm looking for, what do you think will be the principal challenges in completing this search? How long do you estimate it will take to find our placement? And what do you think it will take in compensation to attract the right person?** (Weigh the recruiter's responses in light of your own hunches; and on the compensation issue, realize that to entice a high achiever is always going to involve a premium over what your current internal salary structure is.)

6. **Again, with your knowledge of the marketplace for this individual, what do you estimate your out-of-pocket expenses will run?** (Look for specificity—regardless of its magnitude. It can be an actual dollar range like $5000 to $6000 or a percentage of the professional fee. But watch out for an estimate like 10 to 15 percent of the professional fee on any search where the base salary is over $150,000—unless you also always fly first-class, stay in $400-a-night hotel rooms, and dine at five-star restaurants.)

If you still have an interested and interesting recruiter on the line after posing these questions, this valuable resource should be asked to submit a formal proposal (complete with names of client references). He or she is worth inviting to your offices for a face-to-face visit. You should also invite one or two more. Recruiters do not jump up and down with glee over "shoot outs," as they call them, where they have to compete head-to-head with others. But they're getting increasingly accustomed to them. As employers become more sophisticated in their use of search consultants, and especially as they become smarter in selecting the best-qualified recruiter for a precise need—not just good ol' Mort every time—shoot outs will become the norm, and will ultimately benefit employers and headhunters alike. Even good ol' Mort will eventually settle into his proper market niche.

Your selection process has now wound down to its last stage. It's time to bring in your finalists and get specific with them. Each of them should receive the same overview and interview. Their visits ideally will occur on the same day or in close proximity. This is especially necessary when a search committee is involved or when a group of individuals will be included in the selection process. You want impressions to be fresh in your mind.

Allow about two hours for each recruiter, and have your agenda worked out in advance. If a brief plant tour or some other quick orientation is necessary, do that first. Then proceed to fill in the recruiter on all of the pertinent information to provide an accurate picture of your need. Above all, be honest. If others from your organization will be closely involved with the search or the product of that search, be sure to include them in these final screening sessions.

Your purpose is to select not only the recruiter most qualified from a technical aspect, but the individual with whom you and your group are personally most comfortable. Much of your assessment of the recruiter's skills and knowledge of your industry or activity was obtained in your initial telephone call. Now you're judging the intangible factors—the recruiter's sense of your culture, compatibility with you and the others involved, communication skills, intellect, sense of humor, and presence. In short, you're selecting a member of your team. There must be no hidden agendas or surprises for the recruiter down the line. Neither can there be a human resources executive or Personnel Manager who feels threatened by the recruiter's work. Once you make your selection, you and your recruiter are in this project together. Although he or she may be the quarterback on this particular drive, you remain the captain of the team—and for the full season.

Following the recruiters' visits, and after polling those who sat in, you should be able to make the decision about your first choice. Assuming that the preferred recruiter's references have also been favorable, it is time for the advisory call to pass along the good news. The runners-up also deserve the courtesy of a phone call to advise them of your decision and to thank them for taking the time to meet with you. You may retain them one day, too.

Getting These Top Recruiters to Perform Their Best for You

Congratulations. You've done a fine job in picking the right quarterback for your search from the 10,000 others who very likely would not score as well. Does this mean that you can just sit back and watch that recruiter do his or her thing? No way. The best results in any search come when both employer and recruiter interact together through the entire process—and beyond. I have referred previously to the need to function as a team, and that is exactly what it takes to obtain a successful search outcome.

Sounds easy doesn't it? After all, recognizing the importance of your search and what you are paying for it, why wouldn't you want to work as a team? Yet one of the harshest surprises every headhunter sooner or later discovers is that all searches are not truly on the level. There are instances where the client actually wants to see the search come up empty-handed or the candidate, once hired, fail miserably in the job.

Fortunately, such counterplays are not the norm in searches, but they are far more frequent than most would imagine. Especially common is the situation where the client feels threatened by the caliber of the candidates being presented and seeks every possible avenue to disqualify each of them. All recruiters have their share of these types of clients.

There are no hidden agendas in your search, however, so we can get on with cultivating the kind of positive relationship you need with the top recruiter serving you. At the core of this relationship must be *trust*. It must run both ways, between the employer *and* the recruiter. As an employer you must think of your recruiter as though he or she sits on your board of directors. So once you have made the selection of the right recruiter to serve you, it's time to get back together and open up with every bit of pertinent information. This includes sharing with your recruiter your organization's financial situation, the real problems and opportunities you see now and those that are on the horizon, the people relationships and issues that the new hire will have to contend with—in brief, where all the bodies lie in your organization. Especially important in times like these is trusting your recruiter with information as sensitive as the fact that your company may be on the block to be sold, merged, or restructured, or is otherwise susceptible to anything like these disruptive events so common today.

Your recruiter must assimilate all of this and incorporate what is relevant in a *candidate specification*—the vital document that sets forth the ideal personal and professional qualifications the candidate must possess in order to succeed in the job. Much of this outline will highlight personal traits and professional skills, but it must also convey in words the culture of your organization and the nuances of the actual work environment. A good candidate specification is a type of template; only the right candidates pass through it easily.

It is normally the employer's place to provide the *position description,* although on occasion the recruiter is asked to prepare this. The position description, equally important as the candidate specification, details the basic functions of the job, reporting and supervisory responsibilities, coordinative relationships, and major duties and responsibilities in the position. The recruiter uses both the position description and the candidate specification in developing candidates for the job. It is important that both be well crafted and that you agree with what is said in both.

Armed with these materials, and with copies of your annual report and other organizational literature, your recruiter is equipped to sally forth in search of the needle in the haystack. But you want to know one more thing from your search consultant. What is the *work plan?* Although the sequence of the search may have been outlined in your recruiter's proposal letter, do you know more specifically which organizations by name will be probed? Are the right academy companies included? Are there some individuals or organizations on the recruiter's list that would prove awkward or embarrassing to you should they be approached? Do you think that the recruiter is soliciting candidates with the most appropriate titles and from the most appropriate level in their current organizations? Do you know about some organizations that might be good places to look for candidates but do not appear on the recruiter's list? Do you know some individuals who would be helpful *sources*—people who may not be candidates themselves but might offer good suggestions of others? And are there some associations your recruiter should know about, conventions coming up, or trade journals that will prove helpful?

You're in this together. As the search goes forward you may hear of someone who might be a candidate or another good source. Let your recruiter know about that. For a search to go well there cannot be "your" candidates and "the recruiter's" candidates. They are all your team's candidates.

It is the recruiter's job to use all the resources and ingenuity that can be mustered to generate an array of candidates who fit your job specifications to various degrees, some better than others. It is also the recruiter's responsibility to perform the work ethically. One of the very unfortunate byproducts of the pressure on researchers to obtain candidate names or organization information can sometimes take the form of gross deception. There have been several recent incidents where researchers with search firms or with outside research suppliers have been caught using such surreptitious guises as to say they are performing research for an academic project or seeking names for *Who's Who* directories.

It is also the recruiter's responsibility to maintain the confidentiality of a confidential search and an appropriate degree of confidentiality even when a search is not a confidential one. No organization benefits from having its management needs broadcast to the world at large—except in those very rare instances where public awareness can help generate a candidate who might otherwise be nearly impossible to find. For example, searches for commissioners of major sports groups and heads of government agencies are often aided by wide public knowledge of the need.

As the employer, you are responsible for ensuring that the search proceeds on schedule and with regular feedback from you to the recruiter. If you haven't seen your first candidate within five or six weeks from the start of the search, something is awry. Either your recruiter is spending too much time on other assignments or having trouble getting a handle on your industry or area of activity. It's time to reconvene for a heart-to-heart talk. Maybe the marketplace is telling both you and the recruiter that your specifications are unrealistic.

Your role includes seeing that the recruiter you selected is still personally deeply involved with the search. Many search firms employ gifted "rainmakers." These are individuals who are especially accomplished at selling the assignment—they frequently are the ones who brag about "selling over a million dollars a year" in searches—but who are equally skilled at avoiding the trenches where the gruntwork on a good search really takes place. Rainmakers usually surround themselves with gofers, the bag people who do their work for them. Don't forget, *that's not what you contracted for when you selected one of the top recruiters.*

Throughout the search your recruiter has been doing various types of reference checking. Initially it is the kind of quick-and-dirty call or two to references the recruiter knows personally. The recruiter just wants to be sure there are no major flaws or flags with the candidate. The fine-tuned, in-depth references are reserved for your actual finalists, usually not more than one or two. Here's another place where your top recruiter earns his or her pay—and be sure that it is your recruiter doing your reference checking, not just some underling.

Reference checks may not constitute the most critical element in the outcome of a search, but they are everything in predicting the ultimate performance of the candidate once in the job. Quality reference checking is the single most important ingredient in a search well done. Many a candidate, especially one who has had considerable prior interviewing experience, can fool an employer or the most seasoned recruiter in an interview regardless of its length or apparent thoroughness. I repeat, *references are everything.* Regrettably, they are getting much more difficult to check. The privacy of information acts and other regulatory restraints make reference checking difficult to conduct, and too many employers and recruiters alike shy away from any but the most cursory and superficial ones. Do not allow your recruiter to avoid doing in-depth references. Good thorough reference checking can still be accomplished. It just takes the right knowledge, skills, contacts, and the instincts of Peter Falk's Columbo. Speaking personally, I've always felt that thorough reference checking is as much in a candidate's best interest as it is in the employer's. Who in his right mind would ever want to be placed in a job where a limitation in his background that could be uncovered through good reference checking would cause him to fail?

The skills of your top recruiter also come into play when it's time to put together the hiring package with your preferred candidate. It is a bad mistake for employers to get directly involved with a candidate in negotiating a compensation package. Your role as the employer is to give your recruiter the parameters to work with but then trust that the deal can be worked out between candidate and recruiter. You, however, should be the one who extends the ultimate formal offer, not your recruiter.

We work in a time of more job uncertainty and career chaos than in any period since the Great Depression. Megamergers, LBOs, downsizing, spin-offs, takeovers, and other employment discombobulations have wreaked havoc on hundreds of thousands of working professionals. Now, many of these talented but displaced individuals find themselves looking for jobs on their own or with the help of outplacement firms. In the recent past, most employers would turn their noses up at those "in the job market." And they were, to a certain extent, correct in that feeling. This attitude should no longer exist on the part of any hiring organization. Consequently, your recruiter should be encouraged as never before to consider those high achievers who send their resumes over the transom as objectively as any other candidates whom the search identifies. There is almost as much likelihood of finding your perfect placement among the write-ins at the recruiter's office as there is in turning every stone out there in the field of the still-employed.

Working together for the past three months, give or take a few, your team has succeeded in finding and hiring the right individual for your very significant need. Does this mean that you and your recruiter part company until the next search that appears right for him or her? It should not. Even as the new hire comes aboard and settles into your organization, little tips might better be communicated to the placement by your search consultant than by you personally. Call them informal pieces of constructive criticism to correct small habits or traits that might become larger problems worth formal mention later on. Your recruiter is also going to want to speak with you every few months about how the new hire is performing. Like doctors, headhunters' egos need to know not only that the operation was a success but that the patient is thriving.

Early in this chapter I said that there are four major reasons why employers need to know North America's top recruiters. The last of these four suggests that it would be wise to get to know the best headhunters personally—because you, too, someday might find yourself in the ranks of the unemployed. If that motivation is one of the reasons you read this chapter, I suggest that you turn back and peruse very carefully Chapter 2. It will give you all the advice you need.

4

WAR STORIES FROM HEADHUNTER DIARIES

To the outside observer, executive recruiting is an intriguing and mysterious business, but also a predictable and orderly process. After all, headhunters sooner or later always find their placements. Right? If only they knew...

Fred Wackerle, one of America's most accomplished recruiters, took on a search last year for the Chief Operating Officer of a $400 million defense products company. As he tells it, "One of my potential candidates—let's call him Hoss Cartwheel because when I met him he looked a lot like the late Hoss Cartwright of Bonanza fame—sounded interesting on the telephone. Following a lengthy conversation about his track record, we agreed to a face-to-face interview at the Jacksonville, Florida airport. (Interestingly, I hadn't approached him; he had called me after he had heard about my search via the grapevine.)

"We spent almost two hours together, during which time Hoss recited a fabulous set of experiences, named names of superiors, subordinates, peers, and provided a detailed sketch of his company's organization chart, products, and programs. He had worked for three aerospace/defense companies in progressively responsible positions and his educational credentials were perfect for my search:

Georgia Tech, B.S. electrical engineering, 1966
University of Chicago, M.B.A. finance, 1968
Duke University, J.D. law, 1970

His reason for being interested stemmed from current organization changes, which had been well publicized in *The Wall Street Journal*. While his current employer, a *Fortune* 50 company, was considering him for internal transfers, he was openly looking on the outside.

"Hoss Cartwheel gave me the direct telephone numbers and names of his immediate and past superiors plus the parent company chief operating officer and a major customer as references. He said I'd be free to talk to any of them, but only after mutual interest had been established. I revealed our client's identity and he gave me permission to present his credentials to my client. I then asked my routine last question: 'Are there any skeletons in your closet?' and he answered 'no.'

"He seemed to be a perfect candidate. I rushed his candidate report with my interview notes to our client. They were interested. I then called Hoss to arrange a preliminary meeting with the client and we set some dates. A few days later he telephoned, and, much to my surprise, withdrew, stating that he had another opportunity in a more desirable location and had decided to pursue it rather than string along my client. I persisted, but he said no. As we always do, I then entered his background into our retrieval system for future searches. Now comes the interesting part.

"A few months ago, during a routine file updating procedure, my assistant said to me, 'I'm trying to update the file of this person named Hoss Cartwheel but can't seem to find him. What should I do?' I reviewed the file and remembered him from the above search. I suggested that we check with Duke University, the University of Chicago, and Georgia Tech as a first step. Perhaps their alumni files would be current. We discovered that:

- Duke University never had him as a student!
- Georgia Tech never had him as a student!
- The University of Chicago never had him as a student, and reported they receive upwards of ten calls a year attempting to verify his degree!

- The telephone numbers, both home and office, in Jacksonville had been disconnected with no forwarding numbers.
- I called the chief operating officer he had previously given me as a reference and he had never heard of Hoss Cartwheel.
- I called his two previous immediate superiors and they too had never heard of Hoss Cartwheel.

"I knew the corporate head of personnel of Cartwheel's last purported employer and called him to relate the above experience. There was utter silence on the other end of the phone. Then, he began to unfold a story. I was the third search consultant in the last year to tell him the same tale! Hoss Cartwheel was a complete fabrication...a true counterfeit executive."

This book was written essentially for only two groups of individuals—our most talented professionals and the employers who seek them. But the book, above all, is written *about* some of the accomplished individuals who bring these two parties together. No discussion of the demographics or the individual profiles of the Top 150 can begin to do justice to portraying the day-to-day work of North America's retained recruiters. Some idea of what they deal with may be instructive for job seekers and employers alike because in few other vocations are the frailties of human nature as nakedly displayed. After all, how many other human decisions put at risk a job, earnings, family, community, and emotional and physical well-being all at one time?

The personal experiences—one might aptly call them war stories—of the recruiters in this book could fill volumes. Having largely exhausted my own collection of anecdotes in the first edition, Fred Wackerle and a number of the other top recruiters profiled in these pages have kindly supplied me with some of their own. All of these war stories are true: Only the names of certain clients, candidates, and fellow recruiters have been changed to protect their further discreditation. Although it is unlikely that any of these events will ever happen to you, there are messages for all of us—professionals, employers, and recruiters—in what they tell us about the real world of headhunting.

Perhaps a few of the following vignettes will quickly clear up the misconception that headhunters themselves can do no wrong.

Recruiters . . . The Heros (and Heroines) of These
Skirmishes—or Are They?

Gerry Roche, a true legend in his own time among executive recruiters, tells the story of flying to Cleveland to meet a key candidate for one of his many top-level searches. "Against my better judgment, my candidate convinced me that, instead of having dinner at the airport or at some restaurant in the area, we should go to his home for dinner . . . probably to show off his bride and domestic tranquility. I accepted his invitation, rented a car at the airport, and followed him out of the airport parking lot. It was dark and raining and visibility was rotten. Nevertheless, I spotted my candidate's car and proceeded to trail him out to the remotest part of the Cleveland boonies. After about 20 minutes his car started going faster, and faster, and then even faster. I couldn't imagine what this man was up to. He was acting as though he was trying to lose me. Now halfway to Akron he finally pulled into his driveway and I pulled up behind him. Before I could get out of my rented car, he ran into the house. I walked up the driveway and the poor chap just about attacked me. He had even called the police. He couldn't understand why I had been following him. Of course, I had followed the wrong car. It took a fair amount of my best powers of persuasion to convince him that I was only a poor recruiter, not a kidnapper. When last heard from, my real candidate was still circling the airport looking for me."

Gerry Roche, who didn't become chairman of Heidrick & Struggles by being unaggressive and slow to close, recites another incident that, to the party on the other end of the phone line, must have sounded like he had just won the lottery. "I had been working on a search for four months and finally got the client to decide on a candidate after weeks of excruciating meetings, reference checks, and salary negotiations. We were down to the offer stage, and, admidst the excitement of the deal-making moment, closing this search and making the placement were the only things in my mind. Just then, in comes a call from my candidate, Joe Glow.

" 'Hello, Joe!' I exult. 'Okay, we're ready. Here's the deal.' I proceed through the entire offer, covering a high six-figure base salary, bonus, stock options, severance clause, relocation allowances, timing . . . the complete deal in exquisite detail. Being somewhat dismayed by the relative lack of enthusiasm I sensed on the other end of the phone, I gave it my best close. I talked about the future, how great this job will be for him, how the children will love living in Anaheim, but still no reaction. Finally, after what seemed like an eternity of silence, I said, 'Well, Joe, what do you think of the deal?' After an equally long and perplexing pause, the only response was 'Hello?' I had extended the offer to the wrong Joe. The poor soul I had on the line was Joe Grow, someone who I had never even spoken to before. He was a job seeker just calling me out of the blue. Thank God he let me withdraw the offer."

Executive recruiting, perhaps more than any other line of work, requires many instant identifications in crowded places of people you've never in your life seen before. Most of these take place in airports as individuals debark from flights. But they also occur in lounges, restaurants, lobbies, and offices other than your own.

Barbara Provus, one of the 12 exceptional women who rank among North America's top recruiters, had just started a search with a colleague to find a department head for a major urban-based university. The two had already met with the president of the school and were to spend the rest of the day talking with other senior level administrators to get their insights on the job to be filled.

"Our schedule was a full one, and it had us moving every 30 minutes to one of three different offices set aside for us for these orientation briefings. After a busy morning of these sessions and a hasty lunch, we were running a few minutes late for our next meeting with the provost.

"My colleague was ahead of me by about 20 paces and dashed into one of the assigned offices. As I entered, I saw that our interviewee was already there, seated at the table. We mumbled apologies about being a little late, and then my partner began to introduce our firm and our purpose in being there. While he was talking I glanced at our schedule and suddenly realized we were in the wrong room.

"I tugged at my partner's sleeve, perhaps too subtly, because he continued with his presentation. Our guest was listening very intently, nodding at all the appropriate spots. I then cleared my throat and tried to interrupt. 'Just a minute, Barbara,' my colleague said politely, 'you'll have your chance!' Our guest continued to smile pleasantly at us both. After what seemed like an extremely long introductory narration, my fellow recruiter finally concluded with his standard question: 'Well, now will you tell us a little about your role at the university?'

" 'Pleased to do so,' he responded with gusto. 'I'm Joe Turner, Department of Sanitation Services. And I'm certainly honored to have the two of you participating in our first on-campus Pick-Up-The-Litter Day. I'm sure the other volunteers will be here shortly!' "

The follies of recruiters could fill a book itself, infallible as they may appear to be to those on the outside. Even the very best can pull some real boners—including their participation in creating this book. To compile the profiles and rankings, a number of multipage questionnaires went back and forth between the top recruiters and my office. Even then, it was more than we bargained for when, in one large, thick overnight mail envelope we received not the questionnaire we had expected but the complete confidential personnel report on one top recruiter's leading candidate for an airline client. (The thoroughly embarrassed recruiter we promptly called offered personally to come to Chicago to retrieve the package, but we air-couriered it to his client for him.)

Candidates... Who Goes There? Are You Friend Or Foe?

Candidates, even more so than clients, are the reason headhunters do not age gracefully.

Lynn Tendler Bignell, a true luminary among North America's top women recruiters, remembers a search some years ago when the firm she cofounded was in its infancy. "We were searching for the National Sales Manager of a specialty chemical company. Our client was in a huge rush and because of scheduling

conflicts urged us to get one of our candidates to them even before we had had the chance to meet him personally. We would
normally refuse this, but hard-pressed as we were by the client
and somewhat comforted by the fact that we had obtained excellent references and had extensive prior telephone conversations
with the candidate, we acquiesced.

"Our client, the Vice President–Sales, was a particularly dap-
per chap, small of stature, and a health fanatic. In his feedback to
us at the end of the day he went out of his way to impress upon
me how open-minded he had tried to be about our candidate.
He added that all of the others who had met with our candidate
before him had tried to do the same. Unfortunately, however, all
came to naught at the end of the day's visit. Just as our candidate
was settling into his seat in the Vice President–Sales' office, the
chair collapsed and our Mr. Perfect ended up flat on the floor,
legs akimbo, and his face beet-red. All 310 pounds of him!"

Candidates sometimes come with other forms of excess bag-
gage. Ms. Bignell is not alone among her fellow headhunters
when it comes to coping with candidates who bring with them
some extraordinary domestic accessories. She remembers one in
particular. "The search had gone exceptionally well. Our lead
candidate was very anxious for the job. He had shared his confidence with his secretary so we were free to leave messages with
her of a confidential nature, and so the recruiting process was
nicely accelerated. It is our practice to speak with the spouse at
some point in the process to make certain that family, geographic,
or dual career issues are addressed and dealt with if possible. The
candidate's spouse in this instance, however, was not accessible to
us. Her husband told us she was wholly in favor of this opportunity but was distracted due to the failing health of her parents and
the constant commuting back and forth to their house some 100
miles away. So when he showed up without her for the look at the
community and the real estate everyone understood. And when
he started work everyone also understood that his wife would
follow in three to six months. The only real surprise came when
it was his trustworthy secretary who made the move instead."

John Lucht, a premier recruiter as well as a best-selling author, found himself in the middle of a domestic situation so im-
probable that it had to be true.

"While my firm is in New York, I was recruiting simultaneously for two out-of-town client companies. I was asked to find the new Senior Vice President and Head of Claims for a life insurance company headquartered in Detroit, and at the same time I was looking for a Group Executive who would become the successor to the founder of a venture-capital concern based in Chicago. Both of these clients would consider candidates from anywhere in the country, but we all knew that New York would be a prime place to look for people to fill either position.

"I had early success in finding several fine candidates on both searches. Clearly, however, the top prospect for my venture-capital assignment was a woman who worked on Wall Street and who had already made a great name for herself. Moreover, my client was especially intrigued with the idea of adding a woman to their top management team. She, like many other independent-thinking women in business, was operating under her maiden name, Shirley Waters. She was interested in our opportunity and everything looked very positive.

"At the same time, I was developing candidates for my claims search in Detroit. Jack Rivers was with an insurance company in midtown Manhattan and appeared to be an ideal finalist. Things were going almost too well. All of my advance checking and references resulted in outstanding comments about both individuals.

"As I spoke further with Ms. Waters about her possible relocation to Chicago, she said, 'Well you might think on the surface it would be a problem, because you know I'm married. Under normal circumstances it would be unacceptable because my husband also has a job here in New York. But as a matter of fact, I'm very seriously considering divorce. I've not told him this yet but I believe that it is inevitable. If this should go through and I should get the job in Chicago—and even if I don't—this would probably be the time to tell him.'

"That was a blow! Every recruiter knows very well that virtually no employer is willing to hire someone with anything as personally disruptive in his or her life as a current divorce. I resolved to find other good candidates for that search, and prepared to interview the most promising prospect for the other search, Mr. Rivers.

"Again, I pointed out the relocation issue. His response practically echoed that of Ms. Waters: 'Well, under normal circumstances it would be out of the question but I'm not entirely happy with my home life. My wife has a carreer here in New York and I've been thinking I really would like a divorce. I haven't brought myself to giving her the bad news yet, but the fact that I'm considering an out-of-town job offer might be just the right reason to make it happen.'

"Later that evening as I was putting my paperwork together, I glanced one more time at the resumes of my two leading candidates who had so rapidly fallen from favor. And there it was in black and white. In a metropolitan area of 12 million people, my fallen duo just happened to reside in the same house in Connecticut. I hadn't noticed their addresses before because my contacts with both of them up to that time had been telephonic, except for my personal interviews. Did either get their job, you ask? No, but they did get their divorce."

Every recruiter would like to forget entirely a few select candidates. John Johnson, the stellar recruiter who heads Lamalie Associates, had an experience early in his career that has left an impression that will probably outlast his career. "We had been working very hard to recruit a senior marketing executive for a major client of ours. Finally, we identified and interested a rising young star from one of my client's top competitors. We put a big rush on this individual, putting him through his paces, introducing him to all our client's top brass, and rolling out the red carpet for him and his wife.

"As we completed our reference checking on this individual, it became increasingly clear that he was not only one of his company's best marketing talents but an individual already pegged for top management. This simply served to heighten the interest of our client. We decided to stretch our original compensation package and talk up his succession possibilities with our client organization.

"After a considerable amount of discussion and renegotiation of details of the offer, he accepted our offer. The transition went smoothly. The new hire and his wife visited our client's city and prepared for the relocation. On his first day on the job he arrived early and immediately met with his immediate subordinates and others with whom he would interact. All impressions were that he was an outstanding selection and that he would provide long-term value to the company.

"Three days later he didn't arrive at work. He called the hiring manager and told him that his wife had become gravely ill, and that he had returned to his recently departed residence. He, of course, had gone back to his former employer and his wife experienced an overnight recovery. Today he is the chief executive officer of a *Fortune* 100 company. But to this day he is known in our firm as our 'now you see him, now you don't' candidate."

As Fred Wackerle found in his tale of the counterfeit executive, reference checking provides more anecdotes than probably any other area of executive recruiting. Fabrications abound particularly in the area of educational credentials. Otis Bowden II, one of America's most highly regarded and experienced recruiters, remembers checking out a candidate for a Vice President of Human Resources position. The man claimed he had both an M.B.A. and an undergraduate degree from a Big Ten university. In addition, the candidate was a regent for this major university system. Alas, as Bowden discovered, the man not only lacked an M.B.A., but had not even completed his undergraduate work.

Leon Farley, one of North America's most respected headhunters, had a similar experience in checking out a candidate to become a partner in a major consulting firm. The candidate cited a B.A., an M.B.A., and an M.S. from the University of Chicago. Recruiter Farley sensed that there might be a bit of excessive education in the man and inquired of the Chicago school's registrar. The answer came back that the candidate's records were "blocked at the student's request, possibly because he never completed his degrees." Interestingly, the man had already risen to partner level in the consulting arm of a Big Eight accounting firm.

The hoops that recruiters are sometimes forced to jump through to accommodate candidate compensation and benefit requirements defy all attempts at justification. Furthermore, many of the stories in this area of dealing with candidates reflect so poorly on all parties that, if told, would result in producing the attitude that some candidates are obscenely greedy, and that some headhunters are crasser wheelers and dealers than are our politicians.

On occasion, candidate requests for special relocation benefits and dispensation from new employers exceed all bounds of reason or imagination. One such situation confronted Lynn Tendler Bignell at the conclusion of a search for a division executive. The chosen individual, in addition to being a successful corporate type, was also a gentleman farmer. There were several hundred acres of land to factor into the relocation package—but on the land happened to graze 100 sheep. Mr. Perfect Candidate was insistent that the sheep follow him. Recruiter Bignell, fortunately for her, had a more compassionate client than I have had in my experience, and the good client agreed to put up the hay—make it grass—to transport all 100 woolly critters to a new pasture in the East.

Regrettably for the poor client, the fleecing did not stop there. Eight weeks slipped away before the move could occur, and, as nature would have it, 25 more little bouncing bundles of woolly joy came into the world. Recruiter Bignell, apparently undaunted, managed to work out a compromise between both client and candidate. All 125 sheep were moved, but it was certainly not the sheepest move in relocation history.

Clients . . . You Pay to Stay Above the Fray. But Do You?

If candidates can cause a recruiter to age less than gracefully, clients can make any headhunter want to pull his or her hair out. In fact, a quick perusal of the portraits in this book will reveal that more than a few—myself included—may have carried this a bit too far.

Robert Dingman, another of North America's premier recruiters, had been asked to find a new chief financial officer for a seriously troubled airline. His client was the president, but this airline was really run by a very domineering chairman. The original specifications for the job called for someone who is highly financing-oriented, not one who had come up through the controls route. Recruiter Dingman dutifully found several good candidates but all were rejected. Back came word from the president that, since they had worked out their lines of credit, the need had shifted now to a controls-oriented person.

Without any adjustment in his fee, Dingman went back to the drawing board to come up with suitable new candidates. In due course he did. But each one was disqualified again by the chairman. In frustration, Dingman asked the president why all of his good candidates were striking out. The president seemed embarrassed as he told Dingman that the search had to be canceled. "Why?" Dingman asked. The president responded, "Frank has a good friend he's secretly wanted as our chief financial officer all along. I had hoped you could find us someone he would accept instead but he won't budge." Adding insult to injury, soon thereafter the airline creatively filed for bankruptcy, leaving Recruiter Dingman out many thousands of dollars.

Bob Dingman was also engaged to assist a major Southern California building materials company in finding a new corporate controller. Fairly quickly an excellent candidate was found and an offer extended and accepted, with the candidate turning down along the way another firm's offer with even higher compensation.

"I was pleased," reports Dingman, "that the candidate would not need to relocate because his eight-year old son had leukemia and perhaps only two years left to live. My happy candidate had already retained a contractor to remodel a part of the house to accommodate their ill son. Then came an evening phone call to my home from my client. It seems that a board member, who happened to chair the client's audit committee, knew the newly hired controller and disliked him. There was no way to salvage things, my client said, so my task was to get the new hire to retract his acceptance of the offer.

"The two hours I spent with the agitated candidate were full of anger, threats of a lawsuit, and palpable fear for himself and his family. But he finally withdrew. I kept up with him for some time until he landed a comparable job. I felt very pleased with what I had been able to do for my client under difficult circumstances and expected a warm, continuing relationship for having extricated them from a potential debacle. Instead, my presence served as a reminder of their gaffe and they soon switched to another search firm."

So, I ask, after episodes like these, why does Bob Dingman still have so much hair?

Handling six to eight searches at a time is a full platter for any recruiter. But can you imagine what it was like for Pendleton James, another of North America's most gifted recruiters, when he was assigned to do the staffing for newly elected President Ronald Reagan? As Recruiter James puts it, "Having just a few weeks to get a cabinet together, find 650 members of the administration, and fill 4,000 jobs that the president has the authority to appoint is a nightmare of daunting proportion. I doubt any other recruiter has faced anything similar. After serving on the White House staff and then returning to private practice with my own search firm, anything from this point on is a cakewalk."

Lynn Tendler Bignell did not have to worry about the awesome task of filling 650 key jobs in a few weeks' time—the single one she took on for one of her own clients was enough of a dandy. Ms. Bignell had been retained by a smokestack industry client which had recently acquired a company that manufactured traditional consumer dinnerware. The new owners of the company wanted to add a highly contemporary line to the mainstay dinnerware line and open up a new customer base. To do that they needed a director of design. It was Recruiter Bignell's suggestion that they look outside the tabletop industry and probe companies where pattern and color were key, namely, the fashion industry.

"As the search progressed, it became clear that these candidates from the fashion industry—replete in their sandals, peasant skirts, flowered shirts, and long hair—would have a difficult transition to make into the corporate mold. We kept at it, though, and eventually located someone who appeared to be a perfect candidate. Not only was he a highly regarded designer but he wore a suit and tie, his hair was regulation length, and he understood the business of design as well. Since like many big city dwellers he did not own a car, he would rent one and drive to his interview with our client 50 miles away.

"I could hardly wait for the feedback after the visit because I felt so good about the candidate we had found. But what my client told me caused my heart to sink. My ideal candidate arrived for his interview in a white suit and shocking pink tie. On top of this he pulled up in a chauffeur-driven white stretch limousine that waited for him the entire day. It turned out that the real reason the candidate didn't have a car was that he couldn't drive. I was just at the point of telling my client that we had other good candidates in the pipeline.

"Then it came out. They loved him! He was exactly what they were looking for. He was just enough outside the corporate culture to make a difference, they felt, and he was certainly a risk taker. In fact, they had already made him an offer and he had accepted on the spot. Obviously, any caution or counsel from me at that point was too late. The deal was done.

"I had my trepidations. Was the client really going to be able to absorb this maverick? The candidate had certainly demonstrated a different persona than the one I saw when I first interviewed him. I tried to express my reservations to the client but they would hear none of it. Regrettably for the client, candidate, and ourselves, my concerns proved well founded. After eight increasingly difficult months of seeing the white limousine pull up and disgorge my placement, and paying for the chauffeur, our client issued him a pink slip to go with his pink tie and gave him a one-way fare home."

I'm happy to report that fewer and fewer clients discriminate on the basis of such illogical things as age, sex, race, creed, or national origin. They discriminate on more significant things. For instance, we had a client in the private-club field whose first name is Mel. Mel will not interview anyone whose first name is Bruce. There are others, of course.

John Johnson of Lamalie Associates also had a client with an interesting bias. "I was called upon to recruit a senior planning executive for an Indiana-based company which was headed by a very sharp young executive. When I undertook the search I knew that we would have to produce some truly exceptional candidates to satisfy him. After months of work, I had developed three executives who were outstanding matches with our client's specifications. Following the last of the candidate interviews with our client I called for his feedback. I was very confident of some highly complimentary comments. Needless to say, when I heard that none of my candidates was satisfactory I was shocked. I got feedback like, 'He's not a right fit for the organization,' 'I don't think it would work,' 'The division president wasn't taken by him,' and on and on—all meaningless input which was of no help to me as I screened new candidates.

"I called the Vice President–Human Resources and asked if we could get together to find out what I was missing. He was one of these busy personnel types who could never quite finish a meeting because he was running off to another. When I did get him to sit down with me, and pointed out how closely our candidates fit the job specifications, he started to play back to me the innocuous comments which had already been passed on to me. I challenged him to translate them into meaningful screening criteria. Without a blink he stated that nobody made it in the organization if the president had to look down at the individual. In fact, all candidates had to be near physical and professional clones of the president. In brief, they had to be 6'3" or taller and to have come from a major consulting firm. Now with the real calipers I had on the job, it was easy to make the placement."

In the pages that follow, you will see the faces and backgrounds of North America's most accomplished recruiters. They've all weathered many a campaign and facilitated matches between clients and candidates that have changed the faces of enterprises and organizations for most of the twentieth century. There is a tendency for them to have become in their work a bit calloused, suspicious, and super-critical of the two parties with whom they must interact so precisely and so sensitively. But there is a psychic reward that goes far beyond the fees they collect for their expertise. I particularly like what Leon Farley has to say about this:

> We all have stories of the rogues and the rascals. I have much more pleasant recollections of the brilliant executives, the driving entrepreneurs, the founders of companies, and the great leaders who have formed our recruiting base over the years and whom we have been honored to serve both as clients and candidates.

PART II

AMERICA'S TOP EXECUTIVE RECRUITERS

5

PROFILES OF THE TOP 150 EXECUTIVE RECRUITERS

JOHN R. AKIN
President
J.R. Akin & Company
183 Sherman Street
Fairfield, CT 06430
Telephone: (203) 259-0007

Date of Birth: January 25, 1937
Grew up in: Wakefield,
   Massachusetts

HIGHER EDUCATION:
Boston College
   B.S. degree, business administration/finance, 1959
Northeastern University
   M.B.A. degree, behavioral science, 1970

MILITARY:
First Lieutenant, United States Army Signal Corps, 1960 to 1962

EMPLOYMENT HISTORY:
1983 to present: J.R. Akin & Company
1979 to 1982: Partner, Antell Wright & Nagel
1978 to 1979: Vice President Human Resources, Burndy Corporation
1959 to 1978: Various positions to Director Human Resources, Information Systems, GTE

PRIVATE CLUBS:
Williams Club

ASSOCIATIONS/ PROFESSIONAL SOCIETIES:
Association of Executive Search Consultants
International Association of Corporate and Professional Recruiters

SPECIAL INTERESTS AND HOBBIES:
Boating, fishing, running

REPRESENTATIVE AND SIGNIFICANT PLACEMENTS:
Ronald Turcotte, Assistant General Manager Canada, now Executive
   Vice President and Chief Operating Officer
   Trans-Lux Corporation

Joseph D. Williams, Senior Vice President, Chief Financial Officer and
   Treasurer
   Mutual of America
Robert Rohrer, President
   Gray Line Worldwide
Albert Del Gardo, Vice President Information Systems
   Gibson Greetings
Peter Yeatman, President
   Radstone Technologies

WHAT I LOOK FOR IN GENERAL IN A CANDIDATE

In the selection of executive talent, the interview focus is on accomplishments. What was done and what was the impact on the company's profit and loss statement? In addition, emphasis is placed on activities and accomplishments that are indicative of superior intelligence, ambition, people skills such as team building and effective selection and retention, and adaptive skills and flexibility.

Retained executive search is basically a simple business. It is a function of listening carefully and asking dozens of appropriate questions of the client organization (all of the key executives participating in the selection process) and, in particular, the hiring manager.

The next step is a thoughtful development of a description of both the position and duties and the personal traits and characteristics of the successful candidate. The draft is submitted for intensive review by the client. Following approval of the description, a well-disciplined search follows. There is no substitute for hard work, sharp focus, and exercise of discipline and excellence in selection criteria at this point.

The rest of the search process follows, including active participation in the offer process on the part of the search consultant and frequent contact with the placed executive after he/she starts the new position. We at J.R. Akin & Company feel that one of the most important ingredients in this process is the continuity of having one consultant doing the soliciting, telephone interviewing, and personal interviewing.

GEOGRAPHIC SCOPE OF RECRUITING ACTIVITIES:
Serve clients nationwide and in Europe, Hong Kong, and Taiwan

TOTAL YEARS OF RETAINER-TYPE RECRUITING EXPERIENCE:
13 years

DONALD T. ALLERTON
Partner
Allerton Heneghan & O'Neill
208 South LaSalle Street,
   Suite 766
Chicago, IL 60604
Telephone: (312) 263-1075

Date of Birth: January 4, 1940
Grew up in: New Jersey

Stuart–Rodgers–Reilly Photography

HIGHER EDUCATION:
   Farleigh Dickinson University, Rutherford, NJ
      B.S. degree, business administration, 1965

EMPLOYMENT HISTORY:
   1978 to present: Allerton Heneghan & O'Neill
   1975 to 1978: Vice President and General Manager–Midwest, Staub
      Warmbold
   1972 to 1975: Director, Corporate Employment, G.D. Searle & Com-
      pany
   1969 to 1972: Celanese Corporation
   1965 to 1969: Warner-Lambert Company

REPRESENTATIVE AND SIGNIFICANT PLACEMENTS:
   Executive Vice President, Research and Development
      Major pharmaceutical company
   President and Chief Operating Officer
      Drug delivery company
   Executive Vice President and Assistant Director Personnel
      Leading electronics company
   Vice President–Strategic Marketing
      European-based pharmaceutical company
   Director–Cultural Diversity
      Fortune 100 consumer products company

WHAT I LOOK FOR IN GENERAL IN A CANDIDATE

Experience has taught me that executives with certain core qualities tend to be the most successful over time. These qualities include:

Innate intelligence and common sense

Effective communication skills to articulate a sense of purpose and goals

Proven leadership skills to inspire people to achieve a vision

Unquestioned personal integrity and honesty

Broad business perspective to learn from others and take advantage of global opportunities

Sense of humor, because taking yourself too seriously stifles creativity and takes the fun out of working

The position and the client determine what I specifically look for in a candidate. Each assignment requires recruiting a person with a unique blend of accomplishments, experience, and expertise. However, a successful match demands compatible chemistry. Candidate and client must experience a sense of positive chemistry or all the candidate's other positive attributes will place a distant second.

GEOGRAPHIC SCOPE OF RECRUITING ACTIVITIES:

Serve clients nationwide and in Europe, Canada, Mexico, and Brazil

TOTAL YEARS OF RETAINER-TYPE RECRUITING EXPERIENCE:

16 years

GERRY BAKER
President
Baker Harris & Partners Limited
130 Adelaide Street West,
   Suite 2710
Toronto, Ontario, M5H 3P5
Telephone: (416) 947-1990

Date of Birth: October 11, 1938
Grew up in: Windsor, Ontario

HIGHER EDUCATION:
   University of Windsor
      Bachelor of Commerce, 1961

EMPLOYMENT HISTORY:
   1979 to present: Baker Harris & Partners Limited (prior to October 1,
      1991, Gerry Baker & Associates)
   1970 to 1979: Director of Executive Search, Coopers & Lybrand

PRIVATE CLUBS:
   Mississauga Golf and Country Club

ASSOCIATIONS/PROFESSIONAL SOCIETIES:
   Institute of Certified Management Consultants of Ontario

SPECIAL INTERESTS AND HOBBIES:
   Golf, tennis, skiing, cottage life

REPRESENTATIVE AND SIGNIFICANT PLACEMENTS:
   Senior Vice President–Sales and Marketing
      Mitel Corporation
   Vice President–Sales
      Systemhouse Canada
   Vice President–Marketing
      Digital Equipment Corporation
   President
      Baker Lovick Advertising
   Executive Vice President
      NovAtel Communications

WHAT I LOOK FOR IN GENERAL IN A CANDIDATE

Our belief is that people make the difference in the success of any organization, and our mission is to ensure that our clients hire key personnel who will contribute to their success.

Our candidate selection criteria depend on the job, the company, the issues, and what needs to be accomplished. However, without exception, we look for candidates who have performed well and who are motivated to perform well in the future.

One client might need a visionary leader, another might need someone who can open up new markets, and a third, someone who can drive product development. The key is to know what skills are truly needed for success and then to focus on finding and selecting those skills.

GEOGRAPHIC SCOPE OF RECRUITING ACTIVITIES:

Serve clients in Canada, the United States, and the United Kingdom

TOTAL YEARS OF RETAINER-TYPE RECRUITING EXPERIENCE:

25 years

O. WILLIAM BATTALIA
Chairman
Battalia Winston International,
   Inc.
275 Madison Avenue
New York, NY 10016
Telephone: (212) 683-9440

Date of Birth: December 18, 1928
Grew up in: Brooklyn, New York

Catherine—Noren Photography

HIGHER EDUCATION:
   Cathedral College
      B.A. degree, social science, 1951
   Columbia University Graduate School of Business
      M.B.A. degree, 1956

MILITARY:
   Corporal, United States Army Security Agency, 1951 to 1953

EMPLOYMENT HISTORY:
   1963 to present: Battalia Winston International
   1959 to 1963: Director, Personnel, ITT Information Systems Division
   1956 to 1959: Employment Supervisor, Unisys, Sperry Division

PRIVATE CLUBS:
   University Club of New York

ASSOCIATION/ PROFESSIONAL SOCIETIES:
   Association of Executive Search Consultants

SPECIAL INTERESTS AND HOBBIES:
   Swimming, jogging, tennis, skiing, theater, reading, music

REPRESENTATIVE AND SIGNIFICANT PLACEMENTS:
   Peter Browning, Executive Vice President to Chairman and Chief
      Executive Officer
      National Gypsum
   Edward Leinss, President and Chief Executive Officer
      Ahlstrom Filtration, Inc.

Charles L. Bradford, Vice President and General Manager, Container
  Division
  Jefferson Smurfit Corporation
Francis G. Guiliano, President
  PCL Industries, Inc.
Douglas Daniels, President
  Dexter Corporation, Non-Wovens Division

WHAT I LOOK FOR IN GENERAL IN A CANDIDATE

I look for a candidate who fits the specification, not loosely but
tightly. I try to find the person who has the right number of years in
the right function in the right industry.

Beyond that, I look for intelligence, motivation, management style,
integrity, creativity, promotability, people skills, judgment, and mind set.
Over and above these "hard" and "soft" criteria is the need to match an
individual to an environment—both the company as a whole and the
group with which the person will interface on a daily basis.

GEOGRAPHIC SCOPE OF RECRUITING ACTIVITIES:
Serve clients nationwide

TOTAL YEARS OF RETAINER-TYPE RECRUITING EXPERIENCE:
28 years

MARTIN H. BAUMAN
President
Martin H. Bauman Associates,
Inc.
410 Park Avenue
New York, NY 10022
Telephone: (212) 752-6580

Date of Birth: December 26, 1929
Grew up in: New York, New York

Bill—Stone Photography

HIGHER EDUCATION:
New York University
B.S. degree, personnel management, 1956
M.B.A. degree, management, 1961

MILITARY:
Corporal, United States Army Signal Corps, 1951 to 1953

EMPLOYMENT HISTORY:
1968 to present: Martin H. Bauman Associates, Inc.
1965 to 1968: Assistant Personnel Director, United Merchants & Manufacturers
1961 to 1965: Vice President, Personnel, Branch Motor Express
Five years prior experience in personnel, training, and development in retailing and manufacturing

PRIVATE CLUBS:
North Shore Health Club

ASSOCIATIONS/ PROFESSIONAL SOCIETIES:
Association of Executive Search Consultants
International Association of Corporate and Professional Recruiters
Society for Human Resource Management
New York Personnel Management Association
American Trucking Association
Non-Prescription Drug Manufacturers Association

SPECIAL INTERESTS AND HOBBIES:
Outdoors and swimming

REPRESENTATIVE AND SIGNIFICANT PLACEMENTS:
Frank Pizzitola, Board of Directors
  Grand Metropolitan, London
A.B. "Ted" Ruhly, Assistant to President to President and Chief
  Executive Officer
  Maersk, Inc.
Doug Reid, Senior Vice President–Human Resources
  Colgate-Palmolive
Don Marshall, Regional Manager to Chairman, CEO, and part-owner
  Sun Distributors
Robert Davis, President
  Sequa Corporation

WHAT I LOOK FOR IN GENERAL IN A CANDIDATE

There are no specific criteria! Each recruit, each function, and each company have different sets of criteria—no two jobs are ever alike! Always critical, however, are intelligence, judgment, motivation, value systems, and management style.

GEOGRAPHIC SCOPE OF RECRUITING ACTIVITIES:
Serve clients nationwide and internationally

TOTAL YEARS OF RETAINER-TYPE RECRUITING EXPERIENCE:
22+ years

JEFFREY G. BELL
Managing Director
Norman Broadbent Interna-
  tional, Inc.
200 Park Avenue
New York, NY 10166
Telephone: (212) 953-6990

Date of Birth: August 28, 1945
Grew up in: Montclair, New Jersey

HIGHER EDUCATION:
  Wesleyan University
    B.A. degree, 1968
  University of Pennsylvania, Wharton School
    M.B.A. degree, 1973

MILITARY:
  Captain, United States Marine Corps, 1969 to 1972

EMPLOYMENT HISTORY:
  1987 to present: Norman Broadbent International Inc.
  1983 to 1987: President, Morgan Research Inc.
  1976 to 1982: Vice President, Russell Reynolds Associates, Inc.
  1975 to 1976: Associate, Corporate Finance, Blyth Eastman Dillon &
    Co., Inc.
  1973 to 1975: Administrative Officer, Brown Brothers Harriman &
    Co.

PRIVATE CLUBS:
  Union Club
  Princeton Club
  Doubles

ASSOCIATIONS/ PROFESSIONAL SOCIETIES:
  British American Chamber of Commerce
  Association of Executive Search Consultants

SPECIAL INTERESTS AND HOBBIES:
Vestryman, St. Bartholomew's Episcopal Church, New York

REPRESENTATIVE AND SIGNIFICANT PLACEMENTS:
Michael D. Madden, Managing Director/Co-Head, Investment Banking Division
Shearson Lehman Brothers
Eric J. Gleacher, President
Gleacher Morgan Grenfell (joint venture between Morgan Grenfell Group PLC and Gleacher & Co.)
John J. Hopkins, Managing Director/Head-Financial Institutions Group
Shearson Lehman Brothers
Robert I. Israel, Managing Director/Head-Energy Group
Wertheim Schroder & Co, Inc.
Roger M. Widmann, Managing Director/Head-Investment Banking
Chemical Bank

WHAT I LOOK FOR IN GENERAL IN A CANDIDATE

I always look for a combination of technical expertise and personal attributes which translate into a track record of accomplishment over time. The more junior the requirement, the more I weight the technical skill sets required in the position specification. For senior positions, I look for "leadership by example," that is, the ability to set standards, motivate colleagues, and discharge one's responsibilities in a highly professional manner. While organizational ability, technical competence, creativity, effective interpersonal skills, and a strong work ethic are highly desirable attributes, a demonstrated commitment to sound business ethics combined with personal integrity are critical and will always determine whether or not I introduce a prospect to a client.

GEOGRAPHIC SCOPE OF RECRUITING ACTIVITIES:
Serve clients nationwide and in the UK, continental Europe, and Hong Kong

TOTAL YEARS OF RETAINER-TYPE RECRUITING EXPERIENCE:
15 years

LYNN TENDLER BIGNELL
(formerly **LYNN GILBERT**)
Principal/Co-Founder
Gilbert Tweed Associates, Inc.
630 Third Avenue
New York, NY 10017
Telephone: (212) 697-4260

Date of Birth: **April 26, 1938**
Grew up in: **Metropolitan New
York and Miami Beach**

Gilbert Tweed Associates, Inc.

HIGHER EDUCATION:
University of Florida
B.A. degree, mathematics, 1959

EMPLOYMENT HISTORY:
1972 to present: Gilbert Tweed Associates, Inc.
1963 to 1967 and 1970 to 1972: Director, Technical Recruiting, Dunhill Personnel
1960 to 1963: Associate, Personnel Associates

ASSOCIATIONS/PROFESSIONAL SOCIETIES:
International Association of Corporate and Professional Recruiters
Chairman, 1990 and President, 1989
Outward Bound USA, past member of Advisory Board

SPECIAL INTERESTS AND HOBBIES:
Adventure travel, crafts, antiques
Author and frequent lecturer

REPRESENTATIVE AND SIGNIFICANT PLACEMENTS:
Jack Allen, Senior Vice President/C-E Environmental
Combustion Engineering
Terry Thompson, Vice President and General Manager
Medco Containment Services
Jacqueline Renner, Marketing Manager–Phosphorus Chemicals
FMC Corporation

Gary Whitehouse, Chief Operating Officer
  Advanced Polymer Systems, Inc.
Martin Wiley, Vice President Sales–Hong Kong
  Loctite Corporation

WHAT I LOOK FOR IN GENERAL IN A CANDIDATE

I believe that my clients deserve candidates who can serve aces, spin straw into gold, and turn dreams into reality. I further believe that it is my responsibility to make certain that they settle for nothing less. I feel every candidate I recommend should add value to my client's organization.

Requisite skills, experience, chemistry, and cultural fit notwithstanding, it is a given that my candidates meet my clients' immediate needs. But, more importantly, they must be able to contribute to the organization's ultimate long-term strategic objectives.

Accordingly, I must make certain that my candidates have that something extra to contribute—perspective, insight, vision, innovation. They must have unique skills and experience beyond what is needed today. My candidates aren't just bodies that fill today's position specifications; they are value-added individuals who must be a resource to my clients, contributing to the future fabric of their organizations.

GEOGRAPHIC SCOPE OF RECRUITING ACTIVITIES:
  Serve clients nationwide and in Canada, Asia, South America, and through INESA Federation of offices in the UK, France, Spain, Germany, Switzerland, Belgium, Italy, and Sweden

TOTAL YEARS OF RETAINER-TYPE RECRUITING EXPERIENCE:
  19 years

OTIS H. BOWDEN, II
President
Bowden & Company, Inc.
5000 Rockside Road, Suite 120
Cleveland, OH 44131
Telephone: (216) 447-1800

Date of Birth: January 2, 1928
Grew up in: Stuttgart, Arkansas

HIGHER EDUCATION:
   Washington University, St. Louis, Missouri
      B.S. degree, business administration, 1950
      M.B.A. degree, 1953

EMPLOYMENT HISTORY:
   1972 to present: Bowden & Company, Inc.
   1967 to 1971: Vice President, Butler Associates, Inc.
   1963 to 1967: Director—Mass Transit Center, BF Goodrich Co.
   1953 to 1963: District Manager, TRW Inc.
   1950 to 1953: Financial Analyst, St. Louis Union Trust Co.

PRIVATE CLUBS:
   The Union Club, Cleveland
   Red Apple Country Club, Eden Isle, AR
   Rotary—Paul Harris Fellow

ASSOCIATIONS/ PROFESSIONAL SOCIETIES:
   Association of Executive Search Consultants, Director
   American Marketing Association
   Society of Automotive Engineers
   Society of Human Resource Management

SPECIAL INTERESTS AND HOBBIES:
   Biking, photography, sailing

REPRESENTATIVE AND SIGNIFICANT PLACEMENTS:
   Richard McFerson, Controller to President, Property/Casualty
      Companies
      Nationwide Insurance

Stephen Huggins, Group Vice President
  BF Goodrich Aerospace
Charles Ennis, Vice President and General Counsel
  GenCorp
James C. Leslie, Vice President–Engineering to Vice President–Marketing
  TRW Inc.
Thomas N. Tower, Vice President–Marketing
  The East Ohio Gas Co.

WHAT I LOOK FOR IN GENERAL IN A CANDIDATE

The results-oriented quality match between the client's criteria and the candidate is my search goal. This is accomplished by:

A thorough understanding of client's criteria
Original research for the best-qualified candidates
The interview and screening process
Persistent, ongoing client and candidate communication

Integrity, intellect, and a positive career performance record must be supported by decisive fundamental leadership, motivating, communicating, planning, organizing, staffing, directing, controlling, listening, evaluating, and interpersonal skills. These should be appropriately enriched with vision, enthusiasm, creativity, tact, loyalty, and a sense of humor. These are the factors which concern me the most as I seek out and evaluate the quality-match candidates.

GEOGRAPHIC SCOPE OF RECRUITING ACTIVITIES:
  Serve clients nationwide and in Canada, Great Britain, Germany, Austria, Finland

TOTAL YEARS OF RETAINER-TYPE RECRUITING EXPERIENCE:
  24 years

WILLIAM J. BOWEN
Vice Chairman
Heidrick and Struggles, Inc.
125 S. Wacker Drive, Suite 2800
Chicago, IL 60606
Telephone: (312) 372-8811

Date of Birth: May 13, 1934
Grew up in: New York, New York

Heidrick and Struggles, Inc.

HIGHER EDUCATION:
Fordham University, New York
  B.S. degree, Economics, 1956
New York University
  M.B.A. degree, investments, 1963

MILITARY:
First Lieutenant, United States Air Force, 1956 to 1959

EMPLOYMENT HISTORY:
1973 to present: Heidrick and Struggles, Inc.
1969 to 1973: 1st Vice President, Shearson Hammill & Co., Inc.
1967 to 1969: Institutional Salesman, Hayden Stone, Inc.
1961 to 1967: Assistant Vice President, First National City Bank, New
  York
1959 to 1961: Trainee, Smith Barney & Co.

PRIVATE CLUBS:
Metropolitan Club, Chicago
Chicago Club
Union League Club of New York
Marco Polo, New York
Onwentsia Club, Lake Forest, Illinois

ASSOCIATIONS/ PROFESSIONAL SOCIETIES:
New York Society of Security Analysts

SPECIAL INTERESTS AND HOBBIES:
Golf, baseball, photography

REPRESENTATIVE AND SIGNIFICANT PLACEMENTS:
Lattie Coor, President
  Arizona State University
Frank Rhodes, President
  Cornell University
Vartan Gregorian, President
  Brown University
Peter Buchanan, President
  Council for Advancement and Support of Education (CASE)
Peter Stanley, President
  Pomona College

WHAT I LOOK FOR IN GENERAL IN A CANDIDATE

Integrity, leadership: a person with a "can do" attitude. While executives should have a high degree of self-confidence, you want someone who can lead and motivate others as well as share the success—not an "I, I, I" type. A sense of humor doesn't hurt.

GEOGRAPHIC SCOPE OF RECRUITING ACTIVITIES:
Serve clients nationwide

TOTAL YEARS OF RETAINER-TYPE RECRUITING EXPERIENCE:
18 years

MICHAEL D. BOXBERGER
Managing Director North America
Korn/Ferry International
120 S. Riverside Plaza, Suite 918
Chicago, IL 60606
Telephone: (312) 726-1841

Date of Birth: August 19, 1946
Grew up in: Elgin, Illinois

HIGHER EDUCATION:
University of Denver
    B.A. degree, biological sciences, 1968
University of Texas at Austin
    M.B.A. degree, finance, 1972

EMPLOYMENT HISTORY:
1986 to present: Korn/Ferry International
1985 to 1986: Partner and Manager–Dallas, Heidrick and Struggles, Inc.
1983 to 1985: Vice President Corporate Development, Kellogg-Rust, Inc.
1981 to 1983: President, McFaddin Ventures, Inc.
1977 to 1981: Senior Vice President and Manager–Houston, Heidrick and Struggles, Inc.
1974 to 1977: Senior Vice President, Capital National Bank
1972 to 1974: Account Executive, the Northern Trust Company

PRIVATE CLUBS:
Chicago Club
River Club of Chicago
Houston Club

ASSOCIATIONS/ PROFESSIONAL SOCIETIES:
The Lincoln Park Zoological Society, Chicago

SPECIAL INTERESTS AND HOBBIES:
Bird shooting, fishing, running, reading

REPRESENTATIVE AND SIGNIFICANT PLACEMENTS:
George V. Bayly, President and Chief Executive Officer
Ivex Corporation
J. Thomas Bouchard, Senior Vice President and Chief Human
Resources Officer
U.S. West, Inc.
Joe S. Farmer, President and Chief Operating Officer
Union Texas Petroleum
Arthur L. Patch, President and Chief Executive Officer
AppleTree Markets, Inc.
Charles E. Perry, President and Chief Executive Officer
The Friedkin Companies

WHAT I LOOK FOR IN GENERAL IN A CANDIDATE

To understand what I look for in a candidate, one must start with the assumption that I genuinely understand my client's business and culture and the specific requirements of the position. Once I am "behind the client's eye" and feel competent as an extension of my client in the marketplace, I look for the following:

- A consistent history of success throughout one's entire life
- The creativity to generate profits or truly "make a difference" regardless of the circumstances
- Leadership by example
- Self-confidence tempered with humility and tact
- A high energy level coupled with a singular focus and commitment to accomplish one's objective
- A proven ability to succeed in complex, difficult situations and to bounce back from adversity and win in the end
- Through it all, the good judgment that maintains a balance in one's life
- Values and ethics that are totally above reproach

GEOGRAPHIC SCOPE OF RECRUITING ACTIVITIES:
Serve clients nationwide and in Europe, Asia, Africa, Middle East

TOTAL YEARS OF RETAINER-TYPE RECRUITING EXPERIENCE:
10 years

ROBERT M. BRYZA
Chairman and President
Robert Lowell International
12200 Park Central Drive,
   Suite 120
Dallas, TX 75251
Telephone: (214) 233-2270

Date of Birth: April 17, 1926
Grew up in: Chicago, Illinois

Robert Lowell International

HIGHER EDUCATION:
Northwestern University, School of Commerce
   B.S. degree, business administration, 1956
Xavier University
   M.B.A. degree, personnel administration, 1960

MILITARY:
Captain, United States Air Force, 1943 to 1966

EMPLOYMENT HISTORY:
1977 to present: Robert Lowell International
1976 to 1977: Vice President–Human Resources, Corporate Officer,
   Houdaille Industries
1963 to 1976: Corporate Manager, Labor Relations, Dresser Industries, Inc.
1961 to 1963: General Manager, Relations Division, Elgin National
   Watch Co.
1960 to 1961: Consultant, Industrial Relations, A.T. Kearney & Co.
1956 to 1960: Personnel Director, Burton Rodgers
1948 to 1956: Plant Personnel Manager, Combustion Engineering

ASSOCIATIONS/PROFESSIONAL SOCIETIES:
Rotary International
Dallas Chamber of Commerce
Dallas Better Business Bureau

SPECIAL INTERESTS AND HOBBIES:
Golf, bowling, horseback riding

REPRESENTATIVE AND SIGNIFICANT PLACEMENTS:
Ronald J. Woods, President
  Universal Rundle
John Platt, President
  Dresser-Clark
William Reid, President
  M&S Systems, Inc. (Nortek)
Lowell Hill, Director–Employee Relations to Vice President–Employee
  Relations
  Harvard Industries
William Thornton, Vice President–Marketing–North America
  Spectus Systems-USA

WHAT I LOOK FOR IN GENERAL IN A CANDIDATE

1. Initially I look for a personality and management style that will blend well with my client's culture, values, and objectives.
2. Does the candidate communicate orally and in writing in a manner that displays imagination, a broad vocabulary, and complete understanding of the subject?

Then, I look for:

- The ability to lead, motivate, and be a team player
- A solid track record of completing assignments and meeting profit plan targets on time according to plan
- Longevity and accomplishments in each of the previous positions
- A healthy, mature mental and moral attitude in both the candidate's business and personal life
- The required education, knowledge, background, vision, and hands-on experience to be successful in the position; determine if there is true interest in the position or is the candidate using the situation for political purposes

GEOGRAPHIC SCOPE OF RECRUITING ACTIVITIES:
Serve clients nationwide and in Canada, France, Spain, Germany, and
  England

TOTAL YEARS OF RETAINER-TYPE RECRUITING EXPERIENCE:
14 years

SKOTT B. BURKLAND
President
Skott/Edwards Consultants
201 Route 17 North
Rutherford, NJ 07070
Telephone: (201) 935-8000

Date of Birth: May 25, 1942
Grew up in: Media, Pennsylvania

Skott/Edwards Consultants

HIGHER EDUCATION:
Dickinson College
A.B. degree, political science, 1964

MILITARY:
Staff Sergeant, United States Army, 1965 to 1971

EMPLOYMENT HISTORY:
1974 to present: Skott/Edwards Consultants
1970 to 1974: Vice President–Personnel–U.S. Consumer Products, The Singer Company
1969 to 1970: Personnel Manager–Area II Operating Group, Citibank
1968 to 1969: Director of Recruiting, W.R. Grace & Co.
1966 to 1967: Recruiter, The Sun Oil Company
1964 to 1966: Financial Analyst, E.I. DuPont DeNemours & Co.
1964 to 1966: Financial Analyst, E.I. DuPont DeNemours & Co.

PRIVATE CLUBS:
The New York Yacht Club
Porsche Club of America

ASSOCIATIONS/PROFESSIONAL SOCIETIES:
Association of Executive Search Consultants
International Association of Corporate and Professional Recruiters
New York Biotechnology Association

SPECIAL INTERESTS AND HOBBIES:
Ocean sailing, Porsche racing

REPRESENTATIVE AND SIGNIFICANT PLACEMENTS:
David F. Hale, President and Chief Executive Officer
Gensia Pharmaceuticals, Inc.
Gerald Z. Gibian, Corporate Vice President–Taxes and Real Estate
Estee Lauder Companies
Robert T. Abbott, Ph.D., President and Chief Executive Officer
Viagene, Inc.
Rodney G. Hilton, President and Chief Executive Officer
Ohmicron Corporation
Samuel K. Ackerman, M.D., Senior Vice President–Medical and
Regulatory Affairs
Xoma Corporation

WHAT I LOOK FOR IN GENERAL IN A CANDIDATE

I look for an established, consistent previous track record because prior performance is a strong indicator of the future. Intelligence and a complete understanding of the business process, including how to read a profit and loss statement, are additional critical factors in selection criteria. Energy, communication skills, appearance, loyalty, and a sense of humor round out candidates for important positions.

GEOGRAPHIC SCOPE OF RECRUITING ACTIVITIES:
Serve clients nationwide and in Europe

TOTAL YEARS OF RETAINER-TYPE RECRUITING EXPERIENCE:
18 years

C. DOUGLAS CALDWELL
Chairman
The Caldwell Partners International
64 Prince Arthur Avenue
Toronto, Ontario M5R 1B4
Telephone: (416) 920-7702

Date of Birth: January 26, 1937
Grew up in: Carleton Place,
  Ontario

The Caldwell Partners Internatinal

HIGHER EDUCATION:
  University of New Brunswick
    Bachelor of Business Administration, 1960

EMPLOYMENT HISTORY:
  1970 to present: The Caldwell Partners International
  1967 to 1970: Consultant, Hickling-Johnston Limited
  1965 to 1967: Marketing Manager, Monsanto Fibers
  1962 to 1965: Contract Specialist, Harding Carpets
  1960 to 1962: Sales Representative, Shell Oil

PRIVATE CLUBS:
  Royal Canadian Yacht Club
  Badminton & Racquet Club (Toronto)
  Georgian Peaks Ski Club

ASSOCIATIONS/PROFESSIONAL SOCIETIES:
  Association of Executive Search Consultants, international member-
    ship

SPECIAL INTERESTS AND HOBBIES:
  Skiing, sailing

REPRESENTATIVE AND SIGNIFICANT PLACEMENTS:
  Harry Rogers, Comptroller General, Office of the Privy Council
    Government of Canada
  Lionel G. Dodd, Chief Operating Officer
    Olympia & York Enterprises Corporation

John Cassaday, President and Chief Executive Officer
  CTV Television Network Limited
Lynton R. Wilson, President and Chief Operating Officer
  BCE Inc.
Donald H. Lander, President and Chief Executive Officer
  Canada Post Corporation

WHAT I LOOK FOR IN GENERAL IN A CANDIDATE

First, we look for attitudes and styles that fail:

- Any sign of *laziness*, which often is cunning and dangerous.
- A person whose *emphasis* is on appearance rather than substance.
- A process-oriented person rather than *results-driven*.
- Any fear of selling (one's ideas and leadership).
- Arrogance!
- Indication of failure to hire *strong, smart staff.*

On the positive side:

- A person with few obvious flaws; a person who has an understanding of people and their frailties, who is good at dealing with people.
- Above average *social skills* and *people skills* with the power to *influence.*
- High *self-confidence* but *subtle* in contests, *tactful* and *well-mannered.*
- High integrity, *likes work* and is a *hard worker*, great stamina.
- A good chairperson or *"head of meeting"* leader, yet detail minded.

Early jobs and repeated ability to get things done. Strengths should include being intensely human, intelligent, and thoughtful—a giver, a touch of single-mindedness and toughness to handle today's challenges. Strategic thinker and planner. Team player who is innovative and ambitious. Participative with strong loyalties to people and the community. Entrepreneurial spirit with commitment and dedication.

GEOGRAPHIC SCOPE OF RECRUITING ACTIVITIES:
Serve clients in Canada, Asia Pacific, Europe, the Americas

TOTAL YEARS OF RETAINER-TYPE RECRUITING EXPERIENCE:
22 years

ROBERT M. CALLAN
Partner
Callan Associates, Ltd.
1550 Spring Road
Oak Brook, IL 60521
Telephone: (708) 832-7080

Date of Birth: September 26,
1936
Grew up in: New York City

Callan Associates, Ltd.

HIGHER EDUCATION:
Fordham University
B.S. degree, business administration, 1958
New York University
M.B.A. degree, 1966

MILITARY:
First Lieutenant, United States Army, 1958 to 1960

EMPLOYMENT HISTORY:
1982 to present: Callan Associates
1981 to 1982: Partner, McFeely Wackerle
1973 to 1981: Senior Vice President and Partner, SpencerStuart Associates
1968 to 1973: Associate, Booz, Allen & Hamilton Inc.
1964 to 1968: Personnel Manager–Research, Hoffmann-La Roche Inc.
1961 to 1964: Employee Relations Manager, Continental Can Company

PRIVATE CLUBS:
Glen Oak Country Club
The DuPage Club

ASSOCIATIONS/PROFESSIONAL SOCIETIES:
International Association Corporate & Professional Recruiters
Illinois Management and Executive Search Consultants

SPECIAL INTERESTS AND HOBBIES:
Family, Hospital, and Community College Board Memberships

REPRESENTATIVE AND SIGNIFICANT PLACEMENTS:
Vice President–Corporate Planning to Executive Vice President and
   Director
   Major international health care company
Corporate Vice President–Marketing to President–North American
   Operations
   Major international capital equipment company
Controller to Vice President and General Manager
   International packaging company
President
   Major furniture company
President and Chief Executive Officer
   Major food company

WHAT I LOOK FOR IN GENERAL IN A CANDIDATE

- A striving for excellence and achievement in school, athletics, extra-curricular activities
- High ethics and personal honesty
- Natural leadership; someone who attracts a following and inspires loyalty
- Intelligence—not necessarily brilliance but a quick study, who homes in on key issues and identifies the right course of action
- Excellent communication skills and the ability to persuade and motivate
- Good judgment, patience, persistence, tenacity
- Success in business in both an up and down economy
- An executive who will really make a substantial difference for my client
- A healthy lifestyle and family environment that is supportive of senior executive responsibility

GEOGRAPHIC SCOPE OF RECRUITING ACTIVITIES:
Serve clients nationwide and in Europe

TOTAL YEARS OF RETAINER-TYPE RECRUITING EXPERIENCE:
23 years

JOHN H. CALLEN, JR.
Chairman and
** Chief Executive Officer**
Ward Howell International, Inc.
99 Park Avenue
New York, NY 10016
Telephone: (212) 697-3730

Date of Birth: June 19, 1932
Grew up in: New Jersey

Ward Howell International, Inc

HIGHER EDUCATION:
  Trinity College
    B.A. degree, history, 1955

MILITARY:
  First Lieutenant, United States Marine Corps, 1955 to 1958

EMPLOYMENT HISTORY:
  1977 to present: Ward Howell International, Inc.
  1958 to 1977: Burlington Industries
    1974 to 1977: President, Burlington Sportswear
    1973 to 1974: President, Galey and Lord
    1960 to 1973: Executive VP—Marketing, Burlington Madison Yarn
    Co.
    1958 to 1960: Sales Representative, Peerless Woolen Mills

PRIVATE CLUBS:
  Rumson Country Club, New Jersey
  Williams Club, New York

ASSOCIATIONS/PROFESSIONAL SOCIETIES:
  Association of Executive Search Consultants

SPECIAL INTERESTS AND HOBBIES:
  Golf, paddle tennis, cross-country skiing, hiking, the environment

REPRESENTATIVE AND SIGNIFICANT PLACEMENTS:
  Director of Engineering
    Saudi Arabian government agency

Chief Operating Officer (later promoted to President)
  Major textile knit fabric producer (acquired by a major holding company)
Executive Director
  Influential environmental advocacy organization
Chief Operating Officer (later promoted to President)
  Well-established, privately owned men's tailored clothing manufacturer
President
  Private college

WHAT I LOOK FOR IN GENERAL IN A CANDIDATE

I look for signs of energy, intelligence, self-motivation, creative problem-solving ability, and, if a high-level position, stature becomes important. In this era, I also look for evidence of strong interpersonal skills, a sense of humor, and an international content in past experience, which is becoming more and more important. Further, I tend to favor candidates who are active in their community or have strong away-from-work interests.

When filling corporate positions in highly competitive industries, I like to see evidence of a competitive spirit—particularly when filling marketing and general management positions.

GEOGRAPHIC SCOPE OF RECRUITING ACTIVITIES:
  Serve clients nationwide and internationally

TOTAL YEARS OF RETAINER-TYPE RECRUITING EXPERIENCE:
  14 years

MICHAEL D. CAVER
Partner, Health Care Practice
Heidrick and Struggles, Inc.
125 S. Wacker Drive, Suite 2800
Chicago, IL 60606
Telephone: (312) 372-8811

Date of Birth: April 7, 1942
Grew up in: Washington, DC and
Richmond, Virginia

Bachrach

HIGHER EDUCATION:
Hampden-Sydney College, Virginia
B.S. degree, modern European history, 1964

EMPLOYMENT HISTORY:
1979 to present: Heidrick and Struggles, Inc.
1977 to 1979: Director, International Personnel, Baxter-Travenol Laboratories.
1976 to 1977: Manager International Personnel Administration, Procter & Gamble Co.
1972 to 1976: Director of Personnel Administration, Procter & Gamble Co. of Canada, Ltd.
1967 to 1972: Various Marketing, Sales and Personnel, Procter & Gamble Co.

PRIVATE CLUBS:
Metropolitan Club

ASSOCIATIONS/PROFESSIONAL SOCIETIES:
American College of Healthcare Executives
American Association of Healthcare Consultants

SPECIAL INTERESTS AND HOBBIES:
Photography, classical music, international travel, fishing

REPRESENTATIVE AND SIGNIFICANT PLACEMENTS:
Richard J. Davidson, President and Chief Executive Officer
American Hospital Association

C. Thomas Smith, President and Chief Executive Officer
  Voluntary Hospitals of America
Richard J. Kramer, President and Chief Executive Officer
  Catholic Healthcare West
Leighton Smith, M.D., President and Chief Executive Officer
  Lutheran General Medical Group
Robert J. Baker, President and Chief Executive Officer
  University Hospital Consortium, Inc.

WHAT I LOOK FOR IN GENERAL IN A CANDIDATE

My objective is to identify candidates whose unique blend of intellect, experiences, concrete accomplishments, values, personality, style, ambitions, and family goals most closely match my client's *total* opportunity.

Given that our client organizations are almost always undergoing fundamental change, we are retained to help them achieve "critical mass" in senior executive strength. Therefore, it is essential that candidates have demonstrated they consistently accomplish priority objectives while anticipating the future and properly positioning their organizations for future successes.

Our clients depend on our ability to present candidates of conspicuous character, values, and integrity; well respected by their peers; committed to continuing professional development; balanced between collegial, participative, and directive styles as appropriate; with strong common sense and good humor; passionate about their commitments; and who inspire and develop others. Such candidates are thoughtful about their affiliations, reluctant to leave as long as they are contributing, and invariably make major impacts in all their involvements.

Especially appealing are those candidates who know themselves well and confidently share their limitations and frustrations, as well as their strengths, accomplishments, and aspirations.

GEOGRAPHIC SCOPE OF RECRUITING ACTIVITIES:
Serve clients nationally and internationally

TOTAL YEARS OF RETAINER-TYPE RECRUITING EXPERIENCE:
12 years

DAVID E. CHAMBERS
President
David Chambers & Associates,
 Inc.
6 East 43rd Street
New York, NY 10017
Telephone: (212) 986-8653

Date of Birth: March 6, 1938
Grew up in: Mason City, Iowa

David Chambers & Associates, Inc.

HIGHER EDUCATION:
 University of Arizona
  B.S. degree, business administration, 1961

MILITARY:
 Specialist Fourth Class, United States Army, 1961 to 1963

EMPLOYMENT HISTORY:
 1974 to present: David Chambers & Associates, Inc.
 1973 to 1974: President, Executive Search Division, Fry Consultants,
  Inc.
 1969 to 1973: Partner, Antell, Wright & Nagel
 1968 to 1969: Employment Director, Allied Chemical
 1967 to 1968: President, David Chambers Company
 1966 to 1967: Associate, Booz, Allen & Hamilton
 1965 to 1966: Employment Supervisor, Xerox Corporation
 1961 to 1965: Employment Representative, Pan American World Air-
  ways

PRIVATE CLUBS:
 Winged Foot Golf Club, New York
 The Boardroom, New York
 Union League Club, New York and Chicago
 Capital Hill, Washington, DC

SPECIAL INTERESTS AND HOBBIES:
 Golf, travel, theater, people

REPRESENTATIVE AND SIGNIFICANT PLACEMENTS:
 Stephen P. Munn, President and Chief Executive Officer
   Carlisle Companies, Inc.
 Patricia G. Campbell, Executive Vice President
   Times Mirror Magazines, Inc.
 John E. Pomeroy, President and Chief Executive Officer
   Dover Technologies, Inc.
 General Charles E. Williams, Chief Operating Officer
   Tollroad Corporation of Virginia
 Dr. Kathleen B. Cooper, Chief Economist
   Exxon Corporation

WHAT I LOOK FOR IN GENERAL IN A CANDIDATE

In addition to personal chemistry and specific background and experience required on each search assignment, I am interested in the candidate's maturity, energy level, appearance, leadership skills, and other personal attributes.

Other considerations include family home life, outside interests, and other matters which will show the person's "balance" of make-up and how he or she projects himself or herself.

GEOGRAPHIC SCOPE OF RECRUITING ACTIVITIES:
 Serve clients nationwide and in Canada, Mexico, and Europe through
   affiliates

TOTAL YEARS OF RETAINER-TYPE RECRUITING EXPERIENCE:
 23 years

DAVID H. CHARLSON
President and Chief Executive
  Officer
Chestnut Hill Partners, Ltd.
2345 Waukegan Road,
  Suite S-165
Deerfield, IL 60015
Telephone: (708) 940-9690

Date of Birth: May 26, 1947
Grew up in: Pittsburgh, Pennsylvania

Chestnut Hill Partners

HIGHER EDUCATION:
  University of Arizona, Tucson
    B.S. degree, business administration, 1969

EMPLOYMENT HISTORY:
  1989 to present: Chestnut Hill Partners
  1984 to 1989: Executive Vice President–Managing Director, Richards
    Consultants
  1976 to 1984: Managing Director–Central Region, Korn/Ferry Inter-
    national
  1975 to 1976: Staff Vice President, Staub Warmbold & Associates
  1974 to 1975: Manager–Corporate Employment, General Foods Cor-
    poration
  1970 to 1974: Personnel Director–International, Bank of America
  1969 to 1970: Marketing Officer, Wells Fargo Bank

PRIVATE CLUBS:
  University Club of Chicago
  Bannockburn Bath & Tennis Club

ASSOCIATIONS/PROFESSIONAL SOCIETIES:
  Illinois Executive Recruiting Council
  Chicago Council on Foreign Relations

SPECIAL INTERESTS AND HOBBIES:
  Tae kwon do, auto racing, golf

REPRESENTATIVE AND SIGNIFICANT PLACEMENTS:
James Armstrong, President and Chief Operating Officer
    Norwest Bank Corporation
O.B. Parrish, President–Pharmaceutical Group
    G.D. Searle
Dr. Joseph Davies, President–Searle Research and Development
    G.D. Searle
Dr. Frank Steinberg, President
    Lorex
Edward Grosso, President and Chief Executive Officer
    AMP/Akzo

WHAT I LOOK FOR IN GENERAL IN A CANDIDATE

I try to see a candidate through the eyes of my client and match as closely as possible his/her management style, work ethic, and personality to that of my client organization. I look for a demonstrated track record of success in more than one environment, as well as individuals who are bright, energetic, and articulate in both oral and written form. They must be self-assured and not easily threatened or intimidated and have the proven ability to recruit, hire, lead, manage, and control other professionals.

I look for candidates who can add value to my client's organization and have the ability to grow beyond the assignment they may be hired to perform.

Finally, I look for someone whose management style and expertise most closely align themselves with those of my client's organization.

GEOGRAPHIC SCOPE OF RECRUITING ACTIVITIES:
Serve clients nationwide and in England, Spain, Switzerland, Germany, France, Japan, Korea, Brazil, Mexico, and Canada

TOTAL YEARS OF RETAINER-TYPE RECRUITING EXPERIENCE:
17 years

JOHN R. "JACK" CLAREY
President
Jack Clarey Associates, Inc.
1200 Shermer Road, Suite 108
Northbrook, IL 60062
Telephone: (708) 498-2870

Date of Birth: June 5, 1942
Grew up in: Des Moines, Iowa

Furla Studios

HIGHER EDUCATION:
Iowa State University
    B.S. degree, industrial administration, 1965
University of Pennsylvania, Wharton School
    M.B.A. degree, corporate finance, 1972

MILITARY:
Lieutenant, United States Navy, 1965 to 1970

EMPLOYMENT HISTORY:
1982 to present: Jack Clarey Associates, Inc.
1976 to 1982: Vice President and Partner, Heidrick and Struggles, Inc.
1974 to 1976: Manager, Price Waterhouse
1972 to 1974: Financial Analyst, Ford Motor Company

PRIVATE CLUBS:
Mid-America Club
Union League Club of Chicago
Sunset Ridge Country Club

ASSOCIATIONS/ PROFESSIONAL SOCIETIES:
Association of Executive Search Consultants, Director
International Association of Corporate and Professional Recruiters, Director–Midwest

SPECIAL INTERESTS AND HOBBIES:
Flying, tennis, microcomputers, Lifeline Pilots (charity)

REPRESENTATIVE AND SIGNIFICANT PLACEMENTS:
President and Chief Executive Officer
   Industrial products holding company
President and Chief Operating Officer
   Consumer durables manufacturer
President and Chief Executive Officer
   Industrial products manufacturer
President
   Consumer packaged goods company
Chief Operating Officer
   International law firm

WHAT I LOOK FOR IN GENERAL IN A CANDIDATE

Obviously, for each assignment the required background and experience differ. Additionally, personal attributes will vary significantly depending on the client's "culture." For example, there must be compatibility in style, values, and priorities. On the other hand, regardless of the assignment, the following are characteristics I seek in each candidate:

- Absolute integrity
- Pattern of consistent achievement
- Common sense
- High energy level and skill in focusing that energy
- Balance between professional and personal interests
- Sense of humor
- Sense of responsibility and accountability for one's own actions
- Realistic acknowledgment of own weaknesses as well as strengths
- Breadth of perspective
- Willingness to listen and to see the other person's point of view
- Ability to deal with adversity or failure by becoming stronger for the experience

GEOGRAPHIC SCOPE OF RECRUITING ACTIVITIES:
Serve clients nationwide

TOTAL YEARS OF RETAINER-TYPE RECRUITING EXPERIENCE:
17 years

WILLIAM B. CLEMENS, JR.
Managing Director
Norman Broadbent International
Inc.
200 Park Avenue
New York, NY 10166
Telephone: (212) 953-6990

Date of Birth: May 6, 1944
Grew up in: Lynchburg, Virginia

Ken Korsh Photographers

HIGHER EDUCATION:
Bloomfield College, New Jersey
　B.A. degree, political science, 1967

EMPLOYMENT HISTORY:
1987 to present: Norman Broadbent International
1979 to 1987: Managing Director, Russell Reynolds Associates, Inc.
1972 to 1979: Director of Staffing, McKinsey & Company, Inc.
1969 to 1972: Personnel Manager, NL Industries
1967 to 1969: Recruiting Coordinator, Squibb Corporation

PRIVATE CLUBS:
University Club, NY
Norwalk Yacht Club, CT
Orchid Island Golf and Beach Club, Vero Beach, FL

ASSOCIATIONS/PROFESSIONAL SOCIETIES:
Association of Executive Search Consultants

SPECIAL INTERESTS AND HOBBIES:
Sailing, skiing, racquet sports, traveling, theater

REPRESENTATIVE AND SIGNIFICANT PLACEMENTS:
Steven Goldstein, President and Chief Executive Officer
　American Express Bank Ltd.
Frank J. Jones, Senior Vice President/Chief Investment Officer
　The Guardian Life Insurance Company of America

Donald G. Ogilvie, Executive Director
  American Bankers Association
Ian Heap, Chairman and Chief Executive Officer
  Exel Corporation
Quentin Smith (Retired Chairman, TPF&C), Member, Board of
  Directors
  Guardian Life Insurance Company

WHAT I LOOK FOR IN GENERAL IN A CANDIDATE

Our profession is an art, not a science. The quality of creative thinking the recruiter brings to his art, the judgment he uses in assessing prospects against client requirements, and the skill to close in a manner beneficial to the client and candidate come only from experience. There is simply no substitute for experience.

One evaluates candidates against specific client needs; personal characteristics, business skills, and personality traits are in part driven by the nature of the organization and the role for which we are recruiting. Nonetheless, there are certain characteristics I look for in every candidate. Not necessarily in order, they are stable personal and professional history, series of successive accomplishments in their chosen field, strong sense of self, sense of humor, personal and professional ambition, positive and genuine personality but with a competitive edge, willingness to make decisions, ability to attract and develop people, intellectual curiosity, understanding the economics of a business and how to make money, get things done, self-directed, highly motivated. To generalize is to overstate the obvious; where we add value is in assisting a client within a given set of candidate parameters and selecting the most appropriate prospect in a timely fashion.

GEOGRAPHIC SCOPE OF RECRUITING ACTIVITIES:
Serve clients nationwide and in Europe

TOTAL YEARS OF RETAINER-TYPE RECRUITING EXPERIENCE:
24 years

W. HOYT COLTON
President, W. Hoyt Colton Asso-
  ciates
67 Wall Street
New York, NY 10005
Telephone: (212) 956-2006

Date of Birth: September 13,
  1939
Grew up in: Huntington, Long
  Island, NY

Colton

HIGHER EDUCATION:
  Long Island University
    B.S. degree, business, 1966

MILITARY:
  First Lieutenant, United States Army Reserves, 1962 to 1968

EMPLOYMENT HISTORY:
  1979 to present: W. Hoyt Colton Associates
  1975 to 1979: Vice President, Director Human Resources, Smith Bar-
    ney & Co.
  1971 to 1975: Assistant Vice President, Regional Personnel Manager,
    Dean Witter & Co.
  1970 to 1971: Employment Manager, Brown Brothers Harriman &
    Co.
  1968 to 1970: Employment Manager, Walston & Co.
  1966 to 1968: Employment Representative, United Airlines

ASSOCIATIONS/PROFESSIONAL SOCIETIES:
  Veterans of the Seventh Regiment, S.A.R.
  Trustee and President of The Stony Brook School Alumni Association

SPECIAL INTERESTS AND HOBBIES:
  Golf, sailing, tennis, skiing
  The Stony Brook School

REPRESENTATIVE AND SIGNIFICANT PLACEMENTS:
Managing Director–Private Placements
    Investment bank
Managing Director–Fixed Income Research
    Investment bank
Vice President–Municipal Finance
    Major commercial bank
Chief Economist
    Major commercial bank
Chief Financial Officer
    Brokerage firm

WHAT I LOOK FOR IN GENERAL IN A CANDIDATE

I look for people who command respect in their chosen vocation at their current level of achievement; people who will bring creativity, energy, leadership, and vision to the new assignment.

The criteria I establish in the candidate's ideal profile are a directed drive, presence, a strong work ethic, personal substance, and a progressively successful track record.

Excellent interpersonal skills, a sense of self, intelligence, stability, honesty, integrity, and personal balance are musts. But above all, that person should have common sense, a natural manner and a style and direction that is consistent with the client's culture and management philosophy.

GEOGRAPHIC SCOPE OF RECRUITING ACTIVITIES:
Serve clients nationwide

TOTAL YEARS OF RETAINER-TYPE RECRUITING EXPERIENCE:
12 years

PETER D. CRIST
Managing Director/Branch Manager
Russell Reynolds Associates, Inc.
200 S. Wacker Drive, Suite 3600
Chicago, IL 60606
Telephone: (312) 993-9696

Date of Birth: March 8, 1952
Grew up in: Piqua, Ohio

Bachhrach

HIGHER EDUCATION:
  Brown University
    A.B. degree, political science, 1974

EMPLOYMENT HISTORY:
  1977 to present: Russell Reynolds Associates, Inc.
  1976 to 1977: Manager of Public Relations, Household Finance Corporation
  1974 to 1976: Director, E.F. McDonald Company

PRIVATE CLUBS:
  Union League Club of Chicago
  River Club

ASSOCIATIONS/PROFESSIONAL SOCIETIES:
  Economic Club of Chicago
  Brown University Alumni Association
  Northwestern Memorial Corporation, Board Member
  United Charities, Board Member

SPECIAL INTERESTS AND HOBBIES:
  Coaching Little League baseball

REPRESENTATIVE AND SIGNIFICANT PLACEMENTS:
  S. Waite Rawls III, Vice Chairman
    Continental Bank Corporation
  James E. LeBlanc, Chairman and Chief Executive Officer
    Whirlpool Financial Corporation

Ronald L. Kerber, Executive Vice President and Chief Technology
  Officer
  Whirlpool Corporation
Larry C. Klumpp, Chairman and Chief Executive Officer
  Pettibone Corporation
Bernard Walch, President
  Bartlett Grain Company

WHAT I LOOK FOR IN GENERAL IN A CANDIDATE

There are certain characteristics that I look for in each and every
candidate. Regardless of the project, I want a person who has a strong
self-awareness and an ability to recognize his or her own strengths and
weaknesses. The more the intellectual honesty, the more attractive the
candidate.

Sensitivity to people, a sense of the subtle, and an ability to project
one's thought process out in situation-management issues are important
features. A positive and genuine personality, intellectual curiosity, and
motivation are important, as is a fundamental sense of humor.

Leadership traits such as the ability to assess risk in both sit-
uational and market-oriented applications, competitiveness, decision-
making skills, energy, and professional ambition have to be balanced
with common sense, humility, and the demeanor to relate with others.
Good listeners who combine the qualities of a team player with a strong
sense of purpose are most attractive.

Strong morals and a balanced family life are pieces of the multidi-
mensional personality which I seek.

GEOGRAPHIC SCOPE OF RECRUITING ACTIVITIES:
Serve clients nationwide and in the UK

TOTAL YEARS OF RETAINER-TYPE RECRUITING EXPERIENCE:
14+ years

RICHARD J. CRONIN
President
Hodge-Cronin & Associates, Inc.
9575 W. Higgins Road, Suite 503
Rosemont, IL 60018
Telephone: (708) 692-2041

Date of Birth: October 4, 1930
Grew up in: Chicago, Illinois

Hedge Cronin Assoc.

HIGHER EDUCATION:
Xavier University
B.S. degree, education, 1974

MILITARY:
Specialist Third Class, United States Army, 1953 to 1955

EMPLOYMENT HISTORY:
1963 to present: Hodge-Cronin & Associates, Inc.
1958 to 1963: Manager–Employment, ITT Telecommunications
1956 to 1958: Manager–Employment, Admiral Corporation

PRIVATE CLUBS:
Cincinnati Club
Chicago:
   Meadow Club
   Metropolitan Club
   Monroe Club
   410 Club
   Plaza and River Clubs

ASSOCIATIONS/PROFESSIONAL SOCIETIES:
International Association of Corporate and Professional Recruiters,
   Board Member
Society of Human Resource Management
Consultants Group Benefit Trust, Trustee

SPECIAL INTERESTS AND HOBBIES:
Family

REPRESENTATIVE AND SIGNIFICANT PLACEMENTS:
  Tec Eischeid, Senior Vice President–Finance to President
    Revel/Monogram
  James Sheridan, President and Chief Executive Officer
    Victor Comptometer Corporation
  Robert MacNally, President
    Tommy Armour Golf Company
  J. Dennis Burns, Vice President/General Manager to President
    American Biltrite, Inc., Tape Products Division
  F.M. Taylor, Jr., President
    Victor Recreational Products Company

WHAT I LOOK FOR IN GENERAL IN A CANDIDATE

There are four basic factors in each individual's makeup, namely, intelligence, motivation, personality, and knowledge/experience. Over the past 30 years, I have developed a structured interview format directed at determining a candidate's intellectual skills and aptitudes, motivational characteristics, personality strengths and limitations, and knowledge/experience. After coupling this with the particular position specifications we have developed during meetings with the client and after three to four hours spent in interviewing a candidate, we can and do make an objective decision as to whether this candidate is qualified for what our client is seeking. For those candidates we feel are qualified, we conduct extensive reference checks.

GEOGRAPHIC SCOPE OF RECRUITING ACTIVITIES:
  Serve clients nationwide and, through member firms belonging
    to International Independent Consultants in Austria, Denmark,
    France, Germany, Italy, the Netherlands, Norway, Singapore, Spain,
    Switzerland, Sweden, and the United Kingdom

TOTAL YEARS OF RETAINER-TYPE RECRUITING EXPERIENCE:
  28 years

O.D. "DAN" CRUSE
**Managing Director Worldwide
 High Technology Practice
SpencerStuart
1717 Main Street, Suite 5300
Dallas, TX 75201
Telephone: (214) 658-1777**

**Date of Birth: March 24, 1939
Grew up in: Texas**

Spencer Stuart

HIGHER EDUCATION:
   University of Dallas
      B.A. degree, liberal arts, 1961

EMPLOYMENT HISTORY:
   1977 to present: SpencerStuart
   1975 to 1977: Vice President–Human Resources, Farah Manufactur-
      ing Company
   1966 to 1975: Vice President–Central Services, Tracor, Inc.
   1963 to 1966: Labor Relations Specialist, General Electric Company

PRIVATE CLUBS:
   Las Colinas Country Club
   Tower Club

ASSOCIATIONS/PROFESSIONAL SOCIETIES:
   Knights of Malta

SPECIAL INTERESTS AND HOBBIES:
   Golf, outdoor activities, including bird hunting and fishing

REPRESENTATIVE AND SIGNIFICANT PLACEMENTS:
   Chief Executive Officer
      High-technology international trade association
   Chief Executive Officer
      NYSE high-technology turnaround
   Chief Executive Officer
      Hotel enterprise owned by one of the nation's leading business
      families

Group Executive
A major business within a NYSE company with a 100-year history/tradition
Chief Executive Officers/Chief Operating Officers
Venture-funded businesses replacing entrepreneurial founders

WHAT I LOOK FOR IN GENERAL IN A CANDIDATE

In general, we make a judgment regarding the executive's ability to make a difference in our client's results. Has the candidate demonstrated the capacity for producing results (beyond the norm of good performance) that will produce a sustainable positive impact within the client organization? Other traits we evaluate include energy and work ethic; self-image; judgment; interpersonal skills; and commitment/dedication. And, finally, will the candidate "fit" in the client's culture even if charged with being a "change agent?"

GEOGRAPHIC SCOPE OF RECRUITING ACTIVITIES:
Serve clients nationwide and in Japan, Germany, France, Spain, Brazil, and Australia

TOTAL YEARS OF RETAINER-TYPE RECRUITING EXPERIENCE:
14+ years

W. MICHAEL DANFORTH
Executive Vice President
Hyde Danforth & Company
5950 Berkshire Lane, Suite 1600
Dallas, TX 75225
Telephone: (214) 691-5966

Date of Birth: August 21, 1941
Grew up in: Longview, Texas

HIGHER EDUCATION:
University of North Texas
B.S. degree, psychology, 1963

Hyde Danforth & Company

MILITARY:
Staff Sergeant, United States Army, Texas National Guard, 1964 to 1970

EMPLOYMENT HISTORY:
1974 to present: Hyde Danforth & Company
1973 to 1974: Vice President, Wescott Associates
1971 to 1973: Vice President and Corporate Secretary, CIC Corporation
1971: Consultant, Booz, Allen & Hamilton, PAR Technology Division
1969 to 1971: Consultant, Peat Marwick Mitchell & Co.
1963 to 1969: Various sales and marketing positions, Hartford Insurance, Ford Motor Company, USM Corp.

SPECIAL INTERESTS AND HOBBIES:
Antique collecting (European furniture and American primitives), travel, theater, bridge

REPRESENTATIVE AND SIGNIFICANT PLACEMENTS:
Partners/Practice Groups
Four of the top ten law firms (eight of the top twenty)
Chief Operating Officer
Major national hotel chain
President
International real estate developer
Dean of the School of Business
Leading private university
Vice President/Director of Research and Development
International telecommunications manufacturer

WHAT I LOOK FOR IN GENERAL IN A CANDIDATE

The closest match to the position/candidate specification. We have created this document in conjunction and collaboration with our client; thus it should reflect the best "picture" of the opportunity and experience required of the candidate—it is the standard against which I measure candidates. Within this framework, specific attributes which I seek include:

- Personal and professional integrity
- Chemistry "fit"—is he or she a proper match with the client
- Proven track record as both a leader and decision-maker
- Perspective—an appropriate sense of the blend of professional, personal, and family values and needs
- Potential—does the candidate have "upward mobility"?
- Sense of humor—ability to laugh at the foibles of life and its unique challenges
- Ability to confront and answer the tough questions, the good sense to realistically identify personal and professional weaknesses, and the demonstrated ability to address and rectify them
- Ability to listen, to hear, and to comprehend what is implied as well as what is said
- Vision and a sense of purpose—a candidate who can effectively communicate his or her goals, ambitions, dreams, and objectives

Executive search, for better or worse, is an art, not a science. To perform professionally as a true consultant, we must not only represent our client and its opportunity (complete with warts), but also be willing to take a firm and objective stand relative to candidates and their true potential, or lack thereof, for that client.

GEOGRAPHIC SCOPE OF RECRUITING ACTIVITIES:
Serve clients nationwide and in Europe

TOTAL YEARS OF RETAINER-TYPE RECRUITING EXPERIENCE:
18 years

DAVID M. deWILDE
Managing Director
Chartwell Partners International,
  Inc.
275 Battery Street, Suite 2180
San Francisco, CA 94111
Telephone: (415) 296-0600

Date of Birth: August 11, 1940
Grew up in: Shiloh, New Jersey

Chartwell Partners International, Inc.

HIGHER EDUCATION:
  Dartmouth College
    A.B. degree, government, 1966
  University of Virginia
    LL.B. degree, 1967
  Stanford University
    M.S. degree, management, 1984

MILITARY:
  Lieutenant, United States Navy, 1962 to 1964

EMPLOYMENT HISTORY:
  1989 to present: Chartwell Partners International, Inc.
  1984 to 1988: Managing Director–Financial Services, Boyden Inter-
    national
  1981 to 1983: Executive Vice President for Policy and Planning, Fan-
    nie Mae
  1977 to 1981: Managing Director, Lepercq deNeuflize and Company
  1976 to 1977: President, Ginnie Mae
  1974 to 1976: Deputy Commissioner of the FHA/Assistant Secretary
    for Housing and Mortgage Credit, HUD
  1972 to 1974: Investment Banker, Lehman Brothers
  1967 to 1972: Attorney, Curtis, Mallet-Prevost, Colt & Mosie

PRIVATE CLUBS:
  Metropolitan Club of Washington, DC
  Belvedere Tennis Club

REPRESENTATIVE AND SIGNIFICANT PLACEMENTS:
Chairman and Chief Executive Officer
  $16 billion privately held financial institution
Chairman and Chief Executive Officer
  $18 billion publicly held financial institution
President and Chief Executive Officer
  Privately held major national mortgage bank
Chief Financial Officer
  Leading West coast merchant bank
Managing Director
  Prominent New York investment bank

WHAT I LOOK FOR IN GENERAL IN A CANDIDATE

I focus on fit. Like Cinderella, it's not sufficient to be a first-rate person unless the glass slipper fits your foot. So, we work closely with our client to carefully define the need. That need, typically, breaks down to a combination of leadership, management, and expertise. We then recruit an executive whose qualities enable her or him to best meet our client's specific need.

Within that framework, I generally look for a consistent record of accomplishment and good judgment. Intelligence is important. Integrity is essential. Energy and enthusiasm should be coupled with commitment and discipline. In a world of imperfection, ability to learn from mistakes is a must.

One of my clients told me, "'Don't bring us a peacetime general." Since then, I've looked for evidence of performance under fire. I am also impressed by executives who have learned to leverage themselves through information technology. Finally, the ability to communicate effectively is an essential skill in any organization. Without it, you cannot lead, manage, or share expertise.

GEOGRAPHIC SCOPE OF RECRUITING ACTIVITIES:
Serve clients nationwide

TOTAL YEARS OF RETAINER-TYPE RECRUITING EXPERIENCE:
7 years

RALPH E. DIECKMANN
President
Dieckmann & Associates, Ltd.
75 East Wacker Drive, Suite 1800
Chicago, IL 60601
Telephone: (312) 372-4949

Date of Birth: March 30, 1944
Grew up in: Cleveland, Ohio

Bachhrach

HIGHER EDUCATION:
  Northwestern University
    B.A. degree, psychology, 1966
  Loyola University of Chicago
    M.S. degree, industrial relations, 1972

EMPLOYMENT HISTORY:
  1981 to present: Dieckmann & Associates, Ltd.
  1973 to 1981: Manager–Executive Search Division, KPMG Peat
    Marwick
  1966 to 1973: Director of Recruiting, R.R. Donnelley & Sons Co.

PRIVATE CLUBS:
  Tavern Club
  East Bank Club

ASSOCIATIONS/PROFESSIONAL SOCIETIES:
  International Search Associates
  International Association of Corporate and Professional Recruiters
  Human Resource Management Association of Chicago
  Employment Management Association

SPECIAL INTERESTS AND HOBBIES:
  Opera, symphony, tennis, cycling, cross-country and downhill skiing,
    sailing, travel, civic and charity boards

REPRESENTATIVE AND SIGNIFICANT PLACEMENTS:
  William H. Bolinder, Chief Executive Officer
    Zurich Insurance Group—United States

Barry Gilway, President–Commercial Division
   Maryland Casualty Company
Newton Allen, President and Chief Executive Officer
   Farm Bureau Services
Glenn E. Stinson, President and Chief Executive Officer
   ABC Rail Corporation
George Welch, President
   Rockford Powertrain

WHAT I LOOK FOR IN GENERAL IN A CANDIDATE

An executive recruiter's greatest value-added service is helping determine which unique candidate talents will have a leveraging effect on client results. Necessary to this process are understanding the complexities of the position within its organizational context and determining the skill sets required to appropriately complement the existing management corps.

Notwithstanding the unique aspects of every search, seventeen characteristics build a foundation for outstanding executive performance.

Communications excellence is the essence of the executive function. *Leadership* requires *charisma* to mobilize the emotional support systems and *drive* to achieve what charisma won't. *Vision* provides the impetus for leadership and *realism* the boundaries to the vision. *Common sense* allows one to lead in the right direction and *intelligence* to lead briskly. *Diversified interests* are a sign of intelligence and a foil for tunnel vision. *Perseverance* multiplies the effectiveness of intelligence. *Self-confidence* and *delegation* permit accepting new responsibilities by entrusting old ones to others. *Decisiveness* combats inertia, the cancer of organizations. *Flexibility* and *creativity* are the primary tools for coping with exponential change, with *staffing finesse* essential to frequent adaptation. Finally, a *sense of humor* is the best outlet for the inevitable stress with which all executives must cope.

GEOGRAPHIC SCOPE OF RECRUITING ACTIVITIES:
   Serve clients nationally and in Europe, South America, Asia, and Australia

TOTAL YEARS OF RETAINER-TYPE RECRUITING EXPERIENCE:
   18 years

ROBERT W. DINGMAN
President
Robert W. Dingman Company, Inc.
32131 West Lindero Canyon Road
Westlake Village, CA 91361
Telephone: (818) 991-5950

Date of Birth: August 23, 1926
Grew up in: Upstate New York

Robt V. Dingman Co. Inc.

HIGHER EDUCATION:
Houghton College, New York
  B.A. degree, 1950

MILITARY:
Private First Class, United States Army, 1944 to 1946

EMPLOYMENT HISTORY:
1979 to present: Robert W. Dingman Co.
1974 to 1979: VP & Partner, Billington, Fox & Ellis
1966 to 1974: VP & Partner, Wilkinson, Sedwick & Yelverton
1950 to 1966: Manager, Arthur Young & Co.
1951 to 1961: Personnel positions in industry, government, and education

PRIVATE CLUBS:
Jonathan Club, Los Angeles
North Ranch Country Club, Westlake Village

ASSOCIATIONS/PROFESSIONAL SOCIETIES:
California Executive Recruiters Association
Association of Executive Search Consultants
Christian Management Association

SPECIAL INTERESTS AND HOBBIES:
Tennis
Author: *The Complete Search Committee Guidebook*
Board Member: Mission Aviation Fellowship

REPRESENTATIVE AND SIGNIFICANT PLACEMENTS:
Vice President–Marketing to President and Chief Executive Officer
   Airline
Senior Vice President–Sales and Marketing to General Manager
   Medical device company
President and Chief Executive Officer
   Computer software company
President/Chief Executive Officer
   Large international relief organization
Executive Vice President to President
   Large regional construction company

WHAT I LOOK FOR IN GENERAL IN A CANDIDATE

What I look for in a candidate varies according to what I have learned about my client. One client may require a highly competitive, intense, and politically adept type of person, while another client may favor someone who is more a team builder, values-oriented person who devotes time to the family and community.

The best possible fit is based on shared values, compatible style, and company goals that allow the candidate to see his or her own goals to be congruent. When there is a shared vision, then the other important factors lie in finding qualities that fit the client's "comfort zone." Search consultants seldom make errors in matters of basic technical competence because these are so easily checked out. Our judgments are of special value as we discern the crucial, though sometimes subtle, things in a firm's culture that make for success.

With all candidates, I look for evidence of leadership, decisiveness, integrity, and how they have rebounded from failures. I have little time for candidates who are less than open with me, cannot identify their limitations, or have only criticism for their past superiors. As I understand that ego space the candidate requires, I can then relate it to that of my client, so that both can have their needs met as they work together.

GEOGRAPHIC SCOPE OF RECRUITING ACTIVITIES:
Serve clients nationwide

TOTAL YEARS OF RETAINER-TYPE RECRUITING EXPERIENCE:
32 years

JOHN P. DiVENUTO
Chairman and Chief Executive Officer
Deven Associates International, Inc.
One Claridge Drive
Verona, NJ 07044
Telephone: (201) 239-5500

Date of Birth: January 22, 1940
Grew up in: Harrison, New Jersey

Deven Associates International, Inc.

HIGHER EDUCATION:
Jersey City State College
B.A. degree, social science, 1965
M.A. degree, education, 1967

MILITARY:
Specialist Fourth Class, United States Army, 1959 to 1962

EMPLOYMENT HISTORY:
1978 to present: Deven Associates International, Inc.
1975 to 1978: Director–Human Resources, Church & Dwight, Inc.
1970 to 1975: Management Consultant, Touche Ross & Co.
1968 to 1970: Compensation Analyst, Thomas J. Lipton, Inc.
1967 to 1968: Teacher, Union New Jersey Township Board of
Education
1965 to 1967: Teacher, Newark New Jersey Board of Education

PRIVATE CLUBS:
Essex County Country Club

ASSOCIATIONS/PROFESSIONAL SOCIETIES:
Institute of Management Consultants
International Association of Corporate and Professional Recruiters
Metro Newark Chamber of Commerce Board of
Directors

SPECIAL INTERESTS AND HOBBIES:
Travel, physical fitness, golf

REPRESENTATIVE AND SIGNIFICANT PLACEMENTS:
Ed May, Vice President–Sales
  AT&T
Michael Cohan, Executive Director
  Casino Reinvestment Development Authority
Thomas Carver, President
  Atlantic City Casino Hotel Association
Al Feigenbaum, President
  Dreyfus Consumer Bank
Robert Kleinschmidt, Managing Partner
  Toqueville Asset Management

WHAT I LOOK FOR IN GENERAL IN A CANDIDATE

I look for confidence and ability to articulate in clear, precise, and well-thought-out responses. I look for one's ability to think quickly on one's feet as well as to respond spontaneously. I look for one's opinions on a broad array of topics including but not limited to social, politics, and so on. I look for social graces. Most importantly, I look for one's principles and value system, which are ascertained through questioning and conversation. I look for one's philosophy, ethics, and manner of conducting business. I am interested in one's hobbies, outside activities, and other interests.

GEOGRAPHIC SCOPE OF RECRUITING ACTIVITIES:
Serve clients nationwide and in the UK, France, Germany, Italy, Taiwan, Thailand, Singapore, and Hong Kong

TOTAL YEARS OF RETAINER-TYPE RECRUITING EXPERIENCE:
21 years

JAMES J. DRURY III
**Managing Director, Midwest
    Region
SpencerStuart
401 N. Michigan Avenue,
    Suite 2500
Chicago, IL 60611
Telephone: (312) 822-0080**

**Date of Birth: March 10, 1942
Grew up in: Chicago, Illinois**

SpencerStuart

HIGHER EDUCATION:
University of Notre Dame
    B.S. degree, aeronautical engineering, 1964
University of Chicago, Graduate School of Business
    M.B.A. degree, marketing and finance, 1966

EMPLOYMENT HISTORY:
1984 to present: SpencerStuart
1979 to 1984: Partner, Nordeman Grimm, Inc.
1974 to 1979: Principal and Director, Marketing Consulting Practice,
    Arthur Young & Co.
1969 to 1974: Management Consultant, Donald R. Booz & Associates
1966 to 1969: Manager of Strategic Planning, The Boeing Company

PRIVATE CLUBS:
The Chicago Club
University Club of Chicago

ASSOCIATIONS/PROFESSIONAL SOCIETIES:
Association of Executive Search Consultants, Board Member

SPECIAL INTERESTS AND HOBBIES:
Polo, fund raising for the Music of the Baroque Orchestra and The
    Nature Conservancy

REPRESENTATIVE AND SIGNIFICANT PLACEMENTS:
  Paul Lustig, President
    Sara Lee Bakery
  Gordon Clemons, President
    Caremark
  John Edwardson, Chief Financial Officer
    Ameritech
  Russell Davis, Chief Financial Officer
    Sears Roebuck
  Robert Niles, Chief Human Resources Officer
    Helene Curtis

WHAT I LOOK FOR IN GENERAL IN A CANDIDATE

The complex business problems our clients face will require more the recruitment of "leaders" than simply "managers." I believe that the 90s will hold the opportunity for some search consultants to serve their clients more as "leadership advisors" than simply as "recruiters." Not every leadership problem will be deserving of a search. Recruiters will have to possess a broader skill set and will need to become students of both leadership and their clients' businesses.

What do I look for in candidates? Leadership capability. Vision and insight. Raw intelligence and common sense. Energy. Self-awareness and assuredness. Honesty and integrity. Sense of urgency and competitive spirit. Humor, listening skills. Likes people. Physical fitness and good health. Sound business judgment.

GEOGRAPHIC SCOPE OF RECRUITING ACTIVITIES:
  Serve clients nationally and occasionally internationally

TOTAL YEARS OF RETAINER-TYPE RECRUITING EXPERIENCE:
  12+ years

CRAIG J. DUDLEY
President
Conrey Interamericana, S.A. de
   C.V.
Prado Sur #240
Col. Lomas de Chapultepec
11000 Mexico, D.F.
Telephone:(525) 540-7507 AL 10

Date of Birth: July 19, 1930
Grew up in: California, Idaho,
   Oregon

Conrey Interamericana, S. A. de C. V.

HIGHER EDUCATION:
   University of Oregon
      B.A. degree, psychology, political science, 1955
   American Graduate School of Foreign Trade-Thunderbird
      Bachelor of Foreign Trade, 1958

MILITARY:
   Corporal, United States Army, 1952 to 1954

EMPLOYMENT HISTORY:
   1983 to present: Conrey Interamericana-Transearch
   1975 to 1983: Vice President Manager Mexico, Heidrick and
      Struggles–Conrey
   1969 to 1975: Vice President, Boyden Latin America
   1958 to 1969: Vice President Manager Mexico, ESB Inc.
   1955 to 1957: Counselor, Marion County Juvenile Department

PRIVATE CLUBS:
   Industrial Club
   San Gaspar Golf

ASSOCIATIONS/PROFESSIONAL SOCIETIES:
   American Chamber of Commerce
   American Society Mexico

SPECIAL INTERESTS AND HOBBIES:
   Golf, hiking, archaeological exploration

REPRESENTATIVE AND SIGNIFICANT PLACEMENTS:
Victor Saracho, Managing Director Mexico, Central America, Northern South America
Sicpa Industries of America, Inc.
Rodolfo Lopez Negrete, President Quality Inn Hotels, Mexico
Xabre Group
Jose Kuri Brena, Vice President Continental Director—Mexico
Caribbean
Texas International
Max Duarte, President International
Sherwin Williams
Jose Carral, Corporate Board Member
Western Airlines

WHAT I LOOK FOR IN GENERAL IN A CANDIDATE

The thought sequence is important. Does this person have the analytical skills and mental disciplines to rationally and intelligently solve problems? Does he make his point concisely? How broad are his interests? Does he know what is going on in the world, or is his world just his territory of work? This also is part of his ability to see both the broad picture and detail at the same time.

Job stability while showing professional development is important. A stable personal life. Energy and willingness to use it to achieve established goals. Are his goals justifiable?

GEOGRAPHIC SCOPE OF RECRUITING ACTIVITIES:
Serve clients in Latin America, United States, Mexico, and Central America

TOTAL YEARS OF RETAINER-TYPE RECRUITING EXPERIENCE:
22 years

MICHAEL S. DUNFORD
President
Michael S. Dunford, Inc.
478 Pennsylvania Avenue,
  Suite 301
Glen Ellyn, IL 60137
Telephone: (708) 858-3330

Date of Birth: October 7, 1944
Grew up in: Appleton, Wisconsin

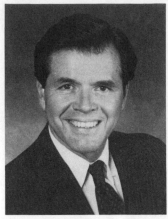

Michael S. Dunford, Inc.

HIGHER EDUCATION:
Stout State University
  B.S. degree, business administration, 1968
University of Wisconsin
  M.B.A. degree, marketing, 1971

MILITARY:
Ensign, United States Navy, 1968 to 1969

EMPLOYMENT HISTORY:
1989 to present: Michael S. Dunford, Inc.
1978 to 1989: Partner, Lamalie Associates, Inc.
1973 to 1978: Associate, Booz, Allen & Hamilton, Inc.
1971 to 1973: Marketing Manager–Refrigerated Foods Division, The
  Pillsbury Co.
1971: Marketing Representative–Computer System Division, The
  RCA Corporation

PRIVATE CLUBS:
Knights of Columbus
Christian Business Men's Committee of USA

SPECIAL INTERESTS AND HOBBIES:
Church programs, American Legion participation, running, tennis

REPRESENTATIVE AND SIGNIFICANT PLACEMENTS:
John W. Roblin, Senior Vice President and Chief Information Officer
  USF&G Corporation
Judd R. Cool, Vice President–Human Resources
  Inland Steel Industries, Inc.

Thomas Herskovitz, President–Frozen Foods, Kraft General Foods, Inc.

Philip Morris Companies, Inc.

Robert E. Naylor, Regional Director–North America
Rohm and Haas Co.

Jack W. Simpson, President
Mead Data Central, Inc., Mead Corporation

WHAT I LOOK FOR IN GENERAL IN A CANDIDATE

Each assignment naturally comes with its specific requirements; however, there are several key elements that we look for in all executive candidates. These can be divided into three categories: personality traits, professional capabilities, and personal interests. Our primary focus centers on the individual's personality and character. Integrity, positive attitude, maturity, and strong communication and listening skills are heavily weighted. We look for a balance between these traits and humility, common sense, demeanor, confidence, and the ability to relate with others.

Professionally speaking, we examine previous employment experiences as an indication of current functional and industry knowledge and future potential. Decision-making abilities, judgment, leadership and management skills, a team orientation, and how one handles financial and corporate success/disappointment are also key factors. The individual's major strengths and developmental areas along with career interests and motivations are evaluated and identified.

Personal responsibilities and interests, such as family, religious activities, community involvement, and hobbies demonstrate the balanced lifestyle that we seek in a healthy, integrated executive.

GEOGRAPHIC SCOPE OF RECRUITING ACTIVITIES:
Serve clients nationwide

TOTAL YEARS OF RETAINER-TYPE RECRUITING EXPERIENCE:
14 years

BERT H. EARLY
President
Bert H. Early Associates, Inc.
55 East Monroe Street, Suite 4530
Chicago, IL 60603-5805
Telephone: (312) 236-6868

Date of Birth: July, 17, 1922
Grew up in: Huntington, West
  Virginia

HIGHER EDUCATION:
  Duke University
    A.B. degree, history, 1946
  Harvard Law School
    LL.B. degree, converted to J.D., 1949

Stuart-Rodgers-Reilly

MILITARY:
  First Lieutenant, United States Army Air Corps, 1943 to 1945

EMPLOYMENT HISTORY:
  1985 to present: Bert H. Early Associates, Inc.
  1981 to 1985: President, Wells International
  1962 to 1981: Executive Director, American Bar Association
  1957 to 1962: Associate General Counsel, Island Creek Coal Company
  1949 to 1957: Associate, Fitzpatrick, Marshall, Huddleston & Bolen
  1950 to 1953: Instructor in Labor Law and Economics, Marshall University

PRIVATE CLUBS:
  University Club of Chicago
  Hinsdale Golf Club
  Harvard Club of New York
  Metropolitan Club of Washington
  Economic Club of Chicago

ASSOCIATIONS/PROFESSIONAL SOCIETIES:
  American Bar Association, Member of House of Delegates
  Life Member of American Law Institute
  American Bar Endowment, Vice President
  Fellow of the American Bar Foundation
  Life Member of American Judicature Society
  International Bar Association

SPECIAL INTERESTS AND HOBBIES:
  Music, theater, travel

REPRESENTATIVE AND SIGNIFICANT PLACEMENTS:
Francis S. Blake, Vice President and General Counsel of Industrial
and Power Systems Group
General Electric Company
Thomas E. Palmer, Vice President, Legal and General Counsel
The Mead Corporation
Kenneth L. Spangler, Senior Vice President and General Counsel
Blount, Inc.
Eugene L. Hohensee, Partner
Arnold & Porter
Walter A. Suhre, Jr., Vice President and General Counsel
Anheuser-Busch Companies, Inc.

WHAT I LOOK FOR IN GENERAL IN A CANDIDATE

After carefully evaluating and determining our client's needs
through a series of comprehensive interviews, we develop search specifications to guide our research in identifying those who most closely
match the needs of the client. We evaluate practice experience and professional accomplishment evidenced by:

- Academic achievement in both undergraduate and law schools
- Broad and comprehensive legal practice experience
- Policy-level and government service practice exposure
- Managerial experience
- Community and professional organization participation
- Reputation as a team player and for superior people skills
- Affirmative, or "can-do," approach to resolving legal issues
- Reputation for integrity and adherence to the highest standards of
  legal profession

Our assessment is based on a careful evaluation of each candidate's written autobiographical statement, comprehensive in-person interviews, and thorough reference checks.

Our goal is to present candidates who are qualified not only by
academic achievement and professional experience, but who are most
likely to be compatible with the culture, style, and traditions of each
client.

GEOGRAPHIC SCOPE OF RECRUITING ACTIVITIES:
Serve clients nationwide

TOTAL YEARS OF RETAINER-TYPE RECRUITING EXPERIENCE:
10 years

GEORGE R. ENNS
President
George Enns Partners Inc.
70 University Avenue, Suite 410
Toronto, Ontario M5J 2M4
Telephone: (416) 598-0012

Date of Birth: August 10, 1936
Grew up in: Windsor, Ontario

George Enns Partners Inc.

HIGHER EDUCATION:
University of Western Ontario
B.A. degree, business administration, 1959

EMPLOYMENT HISTORY:
1983 to present: George Enns Partners Inc.
1978 to 1983: Partner, Herman Smith Inc.
1976 to 1978: President, Bigelow Canada Ltd.
1974 to 1976: President, Canadian Facts Ltd.
1970 to 1974: General Manager, The Mennen Co., Ltd.
1968 to 1970: Vice President Marketing, The Borden Company Ltd.
1959 to 1968: Various marketing positions, General Foods Ltd.

PRIVATE CLUBS:
The Royal Canadian Yacht Club
The Fitness Institute

ASSOCIATIONS/PROFESSIONAL SOCIETIES:
Association of Executive Search Consultants

SPECIAL INTERESTS AND HOBBIES:
Skiing, tennis, fitness, art

REPRESENTATIVE AND SIGNIFICANT PLACEMENTS:
Larry Jackson, President and Chief Executive Officer
Brewers Retail Inc.
Peter Barnard, President and Chief Executive Officer
Peat, Marwick, Stevenson & Kellogg

Richard Peddie, President and Chief Executive Officer
  Pillsbury Canada Limited
Jim McCoubrie, President and Chief Executive Officer
  Telemedia Inc.
Bob Dolan, Vice President–Human Resources
  John Labatt Limited

WHAT I LOOK FOR IN GENERAL IN A CANDIDATE

I look for logical progression in a career path; quality in the organizations the person has worked in; the person's value system; interpersonal characteristics; and the expertise and experience required by the position profile.

I put a lot of emphasis on the person's values and style and my judgment of his or her ability to be effective in my client's environment.

GEOGRAPHIC SCOPE OF RECRUITING ACTIVITIES:
Serve clients nationally and internationally

TOTAL YEARS OF RETAINER-TYPE RECRUITING EXPERIENCE:
13 years

LEON A. FARLEY
Managing Partner
Leon A. Farley Associates
468 Jackson Street
San Francisco, CA 94111
Telephone: (415) 989-0989

Date of Birth: May 6, 1935
Grew up in: Southern California

HIGHER EDUCATION:
University of California at Los Angeles
B.A. degree, English literature, 1956
University of California School of Law
J.D., 1959

EMPLOYMENT HISTORY:
1976 to present: Leon A. Farley Associates
1972 to 1976: Regional Vice President, Korn/Ferry International
1970 to 1972: Executive Vice President–Business Development, ITT
Aerospace Optical Division
1969 to 1970: Marketing Manager–WDL Division, Ford Aerospace
1967 to 1968: Financial Operations Manager–WDL Division, Ford
Aerospace
1963 to 1967: Contracts Manager, Ford Aeronutronic Division
1959 to 1963: Contract Supervisor, Hughes Aircraft

PRIVATE CLUBS:
San Francisco Tennis Club

ASSOCIATIONS/PROFESSIONAL SOCIETIES:
Association of Executive Search Consultants, Past President, Current
Director
Recipient: Distinguished Contribution to the Profession, 1985
International Association of Corporate and Professional Recruiters
California Executive Recruiters Association, Advisory Director

SPECIAL INTERESTS AND HOBBIES:
Rugby, soccer, theater, tennis, travel

REPRESENTATIVE AND SIGNIFICANT PLACEMENTS:
Gerard Gorman, President–International
   Woodward-Clyde Consultants
Pierre Madon, Director–Engineering
   Intelsat
John Gaulding, President and Chief Executive Officer
   Automotive Claims Services Group, ADP
Richard N. Latzer, Senior Vice President and Chief Investment
   Officer
   Transamerica Corporation
Robert J. Duarte, Executive Vice President
   Sumitomo Bank of California

WHAT I LOOK FOR IN GENERAL IN A CANDIDATE

Every corporate search is a response to a client problem, challenge, and opportunity. To be successful as a search consultant, I must deliver candidates who have the ability to address my client's business needs— but more important—whose successful performance is predictable.

The initial telephone calls establish the candidate's technical competence, functional knowledge, and experience. The personal interviews confirm these basic prerequisites but focus particularly on personal characteristics, management style, and motivation. How intelligent is the candidate? What is her executive style? Are we seeking a leader, a manager, or an administrator to resolve our particular management puzzle? Motivation is vital.

I explore the childhood and adolescent years in some depth to evaluate character development. Personally, I favor candidates who have conquered adversity, as tough experiences tend to temper the steel of executive performance. Further, I value intellectual curiosity and sense of humor.

Unlike the psychologist who uses specific tools to gauge behavior, I, as a search consultant, rely on intuition, judgment, and the dramatist's broader perspective of life to select the best candidate.

GEOGRAPHIC SCOPE OF RECRUITING ACTIVITIES:
Serve clients nationwide. International assignments are through affiliates in London, Toronto, Melbourne, and Hong Kong.

TOTAL YEARS OF RETAINER-TYPE RECRUITING EXPERIENCE:
20 years

ANNE M. FAWCETT
Partner
The Caldwell Partners International
64 Prince Arthur Avenue
Toronto, Ontario M5R 1B4
Telephone: (416) 920-7702

Date of Birth: September 30,
1945
Grew up in: Grimsby, Ontario

The Caldwell Partners International

HIGHER EDUCATION:
University of Western Ontario
B.S. degree, 1967

EMPLOYMENT HISTORY:
1975 to present; The Caldwell Partners International
1973 to 1975: Search Consultant, John D. Crawford & Co.
1969 to 1973: Search Consultant, Peat, Marwick & Partners
1967 to 1969: Accounting Assistant, The Bermudiana Hotel Group

PRIVATE CLUBS:
The McGill Club

ASSOCIATIONS/PROFESSIONAL SOCIETIES:
YMCA of Metropolitan Toronto, Board Chair
Faculty of Administrative Studies, York University, Member Advisory
 · Board

SPECIAL INTERESTS AND HOBBIES:
Swimming, hiking, reading, volunteer work

REPRESENTATIVE AND SIGNIFICANT PLACEMENTS:
Chuck Shultz, President and Chief Executive Officer
Gulf Resources Ltd.
Stanley Hartt, Chairman, President and Chief Executive Officer
Campeau Corporation
Donald Lander, President and Chief Executive Officer
Canada Post Corporation

Lynton R. Wilson, President and Chief Operating Officer
  Bell Canada Enterprises Ltd.
John Cassaday, President and Chief Executive Officer
  CTV Television Network

WHAT I LOOK FOR IN GENERAL IN A CANDIDATE

Personal qualities: Solid sense of self worth, quality and duration of relationships, energy, stamina, hard work ethic, signs of striving and self development, good listener, personal impact and salesmanship, a giver rather than a taker, optimist, pragmatist

Track record: Life history of leadership, risk taking—successes /failures, development of people and productive, happy organizations, community contribution, family circumstances, signs of creativity/innovation

Vision: Ability to dream, execution and achievement of dreams in any aspect of life, diverse interests, curiosity, sense of humor

GEOGRAPHIC SCOPE OF RECRUITING ACTIVITIES:

Serve clients in Canada, the United States, and the United Kingdom

TOTAL YEARS OF RETAINER-TYPE RECRUITING EXPERIENCE:

22 years

RICHARD M. FERRY
President
Korn/Ferry International
1800 Century Park East,
  Suite 900
Los Angeles, CA 90067
Telephone: (213) 879-1834

Date of Birth: September 26,
  1937
Grew up in: Ohio

Korn/Ferry International

HIGHER EDUCATION:
  Kent State University,
    B.S. degree, honors in accounting, 1959

EMPLOYMENT HISTORY:
  1969 to present: Korn/Ferry International
  1965 to 1969: Various titles to Partner, Peat, Marwick, Mitchell & Co.

PRIVATE CLUBS:
  Regency Club
  The California Club
  Valley Hunt Club
  Los Angeles Country Club
  Vintage Club

ASSOCIATIONS/PROFESSIONAL SOCIETIES:
  Numerous civic and charitable activities:
    Trustee, California Institute of Technology (Caltech)
    Trustee, Occidental College
    Trustee, the Education Foundation of the Archdiocese of Los
      Angeles
    Director, Catholic Charities
    Director, Paulist Productions
    Director, Los Angeles Chamber of Commerce
  Board of Directors:
    Avery Dennison, Pasadena, CA
    Dole Food Company, Los Angeles
    1st Business Bank, Los Angeles
    Pacific Mutual Life Insurance Company, Newport Beach

SPECIAL INTERESTS AND HOBBIES:
Golf and running

REPRESENTATIVE AND SIGNIFICANT PLACEMENTS:
Lawrence A. Del Santo, Chairman and Chief Executive Officer
Lucky Stores
John F. Grundhofer, President
First Bank System, Inc.
Lawrence Hirsch, Chairman and Chief Executive Officer
Centex Corporation
Ray Irani, Chairman, President and Chief Operating Officer
Occidental Petroleum, Inc.
Richard M. Kovacevich, President and Chief Operating Officer
Norwest Corporation

WHAT I LOOK FOR IN GENERAL IN A CANDIDATE

I look for candidates who are preeminent in their field and who possess the personal qualities and passion to be chief executive officers. They must be bright, goal oriented, creative, enthusiastic, singularly motivated, and have proven themselves in complex, demanding situations. In addition to being superb executives, they must be visionaries with superor communication skills to motivate their troops. They also must be outstanding human beings. I cannot overemphasize this point and the need to be ethical and absolutely above reproach. They must lead by example and must have a keen sense of social responsibility. Society will hold them accountable for their social actions, as Wall Street does for their financial performance.

GEOGRAPHIC SCOPE OF RECRUITING ACTIVITIES:
Serve clients nationwide and in other countries served by the Korn/Ferry network of offices in Amsterdam, Bangkok, Brussels, Budapest, Buenos Aires, Caracas, Copenhagen, Frankfurt, Geneva, Hong Kong, Kuala Lumpur, London, Madrid, Melbourne, Mexico City, Milan, Monterrey, Paris, Rome, San Juan, Sao Paulo, Singapore, Tokyo, Toronto, and Zurich

TOTAL YEARS OF RETAINER-TYPE RECRUITING EXPERIENCE:
25 years

ROBERT M. FLANAGAN
President
Robert M. Flanagan & Associates, Ltd.
Fields Lane
North Salem, NY 10560
Telephone: (914) 277-7210

Date of Birth: March 19, 1940
Grew up in: Concord, New
  Hampshire

Robert M. Flanagan & Associates, Ltd.

HIGHER EDUCATION:
  Saint Anselm College, New Hampshire
    A.B. degree, economics, 1962

EMPLOYMENT HISTORY:
  1991 to present: Robert M. Flanagan & Associates, Ltd.
  1980 to 1991: Paul Stafford Associates, Ltd.
  1966 to 1980: Principal, Booz, Allen and Hamilton
  1965 to 1966: Operations Manager, Milton Bradley Co.
  1963 to 1965: Systems Analyst, American Mutual Insurance Co.
  1962 to 1963: Operations Trainee, New England Merchants National
    Bank

PRIVATE CLUBS:
  The Union League Club of New York
  Mount Kisco Country Club, New York

ASSOCIATIONS/PROFESSIONAL SOCIETIES:
  Association of Executive Search Consultants, former Director

SPECIAL INTERESTS AND HOBBIES:
  Golf

REPRESENTATIVE AND SIGNIFICANT PLACEMENTS:
  President
    Major consumer services company
  President
    Major resort property
  President
    Major trust company

Group Executive
  Information services company
President and Chief Executive Officer
  Not-for-profit association

WHAT I LOOK FOR IN GENERAL IN A CANDIDATE

- Specific accomplishments in his/her field of endeavor
- Quality of the candidate's background vis-á-vis education; organizations he/she has been associated with; outside interests including civic and public service activities
- An appropriate "fit" with the client organization relative to his/her experience in dealing with issues, problems, circumstances that the candidate will be facing if appointed to the position
- A record of success in the candidate's background beginning early in his/her career and including academic, athletics, early work experience, and progression through his/her professional career
- Leadership skills

GEOGRAPHIC SCOPE OF RECRUITING ACTIVITIES:
  Serve clients nationwide and in Europe and the United Kingdom

TOTAL YEARS OF RETAINER-TYPE RECRUITING EXPERIENCE:
  18 years

DULANY "DUKE" FOSTER, JR.
Senior Vice President
Korn/Ferry International
One Landmark Square
Stamford, CT 06901
Telephone: (203) 359-3350

Date of Birth: October 28, 1934
Grew up in: Baltimore, Maryland

Korn/Ferry International

HIGHER EDUCATION:
Colgate University
B.A. degree, liberal arts, 1956
Hofstra University
M.B.A. degree, management, 1964

MILITARY:
United States Air Force, 1956 to 1959

EMPLOYMENT HISTORY:
1971 to present: Korn/Ferry International
1965 to 1971: Manager—Executive Search, Touche Ross & Co.
1959 to 1965: Manager—Planning and Control, Grumman Aircraft
Engineering Corp.

PRIVATE CLUBS:
Woodway Country Club
Landmark Club

ASSOCIATIONS/PROFESSIONAL SOCIETIES:
International Association of Corporate and Professional Recruiters,
Past Chairman
Metropool, Past Chairman and Director
SACIA—The Business Council of Southwestern Connecticut, Past Di-
rector

SPECIAL INTERESTS AND HOBBIES:
Tennis, travel, board of directors service

REPRESENTATIVE AND SIGNIFICANT PLACEMENTS:
Steven C. Mendenhall, Vice President—Human Resources
American Brands, Inc.
Carl M. Vorder Bruegge, Senior Vice President—Sales and Marketing
MCI Communications Corporation
Thomas M. St. Clair, Senior Vice President—Finance, Chief Financial
Officer
Phelps Dodge Corporation
David P. McNicholas, Executive Vice President—Systems Marketing
and Development
Avis, Inc.
John M. Sullivan, Chairman and President
Prince Manufacturing Company, Inc.

WHAT I LOOK FOR IN GENERAL IN A CANDIDATE

The very best fit between the individual and the specific position.
The general areas that are key to my candidate evaluation include:

First impression—appearance, confidence, presence, openness,
friendliness, and honesty
Leadership—ability to articulate a vision, gain the team's support,
organize, inspire, and lead the team
Management—a track record of planning, recruiting, developing,
controlling, and winning in a competitive business environment
Knowledge—having accumulated through education and experi-
ence the required body of knowledge to excel
Balance—between family, personal, and business needs and pres-
sures
Fit—with the company culture, or if required, the ability to change
Intelligence—quickly grasps the essentials; demonstrably bright; in-
tuitive
Communications—superior oral and written skills
Luck—"To deserve victory"

GEOGRAPHIC SCOPE OF RECRUITING ACTIVITIES:
Serve clients nationwide and in Canada

TOTAL YEARS OF RETAINER-TYPE RECRUITING EXPERIENCE:
25 years

JOHN W. FRANKLIN, JR.
Managing Director
Russell Reynolds Associates, Inc.
1850 K Street, N.W., Suite 365
Washington, DC 20006
Telephone: (202) 628-2150

Date of Birth: May 24, 1941
Grew up in: Darien, Connecticut

Russell Reynolds Associates, Inc.

HIGHER EDUCATION:
Amherst College
B.A. degree, English, 1963
Johns Hopkins School of Advanced International Studies
M.A. degree, 1968

EMPLOYMENT HISTORY:
1979 to present: Russell Reynolds Associates, Inc.
1973 to 1979: Executive Vice President and Director, Simmons Associates
1968 to 1973: Management Consultant, American Technical Assistance Corp.
1967 to 1968: International Relations Officer, U.S. Department of State, Agency for International Development
1963 to 1965: Volunteer—Nepal Group II, Peace Corps

PRIVATE CLUBS:
Chevy Chase Club, Maryland
Metropolitan Club of Washington, DC

ASSOCIATIONS/PROFESSIONAL SOCIETIES:
Urban Land Institute
National Multi-Housing Council

SPECIAL INTERESTS AND HOBBIES:
Sailing, bicycling, reading, opera

REPRESENTATIVE AND SIGNIFICANT PLACEMENTS:
Terence C. Golden, Chief Financial Officer
The Oliver Carr Company

Herbert D. Ihle, Senior Vice President–Finance and Controller
   Northwest Airlines
Carl W. Stearn, Vice Chairman of the Board and Chief Executive
   Officer
   Provident Bankshares Corporation
John H. Dasburg, Vice President–Tax
   Marriott Corporation
Barton Harvey III, Vice Chairman
   The Enterprise Foundation

WHAT I LOOK FOR IN GENERAL IN A CANDIDATE

After 18 years in the business, one is struck by four things. First, native intelligence often correlates to success, of course depending on the function. Put differently, a hard driver without a quick and sharp brain can be dangerous. I find myself listening to the orderliness and logic of a person's thought process. Second, energy and enthusiasm are contagious and often characteristics of a strong leader. Importantly, they are recognizable in an interview setting. The higher the level of recruiting one does, the more one recognizes the need for these infectious characteristics. Third, interviewing skills are distinctly different from professional competence. I put less emphasis on the interview and more on third-party referrals. The few times I haven't done this have been almost uniformly disappointing. In this day of significant job movement, unemployment, and "high-level" people looking hard for jobs, there are a number of mediocre executives who become quite skillful at interviewing. Our industry places undue importance on first impressions and cosmetic "qualifications." The guts of the recruiting business lies in referencing. The more done before an interview, the better. Fourth, long-term client relationships to us in the recruiting business permit recognition of the personal characteristics which work within a given organization. If one is unfortunate to have lots of clients where one-time transactions are the rule, this calibration is not possible. However, with companies with significant hiring appetites, the recruiter has the opportunity to apply value-added judgment in depth and on a consistent basis.

GEOGRAPHIC SCOPE OF RECRUITING ACTIVITIES:
Serve clients nationwide and in Europe and Asia

TOTAL YEARS OF RETAINER-TYPE RECRUITING EXPERIENCE:
18 years

JAY GAINES
President
Jay Gaines & Company, Inc.
598 Madison Avenue
New York, NY 10022
Telephone: (212) 308-9222

Date of Birth: April 18, 1947
Grew up in: Oceanside, Long
   Island, NY

Jay Gaines & Company, Inc.

HIGHER EDUCATION:
   George Washington University
      B.A. degree, psychology, 1968
   Columbia University
      M.A. degree, industrial psychology, 1970

EMPLOYMENT HISTORY:
   1982 to present: Jay Gaines & Co., Inc.
   1976 to 1982: Vice President, Oliver and Rozner
   1972 to 1976: Associate Recruiter, Halbrecht Associates
   1968 to 1972: Teacher Sixth Grade Special Service School, NY Board
      of Education

ASSOCIATIONS/PROFESSIONAL SOCIETIES:
   Association of Executive Search Consultants

SPECIAL INTERESTS AND HOBBIES:
   Boating, skiing, bicycling, reading

REPRESENTATIVE AND SIGNIFICANT PLACEMENTS:
   Bruce Peterson, Chief Executive Officer
      EJV Partners
   Peter Brown, Executive Vice President/Chief Operating Officer
      Glenmede Trust Corp.
   Ladd Willis, Managing Vice President
      First Manhattan Consulting Group
   Ken Fugate, Chief Information Officer
      First Nationwide
   Jim Hynes, Managing Director
      Fidelity Capital

WHAT I LOOK FOR IN GENERAL IN A CANDIDATE

We look first for performance. The individual should be performing at or near the top of her peer group with a demonstrated record of substantive accomplishments relative to the needs of the particular client and assignment. Accomplishments must demonstrate initiative, staying power, and consistency. How well does the individual hold up under adversity? To what extent will he push for what he thinks is right? We want to know the individual's overall role and how difficult and how important their accomplishments were. Personal and professional integrity are of absolute importance. We are most comfortable with individuals who have a well-developed sense of themselves. That includes understanding where they are today, why they have been successful in the past, recognizing the situations in which they operate best, and understanding the characteristics that differentiate them from their peers.

It also includes an ability to define and articulate a professional value system—what one wants to achieve, the rewards that are meaningful, and how they generally go about achieving it. We look for the accompanying sense of confidence and consistency in how they would approach any situation. We place an extremely high premium on thoughtfulness and insight. We look for and value in-depth professional/functional expertise combined with the instincts that come with seasoning and successful experience. We seek out a work ethic and commitment level that is substantially higher than the norm. However, we value the individual who has successfully managed his or her career along with their personal life. We want someone who ideally can bring an additional dimension and add substantial value to our client organization. Can the individual lead our client, and take them substantially further over time than where they are today? We want that person to deliver and be counted upon over a long period of time.

GEOGRAPHIC SCOPE OF RECRUITING ACTIVITIES:
Serve clients nationwide and in London and Tokyo

TOTAL YEARS OF RETAINER-TYPE RECRUITING EXPERIENCE:
19 years

JOHN T. GARDNER
Managing Partner
Lamalie Associates, Inc.
123 North Wacker Dr., Suite 950
Chicago, IL 60606
Telephone: (312) 782-3113

Date of Birth: June 21, 1943
Grew up in: Racine, Wisconsin
**   and Stuart, Florida**

Stuart—Rodgers—Reilly

HIGHER EDUCATION:
Georgia Institute of Technology
    B.S. degree, industrial management, 1965
Harvard University, Graduate School of Business
    M.B.A. degree, 1970

MILITARY:
First Lieutenant, United States Army, 1966 to 1968

EMPLOYMENT HISTORY:
1986 to present: Lamalie Associates, Inc.
1982 to 1986: Vice President–Ceramics and Planning Manager–
Lighting, General Electric Co.
1980 to 1982: Senior Vice President, Fotomat Corporation
1977 to 1980: General Manager, Opthalmic Instrument Business, Director of Marketing, American Optical Group, Warner Lambert
Company
1973 to 1977: Engagement Manager, McKinsey & Company
1972 to 1973: Vice President–Marketing, Cole National Corporation
1970 to 1972: Divisional Merchandise Manager, Rike's, Federated Department Stores

PRIVATE CLUBS:
Metropolitan Club of Chicago
Harvard Club of New York

ASSOCIATIONS/PROFESSIONAL SOCIETIES:
Harvard Business School Club of Chicago

SPECIAL INTERESTS AND HOBBIES:
Tennis, reading

REPRESENTATIVE AND SIGNIFICANT PLACEMENTS:
Senior Vice President and Group President
$1.2 billion industrial group of a *Fortune* 200 company
President and Chief Executive Officer
$200 million private spin-off from a major international chemical
company
Group Vice President–Marketing
$2 billion consumer goods business
Executive Vice President and Chief Financial Officer
Leading speciality retailer
Member, Board of Directors
$3 billion *Fortune* 200 mining and industrial company

WHAT I LOOK FOR IN GENERAL IN A CANDIDATE

Before any candidate is evaluated, it is important to develop a comprehensive knowledge of the business, the culture of the client, and the job content of the specific position. I then assess the candidate's experience base to ensure the requisite technical skills and background. Second, through a combination of in-depth interviewing and extensive reference checking, I look for a compatible style and value system. Finally, I look for certain individual characteristics that are essential for successful senior executive placements:

- Mental capacity and toughness—the intellect and "street smarts" to get the job done
- Vision and passion—the ability to see and internally feel where the business needs to go and an unswerving drive to get there
- Leadership, self-confidence, communication skills and maturity—the ability to motivate others through diplomacy and personal example
- Integrity—unquestioned on both a personal and professional level

GEOGRAPHIC SCOPE OF RECRUITING ACTIVITIES:
Serve clients nationwide

TOTAL YEARS OF RETAINER-TYPE RECRUITING EXPERIENCE:
6 years

FRANK A. GAROFOLO
President
Garofolo, Curtiss, Lambert &
  MacLean
326 West Lancaster Avenue
Ardmore, PA 19003
Telephone: (215) 896-5080

Date of Birth: May 2, 1938
Grew up in: Camden, New Jersey

Joseph Nettis Photography

HIGHER EDUCATION:
  Drexel University
    B.S. degree, commerce and engineering, 1962

EMPLOYMENT HISTORY:
  1973 to present: Garofolo, Curtiss, Lambert & MacLean
  1971 to 1973: Vice President, Pappas, Coates & DelVecchio
  1969 to 1971: President, Pacesetter Management Systems Inc.
  1967 to 1969: Self-employed insurance broker

SPECIAL INTERESTS AND HOBBIES:
  Sports from the spectator standpoint, reading, working, tennis, spiritual growth

REPRESENTATIVE AND SIGNIFICANT PLACEMENTS:
  Charles Pierce, Assistant Secretary Health of the State of New Jersey
    Delaware Valley Hospital Council
  Joseph Culver, President
    Woodward & Dickinson
  James McCaslin, Chief Operating Officer
    Episcopal Hospital
  Douglas J. Spurlock, President
    Polyclinic Medical Centers
  Maynard R. Stufft, President & CEO
    PHICO Insurance Co.

WHAT I LOOK FOR IN GENERAL IN A CANDIDATE

Each candidate with whom I meet must possess the basic technical requirements, the background, and experience to measure up to the criteria established by our client. There may be exceptions to the rule; however, this is generally step number one. Almost as important is the assessment of the potential personal chemistry that can develop between the candidate and the client and their organization—an equally critical ingredient for a successful search. When the element of positive personal chemistry prevails, inevitable rough spots can be worked out so they do not develop into road blocks.

Once having satisfied that the candidate meets these two basic requirements, I look to the basic individual traits such as personality, leadership, management style, energy, and intelligence. These must be thorough and examined against the needs of the situation as expressed by the client. From my own perspective, I also want to develop a picture of the internal value system of the potential candidate. It is important to me to know how much emphasis they place on the issues such as fair play and equitable treatment. The fundamental moral fiber of the person and what makes him who he is, as well as what is important in his life, are factors that make up the whole person. It is when these are reviewed against my understanding of the client and both the spoken and unspoken requirements of the opportunity that positions me to determine compatibility, hence a recommendation.

GEOGRAPHIC SCOPE OF RECRUITING ACTIVITIES:
Serve clients nationwide

TOTAL YEARS OF RETAINER-TYPE RECRUITING EXPERIENCE:
18 years

RONALD G. GOERSS
Partner
Smith, Goerss & Ferneborg
Ecker Square, 25 Ecker Street
San Francisco, CA 94105
Telephone: (415) 543-4181

Date of Birth: April 10, 1929
Grew up in: Tonawanda, New
  York

HIGHER EDUCATION:
  Concordia Seminary
    B.A. degree, 1951
    Master of Divinity, 1954
  University of Southern California
    M.A. degree, 1961

Elson–Alexandre

EMPLOYMENT HISTORY:
  1980 to present: Smith, Goerss & Ferneborg, Inc.
  1971 to 1980: Associate and Vice President, Heidrick and Struggles,
    Inc.
  1970 to 1971: Vice President, MRG Corporation
  1966 to 1970: Manager of Staff Recruitment, McKinsey & Company,
    Inc.
  1963 to 1966: Pastor, University Lutheran Chapel, University of Cal-
    ifornia, Los Angeles
  1960 to 1963: Pastor, Immanuel Lutheran Church, Valparaiso, Indi-
    ana
  1954 to 1960: Lutheran Campus Pastor, UCLA and USC

PRIVATE CLUBS:
  University Club of San Francisco, Carmel Valley Racquet Club
  Peninsula Golf and Country Club

ASSOCIATIONS/PROFESSIONAL SOCIETIES:
  Association of Executive Search Consultants
  The Newcomen Society
  Commonwealth Club of California

SPECIAL INTERESTS AND HOBBIES:
  Tennis, reading, music (jazz and classical), conversation with interest-
    ing people, family activities

REPRESENTATIVE AND SIGNIFICANT PLACEMENTS:
  President and Chief Executive Officer
    One of the largest heavy construction companies in the United
    States
  Division President
    Leading manufacturer of ophthalmic products
  Vice President, Chief Information Officer
    Major retail chain
  Vice President–Human Resources
    Major rail transportation company
  Senior Vice President, Chief Financial Officer
    Growing biotechnology company

WHAT I LOOK FOR IN GENERAL IN A CANDIDATE

When entrusted with a new search assignment I always listen carefully to the client. I try to keep in mind the problems and opportunities the client emphasizes, the priorities he/she places on skill, experience, personality, and other vital criteria. That sets the standards of evaluating prospective candidates.

Through research and initial telephone conversations with prospective candidates, technical qualifications can be assessed sufficiently to decide whether personal interviews are warranted. In the personal interview I probe an individual's capabilities while simultaneously assessing personality and adaptability for fitting with the client culture. I look for career progression which is outstanding, characterized by achievement and leadership.

The all-important personal qualities are considered from the first handshake. I look for confidence, poise, a healthy self-esteem, energy, curiosity, humor. I expect a candidate to probe, to ask questions that are thoughtful and clear, and to give articulate responses to my questions.

I always find out as much as possible about a candidate's values, personal interests, and avocational pursuits. I look for a sense of responsibility toward society more developed than that of a mercenary. In short, I look for someone who is interesting and stimulating as a person, not simply technically competent.

GEOGRAPHIC SCOPE OF RECRUITING ACTIVITIES:
  Serve clients nationwide

TOTAL YEARS OF RETAINER-TYPE RECRUITING EXPERIENCE:
  20 years

WILLIAM E. GOULD
Managing Director
Gould & McCoy Inc.
551 Madison Avenue
New York, NY 10022
Telephone: (212) 688-8671

Date of Birth: October 23, 1932
Grew up in: Watertown, New
**   York**

Gould & McCoy, Inc.

HIGHER EDUCATION:
Williams College, Massachusetts
    B.A. degree, chemistry, physics, 1957
Harvard Business School
    M.B.A. degree, 1965

MILITARY:
Sergeant, United States Army, 1953 to 1955

EMPLOYMENT HISTORY:
1973 to present: Gould & McCoy Inc.
1969 to 1973: Vice President, Heidrick and Struggles
1965 to 1969: Commercial Director, Mack Amax Aluminum Ltd.,
    Subsidiary of Amax Corp.
1961 to 1965: Sales Manager–Varcum Chemical Division, Reichhold
    Chemicals Corp.
1957 to 1961: New Products Marketing Engineer, Carborundum
    Company

PRIVATE CLUBS:
Harvard Club
Williams Club
Silver Spring Country Club, CT

SPECIAL INTERESTS AND HOBBIES:
International business/cultural relations, geriatrics, life planning

REPRESENTATIVE AND SIGNIFICANT PLACEMENTS:

Alfred A. Piergallini, Chairman, President and Chief Executive
Officer
Gerber Products Company

Daniel E. Gill, Chairman and Chief Executive Officer
Bausch & Lomb

Louis P. Mattis, Chairman, President and Chief Executive Officer
Sterling Drug/Eastman Kodak

Burton A. Dole, Jr., Chairman and Chief Executive Officer
Puritan-Bennett Corporation

James W. Giggey, Senior Vice President–International
Eastman Chemical Company/Eastman Kodak

WHAT I LOOK FOR IN GENERAL IN A CANDIDATE

I look for many elements. Cultural fit with the client is the most important or the person has a high probability of leaving within two years. The person's evolvement as a human being—how does he/she cope with adversity, with superiors/peers/subordinates—how mature is the person? What has the person done with his/her personal life—is the person a total human being or just one dimensional? What is the person's track record? Did he really do what he claimed to do? Is the person a leader or a follower, and how does that fit our client's requirements? What is the person's "life plan?" What are her goals? Does she have goals, and how does that fit with our client? What is the person's relationship with his/her spouse or, if single, is he/she fulfilled personally? Finally, the person should have a sense of humor. In my 22 years of retainer search experience, the successful people always had a sense of humor.

GEOGRAPHIC SCOPE OF RECRUITING ACTIVITIES:

Serve clients nationwide and in Europe, Brazil, and Argentina

TOTAL YEARS OF RETAINER-TYPE RECRUITING EXPERIENCE:

22 years

JOSEPH E. GRIESEDIECK, JR.
U.S. Managing Director
SpencerStuart
333 Bush Street
San Francisco, CA 94025
Telephone: (415) 495-4141

Date of Birth: July 3, 1944
Grew up in: St. Louis, Missouri

Atkinson Business Photography

HIGHER EDUCATION:
Brown University
A.B. degree, classics, 1966

EMPLOYMENT HISTORY:
1985 to present: SpencerStuart
1979 to 1985: Managing Director, Russell Reynolds Associates
1978 to 1979: Group Vice President, Alexander & Baldwin, Inc.
1966 to 1978: President and Chief Operating Officer, Falstaff Brewing
Corporation

PRIVATE CLUBS:
Bohemian Club, San Francisco
St. Louis Country Club

SPECIAL INTERESTS AND HOBBIES:
Automobile racing

REPRESENTATIVE AND SIGNIFICANT PLACEMENTS:
Michael Pharr, Chief Financial Officer
Safeway, Inc.
Amy McCombs, President
KRON-TV, Chronicle Broadcasting Company
Jack Hancock, Executive Vice President, Chief Information Officer
Pacific Telesis
Jack Edwards, President and Chief Executive Officer
Itel Transportation Services
Kenneth McLennan, President and Chief Executive Officer
Machinery and Allied Products Institute

WHAT I LOOK FOR IN GENERAL IN A CANDIDATE

While each search situation dictates relatively specific requirements in terms of candidate experience and behavioral factors, in a more general sense I look for the following qualities:

- Overall breadth of experience, as well as specific accomplishments/achievements (personal as well as professional)
- Quality of experience and education, including the excellence of the institutions which the individual has chosen
- Sound values, with some history of having made a commitment (to anything!)
- Interpersonal skills; an ability to work effectively with and through others
- A degree of entrepreneurial spirit
- How the individual has handled adversity
- Sense of humor and a well-balanced perspective

GEOGRAPHIC SCOPE OF RECRUITING ACTIVITIES:
Serve clients nationwide and in Europe

TOTAL YEARS OF RETAINER-TYPE RECRUITING EXPERIENCE:
13 years

PETER G. GRIMM
Managing Partner
Nordeman Grimm, Inc.
717 Fifth Avenue, 26th Floor
New York, NY 10022
Telephone: (212) 935-1000

Date of Birth: May 23, 1933
Grew up in: Larchmont,
  New York

Bachhrach

HIGHER EDUCATION:
  Cornell University
    B.S. degree, hotel administration, 1955

MILITARY:
  First Lieutenant, Single Engine Jet Instructors Pilot, U.S. Air Force,
    1956 to 1959

EMPLOYMENT HISTORY:
  1968 to present: Nordeman Grimm, Inc.
  1966 to 1968: Partner, Antell Wright & Nagel
  1961 to 1966: Senior Associate, Cresap McCormick & Paget
  1959 to 1961: Registered Representative, Merrill Lynch
  1955 to 1956: Sales, General Foods

PRIVATE CLUBS:
  University Club of New York
  University Club of Larchmont
  Winged Foot Golf Club
  Larchmont Yacht Club
  Loblolly Pines Golf Club

SPECIAL INTERESTS AND HOBBIES:
  Golf, sailing, travel, reading

REPRESENTATIVE AND SIGNIFICANT PLACEMENTS:
  Bruce Allbright, Chairman and Chief Executive Officer
    Dayton Hudson
  Anthony Luiso, Chairman and Chief Executive Officer
    International Multifoods

Brian Kendrick, Senior Vice President and Chief Financial Officer
  Saks Fifth Avenue
Deborah Borda, Executive Director
  New York Philharmonic
Robert Lund, Chairman and Chief Executive Officer
  International Telecharge, Inc.

WHAT I LOOK FOR IN GENERAL IN A CANDIDATE
  The things I look for are:

- Intelligence—a sound and logical thought process
- Presence—the ability to present effectively, one-on-one and in groups
- Energy—high energy is essential in today's competitive environment
- Work ethic—goes hand-in-hand with high energy
- Competitive—in whatever he/she has done in school, business, sports
- Risk tolerance—able to make decision based on incomplete analysis
- Success—the earlier the better
- Luck—I look for the "luck" executive; they usually make their own luck
- Sound basic values—honesty, sensitivity to others
- Consistency—some pattern in their lives/careers
- Balance—something to balance the business part of their lives—home, sports, travel

GEOGRAPHIC SCOPE OF RECRUITING ACTIVITIES:
  Serve clients nationally and in Great Britain and Europe

TOTAL YEARS OF RETAINER-TYPE RECRUITING EXPERIENCE:
  26 years

DAVID O. HARBERT
President
Sweeney, Harbert & Mummert,
Inc.
777 S. Harbour Island Blvd.,
Suite 130
Tampa, FL 33602
Telephone: (813) 229-5360

Date of Birth: April 14, 1940
Grew up in: Shaker Heights,
Ohio

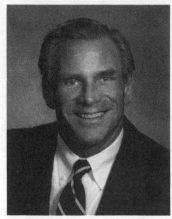

Bob Baggett

HIGHER EDUCATION:
University of Michigan
B.B.A. degree, engineering and business, 1962
M.B.A. degree, finance and statistical methods, 1963

EMPLOYMENT HISTORY:
1991 to present: Sweeney, Harbert & Mummert, Inc.
1986 to 1991: Sweeney Shepherd Bueschel Provus Harbert & Mummert, Inc.
1981 to 1986: Vice President/Managing Director, Lamalie Associates
1979 to 1981: Vice President Finance and Chief Financial Officer, Austin Powder
1977 to 1979: Vice President Finance, Stanwood Corp.
1972 to 1977: President, Advisory Services Inc.
1968 to 1972: Manager Finance, Celanese Corp.
1965 to 1968: Senior Financial Analyst, Standard Oil New Jersey
1964 to 1965: Auditor/Consultant, Arthur Andersen & Co.

PRIVATE CLUBS:
Union Club of Cleveland

ASSOCIATIONS/PROFESSIONAL SOCIETIES:
Financial Executives Institute, Chicago Chapter

SPECIAL INTERESTS AND HOBBIES:
Physical fitness, music, audio/video equipment, travel, movies, automobiles

REPRESENTATIVE AND SIGNIFICANT PLACEMENTS:
President and Chief Executive Officer
Major energy distribution company

President and Chief Operating Officer
  Fortune 500 diversified manufacturing company
Executive Vice President, Finance and Planning
  Fortune 200 manufacturing and distribution company
Senior Vice President, Management Information Systems (Chief
  Information Officer)
  $3 billion distribution company
Vice President, Finance and Chief Financial Officer
  Manufacturer and distributor of household products

WHAT I LOOK FOR IN GENERAL IN A CANDIDATE

Every search assignment is unique, based on the client involved and their specific requirements for the position. To truly achieve a successful, long-term match, candidate evaluations are necessarily comprehensive and move through several levels. The chronology tends to be the following:

1. Technical skills—does the candidate meet the position's technical requirements? Have the appropriate career steps and professional accomplishments successfully taken place? If so, I will then concentrate on:
2. Interpersonal skills and chemistry with my client—does the candidate present himself/herself in a manner compatible with the position and the environment? Typically this will include an evaluation of intelligence, aggressiveness, purpose, professionality, poise, articulation, candor, and sense of humor. Physical presentation is also considered: clothing, physical fitness, mannerisms, and so on. I will then make judgments on:
3. The candidate's interests—will they be served? If not, he/she will probably fail in the position and therefore our client's needs will not be satisfied.
4. Recruitability—as I gain knowledge of the candidate, it is clear he/she can, in fact, be recruited, or are we wasting my client's time?
5. Promotability—what is his/her potential to grow beyond the initial position? Will this be a match in everyone's long-term interest?

GEOGRAPHIC SCOPE OF RECRUITING ACTIVITIES:
Serve clients nationwide

TOTAL YEARS OF RETAINER-TYPE RECRUITING EXPERIENCE:
10 years

ANDREW D. HART, JR.
Managing Director
Russell Reynolds Associates,
   Inc.
200 Park Avenue
New York, NY 10166
Telephone: (212) 351-2000

Date of Birth: May 3, 1929
Grew up in: Charlottesville,
   Virginia

Russell Reynolds Associates Inc.

MILITARY:
First Lieutenant, United States Army, 1951 to 1954

EMPLOYMENT HISTORY:
1970 to present: Russell Reynolds Associates, Inc.
1969 to 1970: Associate, Boyden Associates, Inc.
1962 to 1969: General Sales Manager, Carton Division, Westvaco
   Corp.
1958 to 1962: Eastern Regional Sales Manager–Carton Division, Federal Paper Board Co.
1954 to 1958: Sales Representative, Federal Paper Board Company

SPECIAL INTERESTS AND HOBBIES:
Education, Republican Party politics, fund raising, skiing, golf, tennis,
   reading, the arts

REPRESENTATIVE AND SIGNIFICANT PLACEMENTS:
Robert P. Bauman, Chairman and Chief Executive Officer
   Beecham Group Plc.
Jan Leschly, Chairman–Pharmaceuticals
   SmithKline Beecham Plc.
Reece A. Overcash, Jr., Chairman and Chief Operating Officer
   Associates Corporation of North America (Subs. of Gulf + Western
   Inc.)
William P. Panny, President and Chief Operating Officer
   Bendix Corporation
Maurice Segall, President and Chief Executive Officer
   Zayre Corporation

WHAT I LOOK FOR IN GENERAL IN A CANDIDATE

In personal terms, I look for leadership ability, interpersonal/communication skills, dedication, ambition, self-confidence, integrity, and good judgment. As to professional qualifications, I am interested in self-assessment of one's principal skills and accomplishments, the results of performance appraisals, and one's management philosophy. In general management positions, I probe the extent of one's marketing, manufacturing, financial, and administrative experience as well as the achievements over a period of time in terms of financial results and the steps taken to bring those about. I am particularly interested in the reasons behind job changes and who initiated the change or termination and for what reasons. In the last analysis, I am looking for individuals with a proven record of performance in jobs matching the position requirements.

GEOGRAPHIC SCOPE OF RECRUITING ACTIVITIES:
Serve clients nationwide and in Europe, the Far East, and Latin America

TOTAL YEARS OF RETAINER-TYPE RECRUITING EXPERIENCE:
22 years

GARDNER W. HEIDRICK
Chairman
The Heidrick Partners, Inc.
20 N. Wacker Drive, Suite 2850
Chicago, IL 60606
Telephone: (312) 845-9700

Date of Birth: October 7, 1911
Grew up in: Peoria, Illinois

The Heidrick Partners, Inc.

HIGHER EDUCATION:
   University of Illinois
      B.S. degree, banking and finance, 1935

MILITARY:
   United States Naval Reserve, 1945 to 1946

EMPLOYMENT HISTORY:
   1982 to present: The Heidrick Partners, Inc.
   1953 to 1982: Co-Founder/Chairman Heidrick & Struggles, Inc.
   1951 to 1953: Associate, Booz, Allen & Hamilton
   1942 to 1951: Director of Personnel, Farmland Industries
   1935 to 1942: Industrial District Manager, Scott Paper Company

PRIVATE CLUBS:
   Hinsdale Golf Club
   The Chicago Club
   Tower Club
   DuPage Club
   Country Club of Florida
   The Ocean Club
   The Little Club

ASSOCIATIONS/PROFESSIONAL SOCIETIES:
   Association of Executive Search Consultants
   International Executive Service Corps
   National Association of Corporate Directors

SPECIAL INTERESTS AND HOBBIES:
   Golf, coin collecting

REPRESENTATIVE AND SIGNIFICANT PLACEMENTS:
Chief Executive Officer
   Major diversified cultural not-for-profit organization
House Counsel, later Chairman, Chief Executive Officer
   $3 billion consumer/industrial manufacturer
Director
   Fortune top ten industrial organization
Directors
   Major southwestern telecommunications corporation
Director
   One of the top eastern mutual life insurance companies

WHAT I LOOK FOR IN GENERAL IN A CANDIDATE

In corporate director assignment: what the candidate will bring to the board and his/her visibility. Generally, this is a chairman or a president. Overall, it is compatibility.

Targeted are industries, functional position, geography (ability to attend meetings), minorities, and women.

In general management executives, it is primarily the same. The pattern of the past indicates the pattern of the future.

GEOGRAPHIC SCOPE OF RECRUITING ACTIVITIES:
Serve clients nationwide

TOTAL YEARS OF RETAINER-TYPE RECRUITING EXPERIENCE:
40 years

ROBERT L. HEIDRICK
President
The Heidrick Partners, Inc.
20 N. Wacker Drive, Suite 2850
Chicago, IL 60606
Telephone: (312) 845-9700

Date of Birth: June 8, 1941
Grew up in: Hinsdale, Illinois

The Heidrick Partners

HIGHER EDUCATION:
Duke University
B.A. degree, economics, 1963
University of Chicago
M.B.A. degree, 1971

EMPLOYMENT HISTORY:
1982 to present: The Heidrick Partners, Inc.
1977 to 1982: President, Robert Heidrick Associates, Inc.
1975 to 1977: Vice President, Spriggs & Company
1963 to 1975: Division Vice President–Marketing, American Hospital
Supply Corp.

PRIVATE CLUBS:
The Chicago Club
The Racquet Club
Tower Club
Glen View Club
Firestone Country Club, Akron, OH

SPECIAL INTERESTS AND HOBBIES:
Golf, numismatics

REPRESENTATIVE AND SIGNIFICANT PLACEMENTS:
Chairman, President, and Chief Executive Officer
$3 billion electric and gas utility
Chief Financial Officer
$2.5 billion consumer products company
Chief Executive Officer
$300 million railroad

Head of Manufacturing Technology
  $3 billion industrial products company
Member, Board of Directories
  $700 million industrial products company

WHAT I LOOK FOR IN GENERAL IN A CANDIDATE

First is the executive's image: how well groomed? The person's presentability: assertive, retiring, and so on? In short, the individual's executive presence?

Second, education and compensation are a strong consideration. In most instances, it is important that the individual have a college degree, with graduate work being a plus. However, the older and more experienced the executive, the less important is the education. In terms of compensation, there should be a pattern of good upward progression. For younger people, earnings should be three or four times the person's age.

Ultimately the compatibility of the candidate with the client and the client organization is important. The individual should have "street smarts" along with leadership skills.

Third is the background and experience. Does the person have a track record of success? Is he/she able to articulate accomplishments without overstating or taking too much personal credit? Is there good humility? Does the career progress in a logical fashion?

GEOGRAPHIC SCOPE OF RECRUITING ACTIVITIES:
Serve clients nationwide

TOTAL YEARS OF RETAINER-TYPE RECRUITING EXPERIENCE:
16 years

GEORGE W. HENN, JR.
President
G.W. Henn & Company
85 E. Gay Street, Suite 1007
Columbus, OH 43215
Telephone: (614) 469-9666

Date of Birth: November 13, 1936
Grew up in: Spring Lake, New
  Jersey

G. W. Henn & Company

HIGHER EDUCATION:
Rutgers University
  B.A. degree, American civilization, 1958

MILITARY:
E-4 (Reserve), United States Army, 1959

EMPLOYMENT HISTORY:
1987 to present: G.W. Henn & Company
1980 to 1987: Managing Director–Cleveland, SpencerStuart Associates
1971 to 1980: Partner, Booz, Allen & Hamilton Inc.
1969 to 1971: Associate, David North & Associates
1958 to 1969: Personnel Director, Great American Insurance Co.

PRIVATE CLUBS:
University Club of Columbus

SPECIAL INTERESTS AND HOBBIES:
Breeding and exhibiting American saddlebred horses

REPRESENTATIVE AND SIGNIFICANT PLACEMENTS:
President
  Major international materials handling manufacturing company
Chairman and Chief Executive Officer
  Non-bank subsidiary of major super regional bank
Chief Information Officers (5)
  Recruited for *Fortune* 100 companies

President and Chief Operating Officer
  Major regional bank
President and Chief Executive Officer
  Major leasing company

WHAT I LOOK FOR IN GENERAL IN A CANDIDATE

Our objective in all client assignments is to recruit the best possible candidate for the position—the candidate who can best contribute to the client organization—short and long term.

Leading candidates have a record of significant progression through larger, well-managed companies. In addition to functional skills, the candidates have demonstrated the personal dimension to work effectively in a corporate setting while aggressively and energetically pursuing business goals and objectives.

Successful candidates consistently demonstrate leadership skills and the strategic understanding of key business issues. They are also known and regarded within their industry.

GEOGRAPHIC SCOPE OF RECRUITING ACTIVITIES:
Serve clients nationwide and in Canada

TOTAL YEARS OF RETAINER-TYPE RECRUITING EXPERIENCE:
22 years

WILLIAM A. HERTAN
Chairman and Chief Executive Officer
Executive Manning Corporation
3000 N.E. 30th Place, Suite 405
Fort Lauderale, FL 33306
Telephone: (305) 561-5100

Date of Birth: July 15, 1921
Grew up in: Ridgewood, New Jersey

Tiffany Studio

HIGHER EDUCATION:
New York University
B.S. degree, industrial relations, 1943

MILITARY:
Lieutenant Commander, United States Navy Reserve, 1941 to 1957

EMPLOYMENT HISTORY:
1956 to present: Executive Manning Corporation
1948 to 1956: Owner/President, Harper Associates Employment Agency

PRIVATE CLUBS:
Boca Raton Country Club

ASSOCIATIONS/PROFESSIONAL SOCIETIES:
American Management Association
Newcomen Society

SPECIAL INTERESTS AND HOBBIES:
Boating, fishing, traveling

REPRESENTATIVE AND SIGNIFICANT PLACEMENTS:
Vice President–Environmental Services
$15 billion multinational firm
President and Chief Operating Officer
$5 billion health services organization

President
$350 million aerospace firm
Division President to Executive Vice President
Multibillion dollar multinational electronics corporation
President
$1 billion major aerospace corporation

WHAT I LOOK FOR IN GENERAL IN A CANDIDATE

The most important factors that I personally look for in a candidate include an openness and frankness. The candidate must possess a unique ability to communicate skills both orally and in writing. "Technical" experience and a proven record of achievement in his or her given field is essential. Stability of employment becomes an integral part of the evaluation. Diversity of assignments within a given corporation or no more than three corporate changes in the employment record is used as a basic benchmark. Loyalty to employer and subordinates and the ability to convey loyalty is an essential factor in the evaluation. This becomes more important in today's economy. Family stability is essential and the lack of external stress mandatory. A candidate's ability to comprehend corporate politics is an important factor for a new hire. Character and business references become an integral part of the evaluation. This cannot be limited to only the references supplied by the candidate but a rigorous in-depth check of past and present records becomes a truly essential part of an individual's evaluation.

GEOGRAPHIC SCOPE OF RECRUITING ACTIVITIES:
Serve clients nationwide and in England, Germany, and France

TOTAL YEARS OF RETAINER-TYPE RECRUITING EXPERIENCE:
36 years

WILLIAM G. HETZEL
President
William Hetzel Associates, Inc.
Williamsburg Village
1601 Colonial Parkway
Inverness, IL 60067
Telephone: (708) 776-7000

Date of Birth: May 19, 1933
Grew up in: Miami, Florida and
   Washington, DC

William Hetzel Associatees, Inc.

HIGHER EDUCATION:
University of Miami
   B.B.A. degree, marketing, 1953
Northwestern University
   M.B.A. degree, marketing, 1962

MILITARY:
Lieutenant Junior Grade, United States Navy, 1953 to 1956

EMPLOYMENT HISTORY:
1981 to present: William Hetzel Associates, Inc.
1978 to 1981: Senior Vice President, Eastman & Beaudine, Inc.
1974 to 1978: Vice President, Lamalie Associates, Inc.
1972 to 1974: Division Vice President and General Manager, ITT
   Corp.
1970 to 1972: President, Medelco, Inc.
1969 to 1970: Director of Marketing, Maremont Corporation
1964 to 1969: Various positions, Xerox Corporation
1961 to 1964: Management Consultant, McKinsey & Company
1960 to 1961: Account Executive, Low's Inc.
1956 to 1960: District Sales Representative, Diamond International
   Corp.

PRIVATE CLUBS:
Plaza Club

ASSOCIATIONS/PROFESSIONAL SOCIETIES:
International Association of Corporate and Professional Recruiters
Illinois Management and Executive Search Consultants

SPECIAL INTERESTS AND HOBBIES:
Member, Advisory Board, College of Business Management, Northeastern Illinois University

REPRESENTATIVE AND SIGNIFICANT PLACEMENTS:
Subsidiary President, now Corporate President
  Large paper company
Division Director, Marketing, now Division President
  Fortune 200 conglomerate
Division Director, Marketing, now Division Vice President and General Manager
  Fortune 100 conglomerate
Division Engineering Manager, now Division President
  Fortune 200 conglomerate
Program manager, now Vice President, Program Management and Marketing
  Fortune 100 aerospace company

WHAT I LOOK FOR IN GENERAL IN A CANDIDATE

One of the things that makes my job interesting is the nearly universal insistence of our clients that candidates demonstrate the potential to advance. Also important in our candidate evaluation, and relatively easy to judge, are client requirements of education, technical background, prior experience, and level of responsibility. But even more important to us are the personal characteristics which a candidate will need to succeed within the client organization.

In evaluating candidates, I rely heavily on what I learn in interviews and from references. Candidates must be intelligent, articulate, likeable, mature, poised, and ambitious. They must be results oriented and able to deal with financial information, but able to handle broad concepts as well.

Though it smacks of cliché, our staff agrees that our entire organization of candidates is designed to find the "hand" which will perfectly fit the client's "glove."

GEOGRAPHIC SCOPE OF RECRUITING ACTIVITIES:
Serve clients nationwide

TOTAL YEARS OF RETAINER-TYPE RECRUITING EXPERIENCE:
17 years

JAMES N. HEUERMAN
**Vice President and Senior
  Partner
Korn/Ferry International
600 Montgomery Street,
  31st Floor
San Francisco, CA 94111
Telephone: (415) 956-1834**

**Date of Birth: August 9, 1940
Grew up in: St. Cloud, Minnesota**

Gabriel Maulin Studios

HIGHER EDUCATION:
   University of Minnesota
      B.S. degree, business, 1965
      M.A. degree, hospital and health care administration, 1971

MILITARY:
   Spec-4, United States Army, 1960 to 1962

EMPLOYMENT HISTORY:
   1983 to present: Korn/Ferry International
   1977 to 1983: Vice President and Partner, Booz, Allen & Hamilton
   1972 to 1977: Principal, Arthur Young & Company
   1971 to 1972: Assistant Administrator, Evanston Hospital, Illinois
   1965 to 1970: Marketing Representative, IBM

PRIVATE CLUBS:
   Valley Vista Club

ASSOCIATIONS/PROFESSIONAL SOCIETIES:
   Health Directions Society

SPECIAL INTERESTS AND HOBBIES:
   Tennis, running, cycling, reading

REPRESENTATIVE AND SIGNIFICANT PLACEMENTS:
   Dr. Monroe Trout, President and Chief Executive Officer
      American Healthcare Systems

John G. King, President and Chief Executive Officer
  Legacy Health System
Robert Montgomery, President
  Alta Bates Corporation
C. Duane Dauner, President
  California Association of Hospitals and Health Systems
David A. Reed, President
  St. Joseph Health System

WHAT I LOOK FOR IN GENERAL IN A CANDIDATE

A series of milestones over time, which include:

- Work ethic, usually developed at a young age
- Solid education, good schools, and accomplishment
- Early jobs that refine analytical skills
- Mentors who contribute to style and character
- Employer organizations of quality and reputation
- Demonstrated profit and loss responsibility and results
- A well-developed management philosophy and style
- A vision of one's industry that demonstrates depth of thinking
- An ability to communicate in a clear and meaningful fashion

GEOGRAPHIC SCOPE OF RECRUITING ACTIVITIES:
Serve clients nationwide

TOTAL YEARS OF RETAINER-TYPE RECRUITING EXPERIENCE:
8 years

HENRY G. HIGDON
Managing Director
Higdon, Joys & Mingle, Inc.
375 Park Avenue, Suite 3008
New York, NY 10152
Telephone: (212) 752-9780

Date of Birth: June 1, 1941
Grew up in: Shaker Heights,
  Ohio and Greenwich,
  Connecticut

Higdon, Joys & Mingle, Inc.

HIGHER EDUCATION:
  Yale University
    B.A. degree, American studies, 1964

MILITARY:
  Staff Sergeant, United States Marine Corps Reserve, 1964 to 1970

EMPLOYMENT HISTORY:
  1986 to present: Higdon, Joys & Mingle, Inc.
  1971 to 1986: Executive Vice President, Russell Reynolds Associates, Inc.
  1964 to 1971: Associate, Massachusetts Mutual Life Insurance Co.

PRIVATE CLUBS:
  Yale Club of New York City
  Greenwich Country Club
  California Club
  Racquet and Tennis Club

SPECIAL INTERESTS AND HOBBIES:
  Sports: skiing, running, squash, rugby, coaching Little League baseball; active in church and alumni affairs of Andover and Yale

REPRESENTATIVE AND SIGNIFICANT PLACEMENTS:
  Stephen M. Wolf, President and Chief Operating Officer
    Continental Airlines
  Robert N. Gurnitz, President and Chief Executive Officer
    Northwestern Steel and Wire Company
  James H. Gardner, Executive Vice President and Chief Operating Officer
    Kinder-Care Learning Centers, Inc.

Warren E. Bartel, Executive Vice President and Chief Operating
Officer
Weirton Steel Corporation
Burton J. Megargel, Managing Director and Head of Mergers and
Acquisitions Department
Kidder, Peabody & Company, Inc.

WHAT I LOOK FOR IN GENERAL IN A CANDIDATE
In general, I look for the following characteristics in candidates:

- *Integrity.* While it would appear that this would go without saying, it
  can never be assumed and is the single most important characteristic
  for any candidate.
- *Intelligence.* While a high level of intellect is clearly preferred, basic
  street smarts, savvy, and instincts are as important.
- *High level of energy.* Energy is critically important, and assumes great
  stamina and endurance, and even physical fitness.
- *Team leadership.* While most people look for team players, which is
  important, I believe that it is more important for someone to be able
  to be a team builder and a team leader.
- *Self-confidence and inner security.* I look for self-confidence, which also
  means that an individual can admit that one can make mistakes and
  realizes that one is fallible.
- *Communications ability.* People who are organized in their thought process and can present ideas with clarity and brevity.
- *A sense of humor.* A sense of humor is absolutely essential, as it enables
  people to not take themselves too seriously, to have some grace under
  pressure, and to laugh at themselves.
- *Humility.* Self-effacement can be an important characteristic, especially in today's world of occasionally super-arrogant CEOs who may
  feel they can do absolutely no wrong.
- *Balance.* I look for people who have their lives in balance, meaning
  that their personal, family, business, intellectual, and even spiritual
  existences blend well together. I am not impressed with people who
  are single-dimensional or monomaniacal.

GEOGRAPHIC SCOPE OF RECRUITING ACTIVITIES:
Serve clients nationally and internationally

TOTAL YEARS OF RETAINER-TYPE RECRUITING EXPERIENCE:
20 years

LAWRENCE W. "LARRY" HILL
Managing Director
Russell Reynolds Associates, Inc.
1000 Louisiana Street, Suite 4800
Houston, TX 77002
Telephone: (713) 658-1776

Date of Birth: March 27, 1933
Grew up in: Sebring, Florida

Russell Reynolds Associates, Inc.

HIGHER EDUCATION:
Auburn University
B.S. degree, business administration, 1957

MILITARY:
Corporal, United States Army, 1954 to 1955

EMPLOYMENT HISTORY:
1983 to present: Russell Reynolds Associates, Inc.
1982 to 1983: President/Owner, Lawrence W. Hill & Associates
1963 to 1982: Senior Vice President, Heidrick and Struggles, Inc.
1961 to 1962: Personnel Director, Argus Cameras, Inc.
1957 to 1961: Training Department, Union-Camp Corporation

PRIVATE CLUBS:
Lakeside Country Club, Houston
Coronado Club, Houston

SPECIAL INTERESTS AND HOBBIES:
Trinity Episcopal Church, Galveston, Texas; golf, fishing, computer
programming

REPRESENTATIVE AND SIGNIFICANT PLACEMENTS:
Chairman and Chief Executive Officer
Texas-headquartered, NYSE-listed regional bank holding company
President and Chief Operating Officer
Houston-headquartered, NYSE-listed precious metals mining company

President and Chief Operating Officer
  Houston-headquartered, NYSE-listed manufacturing company, number one in its industry
Vice President and Chief Information Officer
  Denver-headquartered, NYSE-listed world wide manufacturing company
Vice President for Strategic Planning
  Houston-headquartered interstate gas pipeline, one of the largest in United States

WHAT I LOOK FOR IN GENERAL IN A CANDIDATE

The great fascination of the executive search profession is that every search, every client, and every "ideal" candidate is different. Having survived 28 years of dealing with the differences, I've convinced myself that there is a certain commonality of characteristics found among those people who are consistently successful and well respected.

Integrity comes first; it's the hardest characteristic to identify and to quantify but there isn't any substitute for having it and holding to it.

Intellectual capacity, particularly intellectual curiosity, is another very basic ingredient, as is an ability to communicate effectively with a diverse universe of audiences.

Other characteristics that I give great weight to are job stability, and high energy level, and, perhaps most importantly, the ability to make decisions and to stay with them. Almost without exception, successful people have the proverbial "brass balls."

GEOGRAPHIC SCOPE OF RECRUITING ACTIVITIES:
  Serve clients nationwide and in Europe

TOTAL YEARS OF RETAINER-TYPE RECRUITING EXPERIENCE:
  28 years

MICHAEL J. HOEVEL
Partner
Poirier, Hoevel & Company
12400 Wilshire Blvd., Suite 1250
Los Angeles, CA 90025
Telephone: (213) 207-3427

Date of Birth: September 16, 1944
Grew up in: Pasadena, California

Westside Studio

HIGHER EDUCATION:
California State University
B.S. degree, 1967

EMPLOYMENT HISTORY:
1975 to present: Poirier, Hoevel & Company
1972 to 1975: Consultant–Executive Search, Peat Marwick Main & Company
1967 to 1972: Manager of Recruiting, City of Los Angeles
1967: Management Trainee, Shell Oil Company

PRIVATE CLUBS:
Harvard Business School Olde Boys Rugby Club
California River Expeditions

ASSOCIATIONS/PROFESSIONAL SOCIETIES:
California Executive Recruiters Association
Society for Human Resources Management

SPECIAL INTERESTS AND HOBBIES:
Family, travel, river rafting, scuba diving, snow skiing, golf

REPRESENTATIVE AND SIGNIFICANT PLACEMENTS:
Chief Financial Officer
$700 million retail holding company
Chief Executive Officer
$6.5 billion asset management company
Executive Vice President–Marketing
Top ten U.S. financial institution

Five critical tax management positions
  Major multinational subsidiary of *Fortune* 10 company
Top insurance executive to launch nationwide retail insurance sub-
  sidiary in U.S.
  Multi-national Japanese conglomerate

WHAT I LOOK FOR IN GENERAL IN A CANDIDATE

A solid employment history with excellent progression. Good articulation, an easy but slightly aggressive manner, intelligent, a sense of
humor, a life outside of business, and honesty.

The above, coupled with experience which meets or exceeds what
my client is looking for.

Finally, there is a growing trend among my clients to prefer candidates who can work within a highly collaborative and team-oriented
management group, where team accomplishments are more highly valued than individual acts.

GEOGRAPHIC SCOPE OF RECRUITING ACTIVITIES:
  Serve clients nationwide and in Europe and Latin America

TOTAL YEARS OF RETAINER-TYPE RECRUITING EXPERIENCE:
  20 years

DAVID H. HOFFMANN
President
DHR International, Inc.
10 S. Riverside Plaza, Suite 1650
Chicago, IL 60606
Telephone: (312) 782-1581

Date of Birth: August 7, 1952
Grew up in: Washington, Missouri

DHR International, Inc.

HIGHER EDUCATION:
  Central Missouri State University
    B.S. degree, 1974

EMPLOYMENT HISTORY:
  1989 to present: DHR International
  1985 to 1989: Senior Vice President/Managing Partner, Boyden
    International
  1983 to 1985: Vice President/Partner, Korn/Ferry International
  1977 to 1983: Director of Employee Relations, GATX Corporation
  1975 to 1977: Various Human Resource Positions, Pullman Inc.
  1974 to 1975: Various Human Resource Positions, Clark Equipment
    Company

SPECIAL INTERESTS AND HOBBIES:
  Board Member, Lawrence Hall School for Boys
  Youth Athletics (coach various Little League organizations)

REPRESENTATIVE AND SIGNIFICANT PLACEMENTS:
  Senior Vice President to President
    Major food products division
  Vice President–Human Resources to Senior Vice President–Human
    Resources
    Fortune 500 company
  Chief Financial Officer
    Fortune 500 company

President
International division of *Fortune* 500 company
President
Fortune 500 company

WHAT I LOOK FOR IN GENERAL IN A CANDIDATE

An individual who can effect change and be perceived as a change agent. A charismatic leader who achieves results. Exceptional track record of accomplishment. Exceptional communication skills both oral and written. Strong people skills—a total business acumen. A career orientation. Interests outside the job—family, civic, philanthropic, and so on. A well-rounded and grounded individual. A visionary.

GEOGRAPHIC SCOPE OF RECRUITING ACTIVITIES:
Serve clients nationwide and in Europe and Latin America

TOTAL YEARS OF RETAINER-TYPE RECRUITING EXPERIENCE:
9 years

JONATHAN S. HOLMAN
President and Founder
The Holman Group, Inc.
1592 Union Street
San Francisco, CA 94123
Telephone: (415) 751-2700

Date of Birth: May 26, 1945
Grew up in: Washington, DC and
San Juan, PR

Bachrach

HIGHER EDUCATION:
Princeton University
A.B. degree, politics, 1966
Stanford University Graduate School of Business
M.B.A. degree, 1968

EMPLOYMENT HISTORY:
1981 to present: The Holman Group, Inc.
1978 to 1981: Partner, Bacci, Bennett, Gould & McCoy
1971 to 1978: Director of Human Resources, E & J Gallo Winery
1968 to 1971: Personnel Director, Pfizer, Inc.

ASSOCIATIONS/PROFESSIONAL SOCIETIES:
California Executive Recruiters Association

REPRESENTATIVE AND SIGNIFICANT PLACEMENTS:
Robert C. Miller, President and Chief Executive Officer, later Chairman and CEO
Mips Computer Systems, Inc.
Daniel J. Warmenhoven, President and Chief Operating Officer, later Chairman and CEO
Network Equipment Technologies, Inc.
Charles M. Boesenberg, Vice President–U.S. Sales, later Senior Vice President, Apple USA
Apple Computer, Inc.
Anthony S. Tiano, President and Chief Executive Officer
KQED San Francisco, Channel 9
John East, President and Chief Executive Officer
Actel Corporation

WHAT I LOOK FOR IN GENERAL IN A CANDIDATE

Those of us who focus our efforts on chief executive officer level searches face some special dilemmas, most notably the need to satisfy an entire board of directors rather than a single person making a hiring decision. This means that there probably will be countervailing forces as to what defines the "perfect" candidate. The good chief executive officer recruiter will take a strong hand in helping the board define perfection for their special set of circumstances; the task then is to find a chief executive officer whose strengths are those needed and whose weaknesses are irrelevant, fixable, or counterbalanced elsewhere within the hiring organization.

It is easy to get consensus that ideal candidates for almost any role must be smart, diligent, strong communicators, and half a dozen other standard adjectives. For a chief executive officer, I have four particular biases which augment these. First, he or she must know how to make money for the enterprise. If that criterion is not met, the others don't matter. Second, there must not be the slightest issue of business or personal integrity. The chief executive officer sets the tone for the behavior of the organization, and flaws at this level get magnified below. Third, the references from subordinates and peers must be at least as good as those from superiors; it is a lot easier to fool your boss than anyone else. Finally, a sense of humor is essential. Somewhere along the way things will go wrong, and it takes humor to pull through.

GEOGRAPHIC SCOPE OF RECRUITING ACTIVITIES:
Serve clients nationwide and occasionally in Europe

TOTAL YEARS OF RETAINER-TYPE RECRUITING EXPERIENCE:
14 years

WILLIAM C. HOUZE
Partner
William C. Houze & Company
48-249 Vista De Nopal
La Quinta, CA 92253
Telephone: (619) 564-6400

Date of Birth: November 26, 1921
Grew up in: Kentucky

William C. Houze & Company

HIGHER EDUCATION:
Chase College
   B.S. degree, commerce, personnel, 1955
University of Southern California
   M.A. degree, liberal arts, 1976

MILITARY:
Captain, Pilot, United States Air Force, 1942 to 1945

EMPLOYMENT HISTORY:
1984 to present: William C. Houze & Company
1977 to 1984: President, Houze, Shourds & Montgomery, Inc.
1973 to 1977: Partner and Vice President–Operations, Hergenrather & Company
1967 to 1973: Executive director–Management Personnel, Rockwell International
1963 to 1967: Manager–Employee Relations–Computer Division, General Electric Company
1951 to 1963: Various Human Resource positions, Jet Engine Division, General Electric Company

PRIVATE CLUBS:
The Cliff Dwellers
The Los Angeles Athletic Club
MENSA

ASSOCIATIONS/PROFESSIONAL SOCIETIES:
Association of Executive Search Consultants
American Association of University Professors
Society of Automotive Engineers
Armed Forces Communications and Electronics Association
Association of Old Crows
Air Force Association
American Defense Preparedness Association

SPECIAL INTERESTS AND HOBBIES:
Cross-country skiing, classical and jazz music, mountaineering, Anglophilia

REPRESENTATIVE AND SIGNIFICANT PLACEMENTS:
M. Peter Thomas, President and Chief Executive Officer
Ericsson, USA, Inc.
Peter Marino, President and Chief Operating Officer
Fairchild Corporation
James W. Griffith, General Manager—Administration
Toyota Technical Center, USA, Inc.
Aussie Rodgers, Vice President—Human Resources—Retail Operations
Burger King Corporation
Brett Stevenson, Vice Chancellor—Business and Fiscal Affairs
University of California, San Francisco

WHAT I LOOK FOR IN GENERAL IN A CANDIDATE

Over the years I have developed a sequential, three-stage process of evaluating candidates. The first stage is usually the easiest to complete because it measures objective data such as pertinent skills, work experiences, and education—the professional requisites for the position.

Second, a candidate deemed to have the appropriate professional requisites is then evaluated on his or her management style, and how that style will mesh (or clash) with the culture of my client's organization. This second stage requires not only indepth analysis of the candidate, but also several assessments to determine the organization's actual culture.

The third stage serves as a safety net. It assumes that my assessments in the earlier stages may not have been totally correct—that the selected candidates may turn out to be not quite as right as I had predicted. Therefore, before my final "stamp of approval," I probe for bedrock attitudes and behavior patterns such as work ethic, honesty, loyalty, team play, and dedication to the Golden Rule. My experience suggests that a man or woman steeped in such on-the-job behavior can usually overcome marginal shortcomings in specific skills or culture compatibility.

GEOGRAPHIC SCOPE OF RECRUITING ACTIVITIES:
Serve clients nationwide and in England, Western Europe, and the Pacific Rim

TOTAL YEARS OF RETAINER-TYPE RECRUITING EXPERIENCE:
18 years

LOUIS A. HOYDA
Partner
Thorndike Deland Associates, Inc.
275 Madison Avenue
New York, NY 10016
Telephone: (212) 661-6200

Date of Birth: February 7, 1932
Grew up in: Fairfield, Connecticut

Thorndike Deland Associates, Inc.

HIGHER EDUCATION:
   University of Bridgeport
      B.A. degree, history, 1959

MILITARY:
   Corporal, United States Army, 1952 to 1954

EMPLOYMENT HISTORY:
   1986 to present: Thorndike Deland Associates
   1984 to 1985: Vice President–Human Resources, Mastercard International
   1981 to 1984: Vice President, Boyden International
   1971 to 1981: Director–Executive Staffing, AMF Inc.
   1965 to 1971: Manager–Industrial Relations, Perkin Elmer Corporation
   1964 to 1965: Manager–Employment, CBS Laboratories
   1961 to 1964: Human Resources, Avco Corporation

PRIVATE CLUBS:
   Williams Club, New York
   Blackrock Yacht Club, Bridgeport, CT

SPECIAL INTERESTS AND HOBBIES:
   Saltwater fly-fishing, saltwater boating, photography, cuisine, shore bird–carving

REPRESENTATIVE AND SIGNIFICANT PLACEMENTS:
Worthington Linen, President, Direct Marketing, Inc.
   Bertelsmann Music Group
Harry McQuillen, President, Maxwell/Macmillan Publishing
   Company
   Macmillan Inc.
Group Executive, Thomson Information Group
   Thomson Business Information Group
Edward Feder, Senior Vice President–Marketing
   Cigna Worldwide
Senior Vice President–Marketing–Regional Banks
   Chase Manhattan Bank

WHAT I LOOK FOR IN GENERAL IN A CANDIDATE

Balance, intelligence, curiosity, sparkle, accomplishments, analytical capability if appropriate, physical presence, self-confidence, leadership qualities, candor.

A sense of humor
Conversational abilities
Quickness to grasp situations
Excitement, charisma
Quantitative skills

GEOGRAPHIC SCOPE OF RECRUITING ACTIVITIES:
Serve clients nationwide and in Europe, South America, and Australia

TOTAL YEARS OF RETAINER-TYPE RECRUITING EXPERIENCE:
9+ years

SIDNEY A. HUMPHREYS
President
Korn/Ferry International
Scotia Plaza, Suite 1814
40 King Street, West
Toronto, Ontario M5H 3Y2
Telephone: (416) 366-1300

Date of Birth: August 13, 1933
Grew up in: Winnipeg, Manitoba

Peter Caton Gerald Campbell Studios

HIGHER EDUCATION:
University of Manitoba
Chartered Accountant degree, 1959

EMPLOYMENT HISTORY:
1990 to present: Korn/Ferry International
1978 to 1990: Managing Director, SpencerStuart, Toronto
1962 to 1978: Director of Operations Planning, Xerox of Canada, Ltd.
1960 to 1962: Comptroller, Monarch Lumber Company, Winnipeg
1958 to 1960: Chartered Accountant, James N. Chalmers & Co., Winnipeg
1954 to 1958: Student–Manager, Deloitte Haskins & Sells, Chartered Accountants

PRIVATE CLUBS:
Mississaugua Golf and Country Club
Skydome—Founders Club, Fitness Club
Fitness Institute—I.B.M. Tower

ASSOCIATIONS/PROFESSIONAL SOCIETIES:
Youth for Christ Canada, Board Member
Junior Achievement of Canada, Board Member (Past Vice Chairman)
Presidents Association (Canadian Management Association—Affiliate A.M.A.)

SPECIAL INTERESTS AND HOBBIES:
Christian ministries, sports (golf, hockey), travel, reading

REPRESENTATIVE AND SIGNIFICANT PLACEMENTS:
  George Harvey, President and Chief Executive Officer
    Unitel Inc. (formerly CN/CP telecommunications)
  William Gleed, President and Chief Executive Officer
    Citadel Insurance (subsidiary of Winterthur Insurance Co., Switzer-
    land)
  Jerome Huret, Managing Director–France
    Sperry Inc. (France subsidiary of Sperry U.S.)
  Steven Lenard, Executive Vice President–Marketing
    Canadian Imperial Bank of Commerce
  Ronald Smith, President and Chief Executive Officer
    Amdahl Canada Inc.

WHAT I LOOK FOR IN GENERAL IN A CANDIDATE

My first priority is to identify candidates who come as close to the client's position specification as possible. Once I have accomplished this, I have no hesitation in also introducing any candidates who do not completely meet the client's specification, but who I feel have the successful track records that indicate they could do the job. It is important here to know the client culture well, the personalities, strengths, and weaknesses of the executive team.

The major characteristics I look for in candidates are the qualities of leadership and integrity. A track record of building organizations and attaining consistent bottom-line results is a positive indicator. Other personal characteristics that I look for are basic social and communication skills, strong personal drive, and a solid work ethic.

Relative to education, I look for people who are very bright and "street smart," and although university degrees are positive attributes, they are not critical. More and more candidates will be required to have international experience and ideally the capability to converse in more than one language. As a matter of interest, many of the senior executives I have recruited have been reasonably well known to me prior to the specific assignment they take on.

GEOGRAPHIC SCOPE OF RECRUITING ACTIVITIES:
  Serve clients in Canada, the United States, France, the United King-
    dom, Germany, Switzerland, Japan, and Holland

TOTAL YEARS OF RETAINER-TYPE RECRUITING EXPERIENCE:
  13 years

DURANT A. "ANDY" HUNTER
Partner
Gardiner Stone Hunter International, Inc.
One International Place
Boston, MA 02110
Telephone: (617) 261-9696

Date of Birth: November 25, 1948
Grew up in: Williamstown, Massachusetts

Bachrach

HIGHER EDUCATION:
University of North Carolina, Chapel Hill
A.B. degree, American studies, 1971
George Washington University
M.P.A. degree, public administration, 1973

EMPLOYMENT HISTORY:
1989 to present: Gardiner Stone Hunter International
1985 to 1989: Senior Vice President, Boyden International
1983 to 1985: Executive Vice President, HM Consultants International
1981 to 1983: Vice President, James Hunter Machine Company
1974 to 1981: Assistant Vice President, J.P. Morgan
1973 to 1974: Program Director, International Management and Development Institute

PRIVATE CLUBS:
The Country Club, Brookline, MA
The University Club of New York

ASSOCIATIONS/PROFESSIONAL SOCIETIES:
Association of Executive Search Consultants
Council on Foreign Relations

SPECIAL INTERESTS AND HOBBIES:
Boys & Girls Clubs of Boston, international affairs, politics, skiing, golf

REPRESENTATIVE AND SIGNIFICANT PLACEMENTS:
Susan P. Haney, President, The Private Bank
   Bank of Boston
James H. Gately, Senior Vice President–Institutional Sales
   The Vanguard Group
Edmund J. Thimme, Principal–Institutional Sales
   Scudder, Stevens & Clark
Robert C. Dinerstein, General Counsel–North America
   Union Bank of Switzerland
Nicholas G. Lazaris, President and Chief Executive Officer
   M.W. Carr & Co., Inc.

WHAT I LOOK FOR IN GENERAL IN A CANDIDATE

The search for the right executive, much like the search for a marriage partner, is not done "in general." The goal of the recruiter is to find the best available candidate by matching an individual to the unique needs of each client. Having said this, there are qualities and attributes which appear consistently in successful candidates: intelligence, straightforwardness, strong communication and interpersonal skills, organization, energy, focus, humor, professionalism, and motivation.

In matching a candidate to a company, I examine proven accomplishments and potential fit. First, I am looking for a solid record of achievement in a given industry or function. I look much deeper than words on a resume or what a candidate tells me during an interview.

Second, I try to assess whether the match makes sense for everybody. Is the move progressive for the candidate in terms of his/her goals, values, and strengths? Does the candidate measure up to the requirements of the particular industry, company, job, and prospective superiors? Finally, I ask myself, would I like to work with this individual?

GEOGRAPHIC SCOPE OF RECRUITING ACTIVITIES:
Serve clients nationwide and in England, France, and Germany

TOTAL YEARS OF RETAINER-TYPE RECRUITING EXPERIENCE:
6 years

W. JERRY HYDE
President
Hyde Danforth & Company
5950 Berkshire Lane, Suite 1600
Dallas, TX 75225
Telephone: (214) 691-5966

Date of Birth: December 23, 1933
Grew up in: Northeast Texas

Hyde Danforth & Company

HIGHER EDUCATION:
East Texas State University
B.B.A. degree, 1954
M.B.A. degree, personnel administration, 1958

MILITARY:
Personnel Specialist Fourth Class, United States Army, Korea, 1954 to 1956

EMPLOYMENT HISTORY:
1973 to present: Hyde Danforth & Company
1968 to 1973: Manager–Executive Search, Peat Marwick Mitchell & Company
1963 to 1967: Manager–Southwest, Preferred Business Corporation
1958 to 1962: Assistant Director–Personnel, Republic National Life Insurance Co.
1957 to 1958: Business Teaching Assistant, East Texas State University
1956 to 1957: High School Principal, Bland Independent School District, Texas

ASSOCIATIONS/PROFESSIONAL SOCIETIES:
Administrative Management Society, Dallas Chapter (1974 to 1984)
American Society of Personnel Administrators (1968 to 1985)
Accredited Personnel Diplomate (APD) "Consulting accreditation by ASPA"

SPECIAL INTERESTS AND HOBBIES:
Native American history, vegetable gardening, Southwestern art, walking, golf

REPRESENTATIVE AND SIGNIFICANT PLACEMENTS:
Medical Director
   Major southwestern general hospital
Managing Partner
   Very prominent 200-attorney law firm
President
   Significant independent oil company
President
   Major regional Texas bank
Vice President General Counsel
   Multibillion dollar high-technology corporation

WHAT I LOOK FOR IN GENERAL IN A CANDIDATE

Whether he/she is a candidate for an entry-level management position or for chief executive officer, there are certain qualities requisite for on-the-job success. Those attributes include:

1. A professional manner and bearing—the presence for leadership
2. Communications skill—the ability to "sell" an idea orally and to present it effectively in writing
3. Signs of leadership—a track record that historically indicates the ability to motivate and control
4. Client "chemistry"—the carriage to effectively relate with the client's personnel, goals, and objectives
5. "Technical knowledge"—the trait that is both first and last on the list; the experience necessary for excellence

GEOGRAPHIC SCOPE OF RECRUITING ACTIVITIES:
Serve clients nationwide and in Europe

TOTAL YEARS OF RETAINER-TYPE RECRUITING EXPERIENCE:
23 years

HUGH ILLSLEY
Managing Partner
Ward Howell Illsley & Partners
141 Adelaide Street West,
    Suite 1800
Toronto, Ontario M5H 3L5
Telephone: (416) 862-1273

Date of Birth: November 6, 1949
Grew up in: Halifax, Nova Scotia

HIGHER EDUCATION:
  Florida State University
    B.S. degree, 1973

EMPLOYMENT HISTORY:
  1985 to present: Ward Howell Illsley & Partners
  1977 to 1985: President, Wypich Illsley & Associates
  1975 to 1977: Consultant, H.V. Chapman & Associates

PRIVATE CLUBS:
  Lambton Golf Club
  Cambridge Club

SPECIAL INTERESTS AND HOBBIES:
  Golf, squash

REPRESENTATIVE AND SIGNIFICANT PLACEMENTS:
  President
    $2 billion Canadian grocery chain
  President
    $400 million systems integration company
  Chief Operating Officer
    $500 million steel fabricator
  Chief Operating Officer
    Medium-sized financial institution
  Group Vice President
    Major international farm machinery manufacturer

WHAT I LOOK FOR IN GENERAL IN A CANDIDATE

Well-balanced human beings. Self-motivated individuals driven by value systems that best represent the individual, client company, employees, and shareholders.

People who make a difference. Both an ability to lead and to manage. Team builders.

GEOGRAPHIC SCOPE OF RECRUITING ACTIVITIES:

Serve clients mainly in North America; internationally through affiliates

TOTAL YEARS OF RETAINER-TYPE RECRUITING EXPERIENCE:

15 years

D. JOHN INGRAM
Partner
Ingram Inc.
350 Park Avenue, Suite 900
New York, NY 10022
Telephone: (212) 319-7777

Date of Birth: May 15, 1939
Grew up in: Detroit, Michigan

HIGHER EDUCATION:

Michigan State University
B.S. degree, 1964
M.S. degree, 1965

Bachrach

MILITARY:

L/Corporal, United States Marines, 1958 to 1964

EMPLOYMENT HISTORY:

1984 to present; Ingram Inc.
1980 to 1984: Partner, Heidrick and Struggles
1969 to 1980: Senior Vice President, American Express Company
(Fireman's Fund)
1965 to 1969: Supervisor, Bell Telephone Labs
1965 to 1966: Industrial Relations Analyst, Ford Motor Company

PRIVATE CLUBS:

New York Yacht Club
Belle Haven Club

REPRESENTATIVE AND SIGNIFICANT PLACEMENTS:

Andrew L. Lewis, Jr., Chairman and CEO
Union Pacific Corporation
Michael H. Walsh, Chairman and CEO
Union Pacific Railroad
Thomas C. Barry, President and CEO
Rockefeller & Co.
Howard L. Clark, Jr., Executive Vice President and CFO
American Express Company
Morgan Davis, President–Commercial Lines
Fireman's Fund Insurance Company

WHAT I LOOK FOR IN GENERAL IN A CANDIDATE

We seek to be the best. Therefore, we are committed to recruiting the best candidates for our clients' needs. We listen carefully to what our clients intend to accomplish; we strive for excellence in everything we do; our clients' needs always come first.

Moreover, we believe each search is our most important goal; therefore, each search deserves direct intense involvement with a partner. Our clients deserve and pay for the very best effort and experience we offer.

Further, our goal is to develop a partnership with our clients. We expect our clients to listen to our views and we, in turn, value their trust. Our goal is to help our clients recruit the very best executives for their position.

GEOGRAPHIC SCOPE OF RECRUITING ACTIVITIES:
Serve clients nationwide and in Europe and the Far East

TOTAL YEARS OF RETAINER-TYPE RECRUITING EXPERIENCE:
12 years

RICHARD K. IVES
Partner
Wilkinson & Ives
601 California Street, Suite 502
San Francisco, CA 94108
Telephone: (415) 433-2155

Date of Birth: October 22, 1929
Grew up in: Southern California

Wilkinson & Ives

HIGHER EDUCATION:
University of Southern California
B.S. degree, commerce, 1952
Stanford University Graduate School of Business
M.B.A. degree, 1954

MILITARY:
Lieutenant, United States Navy, 1954 to 1957

EMPLOYMENT HISTORY:
1984 to present: Wilkinson & Ives
1975 to 1984: Principal, Richard K. Ives & Company
1972 to 1975: Partner, Bacchi, Bentley, Evans & Gould, Inc.
1970 to 1972: Western Regional Manager, DPF&G
1957 to 1970: Various Sales and Marketing Management Positions,
IBM Corporation

PRIVATE CLUBS:
Jonathan Club
Merchants Exchange Club
Meadow Club

ASSOCIATIONS/PROFESSIONAL SOCIETIES:
California Executive Recruiters Association

SPECIAL INTERESTS AND HOBBIES:
Golf, travel, reading, gourmet cooking

REPRESENTATIVE AND SIGNIFICANT PLACEMENTS:
President of the U.S. Information Processing Subsidiary
    N.V. Phillips, The Netherlands
Chairman and Chief Executive Officer
    Venture capital–funded software company
President and Chief Executive Officer
    Nuclear energy company
Executive Vice President, Research and Development
    Computer workstation company
Vice President, Chief Financial Officer & Member of Board of Directors
    $2 billion high-technology company

WHAT I LOOK FOR IN GENERAL IN A CANDIDATE

In general, I look for a balance between a candidate's professional background and experience, and his/her personal qualities and skills. The following listing (not necessarily in order of priority) contains the traits I look at most closely:

- Record of accomplishment, including specific successes and/or failures
- Education
- Intelligence, and the breadth and depth of thinking
- Maturity and objectivity
- "Presence"—how one comports himself/herself, including dress, posture, and speech
- Creativity and innovative skills
- Leadership qualities
- Ethical and moral values
- Vision, both professionally and personally
- Energy, drive, enthusiasm, ambition
- Communication skills, verbal as well as written
- Work ethic
- Confidence level; a feeling of personal security
- Judgment and common sense

GEOGRAPHIC SCOPE OF RECRUITING ACTIVITIES:
Serve clients nationwide and in Canada, UK, and Europe

TOTAL YEARS OF RETAINER-TYPE RECRUITING EXPERIENCE:
20 years

MIKE JACOBS
President
Thorne, Brieger Associates Inc.
11 East 44th Street
New York, NY 10017
Telephone: (212) 682-5424

Date of Birth: June 6, 1932
Grew up in: Brooklyn, New York

Thorne, Brieger Associates Inc.

HIGHER EDUCATION:
Brooklyn College
B.A. degree, psychology, 1953

MILITARY:
Corporal, United States Army, 1953 to 1955

EMPLOYMENT HISTORY:
1989 to present: Thorne, Brieger Associates
1975 to 1989: President, The Thorne Group
1979 to 1981: Chairman, Kien, Jacobs Associates
1960 to 1975: President, Garnet Associates
1957 to 1960: Counselor, Allen Employment
1955 to 1957: Personnel Assistant, Rotobroil Corp. of America

SPECIAL INTERESTS AND HOBBIES:
Tennis

REPRESENTATIVE AND SIGNIFICANT PLACEMENTS:
Al Andrews, President–Wholesale/Retail Division
Tanner Companies, Inc.
Charles Saldarini, Senior Vice President–Head of Corporate Banking
First Union National Bank
Henry Glass, Division Vice President–Operations
Lightolier
Richard Morrison, Vice President–Sales and Marketing
Maine Rubber
James Schutta, Director of Quality Assurance
Premark International, Food Equipment Group

WHAT I LOOK FOR IN GENERAL IN A CANDIDATE

I look for candidates who are strong enough and smart enough not to be intimidated by the search process or by me.

I look for people who bring the same objectivity to our discussions that I do. They know how to listen. They focus on what is important and ask good questions. They are not turned off by "negatives" but instead put them in perspective.

I look for individuals who will try to manage me ... people who will come to the interview prepared ... who know what they want me to discover about them and what they want to learn about the position ... and who, before the meeting is over, will find a way to accomplish their agenda.

I look for people with a sense of humor who can laugh at themselves but still take their work seriously.

Ultimately, what I always look for in a candidate is someone who not only meets the needs of my client but whose own needs will be equally satisfied by the new position.

GEOGRAPHIC SCOPE OF RECRUITING ACTIVITIES:
Serve clients nationwide

TOTAL YEARS OF RETAINER-TYPE RECRUITING EXPERIENCE:
16 years

THEODORE JADICK
Partner and Member of Executive Committee
Heidrick & Struggles, Inc.
245 Park Avenue
New York, NY 10167
Telephone: (212) 867-9876

Date of Birth: July 16, 1939
Grew up in: Scranton, Pennsylvania

Bachrach

HIGHER EDUCATION:
University of Scranton
B.S. degree, business administration/accounting, 1961

MILITARY:
Specialist, Fourth Class, United States Army, 1962 to 1968

EMPLOYMENT HISTORY:
1975 to present: Heidrick & Struggles, Inc.
1965 to 1975: Senior Vice President, F.W. Hastings Associates
1962 to 1965: Senior Accountant, Deloitte Haskins & Sells

PRIVATE CLUBS:
New York:
Sky Club
Union League Club
Sleepy Hollow Country Club
South Carolina:
Melrose Club

SPECIAL INTERESTS AND HOBBIES:
Squash, tennis, golf; Board of Directors, Calvary Hospital Foundation, Bronx, NY

REPRESENTATIVE AND SIGNIFICANT PLACEMENTS:
Timm F. Cull, President and Chief Executive Officer
Nestle USA, Inc.

Dr. George H. Heilmeier, President and Chief Executive Officer
   Bellcore
James Osterhoff, Chief Financial Officer
   Digital Equipment Corporation
Edwin P. Hoffman, President and Chief Operating Officer
   Household International, Inc.
Bill White, President
   National Baseball League

WHAT I LOOK FOR IN GENERAL IN A CANDIDATE

As I address potential candidates against predetermined search criteria, my prime concern centers around specific, direct, and quantifiable
accomplishments. All of us live and function in a competitive marketplace. What sets some individuals apart are their accomplishments and
the environment in which these results are produced. Personal characteristics also play a major role in my evaluation. Much attention is
given to integrity, values, people skills, creativity, drive, and initiative.
Obviously the ability to get the job done through and with people is an
important measure of success. These qualities are certainly tested in flat
organizations, where the best thinking by a group of people working
together in a positive fashion can result in a well-defined team effort.
Today's shrinking world also places a premium on a global outlook and
candidates with international expertise. More and more the international thread is woven into the fabric of many of our position specifications.

GEOGRAPHIC SCOPE OF RECRUITING ACTIVITIES:
Serve clients nationwide and in Europe

TOTAL YEARS OF RETAINER-TYPE RECRUITING EXPERIENCE:
16 years

E. PENDLETON JAMES
Chairman
Pendleton James and Associates
200 Park Avenue, Suite 3706
New York, NY 10166
Telephone: (212) 557-1599

Date of Birth: October 23, 1929
Grew up in: Midwest and California

The White House

HIGHER EDUCATION:
University of the Pacific
B.A. degree, 1954

MILITARY:
United States Army, 1950 to 1952

EMPLOYMENT HISTORY:
1978 to Present: Pendleton James and Associates
Prior employment: Heidrick and Struggles, Inc.
                        Russell Reynolds Associates

PRIVATE CLUBS:
New York:
    The River Club
    The Economic Club
    Sky Club
    Union League Club
The Metropolitan Club, Washington, DC
Round Hill Club, Greenwich, CT
The California Club, Los Angeles, CA

ASSOCIATIONS/PROFESSIONAL SOCIETIES:
Board Member, Metropolitan Series Fund
Former Board Member, USO World Board of Governors
Chairman, Republican Roundtable of Greenwich
Director, Ronald Reagan Foundation

SPECIAL INTERESTS AND HOBBIES:
Golf, tennis, skiing, reading

REPRESENTATIVE AND SIGNIFICANT PLACEMENTS:
Jim Broadhead, Chairman, President and Chief Executive Officer
    FPL Group, Inc.
Elizabeth Dole, President
    The American Red Cross
Bob Guyett, Senior Vice President, Chief Financial Officer
    Fluor Corporation
Five Members, Board of Directors
    Union Pacific Corporation
Ben Heineman, Senior Vice President, General Counsel
    General Electric

WHAT I LOOK FOR IN GENERAL IN A CANDIDATE

Initial overall appearance—both physical and verbal. How well does candidate present him/herself—his/her background, experiences? What are his/her career goals? What are his/her outside interests? Is his/her personal life stable? Is he/she smart in life? Can he/she handle him/herself at all levels and in all situations? Is candidate flexible? Does candidate respond well to change (not job-hopping change but changes within his/her environment)? Does he/she have a stable work background?

GEOGRAPHIC SCOPE OF RECRUITING ACTIVITIES:
Serve clients nationwide and in the United Kingdom

TOTAL YEARS OF RETAINER-TYPE RECRUITING EXPERIENCE:
23 years

CAROL S. JEFFERS
Vice President and Partner
John Sibbald Associates, Inc.
8725 W. Higgins Road,
  Suite 575
Chicago, IL 60631
Telephone: (312) 693-0575

Date of Birth: July 13, 1942
Grew up in: Western Pennsylvania

John Sibbald Associates, Inc.

EMPLOYMENT HISTORY:
  1975 to present: John Sibbald Associates, Inc.
  1974 to 1975: Associate, Booz, Allen & Hamilton
  1969 to 1974: Real Estate Administrator, Midas International
  1964 to 1969: Credit Manager, U.S. Leasing Corp.

PRIVATE CLUBS:
  Metropolitan Club

ASSOCIATIONS/PROFESSIONAL SOCIETIES:
  National Club Association
  Illinois Management and Executive Search Consultants

SPECIAL INTERESTS AND HOBBIES:
  Collecting cookbooks, modern jazz, entertaining

REPRESENTATIVE AND SIGNIFICANT PLACEMENTS:
  John D.Hightower, General Manager
    The Country Club of Virginia, Richmond
  Karl Peschke, General Manager
    Glen View Club, Golf, Illinois
  Walter Asche, General Manager
    River Oaks Country Club, Houston
  Stephen Foristel, General Manager
    The Alta Club, Salt Lake City
  Stanley Orr, General Manager
    The Union League of Philadelphia

WHAT I LOOK FOR IN GENERAL IN A CANDIDATE

I attempt to spot in every candidate I interview for a given client the qualities which suggest that the candidate will make a genuine difference to the client organization. My work is highly specialized in that I serve only the hospitality industry, especially private clubs and resorts throughout the Western Hemisphere. In seeking people for this field, then, my focus must not only be on the professional skills and credentials they possess but on their sociability and service quotients as well. In these latter aspects, hospitality professionals are different from most other managers and executives. These service-oriented qualities are as necessary for a club's head golf professional as they are for a club general manager. It is not enough for a candidate just to fit a club's distinctive culture. What I get paid for is finding a manager who counts. This is that rare individual who over the years does everything the club called for in its job description but also multiplies the members' pleasure and satisfaction with his or her own good taste, professional skills, and personal character. On top of this, a truly top club manager must always recognize that he or she is ever the employee—and regardless of tenure, reputation, ego, or caliber of clubs—never like a member.

GEOGRAPHIC SCOPE OF RECRUITING ACTIVITIES:
Serve clients nationwide and in Canada and the Caribbean

TOTAL YEARS OF RETAINER-TYPE RECRUITING EXPERIENCE:
12 years

JOHN F. JOHNSON
President and Chief Executive Officer
Lamalie Associates, Inc.
One Cleveland Center
1375 East Ninth Street
Cleveland, OH 44114
Telephone: (216) 694-3000

Date of Birth: April 23, 1942
Grew up in: Brooklyn, New York

Stuart—Rodgers—Reilly

HIGHER EDUCATION:
Tufts University
B.A. degree, economics, 1963
Columbia University
M.B.A. degree, industrial relations, 1964

EMPLOYMENT HISTORY:
1976 to present: Lamalie Associates, Inc.
1967 to 1976: Various Human Resource Positions, General Electric Co.
1964 to 1967: Industrial Relations Analyst, Ford Motor Company

PRIVATE CLUBS:
Union Club
The Club

ASSOCIATIONS/PROFESSIONAL SOCIETIES:
Association for Corporate Growth
Association of Executive Search Consultants
The Human Resource Planning Society
The International Association of Corporate and Professional Recruiters
The Planning Forum

SPECIAL INTERESTS AND HOBBIES:
Wine collecting, big-game fishing, thoroughbred racing

REPRESENTATIVE AND SIGNIFICANT PLACEMENTS:
Roger T. Fridholm, President and Chief Operating Officer
The Stroh Brewery Company

Thomas V. Brown, President
    Caraustar Industries, Inc.
Wallace B. Askins, Executive Vice President and Chief Financial
    Officer (Director)
    Armco Inc.
Joyce E. Hergenhan, Vice President–Corporate Public Relations
    General Electric Company
Jay T. Holmes, Senior Vice President–Corporate Affairs and Secretary
    (Director)
    Bausch & Lomb Inc.

WHAT I LOOK FOR IN GENERAL IN A CANDIDATE

When evaluating candidates for a senior search assignment, I believe that there are four areas which must be explored in detail:

- Intellectual capability
- Functional/technical/industry experience
- Personal values
- Management/leadership style

Each of these factors must be evaluated against both the specification that I developed with my client and my knowledge of the hiring manager and the organization.

Based on education and work history, intellect and experience are easiest to assess. Values and management/leadership capabilities are harder to evaluate and must be sorted out over the course of a two- to three-hour interview. The candidate's value system needs to be compatible with that of the organization, and his or her management/leadership style must enable the individual to function effectively not only in the immediate role but also in broader responsibilities as the individual moves higher in the organization.

Management and leadership skills can become the Achilles' heel of many executives as they rise through an organization. They are the toughest issues to quantify in an interview; and, therefore, I address them in detail when referencing finalist candidates.

GEOGRAPHIC SCOPE OF RECRUITING ACTIVITIES:
Serve clients nationwide

TOTAL YEARS OF RETAINER-TYPE RECRUITING EXPERIENCE:
15 years

DAVID S. JOYS
Managing Director
Higdon, Joys & Mingle, Inc.
375 Park Avenue
New York, NY 10152
Telephone: (212) 752-9780

Date of Birth: July 17, 1943
Grew up in: Wisconsin

Higdon, Joys & Mingle, Inc.

HIGHER EDUCATION:
Amherst College
B.A. degree, economics, 1965
Columbia University Graduate School of Business
M.B.A. degree, finance and marketing, 1967

EMPLOYMENT HISTORY:
1986 to present: Higdon, Joys & Mingle, Inc.
1974 to 1986: Executive Vice President, Russell Reynolds Associates, Inc.
1972 to 1974: Vice President–Marketing Operations and Services, The Hertz Corporation
1967 to 1972: Assistant Vice President–General Sales, American Airlines, Inc.

PRIVATE CLUBS:
Racquet and Tennis Club, New York
Round Hill Club, Greenwich, CT
Marks Club
Verbank Hunting and Fishing Club, Verbank, NY
Anabels, London
Harry's Bar, London

ASSOCIATIONS/PROFESSIONAL SOCIETIES:
Association of Executive Search Consultants

SPECIAL INTERESTS AND HOBBIES:
Hunting/shooting, fly-fishing, golf, squash, impressionist art

REPRESENTATIVE AND SIGNIFICANT PLACEMENTS:
Thomas E. Epley, President and Chief Executive Officer
Technicolor, Inc.
Cary J. Nolan, President and Chief Executive Officer
Picker International, Inc.
Joseph V. Vittoria, Chairman and Chief Executive Officer
Avis, Inc.
G. Michael Hostage, Chairman and Chief Executive Officer
Howard Johnson Company
William J. Hatch, President and Chief Executive Officer
Embarcadero Center, Ltd./Rockefeller & Associates Realty

WHAT I LOOK FOR IN GENERAL IN A CANDIDATE

While each client assignment is unique and requires a tailored solution, most of our senior general management projects require assessment of the following candidate traits, characteristics, and background issues:

- Leadership and team-building skills
- Intelligence *and* common sense
- Personal and professional integrity
- Self-confidence with humility
- Interpersonal and communication skills
- Flexibility/adaptability
- Initiative/motivation/energy/drive
- Judgment
- Ability to listen
- Vision and creativity
- Positive outlook/"can-do" attitude
- Action/results orientation
- Progressive and successful track record of relevant accomplishments
- Balance in life/breadth of interests

GEOGRAPHIC SCOPE OF RECRUITING ACTIVITIES:
Serve clients nationwide and in the U.K., Europe, Canada, and Australia

TOTAL YEARS OF RETAINER-TYPE RECRUITING EXPERIENCE:
18 years

CLAUDIA LACY KELLY
Managing Director
Norman Broadbent International, Inc.
200 Park Avenue, 18th Floor
New York, NY 10166-0003
Telephone: (212) 953-6990

Date of Birth: May 17, 1952
Grew up in: Alexandria, Virginia

Norman Broadbent International, Inc.

HIGHER EDUCATION:
University of Virginia
   B.A. degree, theater, 1974
Columbia University Graduate School of Business
   M.B.A. degree, marketing, 1979

EMPLOYMENT HISTORY:
1989 to present: Norman Broadbent International, Inc.
1984 to 1989: Partner, Nordeman Grimm, Inc.
1979 to 1984: Senior Engagement Manager, McKinsey & Company, Inc.
1978 to 1979: Colgate Palmolive Fellow/Assistant Brand Manager, Colgate Palmolive Co.
1976 to 1977: Appointments Secretary, the office of Senator Jacob K. Javits
1976: Scheduling Staff, the office of President Gerald Ford

PRIVATE CLUBS:
Greenwich Country Club
The Landmark Club

ASSOCIATIONS/PROFESSIONAL SOCIETIES:
Association of Executive Search Consultants

SPECIAL INTERESTS AND HOBBIES:
Family, Board Member Round Hill School, swimming, skiing

REPRESENTATIVE AND SIGNIFICANT PLACEMENTS:
  Althea L. Duersten, Head of Fixed Income Investing
    The Bank of New York
  Patrick Allaway, Head of Foreign Exchange Derivatives Marketing
    Swiss Bank Corporation/O'Connor Services L.P.
  Andrew Mica, Chief Operating Officer
    Guardian Asset Management Corporation
  Michael Pralle, Manager of Business Development
    General Electric Financial Services
  Marketing Advisory Team Members
    Swissair/Swissotel Companies Ltd.

WHAT I LOOK FOR IN GENERAL IN A CANDIDATE

- Consistent, well-established themes in their lives
- Demonstrated track record of success
- Self-reliance
- Genuine human qualities, honesty, warmth, sense of humor, commitment to family and personal ideas
- Mastery of their particular areas of expertise

  However, all of these qualities must be assessed against the criteria established by the client and that indescribable element of "fit" with the business climate and culture of the hiring organization. It is my experience that this last element can frequently be the most ephemeral, the trickiest to assess, and the most critical to success.

GEOGRAPHIC SCOPE OF RECRUITING ACTIVITIES:
  Serve clients nationwide and in Europe and Asia

TOTAL YEARS OF RETAINER-TYPE RECRUITING EXPERIENCE:
  7 years

ROGER M. KENNY
Partner
Kenny, Kindler, Hunt & Howe
and Boardroom Consultants,
Inc.
1 Dag Hammarskjold Plaza,
34th Floor
New York, NY 10017
Telephone: (212) 355-5560

Date of Birth: October 3, 1938
Grew up in: New York, New York

Kenny, Kindler, Hunt & Howe and
Boardroom Consultants, Inc.

HIGHER EDUCATION:
Manhattan College
B.B.A. degree, 1959
New York University Graduate School of Business
M.B.A. degree, 1961

MILITARY:
Specialist Fourth Class, United States Army/National Guard, 1962 to
1968

EMPLOYMENT HISTORY:
1982 to present: Kenny, Kindler, Hunt & Howe and Boardroom Consultants, Inc.
1967 to 1982: Senior Vice President and Partner, SpencerStuart &
Associates
1959 to 1967: Manager-Operations, Port of New York and New Jersey
Authority

PRIVATE CLUBS:
Westchester Country Club, The Board Room, Economic Club

ASSOCIATIONS/PROFESSIONAL SOCIETIES:
Association of Executive Search Consultants; Member Northeast Re-
gional Committee and Nominating Committee
International Association of Corporate and Professional Recruiters

SPECIAL INTERESTS AND HOBBIES:
  Hiking, sports, reading

REPRESENTATIVE AND SIGNIFICANT PLACEMENTS:
  President and Chief Executive Officer
    Retail chain and distribution company
  President and Chief Executive Officer
    Housewares company
  President–North America
    European pharmaceutical company
  Executive Vice President–Marketing
    Multinational information services institution
  Senior-level Board Directors
    Top 50 company

WHAT I LOOK FOR IN GENERAL IN A CANDIDATE

Track record as substantiated by subordinates as well as superiors; multiple views related to leadership. How a person handles adversity; willingness to experiment; and so on.

Since we are dealing with the ninety-fifth percentile of corporate executives, we insist on intelligent contribution as well, so we request speeches, articles. We challenge candidates as to their thinking on current issues. One typical question: What subject would you select that would enable us to determine what is special about you as a business person, a marketer, a financial person, and so forth?

We insist on getting a special handle on each candidate.
What would the candidate have done differently during his/her career?
To whom do they give credit for their own development?

GEOGRAPHIC SCOPE OF RECRUITING ACTIVITIES:
  Serve clients nationwide and in Europe, the Middle East and Far East

TOTAL YEARS OF RETAINER-TYPE RECRUITING EXPERIENCE:
  24 years

DAVID A. KETTWIG
Vice President
A.T. Kearney, Inc.–Executive
　Search
222 South Riverside Plaza
Chicago, IL 60606
Telephone: (312) 648-1939

Date of Birth: March 12, 1941
Grew up in: Joliet, Illinois

Terry Photography

HIGHER EDUCATION:
Joilet Junior College
　A.A.S. degree, business, 1961
Illinois State University
　B.A. degree, 1963

EMPLOYMENT HISTORY:
1989 to present: A.T. Kearney–Executive Search
1982 to 1989: Vice President–Managing Director, Paul Stafford Associates
1981 to 1982: Managing Associate, Korn/Ferry International
1977 to 1981: Senior Manager, Peat Marwick Mitchell & Company
1969 to 1977: Assistant Vice President, American National Bank, Chicago
1967 to 1969: Personnel Manager, Uniroyal
1963 to 1967: Business Teacher, Lincoln-Way High School

PRIVATE CLUBS:
Union League Club of Chicago

ASSOCIATIONS/PROFESSIONAL SOCIETIES:
Association of Executive Search Consultants

SPECIAL INTERESTS AND HOBBIES:
Golf

REPRESENTATIVE AND SIGNIFICANT PLACEMENTS:
Frank Geremia, President
　Kemper Clearing Corporation

Carole McElyea, Vice President—Credit Process
  First Chicago
Ben Gill, General Counsel
  Arthur J. Gallagher & Company
Don Desroches, Senior Vice President
  Zenith Data Systems
Lee Reiser, Vice President—Market Development
  Beatrice Foods

WHAT I LOOK FOR IN GENERAL IN A CANDIDATE

There are three general characteristics I look for in candidates: relevant experience, motivation, and personal traits.

Relevant experience: By relevant I mean the work experience and level of professional attainment as requested by a client. This can be industry specific and/or function specific. In either case, professional achievement is viewed by rank, quality of performance/expertise, amount of experience, achievements, and impact on the organization.

Motivation: Why do candidates do what they do? How did they attain what they have achieved? What *specifically* did they do to achieve this level? What drives them to this level? What long-range aspirations does one have? In what early experiences was the candidate involved, for example, sports, music, academics, part-time or entrepreneurial employment?

Personal traits: While these vary all over the board, it is extremely important to learn about as many traits as possible so that, in the end, our judgment about a "fit," that is, the chemistry, is right between a candidate and a company. This is important because each company has a culture, a style, and a unique personality. An executive search consultant must be very astute at assessing these traits—both the candidate's and the client's—to effect a good fit.

GEOGRAPHIC SCOPE OF RECRUITING ACTIVITIES:
Serve clients nationwide

TOTAL YEARS OF RETAINER-TYPE RECRUITING EXPERIENCE:
14 years

MICHAEL C. KIEFFER
President
Kieffer, Ford & Hadelman, Ltd.
2015 Sprint Road, Suite 510
Oak Brook, IL 60521
Telephone: (708) 990-1370

Date of Birth: December 23, 1942
Grew up in: Kingston, New York

Kieffer, Ford & Hadelman, Ltd.

HIGHER EDUCATION:
Marist College, New York
B.A. degree, liberal arts, 1969
Central Michigan University
M.A. degree, management (health care concentration), 1979

MILITARY:
E-4 SSGT, United States Air Force, 1963 to 1967

EMPLOYMENT HISTORY:
1983 to present: Kieffer, Ford & Hadelman, Ltd.
1977 to 1983: Regional Vice President, Witt Associates
1975 to 1977: Vice President–Human Resources, Geneva General
Hospital
1970 to 1975: Vice President–Human Resources, St. Francis Hospital
1970: Director of Career Counseling, Dutchess Community College
1969 to 1970: Assistant Director, Mid Hudson Career Development
Center

PRIVATE CLUBS:
Aurora Country Club
DuPage Club
Carlton Club

SPECIAL INTERESTS AND HOBBIES:
Golf, sailing, international travel, skiing, tennis

REPRESENTATIVE AND SIGNIFICANT PLACEMENTS:
Ronald Aldrich, President and Chief Executive Officer
Franciscan Health Systems

Thomas Rockers, President and Chief Executive Officer
   Santa Rosa Health Care Corporation
John Johnson, President and Chief Executive Officer
   Berkshire Health System
Jan Jannings, President and Chief Executive Officer
   Millard Fillmore System
Michael Bice, President and Chief Executive Officer
   Allegany Health System

WHAT I LOOK FOR IN GENERAL IN A CANDIDATE

Beyond the basic professional skills and experience to do the job, the following are important to discover in a candidate for a high level executive position: a sense of vision that comes from viewing the world beyond a single industry or discipline; the ability to manage stress and balance one's life; a defined set of values which includes integrity, compassion, strong work ethic, and loyalty. Self-awareness is critical—the introspection to see one's weaknesses and the maturity and self-confidence to admit failures are necessary ingredients in the full development of an executive. Strong relational skills are absolute as is a well-developed sense of humor. At times, the ability to project humanness in adversity and not take oneself too seriously is a definite asset—for the executive and the organization he leads.

GEOGRAPHIC SCOPE OF RECRUITING ACTIVITIES:
Serve clients nationwide

TOTAL YEARS OF RETAINER-TYPE RECRUITING EXPERIENCE:
14 years

RICHARD E. KINSER
President
Kinser & Associates
One Dag Hammarskjold Plaza
New York, NY 10017
Telephone: (212) 207-9820

Date of Birth: May 14, 1936
Grew up in: California

HIGHER EDUCATION:
Stanford University
A.B. degree, economics, 1958

EMPLOYMENT HISTORY:
1986 to present: Kinser & Associates
1983 to 1986: Managing Director, Gould & McCoy Inc.
1981 to 1983: Deputy Director–Personnel, The White House
1979 to 1981: Senior Vice President and Director, William Clark
Associates
1977 to 1979: Partner, Foster Associates
1964 to 1977: Vice President, Booz, Allen & Hamilton
1958 to 1964: Director–Personnel, U.S. Steel Corporation

ASSOCIATIONS/PROFESSIONAL SOCIETIES:
Economics Club of New York
Aspen Institute

SPECIAL INTERESTS AND HOBBIES:
Political science, history, art, photography

REPRESENTATIVE AND SIGNIFICANT PLACEMENTS:
Thomas Page, Chairman, President and Chief Executive Officer
San Diego Gas & Electric Company
Tracey Reiss, Vice President–Communications
RJR Nabisco
John Bohn, President
Moody's Investment Services

Michael Brewer, Vice President–Government Affairs
  Dun & Bradstreet Corporation
Robert Harris, General Counsel
  Thiokol Corporation

WHAT I LOOK FOR IN GENERAL IN A CANDIDATE

Character, intelligence, logic, and clarity of expression are basic candidate qualities that must be evaluated. Who is this person? How does this person think and operate in different circumstances and situations? My discussions with references and candidates are open and free ranging. We cover strategic vision, innovation, management discipline, leadership ability, and relationship skills. Judgment, ability to deal with ambiguity, self-awareness, and adaptability are critical points. Communication skills are more important today than in the past. Drive and level of ambition must fit the situation and the client culture. I look for patterns, personal accomplishments, weaknesses, and a track record. Checking the industry knowledge is the easy part.

As background, it is essential to have a complete understanding of the client's total organization and plans. One cannot compartmentalize a search. Once when conducting searches for a Vice President–Operations and a Chief Financial Officer for the same client, I found a candidate who could fill both positions. We reorganized to give him both responsibilities because he also fit a future requirement. Today he is the chief executive officer of the company.

The final recommendation is based on my analysis of the candidate, my judgment about client and candidate "chemistry," and my instinct about the fit.

GEOGRAPHIC SCOPE OF RECRUITING ACTIVITIES:
  Serve clients nationwide and in Europe

TOTAL YEARS OF RETAINER-TYPE RECRUITING EXPERIENCE:
  25 years

R. PAUL KORS
Partner
Kors Montgomery International
1980 Post Oak Boulevard,
Suite 2280
Houston, TX 77056
Telephone: (713) 840-7101

Date of Birth: June 12, 1935
Grew up in: Pontiac, Michigan

Kaye Marvins Photography

HIGHER EDUCATION:
University of Michigan
B.B.A. degree, 1958
University of Southern California
M.B.A. degree, marketing, 1965

MILITARY:
First Lieutenant, United States Army Reserve, 1958 to 1966

EMPLOYMENT HISTORY:
1978 to present: Kors Montgomery International
1973 to 1978: Managing Partner, Korn/Ferry International
1966 to 1972: Account Manager, Dean Witter & Company
1958 to 1966: Salesman, Nalco Chemical Company

PRIVATE CLUBS:
Houston Racquet Club
Palmas Del Mar Country Club

SPECIAL INTERESTS AND HOBBIES:
Skiing, mountain climbing, tennis, golf, classic films

REPRESENTATIVE AND SIGNIFICANT PLACEMENTS:
Richard A. Bray, Executive Vice President–Board of Directors
BP America
Paul G. Fusco, Senior Vice President–Information Services
Bertelsmann Music Group
C. Russell Luigs, Chairman and Chief Executive Officer
Global Marine Corporation

Robert L. Mandeville, Director of Operations
  King Khaled International Airport
Peter Vicars, President and Chief Executive Officer
  Tekelec Corporation

WHAT I LOOK FOR IN GENERAL IN A CANDIDATE

My criterion for selecting a final candidate is based on evaluation of his or her previous successes and accomplishments. Qualifications and experience are also important but not necessarily key ingredients in predicting whether or not the candidate will prove out with the client company.

I like to start by looking at the kinds of decisions and choices the candidate has had to make in previous assignments. From there, I try to move to an in-depth look at how he/she handles responsibilities similar to those in the new position. You want to look for a gamebreaker for a gamebreaker position and a caretaker for a caretaker position.

It is important to verify his/her past achievements by relating them to the tasks and challenges of the client situation. The candidate really needs to demonstrate that he/she can grasp the issues involved and can articulate how past accomplishments will enable him or her to be successful in the new position.

If all is in sync, I want to make sure there is a reasonable chance the candidate would ultimately accept the opportunity. The key here is to gain some in-depth understanding of the candidate's career aspirations and then make a judgment as to whether or not he or she is consistent with the opportunity.

GEOGRAPHIC SCOPE OF RECRUITING ACTIVITIES:
  Serve clients nationwide and in Europe, Japan, Australia, South America, and Saudi Arabia

TOTAL YEARS OF RETAINER-TYPE RECRUITING EXPERIENCE:
  18 years

GARY L. KREUTZ
President
Kreutz Consulting Group, Inc.
585 North Bank Lane, Suite 3200
Lake Forest, Illinois 60045
Telephone: (708) 234-9115

Date of Birth: February 5, 1945
Grew up in: St. Louis, Missouri

Kreutz Consulting Group

HIGHER EDUCATION:
   St. Louis University
      B.S. degree, commerce, 1967
      M.B.A. degree, 1973

MILITARY:
   E-5 Sergeant, United States Marine Corps Reserve, 1967 to 1972

EMPLOYMENT HISTORY:
   1989 to present: Kreutz Consulting Group, Inc.
   1985 to 1989: Senior Vice President/Partner, Slayton & Kreutz International Inc.
   1984 to 1985: Senior Vice President–Human Resources, Federated Department Stores
   1982 to 1984: Vice President–Human Resources, Sandvik, Inc.
   1981 to 1982: Senior Director–Human Resources, American Can Company
   1974 to 1981: Director–Human Resources, PepsiCo

PRIVATE CLUBS:
   Exmoor Country Club

ASSOCIATIONS/PROFESSIONAL SOCIETIES:
   International Association of Corporate and Professional Recruiters
   National Association of Executive Recruiters
   Human Resources Management Association of Chicago

SPECIAL INTERESTS AND HOBBIES:
   Scuba diving, racquetball, tennis

REPRESENTATIVE AND SIGNIFICANT PLACEMENTS:
Tom Quarton, Senior Vice President–Marketing
    Ameritech Publishing Inc.
Sandy Posa, Vice President–Marketing
    Kraft–General Foods
Jason Wright, Corporate Vice President–Financial Communications
    RJR Nabisco Corporation
Robert Hartley, Vice President Administration–Japan
    Continental Bank
Craig Sinclair, Vice President–Advertising and Marketing Services
    Walgreen Company, Inc.

WHAT I LOOK FOR IN GENERAL IN A CANDIDATE

The candidate has to have a proven record of steady career growth in a level of accomplishment that indicates he/she will be able to successfully perform the role required in the search. On all occasions, the client desires the best possible professional within their financial constraints, but the client frequently does not require the candidate come from the client's industry.

With the "baseline" of accomplishment and success established, I pursue much closer the personality of the candidates such as drive, energy, desire and "passion" for what they believe in. The client wants someone who will, in fact, effect change and make a difference at the end of the day. The candidates have to communicate by demeanor, past record, and individual personality that they will make a difference, that they care to make a difference, and why the client opening is correct for them and their careers. Lastly, the candidate has to mesh very well with the client's culture and complement the hiring manager's personality.

GEOGRAPHIC SCOPE OF RECRUITING ACTIVITIES:
Serve clients nationwide and in Canada, Great Britain, France, Sweden, Germany, Switzerland, Italy, and Southeast Asia

TOTAL YEARS OF RETAINER-TYPE RECRUITING EXPERIENCE:
6 years

IRA W. KRINSKY
President
Ira W. Krinsky & Associates
600 Westgate Street
Pasadena, CA 91103
Telephone: (818) 568-3311

Date of Birth: January 15, 1949
Grew up in: New York

Ira W. Krinsky & Associates

HIGHER EDUCATION:
Hofstra University
    B.A. degree, history, 1971
New York University
    M.A. degree, education, 1974
Harvard University
    Ed.D. degree, 1979

MILITARY:
Specialist E-5 Class, United States Army, 1966 to 1979

EMPLOYMENT HISTORY:
1988 to present: Ira W. Krinsky & Associates
1982 to 1988: Managing Vice President, Korn/Ferry International
1979 to 1982: Deputy Superintendent, Pomona Public Schools, California
1978 to 1979: Assistant Superintendent, Levittown Public Schools, New York
1972 to 1975: Teacher, Administrator, etc., Huntington Public Schools, New York

ASSOCIATIONS/PROFESSIONAL SOCIETIES:
Southwestern University School of Law, Los Angeles, Trustee
Phi Delta Kappa, Harvard Club of Southern California

SPECIAL INTERESTS AND HOBBIES:
Weight training, stamp collecting, history

REPRESENTATIVE AND SIGNIFICANT PLACEMENTS:
Diether Haenicke, President
   Western Michigan University
Joan Raymond, General Superintendent of Schools
   Houston Public Schools
Curt Simic, Vice Chancellor for Development
   University of California at Berkeley
Donald Phelps, Chancellor
   Los Angeles Community College District
Richard Rosette, Dean of Business
   Rochester Institute of Technology, New York

WHAT I LOOK FOR IN GENERAL IN A CANDIDATE

I look for four general qualities in all candidates—intelligence, compassion, courage, and integrity. I also look for sensitivity and exceptional communication skills. What is important is how an individual integrates these qualities with his or her personality in each unique career situation. I try and envision the candidate in the specific role I'm recruiting—on-site and interacting with others within and outside the organization. I then form a "gut-level" reaction which forms the basis of my recommendation.

GEOGRAPHIC SCOPE OF RECRUITING ACTIVITIES:
Serve clients nationwide and in Canada and Mexico

TOTAL YEARS OF RETAINER-TYPE RECRUITING EXPERIENCE:
9+ years

KAI LINDHOLST
Managing Partner
Egon Zehnder International Inc.
One First National Plaza,
  Suite 3300
Chicago, IL 60603
Telephone: (312) 782-4500

Date of Birth: August 25, 1942
Grew up in: Denmark

Pach Bros.

HIGHER EDUCATION:
  Copenhagen School of Business Administration
    M.B.A. degree, marketing, 1966
  University of Pennsylvania, Wharton School of Finance
    M.B.A. degree, marketing, 1968

EMPLOYMENT HISTORY:
  1972 to present: Egon Zehnder International
  1968 to 1972: Senior Associate, McKinsey & Company
  1961 to 1963: Sales Representative, Lindholst & Company

PRIVATE CLUBS:
  University Club of Chicago
  Mid-Day Club, Chicago

REPRESENTATIVE AND SIGNIFICANT PLACEMENTS:
  Dr. Peter Rodgers, President and Chief Executive Officer
    E.J. Brach & Sons
  Dr. Patrick Gage, Chief Scientific Officer
    Genetics Institute
  Kenneth Weg, President–Pharmaceutical Group
    Squibb Corporation
  Jean-Pierre Garnier, President–North America
    SmithKline Beecham
  Dr. John Martin, Senior Vice President–Research and Development
    Gilead Science, Inc.

WHAT I LOOK FOR IN GENERAL IN A CANDIDATE

Each client organization has a management style and culture which must be well understood by the search consultant in order to advise successfully on senior-level appointments. However, key characteristics of successful candidates, irrespective of the size of the company, industry, function, and so on which I value in particular are a high energy level, a balanced self-appraisal, an ability to create enthusiasm, and a "can-do" attitude. The more senior the position, such personality characteristics become more and more sought after. While intellectual capacity and certain functional/technical skills are required to even be considered, leaders who have demonstrated an above-average ability to attract, retain, and motivate good people at many levels within an organization are particularly sought after. Talent is *the* scarce resource in the Western world, and executives who have proven that they can "accumulate" and energize talent in their organization will be particularly sought after in the 1990s.

GEOGRAPHIC SCOPE OF RECRUITING ACTIVITIES:
Serve clients nationwide and in Europe, the Far East/Japan, Mexico/Brazil/Argentina

TOTAL YEARS OF RETAINER-TYPE RECRUITING EXPERIENCE:
19 years

JOHN S. LLOYD
President
Witt Associates Inc.
1211 W. 22nd Street
Oak Brook, IL 60521
Telephone: (708) 574-5070

Date of Birth: February 18, 1946
Grew up in: Jefferson City, Missouri

HIGHER EDUCATION:
University of Missouri
B.S. degree, business administration, 1968
M.B.A. and M.S.P.H. (healthcare management), 1970

EMPLOYMENT HISTORY:
1973 to present: Witt Associates, Inc.
1970 to 1972: Associate, A.T. Kearney

PRIVATE CLUBS:
Hinsdale Golf Club

ASSOCIATIONS/PROFESSIONAL SOCIETIES:
Association of Executive Search Consultants
American College of Healthcare Executives
International Health Policy and Management Institute

SPECIAL INTERESTS AND HOBBIES:
Bicycling, hiking, video production

REPRESENTATIVE AND SIGNIFICANT PLACEMENTS:
Douglas Peters, President
Main Line Health Inc.
Clifford Eldredge, President
Pennsylvania Hospital
Charles Pierce, President
Florida Hospital Association

William Goss, Program Manager—Employee Relations
  General Electric Company
James S. Todd, M.D., Executive Vice President
  American Medical Association

WHAT I LOOK FOR IN GENERAL IN A CANDIDATE

I search for candidates who comprehend the complexities of one of the USA's largest industries—that being healthcare. Our industry is in a great transition—it is very expensive, the aging population is growing, and there is professional unrest. Internationally, as well as domestically, the people of the world want better health services and health and medical products. I look for leaders.

Successful candidates must have displayed leadership traits since their youngest years. Candidates must be intelligent and show interest in continuing to pursue personal education. The successful candidate must be able to formulate and clearly express his/her ideas on corporate mission, goals, and objectives. A sense of humor is absolute. A balance must exist between bottom-line focus and people-motivational skills. Candidates must understand the practices of total quality management and continuous quality improvement as they can be applied in the healthcare industry. The person must be able to manage turmoil and change.

GEOGRAPHIC SCOPE OF RECRUITING ACTIVITIES:
Serve clients nationwide and in Europe, Africa, and Asia

TOTAL YEARS OF RETAINER-TYPE RECRUITING EXPERIENCE:
19 years

JOHN LUCHT
President
The John Lucht Consultancy Inc.
The Olympic Tower
641 Fifth Avenue
New York, NY 10022
Telephone: (212) 935-4660

Date of Birth: June 1, 1933
Grew up in: Reedsburg, Wisconsin

photo by Hugh Williams

HIGHER EDUCATION:
University of Wisconsin
  B.S. degree, 1955
University of Wisconsin Law School
  LL.B. degree, 1960

EMPLOYMENT HISTORY:
1977 to present: The John Lucht Consultancy Inc.
1971 to 1977: Vice President, Heidrick and Struggles Inc.
1970 to 1971: General Manager–Tetley Tea Division, Squibb Beech-Nut Inc.
1969 to 1970: Director of Marketing, W.A. Sheaffer Pen Co.
1964 to 1969: Director of New Product Marketing, Bristol-Myers Co.
1960 to 1964: Account Executive, J. Walter Thompson Co.
1959 to 1960: Instructor, University of Wisconsin Law School

PRIVATE CLUBS:
Metropolitan Club of New York
Canadian Club of New York

ASSOCIATIONS/PROFESSIONAL SOCIETIES:
Association of Executive Search Consultants
International Association of Corporate and Professional Recruiters

SPECIAL INTERESTS AND HOBBIES:
Writing, lecturing, and Pro Bono seminars. Author of the best seller
*Rites of Passage at $100,000+ ... The Insider's Guide to Executive Job
Changing*

REPRESENTATIVE AND SIGNIFICANT PLACEMENTS:
John Backe, President & CEO
  CBS Inc.
Patrick Donaghy, President–Silver Burdett & Ginn
  SFN Corporation
Richard Casabonne, President–Franklin Watts Inc.
  Grolier Inc.
James Knabe, President
  Associated Merchandising Corporation
Erna Zint, Regional VP–Far East (recruited and stationed in Hong
  Kong)
  Associated Merchandising Corporation

WHAT I LOOK FOR IN GENERAL IN A CANDIDATE

For almost every high-level position in almost every industry, a rare
few executives stand out. Their leadership, creativity, expertise, and fine
personal characterstics produce an outstanding performance and reputation, which are observable both outside and inside their organization.

Practicing independently, I make it a point to serve only one company in each industry. That way, I avoid the usual "off-limits" restric-
tions. My clients and I have the luxury of just one simple criterion:
"Who's the best person in the field?" rather than merely, "Who's within
the specifications?"

So I always look for the person my client will be most strengthened
to gain and, unfortunately, a competitive organization will be weakened
to lose. And sometimes, of course, that person is junior and rising,
rather than flying high.

GEOGRAPHIC SCOPE OF RECRUITING ACTIVITIES:
Serve clients nationwide and in Europe and Asia

TOTAL YEARS OF RETAINER-TYPE RECRUITING EXPERIENCE:
20 years

THEODORE E. "TED" LUSK
Partner
Nadzam, Lusk & Associates, Inc.
3211 Scott Boulevard, Suite 205
Santa Clara, CA 95054-3091
Telephone: (408) 727-6601

Date of Birth: September 4, 1932
Grew up in: Kansas, Idaho, Oregon, and California

Nadzam, Lusk & Associates, Inc.

HIGHER EDUCATION:
San Jose State College
B.A. degree, industrial relations, 1957

MILITARY:
Sergeant, United States Marine Corps, 1951 to 1954

EMPLOYMENT HISTORY:
1976 to present: Nadzam, Lusk & Associates, Inc.
1970 to 1976: Director–Employee Relations, Singer–Business Machines
1966 to 1970: Manager, Industrial Relations, Singer–Link
1965 to 1966: Corporate Director–Staffing, Utah Construction and Mining
1964 to 1965: Director–Personnel, Soule Steel
1957 to 1964: Various positions in industrial relations, Aerojet–General

ASSOCIATIONS/PROFESSIONAL SOCIETIES:
Association of Executive Search Consultants, Board Member
California Executive Recruiters Association

SPECIAL INTERESTS AND HOBBIES:
Presbyterian Church—Elder; travel, tennis, gardening, dining

REPRESENTATIVE AND SIGNIFICANT PLACEMENTS:
George Leslie, President
Meitec Corporation

John Migliore, Executive Vice President
    Caere Corporation
Horst Simon, Division General Manager
    NCR Corporation
Marion Horna, President
    GWF Power Systems Company, Inc.
Judith Schliessmann, Director of Manufacturing
    GTE Electronics

WHAT I LOOK FOR IN GENERAL IN A CANDIDATE

Track record, track record, and track record. Leadership and managerial skills. Integrity, sense of ethics, and a good dose of common sense. Image and intelligence. Self-confident but not arrogant. Verbal and writing skills. Strategic and tactical abilities.

GEOGRAPHIC SCOPE OF RECRUITING ACTIVITIES:
Serve clients nationwide and in Europe and Asia

TOTAL YEARS OF RETAINER-TYPE RECRUITING EXPERIENCE:
15 years

WILLIAM H. "MO" MARUMOTO
Chairman of the Board
The Interface Group, Ltd.
1025 Thomas Jefferson
  Street, NW
Suite 410, East Lobby
Washington, DC 20007
Telephone: (202) 342-7200

Date of Birth: December 16, 1934
Grew up in: Santa Ana, California

The Interface Group, Ltd.

HIGHER EDUCATION:
Whittier College
  B.A. degree, sociology, 1957

EMPLOYMENT HISTORY:
1973 to present: The Interface Group, Ltd.
1970 to 1973: Special Assistant to the President, The White House
1969 to 1970: Assistant to the Secretary, U.S. Dept. of Health, Education and Welfare
1969: Senior Consultant, Peat, Marwick & Mitchell Company
1968 to 1969: Vice President–Planning and Development, California Institute of the Arts
1965 to 1968: Associate Director of Development and Alumni Relations, University of California at Los Angeles
1958 to 1965: Director of Alumni Relations, Whittier College

PRIVATE CLUBS:
Congressional Country Club, Maryland
Pisces Club, Washington, DC

ASSOCIATIONS/PROFESSIONAL SOCIETIES:
Association of Executive Search Consultants

REPRESENTATIVE AND SIGNIFICANT PLACEMENTS:
Ramona Banuelos, United States Treasurer
United States Department of the Treasury

Luis Nogales and Bruce Llewelyn
    Adolf Coors Company
Gary Quell, President
    Council for the Advancement and Support of Education
John T. Sloan, Vice President—Human Resources
    The Chicago Tribune
Eugene Knorr, Vice President—Washington Relations
    Philip Morris Companies, Inc.

WHAT I LOOK FOR IN GENERAL IN A CANDIDATE

* Corporate presence and bearing
* People skills/chemistry/personality
* Motivation and self initiative
* Leadership qualities
* Written and verbal communication skills
* Mental toughness
* Integrity
* Intelligence
* Strategic and analytical skills
* Demonstrated record of achievements
* Team player
* Focus
* Ability to fit into new culture/environment
* Creative and innovative skills
* Sense of humor

GEOGRAPHIC SCOPE OF RECRUITING ACTIVITIES:
    Serve clients nationwide and in Asia and Europe

TOTAL YEARS OF RETAINER-TYPE RECRUITING EXPERIENCE:
    22 years

JAMES P. MASCIARELLI
Chairman
Fenwick Partners
57 Bedford Street, Suite 101
Lexington, MA 02173
Telephone: (617) 862-3370

Date of Birth: November 14, 1948
Grew up in: Boston area

Fenwick Partners

HIGHER EDUCATION:
Holy Cross College
A.B. degree, psychology, 1970
Babson College
M.B.A. degree, organizational behavior, 1978

EMPLOYMENT HISTORY:
1983 to present: Fenwick Partners
1981 to 1983: President, The Churchill Group
1979 to 1981: Vice President, Winter Wyman & Company
1974 to 1979: North American Human Resources Manager, Data General Corporation
1973 to 1974: Human Resources Manager, Cramer Electronics
1970 to 1973: Executive Director, Community Health Education Council

PRIVATE CLUBS:
Bass Rocks Country Club, Gloucester, MA

ASSOCIATIONS/PROFESSIONAL SOCIETIES:
Association of Executive Search Consultants

SPECIAL INTERESTS AND HOBBIES:
Music, guitar, travel, reading, chess, hiking, boating

REPRESENTATIVE AND SIGNIFICANT PLACEMENTS:
Patrick Courtin, President and Chief Executive Officer
Proteon Inc.
Ronald Fisher, President and Chief Executive Officer
Phoenix Technologies

Richard Stewart, President and Chief Executive Officer
  Computer Corporation of America
Joseph Gill, President—U.S. Operations
  Bruel & Kjaer
Sheldon Horowitz, President—U.S. Operations
  NEK Cable

WHAT I LOOK FOR IN GENERAL IN A CANDIDATE

I seek the optimum combination of personal factors, resume factors, and motivations for the specific search performed. My background and orientation allow me to evaluate motivational and attitudinal factors that are key to critical success elements for the assignment. Recently, I have been testing and researching ways to evaluate creativity in candidates and hope to publish on that subject within the next three years. I introduce *only* candidates with strong belief, value, and attitudinal systems that can inspire or at least provide professional modeling behavior for their organizations. The search for leadership maturity and the self-esteem and self-awareness that it implies are foremost on my mind.

GEOGRAPHIC SCOPE OF RECRUITING ACTIVITIES:
  Serve clients nationwide and through affiliates in North America and
    Europe

TOTAL YEARS OF RETAINER-TYPE RECRUITING EXPERIENCE:
  10 years

NEAL L. MASLAN
Managing Partner
Ward Howell International
16255 Ventura Blvd., Suite 400
Encino, CA 91436
Telephone: (818) 905-6010

Date of Birth: September 22,
1940
Grew up in: Richmond, Virginia

HIGHER EDUCATION:
University of Virginia
B.A. degree, psychology, 1962

Ward Howell International

Yale University
MP.H. degree, healthcare administration, 1964

MILITARY:
First Lieutenant, United States Army, 1964 to 1966

EMPLOYMENT HISTORY:
1988 to present: Ward Howell International
1986 to 1988: Vice President, Paul R. Ray & Company
1982 to 1986: Senior Vice President, American Medical International
1972 to 1982: Executive Vice President, Hyatt Medical Enterprises—
Subsidiary of Hyatt Corp.
1970 to 1972: Executive Vice President, CENCO Hospital and Con-
valescent Homes Corp.
1966 to 1970: Vice President–Administration, Progressive Care, Inc.

PRIVATE CLUBS:
Regency Club

ASSOCIATIONS/PROFESSIONAL SOCIETIES:
American Hospital Association
Federation of American Health Systems

SPECIAL INTERESTS AND HOBBIES:
Tennis, flying, civic boards

REPRESENTATIVE AND SIGNIFICANT PLACEMENTS:
Richard Gilleland, Chairman and Chief Executive Officer
American Medical International
Dan Kohl, President and Chief Operating Officer
HMSS (Division of Secomerica)

Vic Streufert, Executive Vice President, Chief Financial Officer
  American Health Properties
James Elmslie, President and Chief Executive Officer
  Medical Recruiters of America
Ken Hachikian, Chief Executive Officer
  LINC Medical Imaging

WHAT I LOOK FOR IN GENERAL IN A CANDIDATE

Intellectual ability: The ability to conceptualize what a company can and should become

Integrity: Intense commitment to high moral standards and business ethics

Maturity: The ability to maintain personal control; the capability to think before speaking

Interpersonal skills: A style which builds alliances within the organization, along with the ability to establish and maintain positive/genuine relationships

Results orientation/initiative: The ability to work toward outcomes; a self-starter who sets high standards for self and others and demonstrates an active work pace over a protracted period of time

Risk taker: Ability to deal with uncertainty, to analyze an opportunity and take decisive action; the willingness to take prudent financial and technical risks

Business acumen/experience: a solid foundation in general business skills, an aptitude for business strategy, a solid foundation in one's area of expertise, and an experience base which extends outside of the organization

Impact: The ability to tactfully stand out in a crowd and to make a positive and lasting impression

Managerial style: The ability to plan, organize, and delegate, to bring out the best in other people, to develop people, and to give credit to others

Leadership: The ability to inspire others and to set a positive example for others by providing assistance, direction, recognition, and encouragement

GEOGRAPHIC SCOPE OF RECRUITING ACTIVITIES:
Serve clients nationwide and in the UK and Germany

TOTAL YEARS OF RETAINER-TYPE RECRUITING EXPERIENCE:
6 years

LAURENCE R. MASSE
Managing Partner
Ward Howell International, Inc.
1250 Grove Avenue, Suite 201
Barrington, IL 60010
Telephone: (708) 382-2206

Date of Birth: July 27, 1926
Grew up in: Michigan and
   Louisiana

Ward Howell International

HIGHER EDUCATION:
Hope College
   B.A. degree, English, 1950

MILITARY:
Pharmacist's Mate Third Class, United States Navy, 1945 to 1946

EMPLOYMENT HISTORY:
1976 to present: Ward Howell International, Inc.
1972 to 1976: Managing Director, Consulting Partners/TASA Group
1969 to 1972: Vice President–Industrial Relations, REA Express Inc.
1968 to 1969: Associate, Heidrick and Struggles, Inc.
1966 to 1968: Director–Administration and Personnel–Europe, Middle East, and Africa, ITT
1956 to 1966: Director of Personnel, General Foods Corporation
1953 to 1956: Consultant, General Motors Corporation

ASSOCIATIONS/PROFESSIONAL SOCIETIES:
Foreign Relations Council
Association of Executive Search Consultants

SPECIAL INTERESTS AND HOBBIES:
Music, reading, history, travel, antiquing, sports, gardening

REPRESENTATIVE AND SIGNIFICANT PLACEMENTS:
Jack Rutherford, President
   International Harvester (Navistar)
Dr. M. Blakeman Ingle, President
   IMCERA Group, Inc.

James R. Peterson, President
  Parker Pen Company
Gerald B. Johanneson, Executive Vice President and Chief Operating
  Officer
  Haworth, Inc.
Boyd Wainscott, President
  Pitman-Moore, Inc.

WHAT I LOOK FOR IN GENERAL IN A CANDIDATE

The first thing I look for is whether or not the candidate matches the basic criteria the client has established for the position, in terms of experience, education, and specific skills and know-how. Then I determine if the candidate has a successful track record to date, what has he or she actually accomplished, and how well he or she did it.

Once it has been established that the candidate matches the basic criteria for the position and has a proven, successful record of accomplishments, I concentrate on the more intangible elements, for example, intelligence, ability to communicate, humor, integrity, energy and drive, purpose, commitment, focus, organization, flexibility, and so forth.

Finally, I try to determine how the candidate will relate to my client chemistry-wise. If that isn't right, the rest is somewhat academic.

I have found over the years that my initial impression and instincts are usually right. I usually know after the first five or ten minutes if the candidate is someone I should present. The rest of the interview almost always confirms that judgment.

GEOGRAPHIC SCOPE OF RECRUITING ACTIVITIES:
Serve clients nationally and internationally, mostly in Europe

TOTAL YEARS OF RETAINER-TYPE RECRUITING EXPERIENCE:
16 years

JONATHAN E. McBRIDE
President
McBride Associates, Inc.
1511 K Street, NW
Washington, DC 20005
Telephone: (202) 638-1150

Date of Birth: June 16, 1942
Grew up in: Washington, DC

HIGHER EDUCATION:
Yale University
B.A. degree, American studies, 1964

MILITARY:
Lieutenant, United States Naval Reserve, 1964 to 1968

EMPLOYMENT HISTORY:
1979 to present: McBride Associates, Inc.
1976 to 1979: Vice President, Simmons Associates, Inc.
1972 to 1976: Vice President, Lionel D. Edie & Co.
1968 to 1972: Account Executive, Merrill Lynch, Pierce, Fenner & Smith, Inc.

PRIVATE CLUBS:
Metropolitan Club of Washington, DC
Chevy Chase Club
Yale Club of NYC

ASSOCIATIONS/PROFESSIONAL SOCIETIES:
Association of Executive Search Consultants
International Association of Corporate and Professional Recruiters

REPRESENTATIVE AND SIGNIFICANT PLACEMENTS:
Senior Vice President/Managing Director–Equity Investments
    NYSE buy-side institutional financial services company
Vice President–Corporate Communications/Government Affairs
    Major NYSE-listed pharmaceutical/healthcare company
President and Chief Operating Officer
    ASE-listed transportation equipment leasing company

Division President
  NASDAQ-listed computer services company
President and Chief Executive Officer
  Technical/trade association

WHAT I LOOK FOR IN GENERAL IN A CANDIDATE

It seems to me a hiring manager working with a corporate "headhunter" will be more successful by hunting for hearts, not just heads. Same goes for the headhunter, or perhaps better said, the "hearthunter."

I see myself as a hearthunter. I seek personal as well as professional commitment—a synthesis of emotional and rational considerations—in favor of my client's needs. I also seek integrity—not just "honesty," but a sense of "wholeness"—in those candidates I elect to pursue for clients.

Circumstances will arise in a job that neither client nor candidate can anticipate while still in the recruiting process. A candidate who accepts and takes on a new job because it is a natural expression of who she or he *is* is much more likely to meet the challenges successfully than is one who changes jobs because it "looks good" or just "makes sense."

GEOGRAPHIC SCOPE OF RECRUITING ACTIVITIES:
Serve clients nationwide

TOTAL YEARS OF RETAINER-TYPE RECRUITING EXPERIENCE:
16 years

HORACIO J. McCOY
Senior Officer/Regional Director
Mexico/Latin America
Korn/Ferry International, Inc.
Montes Urales #641
Mexico, D.F. 11000
Telephone: (525) 202-5654

Date of Birth: January 4, 1939
Grew up in: Mexico City

Korn/Ferry International, Inc.

HIGHER EDUCATION:
University of Southern California
B.S. degree, business administration, 1961

EMPLOYMENT HISTORY:
1975 to present: Korn/Ferry International, Inc.
1972 to 1975: Operations Director, Super Mercados, S.A.
1971 to 1972: Senior Associate, McKinsey & Company
1967 to 1971: Assistant General Manager, Bristol Myers Company
1965 to 1967: National Sales Manager, Del Monte Foods
1963 to 1965: Account Executive, McCann Ericson
1961 to 1963: Brand Manager, Procter & Gamble Company

PRIVATE CLUBS:
Mexico City Industrialists Club
Chapultepec Golf Club

ASSOCIATIONS/PROFESSIONAL SOCIETIES:
American British Cowdry Hospital Development Campaign
U.S.-Mexico Bilateral Business Committee

SPECIAL INTERESTS AND HOBBIES:
Bible studying, golf, opera

REPRESENTATIVE AND SIGNIFICANT PLACEMENTS:
Octavio Sanchez-Mejorada, President/Managing Director
Campbell Soup Co., Mexico
Gunther Muller, President/Managing Director
Interamerican Development Corp., Washington, DC

Kenneth May, Vice President of Business Expansion
   PepsiCo Foods International, Dallas, Texas
Peter Rozental, Executive Vice President
   PepsiCo Foods International, Mexico
Eduardo Palacios, Senior Vice President
   Citibank, Mexico

WHAT I LOOK FOR IN GENERAL IN A CANDIDATE

The relative weight of the following elements depends on the specific position, industry, and function involved:

- Communication skills, articulation, eye contact
- Key accomplishments, problem-solving skills, decision-making process
- Interpersonal skills, drive level, dependability
- Strengths and weaknesses as a manager
- Motivation level, energy, dynamism and results orientation
- Intellectual skills based on past experience
- Leadership skills and style
- Cultural fit with client and chemistry match
- Future management potential
- Personal presence and appearance

GEOGRAPHIC SCOPE OF RECRUITING ACTIVITIES:
Serve clients in Mexico, Latin America, and U.S. headquarters for Latin America region

TOTAL YEARS OF RETAINER-TYPE RECRUITING EXPERIENCE:
16 years

MILLINGTON F. McCOY
Managing Director
Gould & McCoy, Inc.
551 Madison Avenue
New York, NY 10022
Telephone: (212) 688-1941

Date of Birth: January 22, 1941
Grew up in: Cape Girardeau,
  Missouri

Bachrach

HIGHER EDUCATION:
  University of Missouri
    B.A. degree, 1962

EMPLOYMENT HISTORY:
  1977 to present: Gould & McCoy, Inc.
  1966 to 1977: Vice President, Handy Associates
  1965 to 1966: Advertising and Marketing Research Analyst, Gardner
    Advertising Agency
  1964 to 1965: Field Market Researcher, The Procter & Gamble Company
    pany

PRIVATE CLUBS:
  Harvard Club, NYC

ASSOCIATIONS/PROFESSIONAL SOCIETIES:
  Committee of 200, Founding Member

SPECIAL INTERESTS AND HOBBIES:
  Horses (dressage), gardening, skiing, study of the Enneagram

REPRESENTATIVE AND SIGNIFICANT PLACEMENTS:
  Clifford Drake, Jr., President
    Avant Petroleum, division of Mitsui & Co. (USA), Inc.
  Ronald D. Glosser, President
    Hershey Trust Company
  James McConnell, President and Chief Executive Officer
    Instron Corporation

Gerard J. McConnell, Chief Executive Officer–Sheetfed Press Division
MAN Roland Inc.
Michel Rapoport, President
Pitney Bowes

WHAT I LOOK FOR IN GENERAL IN A CANDIDATE

Gaining an understanding of the client culture and its requirements for success is the first step in determining what I look for in a candidate. My key to the successful search assignment is the right cultural fit.

For example, in some companies diplomacy, well-developed interpersonal skills, and a non-confrontational approach are essential. Other environments may require political skills or the ability to be confrontational for the candidate to be successful. Candidates must have the appropriate orientation for the culture.

After determining cultural fit, the most important part of the assessment process is to figure out if the candidate is on a positive, upward trend in his/her life and career. I have found that the best way to predict future success is to look for a solid and consistent record of past success, going back to the person's early formative years. Critical qualities I seek in an individual are warmth, a good sense of humor, integrity, strong values, and adaptability. I always look for self-knowledge and self-awareness, including personal strategy and direction.

Relative to the client organization and its needs, the other things I look for in a candidate include the requisite level of intelligence, emotional maturity, drive, vision, risk-orientation, personality type, and skill fit with the position requirements.

Unfortunately, there are no shortcuts to the assessment process. It takes an assessor who is self-aware, mature, and seasoned. Like the best candidates, those of us who learn by our experiences are the ones who get ahead.

GEOGRAPHIC SCOPE OF RECRUITING ACTIVITIES:
Serve clients nationwide

TOTAL YEARS OF RETAINER-TYPE RECRUITING EXPERIENCE:
25 years

RICHARD M. McFARLAND
President
Brissenden, McFarland, Wagoner
  & Fuccella, Inc.
One Canterbury Green
Stamford, CT 06901
Telephone: (203) 324-1598

Date of Birth: September 10,
  1923
Grew up in: Portland, Maine

HIGHER EDUCATION:
Rensselaer Polytechnic Institute
  Bachelor of Chemical Engineering, 1944

MILITARY:
Lieutenant Commander, United States Naval Reserve, 1943 to 1946
  and 1951 to 1953

EMPLOYMENT HISTORY:
1981 to present: Brissenden, McFarland, Wagoner & Fuccella, Inc.
1969 to 1981: Senior Vice President, Heidrick & Struggles, Inc.
1967 to 1969: Vice President and General Manager–Inorganic
  Division, Wyandotte Chemical Co.
1961 to 1967: President, Cumberland Chemical Company
1959 to 1961: Manager–Market Development and Application
  Research, Texas Butadiene & Chemical
1955 to 1959: Product Manager, FMC Corporation
1953 to 1955: Manager–Market Research, Brea Chemical Company

PRIVATE CLUBS:
Landmark Club of Stamford, CT
Cedar Point Yacht Club of Westport, CT

ASSOCIATIONS/PROFESSIONAL SOCIETIES:
Commercial Development Association
American Chemical Society

SPECIAL INTERESTS AND HOBBIES:
Sailing, curling, skiing, golf, history (ancient and American)

REPRESENTATIVE AND SIGNIFICANT PLACEMENTS:
Brian M. Rushton, Vice President–Research and Development
Air Products & Chemicals
Robert A. Roland, President
Chemical Manufacturers Association
E. James Ferland, Chairman and Chief Executive Officer
Public Service Enterprise Group, Inc.
Corbin J. McNeill, President and Chief Operating Officer
Philadelphia Electric
Bernard W. Reznicek, Chairman and Chief Executive Officer
Boston Edison

WHAT I LOOK FOR IN GENERAL IN A CANDIDATE

Before a prospect becomes a candidate, he or she is screened by telephone. At this time pertinent facts are obtained directed toward the requirements of the job and the specification developed with the client. Having passed that screen, next comes the face-to-face, in-depth interview, at which time the highly critical first impressions are observed— physical appearance, speech, bearing, credibility, humor, enthusiasm, charisma. Next comes a detailed questioning of early background, education, service time, if any, family, and professional career. Each job is explored as to responsibilities, reporting relationships, accomplishments, and how these were achieved. Emphasis here is on style, managerial skill, leadership, and knowledge. All during this phase, I test for accuracy, truthfulness, communicating skills, and personal stimulus value. At the conclusion of $2\frac{1}{2}$ to 3 hours of conversation, I decide if the candidate has the requisite knowledge, the desired potential for growth, the right personal chemistry to fit the client's environment.

GEOGRAPHIC SCOPE OF RECRUITING ACTIVITIES:
Serve clients nationwide

TOTAL YEARS OF RETAINER-TYPE RECRUITING EXPERIENCE:
22 years

CLARENCE E. McFEELY
Partner
McFeely Wackerle Shulman
20 N. Wacker Drive
Chicago, IL 60606
Telephone: (312) 641-2977

Date of Birth: May 12, 1929
Grew up in: Chicago, Illinois

HIGHER EDUCATION:
Bradley University, Illinois
    B.S. degree, 1951

MILITARY:
First Lieutenant, United States Marine Corps, 1951 to 1953

EMPLOYMENT HISTORY:
1969 to present: McFeely Wackerle Shulman
1969: Managing Partner, William H. Clark & Associates
1960 to 1969: Principal, A.T. Kearney & Company
1959 to 1960: Representative, Dansk Designs, Inc.
1955 to 1959: Employee Relations, The Budd Company
1953 to 1955: Personnel Supervisor, Campbell Soup Company

PRIVATE CLUBS:
Barrington Hills Country Club
The Tower Club, Chicago

ASSOCIATIONS/PROFESSIONAL SOCIETIES:
Association of Executive Search Consultants

SPECIAL INTERESTS AND HOBBIES:
Golf, classical music, theater, travel

REPRESENTATIVE AND SIGNIFICANT PLACEMENTS:
Chief Executive Officer
    A $10 billion financial services holding company
President and Chief Executive Officer
    Independent major market television broadcasting company

President and Chief Executive Officer
   North American subsidiary of a multibillion dollar European textile
   conglomerate
President and Chief Executive Officer
   North American subsidiary of a major UK medical and research
   products company
President and Chief Executive Officer
   Start-up software application development company

WHAT I LOOK FOR IN GENERAL IN A CANDIDATE

- A high level of personal and professional value standards; integrity
  and ethics
- Perception, intuitiveness, and insight to understanding people
- Ability to lead and motivate others
- Decisiveness and courage to solve difficult problems
- Ability to plan, organize, and set priorities
- A high energy level and commitment to excel
- Good intellectual, educational, and cultural background
- Healthy balance between personal and professional life
- Community commitment and social awareness
- Can handle both success and adversity
- Good health, fitness, and grooming

GEOGRAPHIC SCOPE OF RECRUITING ACTIVITIES:
   Serve clients nationwide and in Hong Kong and United Kingdom

TOTAL YEARS OF RETAINER-TYPE RECRUITING EXPERIENCE:
   31 years

CHARLES M. MENG
Chairman and President
Meng, Finseth & Associates, Inc.
3858 Carson Street, Suite 202
Torrance, CA 90503
Telephone: (213) 316-0706

Date of Birth: October 13, 1937
Grew up in: Los Angeles, California

Meng, Finseth & Associates, Inc.

HIGHER EDUCATION:
El Camino College
A.A.S. degree, 1960
Long Beach State University
B.A. degree, political science, 1963

MILITARY:
Sergeant, United States Army (Army Security Agency), 1956 to 1963

EMPLOYMENT HISTORY:
1985 to present: Meng, Finseth & Associates
1971 to 1985: Chairman and President, Houck, Meng & Company
1967 to 1971: Consultant, KPMG Peat, Marwick

PRIVATE CLUBS:
International City Club
World Trade Club
Touchdown Club of Long Beach

ASSOCIATIONS/PROFESSIONAL SOCIETIES:
Boy Scouts of America, Member Advisory Board
Long Beach State University, Founding Member, Board of Governors
and Immediate Past Chair, Presidents Associates
Pacific International Holding, Inc., Member Board of Directors
Carl Landers Finseth Trust, Trustee

SPECIAL INTERESTS AND HOBBIES:
Tennis, jogging, pleasure travel

REPRESENTATIVE AND SIGNIFICANT PLACEMENTS:
John Claerhout, President and Chief Operating Officer
   Hugh O'Brien Youth Foundation
Ronald Viani, General Manager C.B.U.
   TRW, Inc.
Locke Vass, Senior Vice President
   Mitchell Energy and Development
Paul Romy, Chief Financial Officer
   Marine Terminals Corp.
Gerald Peter Digre, Director—Children's Services
   Los Angeles County

WHAT I LOOK FOR IN GENERAL IN A CANDIDATE

I seek candidates that have the talent, experience, and education to meet my client's exacting criteria. Additionally, I look for leadership, ingenuity, and a sense of presence as demonstrated by past performance and during the evaluation process.

The "art" of our profession is the ability to quickly study and thoroughly understand our client organization's personality and environment. This matching of chemistry or persona is critical in selecting nominees for presentation that will successfully function and manage within our client's setting.

Finally, the candidate must have solid business acumen, judgment, vision, and judicious professional ethics. Those individuals possessing these characteristics will be well suited for today's role, as well as tomorrow's greater challenges and demands.

GEOGRAPHIC SCOPE OF RECRUITING ACTIVITIES:
Serve clients nationwide and in Canada, Mexico, and the UK

TOTAL YEARS OF RETAINER-TYPE RECRUITING EXPERIENCE:
24 years

CARL W. MENK
Chairman
Canny, Bowen Inc.
200 Park Avenue
New York, NY 10166
Telephone: (212) 949-6611

Date of Birth: October 19, 1921
Grew up in: Montclair, New Jersey

Bachrach

HIGHER EDUCATION:
Seton Hall University
   B.S. degree, business administration, 1943
Columbia University
   M.A. degree, 1950

MILITARY:
Second Lieutenant–Pilot, United States Air Force, 1943 to 1946

EMPLOYMENT HISTORY:
1984 to present: Canny, Bowen Inc.
1969 to 1984: President, Boyden Associates, Inc.
1946 to 1969: Senior Vice President, P. Ballantine & Sons

PRIVATE CLUBS:
New Jersey:
   Spring Lake Golf Club
   Montclair Golf Club
Union League Club of New York
Johns Island, Florida

ASSOCIATIONS/PROFESSIONAL SOCIETIES:
Association of Executive Search Consultants
Society for Human Resources Management

SPECIAL INTERESTS AND HOBBIES:
Golf, swimming, oil painting

REPRESENTATIVE AND SIGNIFICANT PLACEMENTS:
Edward A. Fox, Chief Executive Officer
  NL Industries
John J. Shea, President and Chief Executive Officer
  Spiegel, Inc.
James L. Vincent, Chairman and Chief Executive Officer
  Biogen Inc.
Sidney Wentz, Chairman and Chief Executive Officer
  Robert Wood Johnson Foundation
Louis R. Morris, Chairman and Chief Executive Officer
  Simplicity Pattern Co.

WHAT I LOOK FOR IN GENERAL IN A CANDIDATE

- Stature
- Intelligence
- Motivation
- Problem-solving ability
- Interpersonal skills
- Communication skills
- Leadership skills in stress situations

GEOGRAPHIC SCOPE OF RECRUITING ACTIVITIES:
Serve clients nationwide and in Europe, Latin America, Pacific Basin

TOTAL YEARS OF RETAINER-TYPE RECRUITING EXPERIENCE:
22 years

HERBERT T. MINES
President & CEO
Herbert Mines Associates, Inc.
399 Park Avenue
New York, NY 10022
Telephone: (212) 355-0909

Date of Birth: January 30, 1929
Grew up in: West Hartford, Connecticut

Bachrach

HIGHER EDUCATION:
Babson College, Massachusetts
B.S. degree, economics, 1949
Cornell University
M.I.L.R. degree, industrial relations, 1954

EMPLOYMENT HISTORY:
1981 to present: Herbert Mines Associates, Inc.
1972 to 1981: Chairman–Search Division, Wells Management Corp.
1970 to 1972: Vice President–Human Resources, Revlon
1966 to 1970: Senior Vice President–Human Resources, Neiman Marcus
1954 to 1966: Administrator–Training and Organizational Development, Macy's

PRIVATE CLUBS:
Beach Point Club

ASSOCIATIONS/PROFESSIONAL SOCIETIES:
Association of Executive Search Consultants
National Retail Federation

SPECIAL INTERESTS AND HOBBIES:
Tennis, reading, art, education

REPRESENTATIVE AND SIGNIFICANT PLACEMENTS:
Chairman and Chief Executive Officer
$8 billion major department store chain

President and Chief Executive Officer
  $2 billion large discount chain
Two Vice Chairmen
  $1.3 billion higher-priced specialty retailer
President and Chief Executive Officer
  $100 million European specialty retailer of fine jewelry, accessories,
  and watches
Executive Vice President
  $1.2 billion manufacturer of apparel, jewelry, and accessories

WHAT I LOOK FOR IN GENERAL IN A CANDIDATE

- General appearance, dress, manner, stature, and verbal presentation
- The ability to express themselves clearly and concisely and know when they have completed their thoughts
- The willingness to discuss subjects which are embarrassing or failures in their career and to deal with them in a practical, understandable way without blaming others. Self-knowledge and a sense of self-worth which makes it possible to discuss their strengths and weaknesses dispassionately
- An understanding of their own personal psychological profile so they can relate their experiences realistically, particularly where these involve other personalities with whom they were uncomfortable or work situations which did not fit
- Energy, a sense of humor, consistency and clarity in their descriptions of past activities and future objectives
- The understanding of why they made mistakes in the past and how they can be avoided in the future. The perception of how to avoid situations where they are likely to fail and to seek those where their strengths can be best utilized
- The ability to formulate a clear response to the position being discussed and if both sides are interested, to pursue the project with consistency but without being overly aggressive

GEOGRAPHIC SCOPE OF RECRUITING ACTIVITIES:
Serve clients nationwide and in England, France, Germany, Spain, Holland, Canada, and the Far East.

TOTAL YEARS OF RETAINER-TYPE RECRUITING EXPERIENCE:
20 years

P. JOHN MIRTZ
Partner
Mirtz Morice, Inc.
One Dock Street
Stamford, CT 06902
Telephone: (203) 964-9266

Date of Birth: February 22, 1940
Grew up in: York, Pennsylvania

Mirtz, Morice, Inc.

HIGHER EDUCATION:
Miami University
B.A. degree, psychology, 1962

MILITARY:
Captain, United States Marine Corps, 1962 to 1966

EMPLOYMENT HISTORY:
1982 to present: Mirtz Morice, Inc.
1980 to 1982: Vice President and Partner, William H. Clark Associates
1971 to 1980: Senior Vice President and Office Manager–NY, Billington, Fox & Ellis
1966 to 1971: Personnel Manager, Celanese Corporation

PRIVATE CLUBS:
Westchester Country Club

SPECIAL INTERESTS AND HOBBIES:
Reading, athletics

REPRESENTATIVE AND SIGNIFICANT PLACEMENTS:
Bob Pascal, Vice President/General Manager–Business Products
Group Bowater, Inc.
Dick Gochnauer, Executive Vice President/General Manager
The Dial Corporation
John Gillespie, Senior Vice President–Human Resources
Unilever United States
Bill Weintraub, Vice President–Marketing
Tropicana Products, Inc.
John Heid, President
Guinness America Inc.

WHAT I LOOK FOR IN GENERAL IN A CANDIDATE

Evaluating those candidate qualities required by our diverse client group has been a challenging and stimulating process over the last 20 years. Each client has its own culture, professional standards, and unique problems. Finding the correct qualities in candidates requires an understanding of all of those issues combined with integrity, highly professional evaluation skills, and a doggedness that keeps the process going until the right person is found.

The personalities and skills of our candidates are as varied as our client requirements. However, there are certain personal qualities that have always been important to me. Integrity, solid values, a high work ethic, and leadership ability top the list. On the professional side, I have always been impressed by those (rare) individuals who have the capacity to build a business, products, and so on by anticipating future requirements. While pure intellectual horsepower must be coupled with a balanced personality, the "visionary" person has always been at the top of my list.

As we look to the future, that "visionary" will require an even greater multinational perspective.

GEOGRAPHIC SCOPE OF RECRUITING ACTIVITIES:
Serve clients nationwide

TOTAL YEARS OF RETAINER-TYPE RECRUITING EXPERIENCE:
20 years

JAMES M. MONTGOMERY
President
Houze, Shourds & Montgomery, Inc.
Greater Los Angeles World Trade Center
One World Trade, Suite 1840
Long Beach, CA 90831
Telephone: (213) 495-6495

Date of Birth: May 5, 1939
Grew up in: Southern California

MILITARY:
Private First Class, United States Marine Corps, 1957 to 1960

EMPLOYMENT HISTORY:
1978 to present: Houze, Shourds & Montgomery, Inc.
1973 to 1978: Director—Industrial Relations, Rohr Industries
1962 to 1973: Director—Personnel, Corporate, Rockwell International

PRIVATE CLUBS:
Long Beach Yacht Club
Virginia Country Club

ASSOCIATIONS/PROFESSIONAL SOCIETIES:
International Association of Corporate and Professional Recruiters
World Trade Club

SPECIAL INTERESTS AND HOBBIES:
Golf, tennis, running, collecting Southwestern art

REPRESENTATIVE AND SIGNIFICANT PLACEMENTS:
Chairman, Chief Executive Officer and Chief Operating Officer
    $1 billion capital goods manufacturer
Vice Chairman
    International aerospace company
Chairman and Chief Executive Officer
    $1 billion capital goods manufacturer

Vice President and General Manager
  $400 million information services company
President
  $100 million information services company

WHAT I LOOK FOR IN GENERAL IN A CANDIDATE

Baseline requirements are candor, the appearance of substance (or more appropriately the absence of superficiality), intellectual capacity, self-confidence, effective communications skills (the ability to articulate answers to unplanned questions and the ability to be a sensitive and active listener), flexibility, and integrity.

In addition to the baseline requirements, I'm interested in whether or not the candidate has strategic vision, integration and/or implementation skills, potential for higher (or broader) responsibilities, a sense of humor, and enough ego to lead and enough humility to follow.

And finally, experience! The track record! The "ideal" or "perfect" track record doesn't exist, but when all is said and done—the interview assessment formalized, the reference completed—the most reliable predictor of future performance is past performance. Therefore, I am keenly interested in whether or not a candidate can articulate and substantiate a rich and balanced overview of his or her experience. A candidate who is clearly "packaging" his or her background and omits important events is a candidate that raises my anxiety level about his or her suitability.

GEOGRAPHIC SCOPE OF RECRUITING ACTIVITIES:
  Serve clients nationwide and in England, Mexico, and Japan

TOTAL YEARS OF RETAINER-TYPE RECRUITING EXPERIENCE:
  13 years

JAMES L. MORICE
Partner
Mirtz Morice, Inc.
One Dock Street
Stamford, CT 06902
Telephone: (203) 964-9266

Date of Birth: September 25, 1937
Grew up in: Northeastern United States

HIGHER EDUCATION:
Keystone Junior College
A.A.S. degree, engineering, 1958
New York University
B.S. degree, personnel and labor relations, 1964

Mirtz Morice, Inc.

MILITARY:
Specialist Fourth Class, United States Army, 1958 to 1960

EMPLOYMENT HISTORY:
1982 to present: Mirtz Morice, Inc.
1980 to 1982: Vice President and Partner, William H. Clark Associates
1976 to 1980: Vice President and Principal, SpencerStuart
1972 to 1975: Vice President and Partner, Billington, Fox & Ellis, Inc.
1969 to 1972: Manager–Staff Recruitment, McKinsey & Company, Inc.
1964 to 1969: Various positions, Equitable Life Assurance Society of the U.S.
1962 to 1964: Training Assistant, Chemical Bank
1960 to 1962: Copy Boy and News Assistant, New York Times

PRIVATE CLUBS:
Union League Club

SPECIAL INTERESTS AND HOBBIES:
Flying (private pilot), travel (U.S., UK, and Europe), reading, gardening, athletics

REPRESENTATIVE AND SIGNIFICANT PLACEMENTS:
Richard Liddy, President–Life Insurance Group
Continental Corporation
Lawrence P. O'Connor, President–Unigard Insurance Group
John Hancock Financial Services

Richard W. Krant, Executive Vice President–Parts and Components,
J.I. Case Inc.
Tenneco Corporation
Robert G. Kiely, President
Middlesex Hospital
Craig Eisenocher, Senior Vice President–Finance
Prudential Reinsurance Company

WHAT I LOOK FOR IN GENERAL IN A CANDIDATE

In general, style and competence as a manager, skill as a leader, expertise in a functional and/or technical field, effectiveness as a communicator, interpersonal skill, strength of conviction, personal confidence, vigor, and the all-important grouping of honesty, forthrightness, and integrity are at the heart of forming opinions about candidates. The key, of course, is to get the appropriate mix of personal characteristics and experience/achievement factors which respond best to the particular client situations. The "fit," or balance of chemistry and expertise between the successful candidate and key members of the client organization is mostly what determines the success of the recruitment exercise. The process includes satisfying not only the tangibles of the job to be done but also the intangibles of the broader role to be played in the corporation.

Executive search is, or should be, an extension of a business problem-solving exercise (strategic and/or tactical) with clients, not just a hiring exercise. It is relatively simple to systematically identify and attract the attention of prospective candidates to any search. The value added to clients is objective advice and counsel leading to the best, sometimes unique (innovative responsibility, organizational, or work relationship alignments), recruitment solutions which help clients meet competitive challenges and establish and maintain leadership in their industries.

Success in our business/profession is not necessarily a quantitative measure. It is, rather, a result of consistently doing good work—bringing about constructive resolutions to assignments in a timely way.

GEOGRAPHIC SCOPE OF RECRUITING ACTIVITIES:
Serve clients nationwide and in Europe and Southeast Asia

TOTAL YEARS OF RETAINER-TYPE RECRUITING EXPERIENCE:
19 years

FERDINAND NADHERNY
Vice Chairman
Russell Reynolds Associates,
    Inc.
200 S. Wacker Drive, Suite 3600
Chicago, IL 60606
Telephone: (312) 993-9696

Date of Birth: December 12, 1926
Grew up in: Berwyn, Illinois

HIGHER EDUCATION:
Yale University
    A.B. degree, economics, 1950
Harvard University Graduate School of Business
    M.B.A. degree, 1952

MILITARY:
S2/C, United States Navy, 1945 to 1946

EMPLOYMENT HISTORY:
1974 to present: Russell Reynolds Associates, Inc.
1972 to 1974: Vice President, Boyden Associates
1969 to 1972: Executive Vice President, Combined Motivation Education Systems, Inc.
1968 to 1969: Group Vice President, Nationwide Industries
1966 to 1968: Assistant to the President, Science Research Associates
1964 to 1966: Executive Secretary, Office of Economic Opportunity
1952 to 1964: General Manager, Cabot Corporation

PRIVATE CLUBS:
Indian Hill Country Club, IL
Chicago Club
Yale Club of New York City
Country Club of Florida

SPECIAL INTERESTS AND HOBBIES:
Education, reading, international travel, golf

REPRESENTATIVE AND SIGNIFICANT PLACEMENTS:
   Barry Sullivan, Chairman and Chief Executive Officer
      First National Bank of Chicago
   William Goessel, President and Chief Operating Officer to Chairman
      and Chief Executive Officer
      Harnischfeger Industries, Inc.
   Nolan D. Archibald, President and Chief Operating Officer to Chair-
      man and Chief Executive Officer
      The Black & Decker Corporation
   Alger B. Chapman, Chairman and Chief Executive Officer
      Chicago Board Options Exchange
   Ralph Guthrie, Chairman and Chief Executive Officer
      Urban Investment & Development Company

WHAT I LOOK FOR IN GENERAL IN A CANDIDATE

In general, what I look for in a candidate is someone who has had an extremely successful career who has reached a point where it is timely to make a job change and preferably a change in company. I tend to look for people who are bright and have high energy levels. Good people skills are also extremely important, since most people who are successful are able to motivate and relate well to others. They must also be good communicators. Integrity and honesty are a must. Attempting to make sure that an individual candidate would fit well into a company's culture, share a similar business philosophy, and especially have a good chemistry with the board of directors or person to whom one is reporting is also important. I personally like to present candidates who have interests outside of business and are happily married.

GEOGRAPHIC SCOPE OF RECRUITING ACTIVITIES:
   Serve clients nationwide and in Western Europe

TOTAL YEARS OF RETAINER-TYPE RECRUITING EXPERIENCE:
   19 years

THOMAS J. NEFF
President
SpencerStuart
55 East 52nd Street
New York, NY 10055
Telephone: (212) 407-0200

Date of Birth: October 2, 1937
Grew up in: Easton, Pennsylvania

Spencer Stuart

HIGHER EDUCATION:
Lafayette College, Pennsylvania
  B.S. degree, industrial engineering, 1959
Lehigh University, Pennsylvania
  M.B.A. degree, marketing and finance, 1961

MILITARY:
First Lieutenant, United States Army, 1961 to 1963

EMPLOYMENT HISTORY:
1976 to present: SpencerStuart
1974 to 1976: Principal, Booz, Allen & Hamilton, Inc.
1969 to 1974: President, Hospital Data Sciences, Inc.
1966 to 1969: Director of Marketing Planning, TWA, Inc.
1963 to 1966: Associate, McKinsey & Company

PRIVATE CLUBS:
Blind Brook
Links Club
Racquet & Tennis
Round Hill
Field Club
Sky Club
Quogue Field Club
Quogue Beach Club
Mill Reef

ASSOCIATIONS/PROFESSIONAL SOCIETIES:
American Business Conference

SPECIAL INTERESTS AND HOBBIES:
Tennis, golf, jogging

REPRESENTATIVE AND SIGNIFICANT PLACEMENTS:
Lou Gerstner, Chairman and Chief Executive Officer
    RJR Nabisco
David Johnson, President and Chief Executive Officer
    Campbell Soup Company
Michael Walsh, Chairman and Chief Executive Officer
    Tenneco, Inc.
Richard Miller, Chairman and Chief Executive Officer
    Wang Laboratories
Lloyd Johnson, Chairman and Chief Executive Officer
    Norwest Corporation

WHAT I LOOK FOR IN GENERAL IN A CANDIDATE

Each client and each assignment is unique, and it is essential to understand this to ensure that we are recruiting a tailor-made executive and not a generic solution. Generally, clients emphasize leadership more than management, with a balance at senior levels of strategic and operating skills, team building, decisiveness, global perspective.

GEOGRAPHIC SCOPE OF RECRUITING ACTIVITIES:
Serve clients nationally and internationally

TOTAL YEARS OF RETAINER-TYPE RECRUITING EXPERIENCE:
17 years

LAWRENCE F. NEIN
Managing Partner
Nordeman Grimm, Inc.
150 North Michigan Avenue,
Suite 3610
Chicago, IL 60601
Telephone: (312) 332-0088

Date of Birth: April 2, 1936
Grew up in: Ohio

Nordeman Grimm

HIGHER EDUCATION:
Miami University of Ohio
B.S. degree, 1958
Wharton School, University of Pennsylvania
M.B.A. degree, 1963

MILITARY:
Lieutenant Junior Grade, United States Navy, 1958 to 1962

EMPLOYMENT HISTORY:
1984 to present: Nordeman Grimm, Inc.
1982 to 1984: President, Education & Information Systems, Inc.
1976 to 1982: President, Sargent-Welch Scientific Company
1973 to 1976: President, Hartmarx Corporation—Gleneagles Division
1970 to 1973: President, The House Stores, Inc.
1963 to 1970: Management Consultant, McKinsey & Company, Inc.

PRIVATE CLUBS:
The Chicago Club
Sunset Ridge Country Club

SPECIAL INTERESTS AND HOBBIES:
Real estate investment, golf

REPRESENTATIVE AND SIGNIFICANT PLACEMENTS:
Richard Sim, President and Chief Operating Officer to Chief Executive Officer
Applied Power Corporation

Betsy Burton, Chairman and Chief Executive Officer
  Supercuts Inc.
Birendra Kumar, Senior Vice President–Group Treasury
  Dean Witter Financial Services Group, Inc.
Donald Richey, President–Cloth World
  Brown Group, Inc.
Howard Larsen, General Manager–Minnetonka Medical
  Minnetonka Corporation

WHAT I LOOK FOR IN GENERAL IN A CANDIDATE

I look at all candidates with a few key thoughts in mind.

First, what are his or her achievements versus the critical needs of the position I am recruiting for? That is, how do this person's accomplishments match up against the (two or three) things that need to be done really well in the position to get exceptional results?

The second thing I look for is cultural fit. Some organizations and positions call for dashing, aggressive, flamboyant, risk-taking personalities. In others, such a person would fall flat on his face.

In all cases, I look for fervor, energy, and leadership in the sense of letting others shine and not having to take all the credit personally. These are key elements in a true leader at any level, I believe, and are "must haves" in my personal screen.

GEOGRAPHIC SCOPE OF RECRUITING ACTIVITIES:
Serve clients nationwide and in Europe

TOTAL YEARS OF RETAINER-TYPE RECRUITING EXPERIENCE:
7 years

JACQUES C. NORDEMAN
Chairman
Nordeman Grimm, Inc.
717 Fifth Avenue
New York, NY 10022
Telephone: (212) 935-1000

Date of Birth: March 24, 1937
Grew up in: New York, New York

Bachrach

HIGHER EDUCATION:
Colgate University
B.A. degree, fine arts, 1958
Harvard University Graduate School of Business
M.B.A. degree, 1964

MILITARY:
Lieutenant Junior Grade, United States Navy, 1959 to 1962

EMPLOYMENT HISTORY:
1969 to present: Nordeman Grimm, Inc.
1968 to 1969: Partner, Parker Nordeman
1964 to 1968: Account Management, Benton & Bowles

PRIVATE CLUBS:
Shinnecock Hills Golf Club
National Golf Links of America
Deepdale Golf Club
University Club
Union Club

ASSOCIATIONS/PROFESSIONAL SOCIETIES:
Association of Executive Search Consultants
Trustee, Cancer Research Institute
Trustee, Union Theological Seminary
Vice Chairman of Business Committee, Metropolitan Museum of Art
Chairman, Parents Committee, St. Paul's School

SPECIAL INTERESTS AND HOBBIES:
Golf, skiing, Dixieland musician (drummer), photography, theater,
travel

REPRESENTATIVE AND SIGNIFICANT PLACEMENTS:
Laurance R. Hoagland, President and Chief Executive Officer
Stanford Management Company
Robin Burns, President and Chief Executive Officer, Estee Lauder
USA
Thomas Schwarz, President and Chief Executive Officer
Grossman's
John Sawhill, Chief Executive Officer
The Nature Conservancy
William J. White, Chairman and Chief Executive Officer
Bell & Howell, Robert M. Bass Group

WHAT I LOOK FOR IN GENERAL IN A CANDIDATE

As to the basic qualities that separate the extraordinary individuals from the ordinary, I look for:

- People who are real. They are down-to-earth and without pretension. Individuals with the highest personal standards of honesty, integrity, and trust. Genuine people with solid values.
- "Smarts." I am intrigued with a person's intelligence and thought processes and am attracted to (1) individuals who are quick and able to cut through to the heart of an issue; and (2) individuals who demonstrate the use of sound judgment.
- A strong sense of self, combined with a sensitivity to others. I am attracted to individuals with an understated confidence and humility.
- A sense of balance—between family, professional life, and outside interests.
- A strong sense of purpose, combined with creativity, energy, and often a flare or passion for whatever they do.
- Good communicators who express ideas in a logical, forthright, and direct manner.
- A sense of humor; able to keep things in perspective.
- Leadership—usually evident throughout every stage of an exceptional career.

GEOGRAPHIC SCOPE OF RECRUITING ACTIVITIES:
Serve clients nationally and internationally

TOTAL YEARS OF RETAINER-TYPE RECRUITING EXPERIENCE:
22 years

DAYTON OGDEN
Chief Executive Officer
SpencerStuart
695 East Main Street
Stamford, CT 06901
Telephone: (203) 324-6333

Date of Birth: January 11, 1945
Grew up in: New Canaan, Connecticut

Spencer Stuart

HIGHER EDUCATION:
Yale University
  B.A. degree, American studies, 1967

MILITARY:
Lieutenant Junior Grade, United States Navy, 1968 to 1971

EMPLOYMENT HISTORY:
  1979 to present: SpencerStuart
  1975 to 1979: Vice President, Simmons Associates
  1973 to 1975: Personnel Director, Dunham and Smith Agencies
  1967 to 1973: Assistant to Personnel Director, Port Authority of New York and New Jersey

PRIVATE CLUBS:
Woodway Country Club, CT
Racquet and Tennis Club, NY

ASSOCIATIONS/PROFESSIONAL SOCIETIES:
Association of Executive Search Consultants

SPECIAL INTERESTS AND HOBBIES:
Fishing, skiing, sailing, reading, tennis

REPRESENTATIVE AND SIGNIFICANT PLACEMENTS:
Gerrit Venema, Chief Executive Officer
  National Bank of Kuwait
Steven Wheeler, Chief Executive Officer
  First Winthrop Corporation

Paul Karas, Chief Executive Officer, JFK 2000
  Port Authority of New York and New Jersey
James Bigham, Executive Vice President
  Continental Grain Company
Randall M. Griffin, President
  Euro Disney Development

WHAT I LOOK FOR IN GENERAL IN A CANDIDATE

- Strong record of achievement—is there a pattern of success in early life, for example, education, military, business?
- Sense of humor—can the candidate view himself/herself with perspective?
- Vision—the ability to see ideas and outcomes that others don't, to bring creative ways of doing things to fruition
- Strong intellectual dimension—the ability to associate, adapt and move between conceptual benchmarks
- An international perspective—the capacity to operate across geographic boundaries and deal with global markets
- Leadership skills—the ability to persuade and motivate others
- Toughness—is the candidate resilient and equipped to deal with difficult people issues?
- Honesty—is the candidate honest with himself/herself and with others?
- Communications—can the candidate articulate ideas verbally and in writing?
- Salesmanship—can the candidate sell ideas, solutions, products, and so forth?

GEOGRAPHIC SCOPE OF RECRUITING ACTIVITIES:
Serve clients nationwide and internationally

TOTAL YEARS OF RETAINER-TYPE RECRUITING EXPERIENCE:
16 years

THOMAS H. OGDON
President
The Ogdon Partnership
375 Park Avenue
New York, NY 10152
Telephone: (212) 308-1600

Date of Birth: April 16, 1935
Grew up in: Tarrytown, New York
  and Greenwich, Connecticut

New York Times

HIGHER EDUCATION:
  Amherst College
    B.A. degree, English, 1957

EMPLOYMENT HISTORY:
  1987 to present: The Ogdon Partnership
  1980 to 1987: Executive Vice President/Chief Operating Officer,
    Haley Associates
  1979: Vice President, Russell Reynolds Associates
  1975 to 1978: Senior Vice President, Needham Harper & Steers
  1961 to 1975: Senior Vice President, Management Supervisor, Benton
    & Bowles
  1959 to 1961: Copywriter, Grey Advertising
  1958: Trainee, Ted Bates Advertising

PRIVATE CLUBS:
  Union Club
  Indian Harbor Yacht Club
  Brook Club

SPECIAL INTERESTS AND HOBBIES:
  Fishing, tennis, squash, gardening, golf

REPRESENTATIVE AND SIGNIFICANT PLACEMENTS:
  Ronald Davis, Chief Executive Officer
    Perrier
  Gene Bedell, Managing Director of MIS/EDP
    First Boston Corporation

Charles Townsend, President and Chief Executive Officer—Women's
   Publishing Division
   The New York Times Company Magazine Group
Robert Davies, President and CEO
   CHB Foods (at the time of LBO)
John Andersen, President and Chief Executive Officer
   Johanna Dairies, Inc. (subsidiary of John Labatt, Ltd.)

WHAT I LOOK FOR IN GENERAL IN A CANDIDATE

The first thing I look for is the degree to which a candidate is truly comfortable with himself/herself. It's a kissing cousin to self-confidence—but different. Other things we all look for—leadership abilities, a sense of humor, the ability to move all the way to an important decision, and handling difficult interpersonal situations all come naturally to someone with this sense of self. That a person has the proper technical qualifications for the position is of course a given.

GEOGRAPHIC SCOPE OF RECRUITING ACTIVITIES:
Serve clients nationwide and in England, Hong Kong, France, Canada, and Eastern Europe

TOTAL YEARS OF RETAINER-TYPE RECRUITING EXPERIENCE:
12 years

GEORGE W. OTT
President and Chief Executive Officer
Ott & Hansen, Inc.
136 S. Oak Knoll, Suite 300
Pasadena, CA 91101
Telephone: (818) 578-0551

Date of Birth: May 5, 1932
Grew up in: Chicago and Los Angeles

HIGHER EDUCATION:
University of Southern California
B.S. degree, business administration, 1954
M.B.A. degree, 1960
Certified Public Accountant, 1967

MILITARY:
Lieutenant Junior Grade, United States Navy (Reserve), 1954 to 1956

EMPLOYMENT HISTORY:
1976 to present; Ott & Hansen, Inc.
1971 to 1976: Vice President, Member of Executive Committee, Korn/Ferry International
1963 to 1971: Partner, Peat Marwick Mitchell & Company
1961 to 1963: Company Administrator, Plasmadyne Corporation
1959 to 1961: Administrative Engineer, Lear Corporation (later Lear Siegler)
1956 to 1959: Engineering Planner, Douglas Aircraft Company, El Segundo Division

PRIVATE CLUBS:
Annandale Golf Club
Jonathan Club

ASSOCIATIONS/PROFESSIONAL SOCIETIES:
California Executive Recruiters Association, Board Member and President-Elect 1992
USC Associates (Support Group)
National Association of Corporate Directors, Los Angeles Chapter, Board Member

SPECIAL INTERESTS AND HOBBIES:
Active in community affairs; Board Member, Los Angeles Rotary Club; Board Member, Salvation Army Metropolitan Board; running, golf, model railroading

REPRESENTATIVE AND SIGNIFICANT PLACEMENTS:
President and Chief Executive Officer
$200 million public medical products company
President and Chief Executive Officer
Medium-sized diverse real estate development company
Executive Vice President, General Manager
Midwest operation of large general contractor
Executive Director
Significant social service non-profit organization
Numerous Chief Financial Officers and Controllers
Public and private companies

WHAT I LOOK FOR IN GENERAL IN A CANDIDATE

The specifics of what I look for in a candidate will, to a significant degree, be based on the position requirements in conjunction with the company personality, style, size, and industry.

Humans are biographical creatures. The key to evaluating a candidate is to attempt to determine that specific individual's biographical line and see if it matches with the company need. This should uncover the candidate's growth rate, strengths, weaknesses, and so on. I've always told clients they must select a candidate that fits well into their culture and who possesses strengths they must have and weaknesses they can live with.

In establishing an individual's biographical pattern, there are issues over and above experience, education, and other credentials that are important—items such as integrity, work ethic, leadership ability, flexibility, adaptability, and intelligence.

The "art form" in our business is to take this subjective evaluation of both client and candidate and recognize a good fit when you see one, and engineer a placement that's good for both parties.

GEOGRAPHIC SCOPE OF RECRUITING ACTIVITIES:
Serve clients nationwide

TOTAL YEARS OF RETAINER-TYPE RECRUITING EXPERIENCE:
28 years

MANUEL A. PAPAYANOPULOS T.
Vice President
Korn/Ferry International, Inc.
Monte Urales #641
Mexico, D.F. 11000
Telephone: (525) 202-6020

Date of Birth: February 21, 1945
Grew up in: Mexico City

Papayanapolies

EMPLOYMENT HISTORY:
1982 to present: Korn/Ferry International, Inc.
1979 to 1982: Partner, Tasa de Mexico, S.A.
1975 to 1978: Managing Director–Middle Management, Tasa de Mexico, S.A.
1975: Industrial Relations Managing Director, Cajas Corrugadas de Mexico, S.A.
1973 to 1975: Personnel Manager, American Express Company (Mexico) S.A. de C.V.
1969 to 1972: Personnel Assistant, Cyanamid de Mexico, S.A. de C.V.

PRIVATE CLUBS:
Mexico City Industrialist Club
Avandaro Golf Club

ASSOCIATIONS/PROFESSIONAL SOCIETIES:
Mexican Institute of Financial Executives

SPECIAL INTERESTS AND HOBBIES:
Tennis, water skiing, chess

REPRESENTATIVE AND SIGNIFICANT PLACEMENTS:
Orlando Ayala, Director–Latin America
   Microsoft Corporation
Marcos Brown, Managing Director
   Cannon Mills
Agustin Dorantes Y Bravo, General Manager
   Bull HN Sistemas de Informacion

Michael Shaw, Managing Director
  DHL Handling
Jose Gorbea, Managing Director
  Shulton de Mexico

WHAT I LOOK FOR IN GENERAL IN A CANDIDATE

Honesty and intellect are basic essential factors involved in all my candidates' evaluations. In-depth interviewing is conducted in accordance with the requirements of a given client, and, in general terms, my assessment includes the evaluation of the following elements:

- A proven track record of accomplishments. Delivery is a very important issue for most clients.
- Leadership capabilities, a successful team player
- Ambition, initiative, aggressiveness, motivation
- Presence, executive stature
- Communication skills, articulation
- Computer, high-tech skills, orientation
- Internationalization, global management skills, languages
- Scholastic background, cultural, social

GEOGRAPHIC SCOPE OF RECRUITING ACTIVITIES:
Serve clients throughout Mexico and the United States

TOTAL YEARS OF RETAINER-TYPE RECRUITING EXPERIENCE:
16 years

DAVID R. PEASBACK
President and Chief Executive Officer
Canny, Bowen Inc.
200 Park Avenue
New York, NY 10166
Telephone: (212) 949-6611

Date of Birth: March 15, 1933
Grew up in: Mt. Lakes, New Jersey

Bachrach

HIGHER EDUCATION:
Colgate University
    B.A. degree, economics, 1955
University of Virginia Law School
    LL.B. degree, 1961

MILITARY:
Sergeant, United States Marine Corps, 1956 to 1958

EMPLOYMENT HISTORY:
1988 to present: Canny, Bowen Inc.
1972 to 1987: Partner to President and Chief Executive Officer, Heidrick & Struggles, Inc.
1968 to 1972: Vice President of Subsidiary, Bangor Punta Corp.
1965 to 1968: Litigation Attorney, Litton Industries Inc.
1961 to 1964: Associate, Covington & Burling Law Firm
1955 to 1956: Salesman–Case Soap, Procter & Gamble

PRIVATE CLUBS:
Sky Club, NY
Belle Haven Club, Greenwich, CT
Yale Club, NY

ASSOCIATIONS/PROFESSIONAL SOCIETIES:
Association of Executive Search Consultants

SPECIAL INTERESTS AND HOBBIES:
Skiing, tennis, paddle tennis, swimming

REPRESENTATIVE AND SIGNIFICANT PLACEMENTS:
  Robert L. Kirk, President and Chief Executive Officer
    CSX Transportation
  Martin R. Hoffman, Vice President and General Counsel
    Digital Equipment Corporation
  Thomas C. McDermott, President and Chief Operating Officer
    Bausch & Lomb, Inc.
  John P. Frestel, Jr., Senior Vice President–Human Resources
    USAir, Inc.
  Robert C. Butler, Senior Vice President and Chief Financial Officer
    International Paper Company

WHAT I LOOK FOR IN GENERAL IN A CANDIDATE

It is a mistake to evaluate a candidate in a vacuum. The executive must be evaluated on how he/she could be expected to perform for a specific client. Accordingly, once it is determined that the candidate has the requisite function and industry experience, *personal impact* becomes a pivotal issue. I define this as a combination of personality, appearance, and management style, which forms the cornerstone for building acceptance in the new environment. Every organization has a unique culture and the candidate must be comfortable with it and vice versa. The absence of the "fit" explains why an executive with an unblemished record of success sometimes fails when he changes jobs. Personal chemistry, though it is an overworked expression, also must be considered. Although it is related to what I labeled personal impact, personal chemistry is more individualized; for example, will the new Chief Financial Officer or Senior Vice President–Human Resources get along with the CEO?

GEOGRAPHIC SCOPE OF RECRUITING ACTIVITIES:
  Serve clients nationwide and in Europe and Canada

TOTAL YEARS OF RETAINER-TYPE RECRUITING EXPERIENCE:
  19 years

GARY J. POSNER
Vice President
George Kaludis Associates, Inc.
2505 Hillsboro Road, Suite 302
Nashville, TN 37212
Telephone: (615) 297-3880

Date of Birth: December 31, 1946
Grew up in: Stamford,
   Connecticut

George Kaludis Associates, Inc.

HIGHER EDUCATION:
Michigan State University
   B.A. degree, business, 1968
   M.A. degree, administration—higher education, 1971

EMPLOYMENT HISTORY:
1988 to present: George Kaludis Associates
1986 to 1988: President, University Search Consultants
1984 to 1986: Vice President for Administration, University of Pennsylvania
1982 to 1984: Vice President for Human Resources, University of Pennsylvania
1978 to 1982: Director—University Personnel Services, Cornell University
1968 to 1978: Director—Employee Relations and Chief Negotiator, Michigan State University

ASSOCIATIONS/PROFESSIONAL SOCIETIES:
American Council of Education, Executive Search Firm Roundtable
College and University Personnel Association
National Association of College and University Business Officers

REPRESENTATIVE AND SIGNIFICANT PLACEMENTS:
Emita Hill, Chancellor
   Indiana University at Kokomo
Irving Crumlin, Director—Human Resources
   Mount Holyoke College

Peter Humanik, Director—Telecommunications
  Columbia University
Doug Wilson, Vice President—University Relations and External
  Affairs
  Indiana University System

WHAT I LOOK FOR IN GENERAL IN A CANDIDATE

Institutions of higher education are facing unprecedented pressures to work smarter and utilize technology effectively to provide quality education within a limited resource base. In addition to the technical qualifications required for the position, candidates striving to enter senior administrative positions in this environment will want to have:

1. A solid understanding of the academic and political environment of today's colleges and universities
2. An ability to assume a leadership role that transcends their specialty area of expertise
3. A self-confidence tempered with a sensitivity to listen to diverse viewpoints
4. An ability to work in a culturally diverse environment

Candidates who listen rather than volunteer their life experiences, who smile and appear interested in the challenges of the position, tend to move forward quicker in the search process. Higher education chooses "finalists" for senior positions with care and often utilizes search committees, which may add some time to the search process. Candidates should welcome the interview process as a way both for the institution to get to know them and to determine if the position, the culture, and the environment "fits" their needs. A successful search marriage occurs when the institution offers the position ring and the candidate says "I do."

GEOGRAPHIC SCOPE OF RECRUITING ACTIVITIES:
Serve clients nationwide

TOTAL YEARS OF RETAINER-TYPE RECRUITING EXPERIENCE:
6 years

DAVID L. POWELL
President
David Powell, Inc.
2995 Woodside Road, Suite 150
Woodside, CA 94062
Telephone: (415) 854-7150

Date of Birth: February 6, 1937
Grew up in: Westchester County,
   New York

HIGHER EDUCATION:
St. Lawrence University
   B.A. degree, 1959

MILITARY:
Captain, United States Marine Corps, 1959 to 1964

EMPLOYMENT HISTORY:
1976 to present: David Powell, Inc.
1971 to 1976: Vice President, Staub Warmbold & Associates
1970 to 1971: Director–Administration, ElectroPrint, Inc.
1968 to 1970: Director–Human Resources, National Semiconductor
   Corp.
1966 to 1968: Manager–Human Resources, Fairchild Semiconductor
   Corp.
1964 to 1966: Personnel Manager, Del Monte Corp.

PRIVATE CLUBS:
Bankers Club, San Francisco
The Family, San Francisco

ASSOCIATIONS/PROFESSIONAL SOCIETIES:
California Executive Recruiters Association

SPECIAL INTERESTS AND HOBBIES:
Fly-fishing, physical fitness, San Francisco Symphony

REPRESENTATIVE AND SIGNIFICANT PLACEMENTS:
Phil White, President
  Informix Corp.
Bill Patton, Chairman and Chief Executive Officer
  Parallan Corp.
Don Caddes, President and Chief Executive Officer
  Norian Corp.
Jeff Heimbuck, President
  Plus Development Corp.
Carl Neun, Senior Vice President and Chief Financial Officer
  Conner Peripherals

WHAT I LOOK FOR IN GENERAL IN A CANDIDATE

Since most of the searches I do are for chief executive officers, being given the prescribed experience and chemistry details is critical. In the emerging electronics and biotechnology markets we serve, entrepreneurial instincts, flexibility, and innovative thinking are a must.

We target in-depth knowledge of the client organization and business plans as key to a successful match. Then, we make sure the intellectual and cultural bonding potential is there.

GEOGRAPHIC SCOPE OF RECRUITING ACTIVITIES:
Serve clients nationwide and in South America and the Far East

TOTAL YEARS OF RETAINER-TYPE RECRUITING EXPERIENCE:
20 years

WINDLE B. PRIEM
Managing Director
Korn/Ferry International
237 Park Avenue
New York, NY 10017
Telephone: (212) 687-1834

Date of Birth: October 17, 1937
Grew up in: Wellesley, Mas-
sachusetts

HIGHER EDUCATION:
Worchester Polytechnic Institute
    B.S. degree, mechanical engineering, 1959
Babson College
    M.B.A. degree, finance, 1964

MILITARY:
Lieutenant Junior Grade, United States Navy, 1959 to 1962

EMPLOYMENT HISTORY:
1976 to present: Korn/Ferry International
1972 to 1976: Regional Director, U.S. Small Business Administration
1964 to 1972: Vice President, Marine Midland Bank

PRIVATE CLUBS:
Harvard Club of New York
New York Athletic Club
Oyster Harbors Club

ASSOCIATIONS/PROFESSIONAL SOCIETIES:
Trustee, Worcester Polytechnic Institute

REPRESENTATIVE AND SIGNIFICANT PLACEMENTS:
Gary Scheuring, Chairman and Chief Executive Officer
    MidLantic Bank
Norman Blake, Chairman and Chief Executive Officer
    USF&G

Thomas Johnson, President
   Manufacturers Hanover Trust Company
Douglas Ebert, President and Chief Executive Officer
   Southeast Bank
Lawrence Small, President and Chief Operating Officer
   Fannie Mae

WHAT I LOOK FOR IN GENERAL IN A CANDIDATE

As a financial services specialist, I take a businessman's approach to search, meaning that I always have my eye on what impact the individual will have on the bottom line. This is true whether I am recruiting a chief executive officer for a major financial institution or looking for an individual contributor, such as a mergers and acquisitions professional. Whatever the position, I ask myself, "Will this candidate make a difference? Will this individual bring added value to the company? Will corporate governance be served properly?" I am always looking for people who can take the business to the next level of maturity. I want people who are more than their resumes.

GEOGRAPHIC SCOPE OF RECRUITING ACTIVITIES:
Serve clients nationwide and in Europe

TOTAL YEARS OF RETAINER-TYPE RECRUITING EXPERIENCE:
15 years

BARBARA L. PROVUS
Principal and Founder
Shepherd Bueschel &
  Provus Inc.
One S. Wacker Drive, Suite 2740
Chicago, IL 60606
Telephone: (312) 372-1142

Date of Birth: November 20, 1949
Grew up in: Evanston, Illinois

HIGHER EDUCATION:
  Russell Sage College, New York
    B.A. degree, sociology, 1971
  Loyola University
    M.S. degree, industrial relations, 1978

EMPLOYMENT HISTORY:
  1992 to present: Shepherd, Bueschel & Provus, Inc.
  1986 to 1992: Sweeney Shepherd Bueschel Provus Harbert & Mummert Inc.
  1982 to 1986: Vice President, Lamalie Associates
  1980 to 1982: Manager–Management Development, Federated Department Stores
  1973 to 1980: Secretary to Consultant–Executive Search, Booz, Allen & Hamilton, Inc.

PRIVATE CLUBS:
  The Economics Club of Chicago

ASSOCIATIONS/PROFESSIONAL SOCIETIES:
  Association of Executive Search Consultants
  International Association of Corporate and Professional Recruiters
  Human Resources Planning Society
  Chicago Finance Exchange
  Board Member, Anti-Cruelty Society

SPECIAL INTERESTS AND HOBBIES:
  Baseball, modern art, gardening

REPRESENTATIVE AND SIGNIFICANT PLACEMENTS:

Robert Boardman, Vice President and General Counsel
  Navistar International Transportation Corp.
Mary Strohmaier, Vice President, Women's General Merchandising
  Manager
  Mark Shale
William J. Razzouk, Senior Vice President–Sales and Customer Infor-
  mation
  Federal Express Corporation
Christopher Marlin, Director–Training and Development
  Tenneco Automotive
Mary C. Moster, Vice President–Communications
  Navistar International Transportation Corp.

WHAT I LOOK FOR IN GENERAL IN A CANDIDATE

In addition to the predefined requirements of the position, for example, education, industry experience, functional skills, management ability, and so on, I believe there are several additional components the successful candidate should have:

- The ability to "stretch" and challenge the organization. Will this candidate simply fill a functional void—or will he/she bring additional value to the equation? Can he/she be a catalyst to drive the organization beyond the status quo in a positive, productive manner?
- Also, the candidate must be recruitable—and for the "right" reasons. If there's no "acceptable" reason for the candidate to leave his/her current job—you may be going after the wrong candidate. However, part of my role is to *help* the candidate assess his/her current situation and to try to find a "reason" he or she should be attracted to my client's opportunity.
- Third, I look for "humanness." What kind of person is he/she—and will he or she, in some small way, be able to bring good values and people skills to my client, beyond his or her technical abilities?

Finally, I require ethics and integrity, not only in candidates, but in my client's and my own actions.

GEOGRAPHIC SCOPE OF RECRUITING ACTIVITIES:

Serve clients nationwide

TOTAL YEARS OF RETAINER-TYPE RECRUITING EXPERIENCE:

11 years

PAUL R. RAY, JR.
President and Chief Executive
  Officer
Paul Ray & Carré Orban International
301 Commerce Street, Suite 2300
Fort Worth, TX 76102
Telephone: (817) 334-0500

Date of Birth: November 6, 1943
Grew up in: Fort Worth, Texas

HIGHER EDUCATION:
  University of Arkansas
    B.S. degree, business administration, 1966
  University of Texas
    J.D., 1970

EMPLOYMENT HISTORY:
  1978 to present: Paul Ray & Carré Orban International
  1969 to 1978: Various Marketing and Management Positions,
    R.J. Reynolds Tobacco Co.

PRIVATE CLUBS:
  Fort Worth City Club
  Fort Worth Club
  River Crest Country Club

ASSOCIATIONS/PROFESSIONAL SOCIETIES:
  Young President's Organization
  Association of Executive Search Consultants
  American Bar Association

SPECIAL INTERESTS AND HOBBIES:
  Community activities specifically related to education, health care, and
    substance abuse; running, hunting, fishing

REPRESENTATIVE AND SIGNIFICANT PLACEMENTS:
  Philip B. Fletcher, President of Banquet Foods to President and Chief
    Operating Officer,
    ConAgra, Inc.
  William C. Bousquette, Executive Vice President and Chief Financial
    Officer,
    Tandy Corporation
  James K. Leslie, Chief Executive Officer–North America
    SICPA Industries of America
  J. Ron Brinson, President and Chief Executive Officer
    Port of New Orleans
  Gilbert J. Mulhere, Vice President–Human Resources and Adminis-
    tration
    ConAgra Frozen Foods

WHAT I LOOK FOR IN GENERAL IN A CANDIDATE

- A strong record of accomplishment and career progression
- A well-planned career path with aggressive goals, increasing levels of responsibility, and measurable results
- The ability to produce results—and a knack for explaining how, clearly and concisely
- Excellent oral and written communication skills
- Energy, self-confidence, and candor
- Personal warmth, empathy, and humor

GEOGRAPHIC SCOPE OF RECRUITING ACTIVITIES:
  Serve clients in North America, Europe, and Asia

TOTAL YEARS OF RETAINER-TYPE RECRUITING EXPERIENCE:
  13 years

PAUL R. RAY, SR.
Chairman and Founder
Paul Ray & Carré Orban International
301 Commerce Street, Suite 2300
Ft. Worth, TX 76102
Telephone: (817) 334-0500

Date of Birth: April 27, 1918
Grew up in: Minneapolis, Minnesota

Paul Ray & Carré Orban International

MILITARY:
Major, United States Army, 1941 to 1945

EMPLOYMENT HISTORY:
1965 to present: Paul Ray & Carré Orban International
(formerly Paul R. Ray & Company, Inc.)
1962 to 1965: Vice President, Boyden Associates
1959 to 1962: Vice President, Chickasha Cotton Oil Company
1953 to 1959: Vice President and General Manager, Burrus Mills
1950 to 1953: General Manager–Soybean Division, A.E. Staley Manufacturing Co.
1946 to 1950 and 1939 to 1941: Vice President and General Manager, Doughboy Industries
1936 to 1939: Finance Department Trainee, Cargill, Inc.

PRIVATE CLUBS:
Eldorado Country Club, Palm Springs
Minneapolis Club
Fort Worth:
    River Crest Country Club
    Shady Oaks Country Club
    Fort Worth City Club
    Fort Worth Club

ASSOCIATIONS/PROFESSIONAL SOCIETIES:
Knights of Malta
Knights of Holy Sepulchre

SPECIAL INTERESTS AND HOBBIES:
Golf—member United States Seniors Golf Association

REPRESENTATIVE AND SIGNIFICANT PLACEMENTS:
William A. Anders, Chairman and Chief Executive Officer
General Dynamics Corporation
Vic Bonomo, Executive Vice President to Vice Chairman
PepsiCo
Christopher J. Steffen, Executive Vice President–Finance
Honeywell, Inc.
Robert N. Hiatt, President and Chief Executive Officer
Maybelline, Inc.
James R. Tindall, President and Chief Operating Officer
ConAgra Prepared Foods

WHAT I LOOK FOR IN GENERAL IN A CANDIDATE
- Consistent record of achievement
- Strong leadership skills
- Ability to delegate routinely
- Ability to manage in a complete atmosphere of openness
- Effective communication skills
- Builder, not a caretaker
- Solid business strategist
- High integrity

GEOGRAPHIC SCOPE OF RECRUITING ACTIVITIES:
Serve clients in North America, Europe, Pacific Rim

TOTAL YEARS OF RETAINER-TYPE RECRUITING EXPERIENCE:
30 years

ELEANOR H. RAYNOLDS
Partner
Ward Howell International, Inc.
99 Park Avenue, 20th Floor
New York, NY 10016-1699
Telephone: (212) 697-3730

Date of Birth: August 20, 1937
Grew up in: Long Island and
    New York City

Ward Howell International, Inc.

HIGHER EDUCATION:
    Bennett College
        A.A.S. degree, 1957

EMPLOYMENT HISTORY:
    1985 to present: Ward Howell International
    1982 to 1985: Senior Vice President, Boyden Associates
    1981 to 1982: Senior Vice President, Manager–Stamford Office, PA
        International
    1978 to 1981: Vice President, MSL International

PRIVATE CLUBS:
    The Union League Club

ASSOCIATIONS/PROFESSIONAL SOCIETIES:
    British American Chamber of Commerce
    National Association of Career Planners/Recruiters

SPECIAL INTERESTS AND HOBBIES:
    Backpacking, skiing, tennis, canoeing, traveling, rafting

REPRESENTATIVE AND SIGNIFICANT PLACEMENTS:
    John J. Mann, Senior Vice President–Pillsbury Brands
        Grand Metropolitan Food Sector
    John R. Speirs, President–Green Giant Domestic
        Grand Metropolitan Food Sector
    Scott L. Colabuono, Chief Financial Officer
        Burger King

James J. Jernee, Senior Vice President–Human Resources
  Grand Metropolitan Food Sector
Steven Landberg, Vice President, Director–Business Development
  and Planning
  Citibank N.A.

WHAT I LOOK FOR IN GENERAL IN A CANDIDATE

Finding the exceptional leader is the speciality of our team. We take over three hours of interviewing time to learn about the candidate's values, academic career, work history, volunteer efforts, leadership difference, product successes where appropriate, and measurable accomplishments in the field of his or her choice. In essence, we look for a pattern of success in the past, the ability to discriminate in the present, and the energy, imagination, and passion to make the critical difference in the future.

We are aware that a company is only as good as the people who work in it. With this in mind we try our very hardest to understand the essence of the corporate environment. Once we know this—once we understand the strategic directions of our clients—then, and only then, do we start our process.

In looking at the candidates, I make sure that they know absolutely everything that is not confidential about my client. When they arrive for the interview, they go in with knowledge and enthusiasm about the opportunity.

To summarize, we are search consultants for that exceptional talent that may or may not be hidden by corporate hierarchy.

I am lucky enough to enjoy a partnership which encourages excellence. It is within this context that I enjoy success in this wonderful field of ours. I love what I do. The clients know it—so do the candidates.

GEOGRAPHIC SCOPE OF RECRUITING ACTIVITIES:
Serve clients nationally and internationally

TOTAL YEARS OF RETAINER-TYPE RECRUITING EXPERIENCE:
13 years

RUSSELL S. REYNOLDS, JR.
Chairman
Russell Reynolds Associates, Inc.
200 Park Avenue
New York, NY 10166
Telephone: (212) 351-2000

Date of Birth: December 14, 1931
Grew up in: Greenwich, Con-
   necticut

HIGHER EDUCATION:
   Yale University
      B.A. degree, history, 1954

MILITARY:
   First Lieutenant, Navigator-Bombardier, Strategic Air Command,
      United States Air Force

EMPLOYMENT HISTORY:
   1969 to present: Russell Reynolds Associates, Inc.
   1966 to 1969: Partner, William H. Clark Associates, Inc.
   1957 to 1966: Commercial Lending Officer–National Division, Mor-
      gan Guaranty Trust Company

ASSOCIATIONS/PROFESSIONAL SOCIETIES:
   Executive Search Council
   Independent Director, Oppenheimer Mutual Funds
   Trustee, Mystic Seaport Museum
   Trustee, Greenwich Historical Society
   Life Trustee, International House
   Trustee, Naval War College Foundation, Inc.
   Republican Eagle

SPECIAL INTERESTS AND HOBBIES:
   Sailing, skiing, squash, tennis

REPRESENTATIVE AND SIGNIFICANT PLACEMENTS:
   Barry Sullivan, Chairman and Chief Executive Officer
      First National Bank of Chicago

William M. Agee, Executive Vice President and Chief Financial Officer
to Chairman, President, and Chief Executive Officer
Bendix Corp.
Robert P. Bauman, Chairman
Beecham Group Plc.
Nigel S. MacEwan, President
Kleinwort Benson Inc.
Sister Mary Rose McGeady, President and Chief Executive Officer
Covenant House

WHAT I LOOK FOR IN GENERAL IN A CANDIDATE

Certainly, the individual's background, technical expertise, and how
he or she interacts with the people in his or her organization is important. Proven results in a candidate's previous positions are evidence of
keen focus, commitment, and perseverance. However, I also look for intangible qualities such as naturalness and comfortableness. Even a nice
smile and a sense of humor are important.

The existence of a strong value system in a candidate is important; values that are compatible with those of the client's organization.
Character is an indication of a candidate's leadership potential—how
well he can get along with, communicate with, and motivate people. In
addition, commitment to family, career, and community show a healthy
balance of priorities.

GEOGRAPHIC SCOPE OF RECRUITING ACTIVITIES:
Serve clients nationally and in the UK, Europe, Hong Kong, and
Japan

TOTAL YEARS OF RETAINER-TYPE RECRUITING EXPERIENCE:
24 years

FRANK RICO, JR.
**Vice President
J.R. Akin & Company
183 Sherman Street
Fairfield, CT 06430
Telephone: (203) 259-0007**

**Date of Birth: July 16, 1939
Grew up in: Long Island, New
York**

J.R. Akin & Company

HIGHER EDUCATION:
Adelphi University
B.A. degree, government/history, 1962

EMPLOYMENT HISTORY:
1984 to present: J.R. Akin & Company
1981 to 1983: Director—Human Resources, Playtex U.S., International
Playtex
1979 to 1980: Vice President, Wilkinson Match North America
1969 to 1979: Director—Personnel, Chesebrough-Pond's Inc.
1968 to 1969: Senior Compensation Analyst, Ebasco Services
1965 to 1968: Senior Probation Officer, Nassau County, New York
Probation Department

ASSOCIATIONS/PROFESSIONAL SOCIETIES:
International Association of Corporate and Professional Recruiters
Association of Executive Search Consultants
American Compensation Association
Employment Management Association
New York Personnel Management Association

SPECIAL INTERESTS AND HOBBIES:
Photography, skiing, Don Quixote collecting

REPRESENTATIVE AND SIGNIFICANT PLACEMENTS:
David Harkelroad, Country Manager—China
Textron Lycoming (Avco Lycoming)
Paul Wybrow, General Manager—Far East
LPL Technologies, Inc.

George Sullivan, Director–Education
  Miles Diagnostic Business Group (Technicon Instrument Corp.)
Keith Trowbridge, Senior Vice President–Marketing and Sales
  Continental Health Affiliates
Anthony Asalone, Division Manager–Gardena, CA Division
  Barnes Group

WHAT I LOOK FOR IN GENERAL IN A CANDIDATE

Given that the candidate has the requisite education and experience, I am concerned with the candidate's intelligence and, more important, how it is utilized. Is the candidate an intellectual bully? Is he or she well informed about his/her discipline, industry, and business, and the world in general? One of my personal views is that one of the keys to renewing the prominence of American industry is to reestablish the team concept in running businesses and hopefully to lay to rest forever what I feel has been more of a "me" approach over the past few decades. Therefore, the candidate must be a team player.

It is important that the candidate be "open"; that is, have a willingness to consider and when appropriate adopt and utilize new ideas and approaches. Equally important and in the same vein, the candidate must be open to developing and establishing relationships with new people he or she will meet and will have to work with.

In order to make the job change process successful and in order to have a successful career, an individual must have adaptive skills as well as the ability to communicate ideas and feelings. With senior executives, I am concerned about their sensitivity to people in general and subordinates in particular. Do they treat others with dignity and respect?

Finally, but by no means least, is the candidate ethical? Is he/she a principled business person? Does his/her life have balance?

GEOGRAPHIC SCOPE OF RECRUITING ACTIVITIES:
  Serve clients nationwide and in Europe, the Western Hemisphere, and the Far East

TOTAL YEARS OF RETAINER-TYPE RECRUITING EXPERIENCE:
  7 years

NORMAN C. ROBERTS
President
Norman Roberts & Associates,
  Inc.
12424 Wilshire Blvd., Suite 850
Los Angeles, CA 90025
Telephone: (310) 820-4600

Date of Birth: March 28, 1941
Grew up in: Los Angeles

Norman Roberts & Associates, Inc.

HIGHER EDUCATION:
  University of California, Los Angeles
    B.A. degree, political science, 1962
  University of Southern California
    M.S. degree, public administration, 1967

EMPLOYMENT HISTORY:
  1988 to present: Norman Roberts & Associates, Inc.
  1976 to 1988: Senior Vice President, Korn/Ferry International
  1971 to 1976: Principal Consultant, Arthur D. Little, Inc.
  1969 to 1971: Senior Consultant, Peat, Marwick, Mitchell and Company
  1966 to 1969: Supervisor of Contracts and Management Services, Economic and Youth Opportunities Agency
  1965 to 1966: Assistant City Administrator, City of Lomita, California
  1962 to 1965: Administrative Assistant/Board of Public Works, City of Los Angeles

PRIVATE CLUBS:
  Regency Club

ASSOCIATIONS/PROFESSIONAL SOCIETIES:
  California Executive Recruiters Association
  International City Management Association
  International Personnel Management Association
  American Society for Public Administration
  Western Governmental Research Association

SPECIAL INTERESTS AND HOBBIES:
Children's Institute International, Board Member and past President;
basketball, tennis

REPRESENTATIVE AND SIGNIFICANT PLACEMENTS:
Peter Ueberroth, President
Los Angeles Olympic Organizing Committee
Neil Peterson, Executive Director
Los Angeles County Transportation Commission
Sylvester Murray, City Manager
City of Cincinnati, Ohio
Jorge Carrasco, General Manager
East Bay Municipal Utility District
Joseph Shuldiner, Executive Director
Housing Authority of the City of Los Angeles

WHAT I LOOK FOR IN GENERAL IN A CANDIDATE

I first look for appropriate training and competency, as demonstrated by the education and experience of the candidate. Thereafter, I focus on personal attributes and management style/abilities. Typically, these include good communication skills, a professional presence, self-confidence, honesty and integrity, and the ability to listen. The accuracy and completeness of information provided to me is indicative of the individual's integrity, and I view this as critical. I am also generally interested in the candidate's enthusiasm, the compatibility of the person's long-term goals with the position we are trying to fill, the appropriateness of his or her salary requirements, and the lack of barriers for accepting a job offer (for example, housing, family commitments, and so on). Finally, the quality of the references provided is a key indicator, as is the content of the background checks.

GEOGRAPHIC SCOPE OF RECRUITING ACTIVITIES:
Serve clients nationwide

TOTAL YEARS OF RETAINER-TYPE RECRUITING EXPERIENCE:
22 years

JOHN H. ROBISON
President
Robison & McAulay
1350 First Citizens Plaza
128 S. Tryon Street
Charlotte, NC 28202
Telephone: (704) 376-0059

Date of Birth: September 25,
1930
Grew up in: Salisbury, North Carolina

Robison & McAulay

HIGHER EDUCATION:
University of North Carolina, Chapel Hill
B.S. degree, business administration, 1952
Rutgers University
Stonier Graduate School of Banking, 1964

MILITARY:
Captain, United States Army, 1952 to 1955

EMPLOYMENT HISTORY:
1979 to present: Robison & McAulay
1975 to 1979: President, Locke & Robison
1973 to 1975: Principal, Woodward, Harris, Robison & Associates
1967 to 1973: Executive Vice President, Bankers Trust of South Carolina (now NCNB)
1952 to 1967: Senior Vice President, North Carolina National Bank

PRIVATE CLUBS:
Charlotte Country Club
Charlotte City Club

ASSOCIATIONS/PROFESSIONAL SOCIETIES:
Association of Executive Search Consultants, past Director

REPRESENTATIVE AND SIGNIFICANT PLACEMENTS:
Paul E. Welder, Executive Vice President, Chief Financial Officer
   Greenwood Mills
Robert L. Shaffer, Vice President–Corporate Communications
   United Dominion Industries
Robert S. Goodale, President
   Harris-Teeter Super Markets
James N. West, D.D., Vice President–Institutional Advancement
   Lutheran Theological Southern Seminary
E.P. Wilkinson (Vice Admiral, Ret.), President
   Institute of Nuclear Power Operations (INPO)

WHAT I LOOK FOR IN GENERAL IN A CANDIDATE

The characteristics and qualifications which I believe are important for selection of finalists for client presentation have changed little over the years and, as have been previously published, have fallen into three categories: assessment of technical competence, matching of personal characteristics with the client's culture, and appropriate evaluation of potential. As these categories are simply stated, they would seem to warrant no further elaboration, and, hopefully, the recruiter becomes more discerning through repeated experience.

Implicd with the three, but possibly necessary to mention, is the basic quality of good character and high integrity—ascertaining that a candidate is of the same caliber and manifests the high standards that we expect of our clients is essential and critical to the process.

GEOGRAPHIC SCOPE OF RECRUITING ACTIVITIES:
Serve clients nationwide and in England, Germany, Switzerland, Finland, France

TOTAL YEARS OF RETAINER-TYPE RECRUITING EXPERIENCE:
18 years

GERARD R. ROCHE
Chairman
Heidrick & Struggles, Inc.
245 Park Avenue
New York, NY 10167-0152
Telephone: (212) 867-9876

Date of Birth: July 27, 1931
Grew up in: Scranton, Pennsylvania

Bachrach

HIGHER EDUCATION:
University of Scranton,
    B.S. degree, accounting, 1953
New York University,
    M.B.A. degree, 1958
University of Scranton
    Honorary Doctor of Laws, 1982

MILITARY:
Lieutenant Junior Grade, United States Navy, Mediterranean, 1953 to 1955

EMPLOYMENT HISTORY:
1964 to present: Heidrick & Struggles, Inc.
1959 to 1963: Marketing Director–Kordite, Mobil Oil Company
1956 to 1958: Account Executive, American Broadcasting Company
1955 to 1956: Management Trainee, American Telephone and Telegraph

PRIVATE CLUBS:
University Club of New York
Sky Club of New York
Yale Club of New York
Blind Brook Country Club
Sleepy Hollow Country Club
The Loxahatchee Club
Member of the Knights of Malta

ASSOCIATIONS/PROFESSIONAL SOCIETIES:
Executive Board, The Wharton Graduate School
Board of Directors, Morrison-Knudsen Corporation
Board Member, Regents of the Catholic University of America
Past Chairman of the Board of Trustees, University of Scranton
Past President, Association of Executive Recruiting Consultants

SPECIAL INTERESTS AND HOBBIES:
Golf, tennis, reading

REPRESENTATIVE AND SIGNIFICANT PLACEMENTS:
Lawrence A. Bossidy, Chief Executive Officer
    Allied-Signal, Inc.
Hollis Harris, President and Chief Executive Officer
    Continental Airlines Holdings, Inc.
John M. Harris, President and Chief Executive Officer
    Rockefeller Financial Services, Inc.
John Sculley, Chairman and Chief Executive Officer
    Apple Computer, Inc.
Stephen M. Wolf, Chairman, President and Chief Executive Officer
    UAL Corporation

WHAT I LOOK FOR IN GENERAL IN A CANDIDATE

* Vision, drive, and demonstrated leadership abilities
* Intelligence and honesty
* Unquestionable integrity and ethics
* Solid interpersonal and communication skills
* Track record of success
* Solid personal characteristics and values
* Chemistry with the client... perhaps the most important aspect of all

GEOGRAPHIC SCOPE OF RECRUITING ACTIVITIES:
Serve clients nationwide and in Europe and Asia

TOTAL YEARS OF RETAINER-TYPE RECRUITING EXPERIENCE:
27 years

BRENDA L. RUELLO
Partner and Member of Executive Committee
Heidrick and Struggles, Inc.
245 Park Avenue
New York, NY 10167
Telephone: (212) 867-9876

Date of Birth: December 22,1937
Grew up in: Florence, South Carolina

HIGHER EDUCATION:
Syracuse University
  B.A. degree, fine arts, 1959

EMPLOYMENT HISTORY:
1977 to present: Heidrick and Struggles, Inc.
1975 to 1977: Manager–Executive Search, Peat, Marwick, Mitchell & Co.
1970 to 1975: Consultant/Recruiter, Booz, Allen & Hamilton, Inc.
1964 to 1966: Consultant–Executive Search, Kiernan & Company
1959 to 1964: Personnel Training, Bloomingdale's

PRIVATE CLUBS:
The Metropolitan Club

ASSOCIATIONS/PROFESSIONAL SOCIETIES:
The Women's Forum
The Financial Women's Association

SPECIAL INTERESTS AND HOBBIES:
Photography, gardening, landscaping

REPRESENTATIVE AND SIGNIFICANT PLACEMENTS:
Al Dunlap, Partner
  Sir James Goldsmith
Dennis K. Eck, Vice Chairman and Chief Operating Officer
  The Vons Companies, Inc.

Ronald B. Gordon, President and Chief Operating Officer
  Goody Products, Inc.
Donald R. Midkiff, Chief Executive Officer
  Coopers, Inc.
Jonathan J. Lane, Senior Vice President–Telecommunications
  Shearson Lehman Hutton, Inc.

WHAT I LOOK FOR IN GENERAL IN A CANDIDATE

A leader who manages a business rather than a career...ability to manage change... "fire in the belly"...global vision, with the ability to execute against that vision.

Commitment to developing a strong motivated team, with the ability to achieve a marketplace leadership role with either the company's products or services. Entrepreneurial instincts combined with respect for total quality objectives. Someone who is inspired to reach out for "hidden" star talent. A thinking implementer who is forthright and unpretentious with an easy self-confidence, a good sense of humor, and the energy and tenacity to exert every effort necessary to solve business problems. Someone who responds to crisis situations with immediacy, emotional control, clear thinking, and solid judgment.

GEOGRAPHIC SCOPE OF RECRUITING ACTIVITIES:
  Serve clients nationwide and in France, England, Holland, and Australia

TOTAL YEARS OF RETAINER-TYPE RECRUITING EXPERIENCE:
  15 years

RICHARD D. SBARBARO
President
Lauer, Sbarbaro Associates, Inc.
30 N. LaSalle Street
Chicago, IL 60602
Telephone: (312) 372-7050

Date of Birth: December 16, 1946
Grew up in: Chicago, Illinois

HIGHER EDUCATION:
DePaul University
  B.S.C. degree, marketing, 1967
  M.B.A. degree, marketing, 1971

EMPLOYMENT HISTORY:
1979 to present: Lauer, Sbarbaro Associates, Inc.
1978 to 1979: Principal, Booz, Allen & Hamilton
1971 to 1978: Senior Vice President, Midwest Stock Exchange
1969 to 1971: Senior Consultant, Fry Consultants
1967 to 1969: Sales Manager, Illinois Bell Telephone Company

PRIVATE CLUBS:
Attic Club
St. Charles Country Club

ASSOCIATIONS/PROFESSIONAL SOCIETIES:
Association of Executive Search Consultants, Chicago Chapter
Presidents Association
Human Resource Management Association of Chicago
Beta Gamma Sigma

SPECIAL INTERESTS AND HOBBIES:
Running, cycling, water sports, golf; DePaul University Athletic
  Board; Management Advisory Board and Adjunct Professor, Grad-
  uate School of Business; Director, EMA Partners International

REPRESENTATIVE AND SIGNIFICANT PLACEMENTS:
President
  Nationally recognized health care system

Chief Executive Officer
  Major insurance company
Dean of the Business School
  Prominent Midwestern university
President
  High-tech *Fortune* 500 company
Chief Operating Officer
  Fortune 500 industrial company

WHAT I LOOK FOR IN GENERAL IN A CANDIDATE

Once a technical competence to successfully meet the client's requirements is established, the softer skills become paramount. They include:

- Leadership—a successful track record with increasing success
- Integrity—no matter what the level, this is a *must*
- Common sense—essential for balance both on and off the job
- Intelligence—this will have been established early on in his/her career
- Willingness to learn—every manager can benefit from expanded knowledge
- Sense of humor—genuine and natural
- People skills—a strong motivator, must truly enjoy people and accept and recognize
- Vision and balance—management that can set the course with lofty objectives yet recognize reality
- Energy—very high, but maintainable
- Compassion—recognition of employees as assets and human beings, not just expense

GEOGRAPHIC SCOPE OF RECRUITING ACTIVITIES:
  Serve clients nationwide and through EMA Partners International in the Netherlands, Spain, Belgium, Ireland, Germany, United Kingdom, Italy, France, Austria, Singapore, and Pacific Rim

TOTAL YEARS OF RETAINER-TYPE RECRUITING EXPERIENCE:
  12 years

STEVEN A. SEIDEN
President
Seiden Associates, Inc.
375 Park Avenue, Suite 3201
New York, NY 10472
Telephone: (212) 688-8383

Date of Birth: February 18, 1936
Grew up in: New York and Palm
    Beach, Florida

Bachrach

HIGHER EDUCATION:
Yale University
    A.B. degree, art history, 1958

MILITARY:
Specialist Fourth Class, United States Army, 1961 to 1962

EMPLOYMENT HISTORY:
1984 to present: Seiden Associates, Inc.
1966 to 1984: Co-President, Herzfeld & Stern, Members of New York
    Stock Exchange
1964 to 1966: Vice President, Irving L. Straus Associates
1962 to 1964: Vice President, Louis Sherry, Inc.
1958 to 1962: Vice President, Seiden Holding Co., Inc.

PRIVATE CLUBS:
Yale Club
Mory's Association
Century Country Club
Bond Club of New York

ASSOCIATIONS/PROFESSIONAL SOCIETIES:
International Association of Corporate and Professional Recruiters
TurnAround Management Association
New York Society of Securities Analysts

SPECIAL INTERESTS AND HOBBIES:
Management science, foreign travel, golf, fly-fishing

REPRESENTATIVE AND SIGNIFICANT PLACEMENTS:
William N. Sick, Chief Executive Officer
    American National Can
Frank J. Belatti, President
    Ramada and Howard Johnson Hotels
Barry C. Burkholder, Chief Executive Officer
    United Savings Banks
David Flood, Chief Executive Officer
    Stewart-Warner Corporation
Robert B. Machinist, President
    MMG Patricof Group

WHAT I LOOK FOR IN GENERAL IN A CANDIDATE

Leadership, chemistry, and track record.

Leadership becomes apparent after meeting an executive for just a short while. Robert Browning wrote, "A man's reach should exceed his grasp." A leader embodies that ideal.

The "chemistry" between client and candidate is critical. However, we don't view "chemistry" as a separate issue. Chemistry is the product of mutual respect and esteem which two successful executives—client and candidate—instinctively develop for one another.

A measurable track record is imperative. I maintain an attitude of healthy skepticism in which both references and financial records serve as evidence to corroborate a candidate's past results.

GEOGRAPHIC SCOPE OF RECRUITING ACTIVITIES:
Serve clients nationwide and in the UK

TOTAL YEARS OF RETAINER-TYPE RECRUITING EXPERIENCE:
8 years

JACK SEITCHIK
President
Seitchik Corwin and Seitchik
1830 Jackson Street
San Francisco, CA 94109
Telephone: (415) 928-5717

Date of Birth: May 11, 1927
Grew up in: Philadelphia, Pennsylvania

HIGHER EDUCATION:
Penn State
    B.A. degree, liberal arts, 1947
Pepperdine University
    M.B.A. degree, 1977

EMPLOYMENT HISTORY:
1974 to present: Seitchik Corwin and Seitchik
1973 to 1974: President, Haywood Division of Genesco
1972 to 1973: Operations Manager, Levi Strauss of Mexico
1969 to 1972: Owner, Confecciones de USA and Casa Central/Dominican Republic
1947 to 1969: Vice President, W. Seitchik & Sons, Inc.

PRIVATE CLUBS:
Golden Gateway Tennis Club
Countryside Racquet Club

SPECIAL INTERESTS AND HOBBIES:
Tennis, fitness

REPRESENTATIVE AND SIGNIFICANT PLACEMENTS:
President
    Widely recognized licensed women's sportwear business
President
    Leading national home and office furniture rental company
Vice President and Chief Operations Officer
    $100 million T-shirt and sportswear screenprinter

President
A leading knit fabric manufacturer
Senior Vice President
One of the top three athletic footwear companies

WHAT I LOOK FOR IN GENERAL IN A CANDIDATE

The important part of retainer search is that each assignment is customized; however, there are certain characteristics that are common to all searches.

1. I am looking for someone who is doing what our client needs done and is doing it well currently for someone else.
2. I am looking for people who are bright and motivated.
3. The candidate should have researched the prospective employer and be well rounded.
4. Since the technical qualifications for each candidate have been verified prior to my meeting, I am looking for a behavioral match. Every company has a different personality. Some people work well in one and not in another. I am looking for the person who most closely matches the corporate culture.

GEOGRAPHIC SCOPE OF RECRUITING ACTIVITIES:
Serve clients nationwide and in Europe and Central and South America

TOTAL YEARS OF RETAINER-TYPE RECRUITING EXPERIENCE:
17 years

DANIEL M. SHEPHERD
Principal
Shepherd Bueschel &
  Provus, Inc.
One South Wacker Drive,
  Suite 2740
Chicago, IL 60606
Telephone: (312) 372-1142

Date of Birth: April 8, 1939
Grew up in: Ashland and Lexington, Kentucky

Shepherd Bueschel & Provus, Inc.

HIGHER EDUCATION:
  University of Kentucky
    B.S. degree, civil engineering, 1962
  Harvard University
    M.B.A. degree, 1964

MILITARY:
  Captain, United States Army Corps of Engineers, 1964 to 1966

EMPLOYMENT HISTORY:
  1991 to present: Shepherd Bueschel & Provus, Inc.
  1986 to 1991: Sweeney Shepherd Bueschel Provus Harbert & Mum-
    mert, Inc.
  1982 to 1986: Vice President, Lamalie Associates, Inc.
  1978 to 1982: Vice President, Heidrick and Struggles, Inc.
  1976 to 1978: Vice President–Product/Market Management, Masonite
    Corporation
  1973 to 1976: Vice President, General Manager–Thunderbird Boats,
    Corporate Director–Operations, Fuqua Industries, Inc.
  1970 to 1973: Various positions, Mattel, Inc.
  1966 to 1970: Various positions, Procter & Gamble Company

PRIVATE CLUBS:
  Union League Club of Chicago
  Harvard Business School Club of Chicago

ASSOCIATIONS/PROFESSIONAL SOCIETIES:
Association of Executive Search Consultants

SPECIAL INTERESTS AND HOBBIES:
My children, coin and art collecting, skiing, Chicago Cubs, exceptional
food and wine

REPRESENTATIVE AND SIGNIFICANT PLACEMENTS:
Ronald H. Yocum, Executive Vice President, President USI Division
Quantum Chemical Company
Stephen R. Wilson, Senior Vice President and Chief Financial Officer
CF Industries, Inc.
Jayne L. Fenton, Vice President–Map & Atlas Publishing Division,
Publishing Group
Rand McNally & Company
Gary M. Christensen, Senior Vice President–Marketing and Sales
Rolscreen Company
Henry J. Feinberg, President, Rand McNally-TDM, Inc.
Rand McNally & Company

WHAT I LOOK FOR IN GENERAL IN A CANDIDATE
- A value-added twist in matching a candidate's technical skills
with the client's needs
- Intellectual efficiency and capacity; mental clarity; common
sense and street savvy; and the ability to reach high levels of
abstraction
- Self-awareness and emotional maturity and stability
- People skills/style in relating to superiors, peers, and subordi-
nates
- The ability to organize and to direct—leadership
- Presence—balance—luck—sense of humor—work ethic—
energy—integrity—skeletons

GEOGRAPHIC SCOPE OF RECRUITING ACTIVITIES:
Serve clients nationwide

TOTAL YEARS OF RETAINER-TYPE RECRUITING EXPERIENCE:
13 years

ANDREW SHERWOOD
Chairman
Goodrich & Sherwood Company
521 Fifth Avenue
New York, NY 10017
Telephone: (212) 697-4131

Date of Birth: January 8, 1942
Grew up in: New Jersey

Goodrich & Sherwood Company

HIGHER EDUCATION:
　Nichols College
　　B.B.A. degree, marketing/management, 1964

EMPLOYMENT HISTORY:
　1971 to present: Goodrich & Sherwood Company
　1967 to 1971: Executive Vice President, Ward Clancy Associates
　1965 to 1967: Director, Gilbert Lane

PRIVATE CLUBS:
　Explorer's Club
　University Club
　Commanderie de Bordeaux
　Rolling Rock Club
　Safari Club
　Young Presidents' Organization
　Economics Club

ASSOCIATIONS/PROFESSIONAL SOCIETIES:
　National Association of Corporate and Professional Recruiters
　Association of Outplacement Professionals
　National Human Resources Planning Association, Conference Board

SPECIAL INTERESTS AND HOBBIES:
　Member National Ski Patrol, tennis, hunting, sporting clays, fishing,
　　restoring vintage race cars

REPRESENTATIVE AND SIGNIFICANT PLACEMENTS:
　President
　　Health care company
　Vice President Marketing
　　Food products company
　Executive Vice President
　　Fortune 100 information systems company

President and Vice President—Sales
  Heating, air conditioning, high-tech company
Chief Executive Officer
  Major U.S. charitable service non-profit organization

WHAT I LOOK FOR IN GENERAL IN A CANDIDATE

When interviewing a top-level candidate I look for balance and ability to communicate appropriately to the situation. The better senior executives I have known and recruited are balanced individuals who can manage diversified problems, opportunities, and people simultaneously with skill and diplomacy. With balance and effective communication style and less emotion, volatility, disruption, and extremism, the greater a likelihood for a smooth-running organization, clearly defined objectives, respect, control, and ultimate success. Qualities I look for:

- Integrity, strength of character, a good role model
- Results-oriented. What has the person accomplished? Against what objectives?
- Sense of humor. Do people enjoy interacting with this person? Have they in the past?
- Presence. Will this person represent the company well, both inside and outside the corporation?
- Energy. A sense of urgency, enough to do the job and motivate others without intimidating
- Vision. Will this person build for the future or just maintain?
- Stamina. Enough to handle tough decisions without getting bogged down, sick, or exhausted
- Communicator. Leads by communicating and encouraging
- Loyalty to the company, staff, customers, stockholders, and family
- Well-organized. Does the individual organize thoughts and work and work well?
- Leadership. A person others seek out and follow willingly
- High frustration level. Able to manage without flying off the handle
- Open to new ideas that others sponsor
- Secure with superiors, subordinates alike

GEOGRAPHIC SCOPE OF RECRUITING ACTIVITIES:
Serve clients nationwide and in Europe

TOTAL YEARS OF RETAINER-TYPE RECRUITING EXPERIENCE:
24 years

MARY E. SHOURDS
Executive Vice President
Houze, Shourds & Montgomery, Inc.
Greater Los Angeles World Trade Center
One World Trade, Suite 1840
Long Beach, CA 90831
Telephone: (213) 495-6495

Date of Birth: November 7, 1942
Grew up in: Turtle Creek, Pennsylvania

HIGHER EDUCATION:
  Pepperdine University
    B.S. degree, 1974
  UCLA
    M.B.A. degree, 1983

EMPLOYMENT HISTORY:
  1977 to present: Houze, Shourds & Montgomery
  1975 to 1977: Vice President, Hergenrather & Company
  1964 to 1975: Rockwell International—Various Human Resources positions to Director–Human Resources Information Systems Organization and Corporate Offices

ASSOCIATIONS/PROFESSIONAL SOCIETIES:
  International Association of Corporate and Professional Recruiters
  Founding Member of the Board of Directors, Center for Telecommunications Management at the University of Southern California
  Past Board Member, JIA Management Group, an information systems consulting firm (now part of A.T. Kearney)

SPECIAL INTERESTS AND HOBBIES:
  Sailing, reading, cooking

REPRESENTATIVE AND SIGNIFICANT PLACEMENTS:
  Chief Operating Officer
    Information systems company
  President
    Network services company

President
 Software company
Vice President–Business Development
 Information technology company

WHAT I LOOK FOR IN GENERAL IN A CANDIDATE

Real people aren't perfect—and, thus, neither are real candidates. In addition, some characteristics are more (or less) important given the client, their particular environment, and the specific pressure points inherent in the industry, the company, and the position for which I am recruiting. However, traits I find most important in evaluating candidates for all positions include:

- A well-seasoned value system, for which there is ample evidence of having been tested successfully. I look for high standards; how (and when) a person struggles with gray areas; intellectual integrity; and someone who isn't inclined to cut corners or shade decisions.
- A good sense of humor; that is, someone who doesn't take himself too seriously; and, along with good humor, the good judgment to know how to inject humor appropriate to the place and time.
- Vision—but especially how well it is balanced by personal organization and a sense of follow-through. There is an old Zen saying that goes something like, "First enlightenment, then the laundry," which makes the point that vision, without at least the sense of what it takes to implement it, has somewhat limited value.
- A healthy tolerance for ambiguity coupled with the ability to adapt and respond to unforeseen changes in organization, customers, markets, and so forth.
- Self-assured and people-oriented. By this I mean that the candidate is capable of standing on his own, but, at the same time, he elicits information, involvement, even criticism, from co-workers and subordinates.
- Good balance—a dedication to family; a commitment to the company; and a sense of responsibility to the society at large.

GEOGRAPHIC SCOPE OF RECRUITING ACTIVITIES:
Serve clients nationwide and in England and Japan

TOTAL YEARS OF RETAINER-TYPE RECRUITING EXPERIENCE:
16 years

FRED SIEGEL
President
CONEX Incorporated
919 Third Avenue
New York, NY 10022
Telephone: (212) 371-3737

Date of Birth: April 17, 1941
Grew up in: Gloversville, New
York

HIGHER EDUCATION:
New York City Technical College
A.A.S. degree, accounting, 1966
Long Island University
B.S. degree, accounting, 1969

MILITARY
Airman 2nd Class, United States Air Force, 1961 to 1965

EMPLOYMENT HISTORY:
1988 to present: CONEX Incorporated
1980 to 1988: Partner, Consulting Associates
1976 to 1980: Associate Dean, New York University Graduate School
of Business
1974 to 1976: Recruitment Manager, Arthur Young & Co.
1970 to 1974: Assistant to the Mayor, New York City Office of the
Mayor
1969 to 1970: Auditor, Price Waterhouse & Co.

PRIVATE CLUBS:
Excelsior Club, New York

ASSOCIATIONS/PROFESSIONAL SOCIETIES:
Association for a Better New York
Jan Pierce Foundation
Presidents Advisory Council of Foreign Policy Association

SPECIAL INTERESTS AND HOBBIES:
Politics, a variety of sports

REPRESENTATIVE AND SIGNIFICANT PLACEMENTS:
Jack Kiermaier, President
Foreign Policy Association

Charles Morgan, General Counsel
  Chiquita Brands International
Peter Fay, Vice President–Human Resources
  Chiquita Brands International
Arthur Morgon, Senior Manager–Real Estate
  Arthur Andersen & Co.
Michael Zachey, President
  R&D Trucking

WHAT I LOOK FOR IN GENERAL IN A CANDIDATE

"Fit" is the key but often elusive factor in completing a successful search. Finding the right work experience, educational background, and other elements of a job description is generally the easier part of the assignment. But knowing the candidate and client well enough to ensure success for both sides is where the "best" recruiters excel. I found myself getting better—more focused—on candidate/client fit as I gained more experience during my 11 years as an executive recruiter.

There are other less-than-obvious factors on which I focus when conducting a search. Gaps on resumes or quick turnover of jobs may indicate problems. I spend a good deal of time determining why candidates leave positions, and look for patterns. Also important is can the candidate deal with the pressure of his or her potential new position? Is he a hands-on manager or delegator? Does he have the personality, work habits, demeanor, leadership, and technical skills necessary to do the job? And the candidate's references must be independent and consistent. In 1990, 12.5 percent of my searches were completed with only one candidate being sent to my client. This was the result of spending a great deal of time learning my client's culture as well as the specific job requirements. It's these factors along with superior staff, strong international partners, and cooperative clients that have made CONEX, the firm I created in 1988, successful. Quite simply, we know what to look for in a candidate and our clients appreciate our effort.

GEOGRAPHIC SCOPE OF RECRUITING ACTIVITIES:

Serve clients nationwide and in Europe, Asia, Canada, and Latin America

TOTAL YEARS OF RETAINER-TYPE RECRUITING EXPERIENCE:

11 years

J. GERALD SIMMONS
President
Handy Associates
250 Park Avenue
New York, NY 10177
Telephone: (212) 692-2222

Date of Birth: September 17, 1929
Grew up in: Miami, Florida

Handy Associates

HIGHER EDUCATION:
University of Miami
B.S. degree, marketing, 1956

MILITARY:
Special Agent, United States Army (Counterintelligence Corps), 1951 to 1953

EMPLOYMENT HISTORY:
1976 to present: Handy Associates
1973 to 1976: Vice President–Marketing, Wiltek
1971 to 1973: Vice President and General Manager–Department and Specialty Store Division, Revlon
1956 to 1971: Director of Marketing, IBM Corporation

PRIVATE CLUBS:
University Club
Sky Club
Greenwich Country Club

REPRESENTATIVE AND SIGNIFICANT PLACEMENTS:
President and Chief Executive Officer
A leading mini computer organization
President–International
One of the country's top computer organizations
Chief Information Officer
Major commercial bank

Outside Director
  Major midwestern insurance company
Outside Director
  Major electrical appliance company

WHAT I LOOK FOR IN GENERAL IN A CANDIDATE

In general, I believe there are three distinct areas that are important to understand in evaluating a candidate for a senior-level position:

1. Personal attributes. This wide-ranging subject involves such things as appearance, personality, ability to communicate, initiative, intuitiveness, intelligence, and ability to react to change.
2. Personal values. This would include such important items as integrity, loyalty—up, down and sideways—honesty, and the willingness to admit when a mistake has been made—pick up the pieces and move on.
3. Professional experience. The more senior the executive position, the less important are the technical skills which may have launched someone on to a business career. It is of vital importance to understand from the candidate and from intensive reference checks his past work experiences, failures, and successes. Too many times we focused on what someone has accomplished and not how they accomplished it. In speaking with candidates and references we must sort out the contributions made by the individual versus the contributions made by others and understand what, if any, real impact the individual had on a particular event, project, or organization.

GEOGRAPHIC SCOPE OF RECRUITING ACTIVITIES:
Serve clients nationwide

TOTAL YEARS OF RETAINER-TYPE RECRUITING EXPERIENCE:
15 years

ROBERT W. SLATER
Managing Director
Slater & Associates
12221 Merit Drive, Suite 1325
Dallas, TX 75251
Telephone: (817) 265-3396
(214) 991-6893

Date of Birth: April 18, 1938
Grew up in: Chicago, Illinois

HIGHER EDUCATION:
Cornell College of Iowa
B.A. degree, history and political science, 1960

MILITARY:
Corporal, United States National Guard, 1961 to 1965

EMPLOYMENT HISTORY:
1991 to present: Slater & Associates
1989 to 1991: Managing Director–North America, Korn/Ferry International
1979 to 1989: Managing Director–North America, SpencerStuart
1969 to 1979: Partner–Management Services, Arthur Young & Co.
1962 to 1969: Regional Personnel Manager, Allstate Insurance
1960 to 1962: Admissions Representative, Cornell College (Iowa)

PRIVATE CLUBS:
The Dallas Club

ASSOCIATIONS/PROFESSIONAL SOCIETIES:
Trustee, Cornell College of Iowa
Board Member, University of Texas at Dallas Graduate School of Management

SPECIAL INTERESTS AND HOBBIES:
Tennis, fine art, history

REPRESENTATIVE AND SIGNIFICANT PLACEMENTS:
David Anderson, Executive Vice President and Chief Financial Officer
  Burlington Northern
Clint Alston, Vice President and Director of Information Systems
  Training and Development
  Philips N.V.
John Anderson, Executive Vice President–Marketing and Sales
  Burlington Northern
Jerry Halvorsen, President
  INGAA
John Amerman, Board Member
  Unocal

WHAT I LOOK FOR IN GENERAL IN A CANDIDATE

I seek candidates with the following:

- A record of accomplishment/success as well as the demonstrated ability to function effectively under both ideal and adverse conditions
- General management skills
- Functional/technical knowledge
- Interpersonal/presentation skills, especially the ability to communicate effectively and listen well

In addition to all of this, you've got to look at personal chemistry and how an individual will match up with the hiring executive.

GEOGRAPHIC SCOPE OF RECRUITING ACTIVITIES:
Serve clients nationwide

TOTAL YEARS OF RETAINER-TYPE RECRUITING EXPERIENCE:
22 years

RICHARD C. SLAYTON
President
Slayton International, Inc.
10 S. Riverside Plaza, Suite 312
Chicago, IL 60606
Telephone: (312) 648-0056

Date of Birth: April 3, 1937
Grew up in: Toledo, Ohio

HIGHER EDUCATION:
University of Michigan
B.S. degree, industrial engineering, 1960
M.B.A. degree, 1965

MILITARY:
Rated, United States Naval Reserve, 1954 to 1965

EMPLOYMENT HISTORY:
1985 to present: Slayton International, Inc.
1976 to 1985: Boyden International
1983 to 1985: Senior Vice President and Manager–Midwest Operations
1982 to 1983: Vice President and Manager–Toledo Office
1976 to 1982: Vice President
1970 to 1976: President, Business Technology Associates
1967 to 1970: Associate Director of Consulting, K.W. Tunnell
1960 to 1967: Various positions in manufacturing and marketing, General Electric Company

PRIVATE CLUBS:
Metropolitan Club of Chicago
Executives Club of Chicago

ASSOCIATIONS/PROFESSIONAL SOCIETIES:
Honor Societies:
Beta Gamma Sigma
Phi Kappa Phi
Alpha Phi Mu

American Institute of Industrial Engineers
Economics Club of Chicago
Society of Automotive Engineers
American Production/Inventory Control Society

SPECIAL INTERESTS AND HOBBIES:
Fly-fishing, skeet, bird hunting

REPRESENTATIVE AND SIGNIFICANT PLACEMENTS:
President and Chief Executive Officer
   Fortune 500 automotive company
President and Chief Executive Officer
   Fortune 500 materials company
President and Chief Executive Officer
   Aerospace company
Group President
   Fortune 500 automotive subsidiary
Vice President and Chief Information Officer
   Fortune 500 industrial corporation

WHAT I LOOK FOR IN GENERAL IN A CANDIDATE

Each professional is endowed at birth with certain qualities common to all, namely, intelligence, energy level, appearance, common sense, and feelings. As a professional develops, other qualities are developed namely, knowledge in one's chosen field, integrity, aggressiveness, organization, written and verbal skills, decision-making ability, interpersonal relations, personality, and overall executive stature.

All of the above comprise a total composite of a candidate which, with career accomplishments, must be evaluated and matched with the particular requirements of a client.

GEOGRAPHIC SCOPE OF RECRUITING ACTIVITIES:
Serve clients nationwide and in Europe and the Far East

TOTAL YEARS OF RETAINER-TYPE RECRUITING EXPERIENCE:
18 years

JOHN E. SMITH, JR.
President
Smith Search, S.C.
Barranca Del Muerto 472, Col.
  Alpes
Mexico, D.F. 01010
Telephone: (525) 593-8766

Date of Birth: December 22, 1933
Grew up in: Rhode Island

HIGHER EDUCATION:
  Georgetown University, School of Foreign Service
    B.S. degree, foreign service, 1957

EMPLOYMENT HISTORY:
  1972 to present: Smith Search, S.C.
  1964 to 1972: Director, Noble & Associates
  1959 to 1964: Vice President, Foote Cone & Belding de Mexico

PRIVATE CLUBS:
  University Club of Mexico, A.C.

ASSOCIATIONS/PROFESSIONAL SOCIETIES:
  American Chamber of Commerce of Mexico, A.C.
  Consejo Empresarial Mexicano Para Asuntos Internacionales

SPECIAL INTERESTS AND HOBBIES:
  Bicycling, skiing, family, work

REPRESENTATIVE AND SIGNIFICANT PLACEMENTS:
  Director General, now Area Vice President–Latin America
    Hewlett Packard de Mexico, S.A. de C.V.
  President
    Babcock & Wilcox de Mexico, S.A. de C.V.
  General Manager
    Textiles Morelos, S.A. de C.V. (Burlington Mills)

General Manager
  Hydril, S.A. de C.V.
General Manager
  General de Telecomunicaciones, S.A. de C.V. (Gentel)

WHAT I LOOK FOR IN GENERAL IN A CANDIDATE

The type of executive we will place is most frequently bilingual in Spanish, bicultural (by dint of extended American cultural, corporate, or educational exposure), U.S.-educated (usually at the M.B.A. level), about 35 to 45 years of age, married, settled down, a resident of Mexico City (no small burg at over 20 million but whose high-interest/high-potential executive class is probably no more than 1 percent of that), upscale (not unimportant in what is still a caste society, egalitarian revolution notwithstanding), which means mostly of European descent (we in Mexico don't have to fret about litigious lambastings for thinking or saying these thoughts). He (sometimes she) is usually in the employ of a leadership Mexican industrial or financial group or a multinational corporation. In either case, they are clearly drawn from an intellectual, business, social upper crust geared and galvanized since birth to assume roles of responsibility and leadership within the Mexican infrastructure.

We feel comfortable recruiting Mexicans for American companies operating in Mexico or elsewhere in Latin America. We feel equally comfortable recruiting Mexicans for Mexicans, both always of the leadership stripe/ilk. We also enjoy the challenge of recruiting in the Spanish-speaking market of the United States.

Candidates, irrespective of the search, must be winners, proven problem solvers, achievers, apt and agile in dealing with the increasingly international and increasingly competitive markets of Latin America, especially Mexico. We place a premium on the candidate who is creative, of high energy level and powerful personality.

GEOGRAPHIC SCOPE OF RECRUITING ACTIVITIES:
Serve clients in Mexico, United States, Central America, and northern South America

TOTAL YEARS OF RETAINER-TYPE RECRUITING EXPERIENCE:
19 years

ROBERT L. SMITH
President
Robert L. Smith & Company, Inc.
666 Fifth Avenue, 37th Floor
New York, NY 10103
Telephone: (212) 541-3791

Date of Birth: July 1, 1938
Grew up in: Florida

HIGHER EDUCATION:
  University of Florida
    Bachelor of Industrial Engineering, 1961
  Harvard University
    M.B.A. degree, 1963

EMPLOYMENT HISTORY:
  1989 to present: Robert L. Smith & Company, Inc.
  1975 to 1989: President and Founder, Johnson, Smith & Knisely
  1971 to 1975: Vice President, MBA Resources (Nordeman Grimm)
  1971: Account Executive, Diebold Group, Inc.
  1967 to 1971: Large Account Marketing, IBM Corporation
  1966 to 1967: Sales Coordinator, Burlington House
  1964 to 1966: Sales/Marketing Management, Craftex Mills, Inc.
  1963 to 1964: Sales Representative, Xerox Corporation

ASSOCIATIONS/PROFESSIONAL SOCIETIES:
  Association of Executive Search Consultants
    (various board positions including Chairman for 1989 to 1990)

SPECIAL INTERESTS AND HOBBIES:
  Organizational dynamics/behavior, travel, scuba diving; contributing
    author to *The Executive Search Collaboration*

REPRESENTATIVE AND SIGNIFICANT PLACEMENTS:
  Ray Baxter, President and Chief Operating Officer to Chairman and
    Chief Executive Officer
    Interbake Foods, Inc.

James R. Holland, Jr., President and Chief Executive Officer, also became Chairman
$150 million, 1700 location consumer service company owned by Hong Kong investor group

Carl Yankowski, Vice President–U.S. Consumer Markets to Vice President–Business Imaging
Polaroid Corporation

Carl V. Stinnett, President and Chief Executive Officer
$1 billion sales subsidiary of Campbell Soup Company

Several Senior Consulting Partners
Greenwich Associates (formerly Greenwich Research Associates)

WHAT I LOOK FOR IN GENERAL IN A CANDIDATE

In evaluating candidates I look for the characteristics which my experience shows are vital to the success of any manager assuming a leadership role in a new situation:

- Industry and functional expertise related to the specifics of the client's business strategy
- Compatibility with the management style of the new boss
- Ability to build effective working relationships with other members of the management team
- Stamina and personal energy to infuse her/his organization with a sustained high level of vitality

GEOGRAPHIC SCOPE OF RECRUITING ACTIVITIES:
Serve clients nationally and internationally

TOTAL YEARS OF RETAINER-TYPE RECRUITING EXPERIENCE:
20 years

ROBERT D. SPRIGGS
Chairman
Spriggs & Company, Inc.
1701 Lake Avenue
Glenview, IL 60025
Telephone: (708) 657-7181

Date of Birth: September 10,
    1929
Grew up in: Villa Grove, Illinois

HIGHER EDUCATION:
  University of Illinois
    B.S. degree, 1955
    J.D., 1957

MILITARY:
  Communications Technician, Third Class, United States Navy, 1951
  to 1954

EMPLOYMENT HISTORY:
  1967 to present: Spriggs & Company, Inc.
  1964 to 1967: Vice President, Johnson & Associates, Inc.
  1963 to 1964: Consultant, McKinsey & Company Inc.
  1959 to 1962: Director–Industrial Relations, Robertshaw Corporation
  1958 to 1959: Manager–Salaried Employment, Brunswick Corporation
  1957 to 1958: Labor Relations Staff Assistant, Caterpillar Tractor
  Company

PRIVATE CLUBS:
  Saddle & Cycle Club

ASSOCIATIONS/PROFESSIONAL SOCIETIES:
  International Association of Corporate and Professional Recruiters
  Illinois Management and Executive Search Consultants

REPRESENTATIVE AND SIGNIFICANT PLACEMENTS:
  James N. Vander Brug, President
    Superior Furniture Systems Manufacturing, Inc.

Bruce Gescheider, President
    Beatrice Meats
Robert Weisman, Vice President–Marketing
    Tropicana
Donald McCarthy, President
    Beatrice Canada
Mark de Naray, President
    Magic Pantry

WHAT I LOOK FOR IN GENERAL IN A CANDIDATE

If one assumes that all of the important requirements of a fit have been met, such as industry experience and knowledge, technical skills, and so on, there are a number of common factors which I look for in particular. One of the most important factors is energy. A truly high energy level is the fundamental building block of success. This high energy level must then be coupled with a real grasp of organization so that it is well channeled. The next step in the process is quality of results. If the results are as significantly greater in their impact as the energy and organization required to produce them have been, then you have the potential for geometric gains in progress for a client. The final piece in the puzzle is ego drive and pride. There must be an incredible need to surpass goals that others would not even dare to attempt. Only the real superstars put all of these elements together, but this is the standard by which I measure.

GEOGRAPHIC SCOPE OF RECRUITING ACTIVITIES:
Serve clients nationwide and in Canada, England, and South Africa

TOTAL YEARS OF RETAINER-TYPE RECRUITING EXPERIENCE:
27+ years

WILLIAM K. SUR
Director and Officer
Canny, Bowen Inc.
200 Park Avenue
New York, NY 10166
Telephone: (212) 949-6611

Date of Birth: April 6, 1932
Grew up in: Toledo, Ohio

Canny, Bowen Inc.

HIGHER EDUCATION:
Villanova University
B.S. degree, economics, 1954

MILITARY:
Lieutenant Junior Grade, United States Navy, 1954 to 1958

EMPLOYMENT HISTORY:
1991 to present: Canny, Bowen Inc.
1989 to 1991: President, Stricker, Sur & Associates
1982 to 1989: President, Sollis, Sur & Associates
1966 to 1982: Senior Vice President and Director, SpencerStuart
1961 to 1966: Senior Financial Analyst, Merck & Co., Inc.
1958 to 1961: Sales Representative, Olin Mathieson Chemical Corp.

PRIVATE CLUBS:
The University Club of New York
The Sky Club, New York
Echo Lake Country Club, Westfield, NJ

SPECIAL INTERESTS AND HOBBIES:
Skiing, shooting, antiquing, golf

REPRESENTATIVE AND SIGNIFICANT PLACEMENTS:
President and Chief Executive Officer
$3 billion public chemical company
Head of Marketing and Operations
$8 billion multinational consumer company

Executive Vice President
   $1 billion health care company
President and Chief Executive Officer
   Private subsidiary of multinational communications company
President and Chief Executive Officer
   Private high-technology device manufacturer

WHAT I LOOK FOR IN GENERAL IN A CANDIDATE

In evaluating a candidate, above all, we seek to determine his or her character, principally by the individual's actions in given situations, and secondarily by the views expressed in relation to the person's career successes and failures. Secondly, we are interested in knowing about the candidate's accomplishments, how they were achieved and under what circumstances, both positive and adverse. Thirdly, we seek specific and personal examples of creativity and innovativeness which directionally provide evidence of leadership and indications of managerial style. If these key factors can be ascertained, it is then relatively easy to evaluate other traits (motivations, aspirations, self-perceptions) and professional skills (business knowledge, industry knowledge, planning ability, profit orientation, etc.) in light of the client's environment and needs.

GEOGRAPHIC SCOPE OF RECRUITING ACTIVITIES:
   Serve clients nationwide and in Europe

TOTAL YEARS OF RETAINER-TYPE RECRUITING EXPERIENCE:
   25 years

CHARLES W. SWEET
President
A.T. Kearney Executive Search
222 S. Riverside Plaza
Chicago, IL 60606
Telephone: (312) 648-0111

Date of Birth: June 11, 1943
Grew up in: Chicago, Illinois

A.T. Kearney Executive Search

HIGHER EDUCATION:
Hamilton College
A.B. degree, English, 1965
University of Chicago
M.B.A. degree, 1968

MILITARY:
Officer Candidate, United States Marine Corps, 1966

EMPLOYMENT HISTORY:
1972 to present: A.T. Kearney, Inc.
1971 to 1972: Manager–Human Resources, Marlennan
1969 to 1971: Human Resources Coordinator, R.R. Donnelley
1968 to 1969: Human Resources, Ford Motor Company
1965 to 1967: Salesman, Procter & Gamble Co.

PRIVATE CLUBS:
Barrington Hills Country Club

ASSOCIATIONS/PROFESSIONAL SOCIETIES:
Association of Executive Search Consultants

SPECIAL INTERESTS AND HOBBIES:
Tennis, bridge, reading

REPRESENTATIVE AND SIGNIFICANT PLACEMENTS:
Thomas McKenna, Chief Operating Officer
Moorman Manufacturing Company
James Rainey, Chief Executive Officer
Farmland Industries

Lee Henry, President and Chief Operating Officer
  RTE
Phil Lindsay, General Secretary
  Rotary International
Richard Randazzo, Vice President–Human Resources
  Asea Brown Boveri

WHAT I LOOK FOR IN GENERAL IN A CANDIDATE

The importance of executive search has grown in direct proportion to industry's understanding of the impact that an outstanding individual can have upon an organization. My job is to understand the client and the client organization and to identify and help him/her recruit candidates who fall within the client's parameters. In each case I look for people with a proven record of accomplishment, leadership ability, intelligence, integrity, and communication skills. Two additional qualities must be explained in detail:

- It is critical to analyze how a candidate has dealt with failure. I believe that most people handle success well. Candidates who have gone to the right schools and progressed well in their careers without a hitch give no indication how they will handle the considerable stress imposed upon modern-day key executives. Outstanding people find ways to deal with setback, are resilient, and find ways to find solutions to problems when none is apparent.
- Interpersonal skills are key to the success of almost every job. I have found that if I use my personality as the barometer I can judge pretty accurately if the candidate will get along with the client.

GEOGRAPHIC SCOPE OF RECRUITING ACTIVITIES:
Serve clients nationwide and in Europe

TOTAL YEARS OF RETAINER-TYPE RECRUITING EXPERIENCE:
20 years

J. ROBERT SWIDLER
Managing Partner for Canada
Egon Zehnder International, Inc.
1 Place Ville Marie, Suite 3310
Montreal, Quebec H3B 3N2
Telephone: (514) 876-4249

Date of Birth: September 17,
**   1946**
Grew up in: Montreal

Egon Zehnder International

HIGHER EDUCATION:
McGill University
    Bachelor of Commerce degree, economics, 1968
Cornell University
    M.B.A. degree, finance, 1970

EMPLOYMENT HISTORY:
1989 to present: Egon Zehnder International, Inc.
1979 to 1989: President, J. Robert Swidler Inc.
1970 to 1979: Partner-in-Charge–Consulting, Touche Ross & Company

PRIVATE CLUBS:
University Club
Elm Ridge Country Club

ASSOCIATIONS/PROFESSIONAL SOCIETIES:
Institute of Management Consultants of Quebec
Canadian Club of Montreal, Board of Directors
Montreal General Hospital Foundation
Grand Ballets Canadiens

SPECIAL INTERESTS AND HOBBIES:
All sports, reading, nutrition, nature; above all, family

REPRESENTATIVE AND SIGNIFICANT PLACEMENTS:
John Oltman, Chairman and Chief Executive Officer
    SHL Systemhouse Inc.

Dominic Dallesandro, Executive Vice President–Finance
   Royal Bank of Canada
Alan Kelly, Executive Vice President–Finance and Development
   Bata International, Inc.
Stephen Larson, President–Pulp and Paper Group
   Domtar Inc.
Juergen Bartels, President
   Ramada Inns Inc.

WHAT I LOOK FOR IN GENERAL IN A CANDIDATE

I try to eliminate all of my personal reactions and find candidates who best suit the particular client problem—in other words I seek the right rather than the best candidate.

In general, I seek strong interpersonal and communications skills, high integrity, entrepreneurship, flexibility, and adaptability. Honesty and straightforwardness, rather than salesmanship, are what I value most. Finally, a high intelligence level, the ability to think strategically, and, increasingly, a global mindset.

GEOGRAPHIC SCOPE OF RECRUITING ACTIVITIES:
Serve clients in Canada, the United States, and Europe

TOTAL YEARS OF RETAINER-TYPE RECRUITING EXPERIENCE:
20 years

MAX ULRICH
Consultant
Ward Howell International, Inc.
99 Park Avenue, 20th Floor
New York, NY 10016
Telephone: (212) 697-3730

Date of Birth: March 21, 1925
Grew up in: St. Petersburg,
Florida

HIGHER EDUCATION:
U.S. Military Academy, West Point, New York
B.S. degree, general engineering, 1946
Massachusetts Institute of Technology
M.S. degree, civil engineering, 1951

MILITARY:
Captain, United States Army Corps of Engineers, 1946 to 1954

EMPLOYMENT HISTORY:
1971 to present: Ward Howell International, Inc.
1974 to 1988: Chairman and Chief Executive Officer
1971 to 1974: Principal and Director
1958 to 1971: Corporate Vice President, Consolidated Edison Company of NY
1954 to 1958: Assistant to Managing Director, Edison Electric Institute

PRIVATE CLUBS:
University Club
Sky Club
Rockland Country Club

ASSOCIATIONS/PROFESSIONAL SOCIETIES:
Sigma Xi Honorary Engineering Society

SPECIAL INTERESTS AND HOBBIES:
Golf, fishing, gardening, landscaping, reading

REPRESENTATIVE AND SIGNIFICANT PLACEMENTS:
Chairman and Chief Executive Officer
  $9 billion insurance company
President and Chief Executive Officer
  One of the nation's largest financial services companies
Chairman and Chief Executive Officer
  One of the nation's major energy companies
President and Chief Operating Officer designate
  Multibillion dollar major chemical company
President and Chief Executive Officer
  Major research and engineering company

WHAT I LOOK FOR IN GENERAL IN A CANDIDATE

In general, I look for those characteristics which are common to most successful executives. These would include such things as intelligence, education, articulateness, mental toughness, aggressiveness, initiative, appearance, personality, and self assurance, to name several.

There are, however, five things I consider of particular importance in the evaluation of a candidate:

1. Integrity—this is of prime significance. It can be sensed in interviews, but best determined by careful referencing. I seek people whose word is their bond.
2. Leadership—too often people confuse management with leadership. Leadership takes many forms, but to be a successful top executive requires one who is not only a good manager but also a good leader.
3. Business abilities—this is a quality that all too few executives have. Many are administrators and managers, but relatively few know how to run a business over the long term and make money.
4. Listener—the ability to listen is a key quality in an executive. One seldom learns anything while talking.
5. A failure in one's background. I personally am leery of an executive who has never experienced a failure or serious setback in his or her career. I look for people who have experienced and overcome adversity. It tells a lot about their moral fiber and helps predict their ability to handle tough problems.

GEOGRAPHIC SCOPE OF RECRUITING ACTIVITIES:
Serve clients nationwide and internationally through affiliates

TOTAL YEARS OF RETAINER-TYPE RECRUITING EXPERIENCE:
20 years

GAIL HAMITY VERGARA
Director of Health Care Practice
SpencerStuart
401 N. Michigan Avenue
Chicago, IL 60611
Telephone: (312) 822-0088

Date of Birth: January 6, 1948
Grew up in: Glencoe, Illinois

HIGHER EDUCATION:
   Pine Manor College
      A.A.S. degree, 1968
   University of Colorado
      B.A. degree, 1970
   University of Illinois
      Masters of Social Work, 1973

EMPLOYMENT HISTORY:
   1991 to present: SpencerStuart
   1980 to 1991: Executive Vice President, Witt Associates
   1973 to 1980: Coordinator–Outpatient Psychiatry, Mercy Hospital,
      Chicago

ASSOCIATIONS/PROFESSIONAL SOCIETIES:
   Association of Executive Search Consultants, Board Member
   American Hospital Association
   Nominee, American College of Healthcare Executives
   Catholic Hospital Association

SPECIAL INTERESTS AND HOBBIES:
   Volunteer with shelter for homeless women; horseback riding, tennis,
      jogging

REPRESENTATIVE AND SIGNIFICANT PLACEMENTS:
   Cliff Eldredge, Chief Executive Officer
      Pennsylvania Hospital
   Douglass Peters, Chief Executive Officer
      Mainline Health System, Radnor, Pennsylvania

Alan Brass, Chief Executive Officer
  Children's Hospital of St. Louis
Donald Pochly, M.D., Vice President–Medical Affairs
  Northwest Community Hospital, Illinois
Patrick Wardell, Administrator
  Montefiore Medical Center, Weiler Division, New York City

WHAT I LOOK FOR IN GENERAL IN A CANDIDATE

The healthcare field has gone through continuous turmoil and turnover in its executive ranks. My experience in working closely with hospital boards of trustees in their pursuit of new leaders has convinced me that superb communication skill is the most important quality to look for in candidates. Rarely does a hospital chief executive officer lose his or her position because of technical incompetence. Rather, in 90 percent of these instances, there has been a communication gap. Therefore, excellent verbal skills, the ability to develop quick rapport, charisma, listening skills, and good written communications are the key success skills. In addition, understanding and complying with the corporate culture, and the ability to have vision are also very important traits. To me, technical competence at the executive level should be a given. To be successful one must also be credible, as this quality helps ensure a feeling of trust from all the members of the organization.

GEOGRAPHIC SCOPE OF RECRUITING ACTIVITIES:
Serve clients nationwide

TOTAL YEARS OF RETAINER-TYPE RECRUITING EXPERIENCE:
11 years

JACK H. VERNON
Managing Director/Manager,
** Boston Office**
Russell Reynolds Associates,
** Inc.**
45 School Street
Boston, MA 02108
Telephone: (617) 523-1111

Date of Birth: February 25, 1930
Grew up in: Western New York
** State**

Bachrach

HIGHER EDUCATION:
  Amherst College
    B.A. degree, chemistry, 1952
  Massachusetts Institute of Technology
    M.S. degree, metallurgy and industrial management, 1954

MILITARY:
  Lieutenant, United States Navy, 1954 to 1957

EMPLOYMENT HISTORY:
  1981 to present: Russell Reynolds Associates
  1975 to 1981: Senior Vice President, Heidrick and Struggles, Inc.
  1971 to 1975: President, Scientific Energy Systems
  1962 to 1971: Executive Vice President, General Manager, Instron
    Corp.
  1958 to 1962: Associate, Arthur D. Little Inc.

PRIVATE CLUBS:
  The Country Club, Brookline, MA
  The Yale Club of New York

ASSOCIATIONS/PROFESSIONAL SOCIETIES:
  WGBH Boston Channel 2 Public TV, Overseer
  New England Conservatory, Overseer
  Trustees of Reservations, Advisory Committee

SPECIAL INTERESTS AND HOBBIES:
Athletics, the outdoors, travel, the arts

REPRESENTATIVE AND SIGNIFICANT PLACEMENTS:
Frank O'Keefe, President
  Armstrong Rubber
David Steadman, Chairman and Chief Executive Officer
  GCA Corp.
Robert Johnson, President and Chief Executive Officer
  Grady Hospital
David Levy, President and Chief Executive Officer
  Corcoran Gallery
Alice Ilchman, President
  Sarah Lawrence College

WHAT I LOOK FOR IN GENERAL IN A CANDIDATE

1. Commitment, effort, and integrity
2. Record of increasing responsibility, scope, complexity, and accomplishment
3. Results-oriented combined with concern for human values
4. Good with people
5. Energy, initiative, enthusiasm, positive attitude

GEOGRAPHIC SCOPE OF RECRUITING ACTIVITIES:
Serve clients nationally and internationally, primarily in Europe

TOTAL YEARS OF RETAINER-TYPE RECRUITING EXPERIENCE:
16 years

JUDITH M. VON SELDENECK
Chief Executive Officer
The Diversified Search Compa-
nies
2005 Market Street, Suite 3300
Philadelphia, PA 19103
Telephone: (215) 732-6666

Date of Birth: June 6, 1940
Grew up in: High Point, North
Carolina

The Diversified Search Companies

HIGHER EDUCATION:
St. Marys Junior College
Associate degree, 1960
University of North Carolina
B.A. degree, political science, 1962

EMPLOYMENT HISTORY:
1973 to present: Diversified Search, Inc. and Diversified Health
Search
1963 to 1972: Executive Assistant, Vice President Walter F. Mondale

PRIVATE CLUBS:
Union League of Philadelphia
Racquet Club of Philadelphia
Philadelphia Cricket Club
Sunneybrook Golf Club
Cape May Cottagers and Beach Club

ASSOCIATIONS/PROFESSIONAL SOCIETIES:
Association of Executive Search Consultants, Board Member
Philadelphia Finance Association,
Committee of 200 (Top businesswomen in United States)
National Association of Corporate and Professional Recruiters

SPECIAL INTERESTS AND HOBBIES:
Golf, fishing, reading

REPRESENTATIVE AND SIGNIFICANT PLACEMENTS:
Ralph H. Thurman, Executive Vice President–RPR and President–
RPR Pharmaceuticals
Rhone-Poulenc Rorer
Richard Greenawalt, President
Advanta Corporation
Dr. Brenden Riley, Chairman–Department of Medicine
St. Marys Hospital
David Sparks, Vice Chairman, Chief Financial Officer
Meridian Bancorp
Marion Butler, Senior Vice President–Sales and Marketing
Independence Blue Cross

WHAT I LOOK FOR IN GENERAL IN A CANDIDATE

Probably the most challenging component of the executive search process is the ability to clearly understand and assess the culture of client companies and match that with individuals who will meet expectations. The difficult aspect is to balance your own personal views of what that match should look like with an accurate understanding of the client's expectations. It is difficult to not have one's own prejudices influence these decisions, so, bearing that in mind, I would have to say I look for people who are very bright, well rounded, still interested in succeeding, and good communicators. I like to see people who have successfully dealt with problems, adversity, change, but at the same time have shown some staying power in their professional careers and not have switched jobs every two years. Youth and high energy levels are always attractive attributes, but only if they are balanced by maturity and seasoning and the acknowledgement that maybe you do not have all the answers and there is still more to be learned. In the final analysis, the client is not always right and a critical role of a good search consultant is the ability to help clients understand other perspectives. In the end, like it or not, we are all judged by how well the people we place in jobs perform.

GEOGRAPHIC SCOPE OF RECRUITING ACTIVITIES:
Serve clients nationwide

TOTAL YEARS OF RETAINER-TYPE RECRUITING EXPERIENCE:
11 years

FREDERICK W. WACKERLE
Partner
McFeely Wackerle Shulman
20 N. Wacker Drive
Chicago, IL 60606
Telephone: (312) 641-2977

Date of Birth: June 25, 1939
Grew up in: Chicago, Illinois

HIGHER EDUCATION:
Monmouth College, Illinois
B.A. degree, 1961

EMPLOYMENT HISTORY:
1970 to present: McFeely Wackerle Shulman
1968 to 1970: Vice President, R.M. Schmitz
1966 to 1968: Partner, Berry Henderson & Aberlin
1964 to 1966: Associate, A.T. Kearney Search
1962 to 1964: Assistant Personnel Director, Stewart Warner Corp.
1961 to 1962: Operations Manager, Ball Brothers Co.

PRIVATE CLUBS:
Bob O'Link Golf Club
Chicago Club
Tower Club

ASSOCIATIONS/PROFESSIONAL SOCIETIES:
Association of Executive Search Consultants, Director

SPECIAL INTERESTS AND HOBBIES:
Playing tuba in a Dixieland band, collecting modern art

REPRESENTATIVE AND SIGNIFICANT PLACEMENTS:
President, Chief Operating Officer, now Chief Executive Officer
Fortune 500 medical products manufacturer
President, Chief Operating Officer, now Chief Executive Officer
Fortune 75 conglomerate
Group Vice President
$2 billion aerospace and defense group

Executive Vice President
  NYSE publishing and entertainment company
President, Chief Executive Officer
  Start-up biopharmaceutical IPO

WHAT I LOOK FOR IN GENERAL IN A CANDIDATE

- Unquestioned integrity
- High work ethic
- Ability to handle failure
- Leadership/motivational skill
- High personal values
- Appropriate balance between business and family
- Ability to separate and prioritize
- High self-confidence
- Earnest and truthful
- Willingness to make a tough, or unpopular, decision

GEOGRAPHIC SCOPE OF RECRUITING ACTIVITIES:
  Serve clients in the United States only

TOTAL YEARS OF RETAINER-TYPE RECRUITING EXPERIENCE:
  28 years

J. ALVIN WAKEFIELD
Managing Director
Gilbert Tweed Associates
P.O. Box 1248
Pittsford, VT 05763
Telephone: (802) 483-9356

Date of Birth: July 25, 1938
Grew up in: Columbia, South
  Carolina

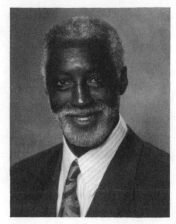

HIGHER EDUCATION:
  New York University
    B.A. degree, English literature, 1960

Gilbert Tweed Associates

MILITARY:
  Captain, United States Air Force, 1961 to 1966

EMPLOYMENT HISTORY:
  1986 to present: Gilbert Tweed Associates
  1984 to 1986: President, Wakefield Enterprises, Inc./Wil-Ern, Inc.
  1981 to 1983: Vice President/Partner, Korn/Ferry International
  1973 to 1981: Vice President Personnel Worldwide, Avon Products,
    Inc.
  1970 to 1972: Manager Recruiting, Singer Company
  1968 to 1970: Supervisor Employee Relations, Celanese Corporation
  1966 to 1968: Employee Relations Assistant, Mobil Oil Corporation

ASSOCIATIONS/PROFESSIONAL SOCIETIES:
  Direct Selling Association, Board of Directors
  New England Board of Higher Education, Board Member
  Direct Marketing Association, Board Member

SPECIAL INTERESTS AND HOBBIES:
  Alpine skiing, tennis, sports cars, classical flute

REPRESENTATIVE AND SIGNIFICANT PLACEMENTS:
  Robert Young, Chief Financial Officer
    Central Vermont Public Service Corporation
  Jack Plaxe, Chief Financial Officer
    Ambase Corporation (formerly City Investing/Home Insurance
    Corp.)
  Peter Von Eisenhart-Rothe, President, Managing Director, Germany
    National Safety Associates
  Charles Stanford, Assistant General Manager–Engineering and Con-
    struction
    Greater Cleveland Regional Transit Authority

)eth Montgomery, President
r..ghlights for Children, Inc.

WHAT I LOOK FOR IN GENERAL IN A CANDIDATE

The selection of the most appropriate executive leadership for an organization is the first, most important decision the enterprise will make—bar none.

The role of the executive recruiter, then, is that of a significant *partner* with the client in providing it with the best alternatives available from which to make this important selection decision. The most important criteria which I use in evaluating a candidate for my client are first, what are the specific candidate *skills* (not experience) required by the client in defining the position? Second, how do the candidate's skills compare with the specific requirements of the position? In other words what is the competence level of each skill when matched against the skill level of the responsibility?

Once skill level and experience have been ascertained, other skills such as how effective a leader is this person? What are her/his management skills and experience? How creative is the person? What is the level of that creativity when measured against the pragmatic aspects of the environment the person will be working in? How strategically does the person think? Is he/she a person of the moment or has the person an ability to stretch himself/herself and those around him? Just as important as each of the above in a management role is the concept of the team player.

Finally, is this a person of honesty and integrity? Do I believe him? Will my client? Should he be believed? And, then finally, assessing and summarizing all of the above, how does this person measure up against the perfect 10? Although a 10 may be difficult to find in every case, my goal is to come as close to a 10 as possible in considering each candidate. Having been myself a client for over 20 years, I know that my client expects no less.

GEOGRAPHIC SCOPE OF RECRUITING ACTIVITIES:

Serve clients nationwide and Europe and South America. Through partnership in International Executive Search Associates, handle client searches through offices in the UK, France, Spain, Germany, Switzerland, Belgium, Italy, and Sweden.

TOTAL YEARS OF RETAINER-TYPE RECRUITING EXPERIENCE:

8+ years

PUTNEY WESTERFIELD
Managing Director
Boyden International
275 Battery Street
San Francisco, CA 94111
Telephone: (415) 981-7900

Date of Birth: February 9, 1930
Grew up in: New Haven, Connecticut

HIGHER EDUCATION:
 Yale University
  B.A. degree, 1951

Arthur Krasinsky

EMPLOYMENT HISTORY:
 1976 to present: Boyden International
  1984 to 1990: Chief Executive Officer
 1973 to 1975: President, Chase World Information Corp., Chase-
  Manhattan
 1957 to 1973: Time Inc.
  1968 to 1973: Publisher, *Fortune*
  1966 to 1967: Assistant Publisher, *Life*
  1965 to 1967: Assistant Publisher, *Time*
  1960 to 1965: Circulation Director
 1953 to 1957: Political Officer, Department of State
 1951 to 1952: Manager–Southeast Asia, Swen Publications Inc.

PRIVATE CLUBS:
 Yale Club of NYC
 Pacific Union Club
 Bohemian Club
 Burlingame Country Club, San Francisco

ASSOCIATIONS/PROFESSIONAL SOCIETIES:
 East Meets West Foundation, Board of Directors
 U.S.-South Africa Leaders Exchange Program, Board of Directors

SPECIAL INTERESTS AND HOBBIES:
 Reading, international affairs, tennis, nature, piano

REPRESENTATIVE AND SIGNIFICANT PLACEMENTS:
 President
  Apparel company

President
  Cable television company
President and Chief Executive Officer
  Multinational conglomerate
President
  Multimedia company
Presidents
  Alaskan native corporations (4)

WHAT I LOOK FOR IN GENERAL IN A CANDIDATE

I make judgments about candidates in these five key areas:

1. Problem solving
   - Problem analysis—grasps the nature of a problem
   - Judgment—reaches appropriate conclusions
2. Communication
   - Dialogue skills—effectiveness of discussion and expression
   - Listening skills—attends to what others are saying
   - Presentation skills—expresses ideas effectively
   - Writing skills
3. Motivation
   - Initiative—self-starting behavior; readiness to be the first to start
   - Drive—sustained energy in accomplishing objectives
   - Reaction to pressure—effective under stress
   - Commitment to excellence—sees that tasks will be done well
4. Interpersonal
   - Leadership—directs behavior of others toward achievement of common goals by charisma, insights, or assertion of will
   - Sensitivity—considers the needs and feelings of others
   - Impact—creates positive impression of self-assurance
5. Administrative
   - Planning and organization—anticipates situations and problems
   - Delegation—assigns work and responsibility effectively

GEOGRAPHIC SCOPE OF RECRUITING ACTIVITIES:
Serve clients nationally and internationally

TOTAL YEARS OF RETAINER-TYPE RECRUITING EXPERIENCE:
15 years

WILLIAM R. WILKINSON
Partner
Wilkinson & Ives
601 California Street, Suite 502
San Francisco, CA 94108
Telephone: (415) 433-2155

Date of Birth: February 5, 1932
Grew up in: Upstate New York

HIGHER EDUCATION:
St. Lawrence University, New York
B.A. degree, sociology, 1953

MILITARY:
Sergeant, United States Army, 1953 to 1955

EMPLOYMENT HISTORY:
1984 to present: Wilkinson & Ives
1971 to 1984: President, William R. Wilkinson & Company, Inc.
1961 to 1971: Chief Executive Officer (Founder), Wilkinson, Sedwick
& Yelverton, Inc.
1956 to 1961: Vice President, McMurry, Hamstra & Company

PRIVATE CLUBS:
Orinda Country Club
World Trade Club
Lakeview Club

ASSOCIATIONS/PROFESSIONAL SOCIETIES:
California Executive Recruiters Association, Past President and Past
Director

SPECIAL INTERESTS AND HOBBIES:
Author, *Executive Musical Chairs*; four directorships with client companies; tennis, walking, bicycling, reading, family activities

REPRESENTATIVE AND SIGNIFICANT PLACEMENTS:
Patrick S. Johnston, President
Chef Francisco, Inc.
Gary M. Knight, President Warehouse Products Division,
Johanna Dairies, Inc.
Jacques A. Robinson, President and Chief Executive Officer
Cincinnati Microwave, Inc.
Jon O. Hooper, President and Chief Executive Officer
Array Technologies, Inc.

Robert Ivie, President and Chief Executive Officer
Guild Wineries

WHAT I LOOK FOR IN GENERAL IN A CANDIDATE

My interview style is to be relaxed and informal so as to encourage spontaneous and open response, and to be thorough enough to gain an understanding of the ingrained behavioral patterns that govern the candidate's personal and career performance. People don't change much throughout their lives, and careful probing and attentive listening will reveal their behavioral patterns readily.

In assessing a candidate's qualifications, I seek to learn of appropriate experience and accomplishment, leadership and management styles and skills, and other performance characteristics that are required for effective functioning in the position for which the candidate is being considered. For example, if the position is that of chief executive, then there must be present the ability to manage the unique contribution by the company's board of directors. At almost any level, it is critical that the candidate's thought processes be crisp, clear, and uncluttered. There must be a focus on issues, rather than problems, and, if strategic issues are important, the candidate must be able to set them in tune with the client company's pace, priorities, and capacities. The same might be said for the candidate's management style, vision of the possibilities, and conceptual capacities.

There must also be the health, energy, depth of intellect, and motivation to perform at a consistently high level. Verbal and written communications need to be acute. In these concerned times, ethical and behavioral values need to be above reproach, and judgment and decisiveness cannot be cluttered by hidden agendas. As a manager, and, often, as a leader, the candidate must have proven his worth in creating work cultures that are people-oriented and encourage and reward team play.

High character and personal integrity are always obligatory. A balanced lifestyle is desirable, and a history of personal, avocational, and career successes is compelling.

GEOGRAPHIC SCOPE OF RECRUITING ACTIVITIES:
Serve clients nationwide and in Canada and Europe

TOTAL YEARS OF RETAINER-TYPE RECRUITING EXPERIENCE:
34 years

WILLIAM H. WILLIS, JR.
President
William Willis Worldwide, Inc.
164 Mason Street
Greenwich, CT 06830
Telephone: (203) 661-4500

Date of Birth: December 19, 1927
Grew up in: Washington, DC;
  Miami Beach, Florida; and
  Greenwich, Connecticut

HIGHER EDUCATION:
  Yale University
    B.A. degree, sociology, 1949

MILITARY:
  Sergeant First Class, United States Army, 1950 to 1952

EMPLOYMENT HISTORY:
  1970 to present: William Willis Worldwide, Inc.
  1965 to 1970: Partner, Devine, Baldwin & Willis
  1962 to 1965: Manager, Food Processing Equipment Business, AMF
  1956 to 1962: Marketing Manager, Owens-Corning Fiberglas Corporation
  1953 to 1956: Assistant to Executive Vice President, Heidelberg Eastern, Inc.
  1952 to 1953: Expedition Leader, American Museum of Natural History
  1949 to 1950: Registered Representative, Gordon Graves & Co., Inc.

PRIVATE CLUBS:
  Yale Club of NYC
  Field Club of Greenwich

ASSOCIATIONS/PROFESSIONAL SOCIETIES:
  Association of Executive Search Consultants, Inc.
  Food and Drug Law Institute
  Institute of Food Technologists
  Connecticut Commission on Compensation of Elected State Officers
    and Judges, member

SPECIAL INTERESTS AND HOBBIES
Sailing, tennis, squash, travel

REPRESENTATIVE AND SIGNIFICANT PLACEMENTS:
John Burke, President and Chief Executive Officer
  Automation Industries, Inc. (acquired by Penn Central Corporation)
Daniel P. Davison, Chairman
  Christie's (Christie, Manson & Woods International, Inc.)
Kay K. Clarke, Vice President—Communications
  Connecticut General Life Insurance Company
Darrell G. Medcalf, Ph.D., Vice President—Basic Sciences
  Kraft General Foods Corporation
Jean-Claude Pineau, Directeur General (President)
  Burton-Corblin S.A.

WHAT I LOOK FOR IN GENERAL IN A CANDIDATE

In assessing a candidate, the number one requirement I seek is integrity. Then the critical judgment has to be "do this candidate's qualifications match the requirements of the position?" Key elements I look for include:

- Management and leadership skills
- A record of significant and relevant accomplishments
- Appropriate education
- Effective communication skills
- Technical qualifications and industry knowledge
- Sufficient drive
- A personal chemistry match with the hiring manager
- A fit between the candidate and the client's corporate culture

I see executive search consultants as true matchmakers.

GEOGRAPHIC SCOPE OF RECRUITING ACTIVITIES:
Serve clients nationally and in the UK, Europe, Australia, and Hong Kong

TOTAL YEARS OF RETAINER-TYPE RECRUITING EXPERIENCE:
25 years

THOMAS C. ZAY
President
Zay & Company, Inc.
Two Midtown Plaza, Suite 1740
1360 Peachtree Street, NE
Atlanta, GA 30309
Telephone: (404) 876-9986

Date of Birth: December 2, 1932
Grew up in: Indianapolis, Indiana

HIGHER EDUCATION:
Northwestern University
    B.S. degree, business administration/finance, 1954

MILITARY:
Captain/Naval Aviator, United States Marine Corps, 1954 to 1957

EMPLOYMENT HISTORY:
1982 to present: Zay & Company, Inc.
1968 to 1982: Executive Vice President, Paul R. Ray & Company, Inc.
1966 to 1968: Senior Vice President, Howard W. Voss, Associates
1962 to 1966: Associate, Booz, Allen & Hamilton
1960 to 1962: Manager–Sales Development, Wisconsin Gas Company
1957 to 1960: Territory Sales Manager, Shell Oil Company

PRIVATE CLUBS:
Capital City Club, Atlanta
Commerce Club, Atlanta
Metropolitan Club, New York

ASSOCIATIONS/PROFESSIONAL SOCIETIES:
International Association of Corporate and Professional Recruiters

REPRESENTATIVE AND SIGNIFICANT PLACEMENTS:
Sidney Kirschner, President and Chief Executive Officer
    National Service Industries, Inc.
Robert Gregory, President and Chief Operating Officer
    VF Corporation

William Van Sant, President and Chief Executive Officer
  Blount, Inc.
Ray Lewis, Senior Vice President–Worldwide Marketing
  Holiday Inns Worldwide/Bass P.L.C.

WHAT I LOOK FOR IN GENERAL IN A CANDIDATE

Genuine, open, and self-confident manner that says, "not only do I want you to know everything you need to about me, I want to find out if what I do well is what your client needs." I'm much more impressed with learning the occasions in someone's career when they encountered adversity or made mistakes, but recovered through a personal commitment to succeed and grow than I am by a litany of successive positive achievements that reflect no hard times. Above all, I hope to find an altogether too rare a characteristic—courage—the willingness to expose oneself to the risks involved in stepping into unknown and new territory and to the potential ridicule resulting from adherence to high standards, principles, and objectives.

GEOGRAPHIC SCOPE OF RECRUITING ACTIVITIES:
Serve clients nationwide and in Europe, Australia, and South America

TOTAL YEARS OF RETAINER-TYPE RECRUITING EXPERIENCE:
27 years

JANIS M. ZIVIC
President
The Zivic Group, Inc.
611 Washington Street,
   Suite 2505
San Francisco, CA 94111
Telephone: (415) 421-2325

Date of Birth: July 17, 1942
Grew up in: Mt. Lebanon, Pittsburgh, PA

HIGHER EDUCATION:
   California State College
      B.S. degree, 1964
   University of Pittsburgh
      M.A. degree, 1967

EMPLOYMENT HISTORY:
   1983 to present: The Zivic Group, Inc.
   1982 to 1983: Vice President and Managing Director, William H.
      Clark Associates
   1978 to 1982: Vice President and Partner, Heidrick and Struggles,
      Inc.
   1974 to 1978: Manager–Professional Recruitment, Castle & Cooke,
      Inc.
   1973 to 1974: Management Recruiter, Crown Zellerbach
   1967 to 1972: English Teacher, Upper St. Clair High School, Pitts-
      burgh
   1964 to 1966: English Teacher, Bay Village High School, Ohio

ASSOCIATIONS/PROFESSIONAL SOCIETIES:
   California Executive Recruiters Association, Past President
   International Association of Corporate and Professional Recruiters,
      Board Director
   Family Service Agency of San Francisco, Chair, Board Recruitment
   Options (for women over 40), Chair, Development

SPECIAL INTERESTS AND HOBBIES:
   Writing, reading, tennis

REPRESENTATIVE AND SIGNIFICANT PLACEMENTS:
Representative clients:
Four of five of California's largest and most prestigious medical centers
One of the two leading U.S. biotechnology firms
The largest Health Maintenance Organization in the U.S.
One of the top five private universities in the U.S.
One of the world's largest and oldest environmental organizations

WHAT I LOOK FOR IN GENERAL IN A CANDIDATE

In a personal interview, I try to identify and evaluate the following, in this order:

- A personal style which complements the individual client
- A management style which supports the mission and culture of the client organization
- Personal and professional integrity
- Technological/functional expertise

These criteria are neither unique nor predictable. That the client and candidate must "speak the same language" is common sense, which is fundamental to our business. If the client is impatient, demanding, decisive, expects subordinates to think quickly and act immediately, he or she is unlikely to hire an executive who acts or works differently *unless* (a critical point) the client needs someone to complement his/her style. It is the responsibility of the search consultant to understand and acknowledge this when presenting candidates to the client. The search process is consultative, not transactional.

Sometimes the client is an anomaly within the larger organization and the search consultant must determine whether to match the candidate to the client or the client's organization. The effective decision can only be reached when the client, the consultant, and the candidate recognize and acknowledge this issue. The search consultant must know the organization as well as the client in order to be competent.

GEOGRAPHIC SCOPE OF RECRUITING ACTIVITIES:
Serve clients nationwide and in Europe and Australia

TOTAL YEARS OF RETAINER-TYPE RECRUITING EXPERIENCE:
13 years

6

AREAS OF RECRUITER SPECIALIZATION

This chapter categorizes and ranks all recruiters qualifying for this book according to their *functional* competencies and areas of *organizational or industry* specialization. A recruiter's standing in each category is a function of the number of nominating points from both clients and peers, as well as his or her own individual ranking of organizational and functional skills.

FUNCTIONAL SPECIALIZATION

Categories

General management	Administration
Advertising/promotion	Direct marketing
Director recruitment	Engineering
Finance and accounting	Human resources/personnel
International	Legal
Manufacturing/production/operations	Marketing/sales—consumer
Marketing/sales—industrial	Merchandising
MIS/computer operations	Planning
Public relations/government affairs	Purchasing/materials
Research and development	Women, handicapped, minorities

Those recruiters who work essentially only in specific organizational or industry specializations are identified by the following symbols:

(HE) Health care

(HO) Hospitality

(LE) Legal

(ED) Educational and related fields

GENERAL MANAGEMENT

1. **Gerard R. Roche,** Heidrick & Struggles, Inc., New York
2. **Thomas J. Neff,** SpencerStuart, New York
3. **Frederick W. Wackerle,** McFeely Wackerle Shulman, Chicago
4. **Leon A. Farley,** Leon A. Farley Associates, San Francisco
5. **Robert W. Dingman,** Robert W. Dingman Co., Inc., Westlake Village, CA
6. **William E. Gould,** Gould & McCoy, New York
7. **Windle B. Priem,** Korn/Ferry International, New York
8. **Peter G. Grimm,** Nordeman Grimm, Inc., New York
9. **Roger M. Kenny,** Kenny, Kindler, Hunt & Howe, New York
10. **John F. Johnson,** Lamalie Associates, Cleveland
11. **Jay Gaines,** Jay Gaines & Company, New York
12. **Richard K. Ives,** Wilkinson & Ives, San Francisco
13. **John S. Lloyd,** Witt Associates, Oak Brook, IL (HE)
14. **John P. DiVenuto,** Deven Associates International, Verona, NJ
15. **John Lucht,** The John Lucht Consultancy, New York
16. **E. Pendleton James,** Pendleton James & Associates, New York
17. **Judith M. VonSeldeneck,** The Diversified Search Companies, Philadelphia
18. **Thomas C. Zay,** Zay & Company, Atlanta
19. **Ferdinand Nadherny,** Russell Reynolds Associates, Chicago
20. **Paul R. Ray, Sr.,** Paul Ray & Carré Orban International, Fort Worth

Donald T. Allerton, Allerton, Heneghan & O'Neill, Chicago
Otis H. Bowden II, Bowden & Company, Inc., Cleveland
William J. Bowen, Heidrick & Struggles, Inc., Chicago
Lynn Tendler Bignell, Gilbert Tweed Associates, Inc., New York
Robert M. Bryza, Robert Lowell International, Dallas
John H. Callen, Jr., Ward Howell International, New York
Jack R. Clarey, Jack Clarey Associates, Inc., Northbrook, IL
William B. Clemens, Jr., Norman Broadbent International, New York
W. Michael Danforth, Hyde Danforth & Company, Dallas
Richard M. Ferry, Korn/Ferry International, Los Angeles
Dulany Foster, Jr., Korn/Ferry International, Stamford, CT
Ronald G. Goerss, Smith, Goerss & Ferneborg, Inc., San Francisco
A.D. Hart, Jr., Russell Reynolds Associates, New York
Gardner W. Heidrick, The Heidrick Partners, Inc., Chicago
Robert L. Heidrick, The Heidrick Partners, Inc., Chicago
William G. Hetzel, William Hetzel Associates, Inc., Schaumburg, IL
James Heuerman, Korn/Ferry International, San Francisco (HE)
David Hoffmann, DHR International, Chicago
D. John Ingram, Ingram, Inc., New York
Mike Jacobs, Thorne, Brieger Associates, Inc., New York
Theodore N. Jadick, Heidrick & Struggles, Inc., New York
Carol S. Jeffers, John Sibbald Associates, Inc., Chicago (HO)
David S. Joys, Higdon, Joys & Mingle, New York
Kai Lindholst, Egon Zehnder International, Chicago
James Masciarelli, Fenwick Partners, Lexington, MA
Jonathan E. McBride, McBride Associates, Inc., Washington, DC
Millington F. McCoy, Gould & McCoy, Inc., New York
Clarence E. McFeely, McFeely Wackerle Shulman, Chicago
Carl W. Menk, Canny, Bowen Inc., New York
Herbert Mines, Herbert Mines Associates, Inc., New York

Dayton Ogden, SpencerStuart, Stamford, CT
George W. Ott, Ott & Hansen, Inc., Pasadena, CA
Paul R. Ray, Jr., Paul Ray & Carré Orban International, Fort Worth
Russell S. Reynolds, Jr., Russell Reynolds Associates, New York
Steven A. Seiden, Seiden Associates, New York
Robert Slater, Slater & Associates, Dallas
Robert D. Spriggs, Spriggs & Company Inc., Glenview, IL
J. Alvin Wakefield, Gilbert Tweed Associates, Inc., Pittsford, VT
William R. Wilkinson, Wilkinson & Ives, San Franciso
William H. Willis, Jr., William Willis Worldwide, Inc., Greenwich, CT

ADMINISTRATION

1. **John S. Lloyd,** Witt Associates, Oak Brook, IL (HE)
2. **Michael Kieffer,** Kieffer, Ford & Hadelman, Oak Brook, IL (HE)
3. **Windle B. Priem,** Korn/Ferry International, New York
4. **Ira W. Krinsky,** Ira W. Krinsky & Associates, Pasadena, CA (ED)
5. **Judith M. VonSeldeneck,** The Diversified Search Companies, Philadelphia
6. **Robert W. Dingman,** Robert W. Dingman Co., Inc., Westlake Village, CA
7. **Gary J. Posner,** George Kaludis Associates, Nashville (ED)
8. **Jack R. Clarey,** Jack Clarey Associates, Inc., Northbrook, IL
9. **Jeffrey G. Bell,** Norman Broadbent International, New York
10. **W. Michael Danforth,** Hyde Danforth & Company, Dallas

Michael Boxberger, Korn/Ferry International, Chicago
W. Hoyt Colton, W. Hoyt Colton Associates Inc., New York
Frank A. Garofolo, Garofolo, Curtiss, Lambert & MacLean, Ardmore, PA
Ronald G. Goerss, Smith, Goerss & Ferneborg, Inc., San Francisco
Peter G. Grimm, Nordeman Grimm, Inc., New York
James Heuerman, Korn/Ferry International, San Francisco (HE)
David Hoffmann, DHR International, Chicago
John F. Johnson, Lamalie Associates, Cleveland
David S. Joys, Higdon, Joys & Mingle, New York
Claudia Lacy Kelly, Norman Broadbent International, New York
David Kettwig, A.T. Kearney, Chicago
Jonathan E. McBride, McBride Associates, Inc., Washington, DC
Neal L. Maslan, Ward Howell International, Encino, CA
Charles M. Meng, Meng, Finseth & Associates, Torrance, CA
George W. Ott, Ott & Hansen Inc., Pasadena, CA
Frank Rico, Jr., J.R. Akin & Company, Fairfield, CT
Steven A. Seiden, Seiden Associates, New York
Fred Siegel, Conex, Inc., New York
Robert L. Smith, Robert L. Smith & Company, New York
Janis M. Zivic, The Zivic Group, Inc., San Francisco

ADVERTISING/PROMOTION

1. **William G. Hetzel,** William Hetzel Associates, Inc., Schaumburg, IL
2. **Thomas C. Zay,** Zay & Company, Atlanta
3. **Gary Kreutz,** Kreutz Consulting, Lake Forest, IL
4. **James J. Drury III,** SpencerStuart, Chicago
5. **Thomas H. Ogdon,** The Ogdon Partnership, New York
6. **Brenda L. Ruello,** Heidrick & Struggles, Inc., New York

7. **Louis A. Hoyda,** Thorndike Deland Associates, New York
8. **David E. Chambers,** David Chambers & Associates, Inc., New York

DIRECT MARKETING

1. **J. Alvin Wakefield,** Gilbert Tweed Associates, Inc., Pittsford, VT
2. **Brenda L. Ruello,** Heidrick & Struggles, Inc., New York
3. **Louis A. Hoyda,** Thorndike Deland Associates, New York
4. **Herbert Mines,** Herbert Mines Associates, Inc., New York
5. **Michael J. Hoevel,** Poirier, Hoevel & Company, Los Angeles
6. **Richard Sbarbaro,** Lauer, Sbarbaro Associates, Chicago
7. **Putney Westerfield,** Boyden International, San Francisco
8. **William K. Sur,** Canny, Bowen Inc., New York
9. **Gail Hamity Vergara,** SpencerStuart, Chicago (HE)
10. **Thomas H. Ogdon,** The Ogdon Partnership, New York

DIRECTOR RECRUITMENT

1. **Gerard R. Roche,** Heidrick & Struggles, Inc., New York
2. **Thomas J. Neff,** SpencerStuart, New York
3. **Roger M. Kenny,** Kenny, Kindler, Hunt & Howe, New York
4. **Gardner W. Heidrick,** The Heidrick Partners, Inc., Chicago
5. **Richard M. Ferry,** Korn/Ferry International, Los Angeles
6. **Frederick W. Wackerle,** McFeely Wackerle Shulman, Chicago
7. **John Lucht,** The John Lucht Consultancy, New York
8. **Dayton Ogden,** SpencerStuart, Stamford, CT
9. **Russell S. Reynolds, Jr.,** Russell Reynolds Associates, New York
10. **Martin H. Bauman,** Martin Bauman Associates, Inc., New York

Michael Boxberger, Korn/Ferry International, Chicago
W. Hoyt Colton, W. Hoyt Colton Associates Inc., New York
David M. DeWilde, Chartwell Partners, San Francisco
Leon A. Farley, Leon A. Farley Associates, San Francisco
Robert L. Heidrick, The Heidrick Partners, Inc., Chicago
Durant A. Hunter, Gardiner Stone Hunter International, Boston
D. John Ingram, Ingram, Inc., New York
Theodore N. Jadick, Heidrick & Struggles, Inc., New York
John F. Johnson, Lamalie Associates, Cleveland
David S. Joys, Higdon, Joys & Mingle, New York
Richard Kinser, Kinser & Company, New York
Charles M. Meng, Meng, Finseth & Associates, Torrance, CA
Carl W. Menk, Canny, Bowen Inc., New York
Thomas H. Ogdon, The Ogdon Partnership, New York
David R. Peasback, Canny, Bowen Inc., New York
Frank Rico, Jr., J.R. Akin & Company, Fairfield, CT
Andrew Sherwood, Goodrich & Sherwood Company, New York
Robert Slater, Slater & Associates, Dallas
Max M. Ulrich, Ward Howell International, New York
Judith M. VonSeldeneck, The Diversified Search Companies, Philadelphia

ENGINEERING

1. **Norman C. Roberts,** Norman Roberts & Associates, Inc., Los Angeles
2. **R. Paul Kors,** Kors Montgomery International, Houston

3. **James Masciarelli,** Fenwick Partners, Lexington, MA
4. **Otis H. Bowden II,** Bowden & Company, Inc., Cleveland
5. **Theodore E. Lusk,** Nadzam, Lusk & Associates, Santa Clara, CA
6. **George W. Henn, Jr.,** G.W. Henn & Company, Columbus, OH
7. **Janis M. Zivic,** The Zivic Group, Inc., San Francisco
8. **Richard J. Cronin,** Hodge-Cronin & Associates, Inc., Rosemont, IL
9. **Leon A. Farley,** Leon A. Farley Associates, San Francisco
10. **William C. Houze,** William C. Houze & Co., La Quinta, CA

O. William Battalia, Battalia, Winston International, New York
Lynn Tendler Bignell, Gilbert Tweed Associates, Inc., New York
Robert M. Callan, Callan & Associates, Oak Brook, IL
Peter Crist, Russell Reynolds Associates, Chicago
Robert W. Dingman, Robert W. Dingman Co., Inc., Westlake Village, CA
John P. DiVenuto, Deven Associates International, Verona, NJ
Richard K. Ives, Wilkinson & Ives, San Francisco
Mike Jacobs, Thorne, Brieger Associates, Inc., New York
William H. Marumoto, The Interface Group, Ltd., Washington, DC
Richard M. McFarland, Brissenden, McFarland, Wagoner & Fuccella, Inc., Stamford, CT
David R. Peasback, Canny, Bowen Inc., New York
David Powell, David Powell, Inc., Woodside, CA
John H. Robison, Robison & McAulay, Charlotte, NC
Richard Sbarbaro, Lauer, Sbarbaro Associates, Chicago
Daniel M. Shepherd, Shepherd, Bueschel & Provus, Inc., Chicago
Mary E. Shourds, Houze, Shourds & Montgomery Inc., Long Beach, CA
Richard C. Slayton, Slayton International Inc., Chicago
Robert D. Spriggs, Spriggs & Company Inc., Glenview, IL
Max M. Ulrich, Ward Howell International, New York
William R. Wilkinson, Wilkinson & Ives, San Francisco

FINANCE AND ACCOUNTING

1. **Thomas J. Neff,** SpencerStuart, New York
2. **Leon A. Farley,** Leon A. Farley Associates, San Francisco
3. **Windle B. Priem,** Korn/Ferry International, New York
4. **Frederick W. Wackerle,** McFeely Wackerle Shulman, Chicago
5. **Robert W. Dingman,** Robert W. Dingman Co., Inc., Westlake Village, CA
6. **Jay Gaines,** Jay Gaines & Company, New York
7. **E. Pendleton James,** Pendleton James & Associates, New York
8. **Paul R. Ray, Sr.,** Paul Ray & Carré Orban International, Fort Worth
9. **Jack R. Clarey,** Jack Clarey Associates, Inc., Northbrook, IL
10. **Richard K. Ives,** Wilkinson & Ives, San Francisco

Jeffrey G. Bell, Norman Broadbent International, New York
William B. Clemens, Jr., Norman Broadbent International, New York
Richard J. Cronin, Hodge-Cronin & Associates, Inc., Rosemont, IL
W. Michael Danforth, Hyde Danforth & Company, Dallas
John P. DiVenuto, Deven Associates International, Verona, NJ
Peter G. Grimm, Nordeman Grimm, Inc., New York
A.D. Hart, Jr., Russell Reynolds Associates, New York
David Hoffmann, DHR International, Chicago

John F. Johnson, Lamalie Associates, Cleveland
Roger M. Kenny, Kenny, Kindler, Hunt & Howe, New York
John Lucht, The John Lucht Consultancy, New York
Jonathan E. McBride, McBride Associates, Inc., Washington, DC
Clarence E. McFeely, McFeely Wackerle Shulman, Chicago
Dayton Ogden, SpencerStuart, Stamford, CT
Russell S. Reynolds, Jr., Russell Reynolds Associates, New York
Robert Slater, Slater & Associates, Dallas
Robert D. Spriggs, Spriggs & Company Inc., Glenview, IL
Judith M. VonSeldeneck, The Diversified Search Companies, Philadelphia
William R. Wilkinson, Wilkinson & Ives, San Francisco
Thomas C. Zay, Zay & Company, Atlanta

HUMAN RESOURCES/PERSONNEL

1. John F. Johnson, Lamalie Associates, Cleveland
2. Barbara L. Provus, Shepherd, Bueschel & Provus, Inc., Chicago
3. Windle B. Priem, Korn/Ferry International, New York
4. William E. Gould, Gould & McCoy, Inc., New York
5. Peter G. Grimm, Nordeman Grimm, Inc., New York
6. Richard K. Ives, Wilkinson & Ives, San Francisco
7. Thomas C. Zay, Zay & Company, Atlanta
8. Leon A. Farley, Leon A. Farley Associates, San Francisco
9. Martin H. Bauman, Martin Bauman Associates, Inc., New York
10. Millington F. McCoy, Gould & McCoy, Inc., New York

Donald T. Allerton, Allerton, Heneghan & O'Neill, Chicago
O. William Battalia, Battalia, Winston International, New York
Jack R. Clarey, Jack Clarey Associates, Inc., Northbrook, IL
Robert W. Dingman, Robert W. Dingman Co., Inc., Westlake Village, CA
A.D. Hart, Jr., Russell Reynolds Associates, New York
James Heuerman, Korn/Ferry International, San Francisco (HE)
D. John Ingram, Ingram, Inc., New York
E. Pendleton James, Pendleton James & Associates, New York
Roger M. Kenny, Kenny, Kindler, Hunt & Howe, New York
Michael Kieffer, Kieffer, Ford & Hadelman, Oak Brook, IL (HE)
John S. Lloyd, Witt Associates, Oak Brook, IL (HE)
John Lucht, The John Lucht Consultancy, New York
Jonathan E. McBride, McBride Associates, Inc., Washington, DC
Carl W. Menk, Canny, Bowen Inc., New York
Ferdinand Nadherny, Russell Reynolds Associates, New York
Gary J. Posner, George Kaludis Associates, Nashville (ED)
Frank Rico, Jr., J.R. Akin & Company, Fairfield, CT
Mary E. Shourds, Houze, Shourds & Montgomery Inc., Long Beach, CA
Robert Slater, Slater & Associates, Dallas
William R. Wilkinson, Wilkinson & Ives, San Francisco

INTERNATIONAL

1. William E. Gould, Gould & McCoy, Inc., New York
2. Roger M. Kenny, Kenny, Kindler, Hunt & Howe, New York
3. Gerard R. Roche, Heidrick & Struggles, Inc., New York

4. **Fred Siegel,** Conex, Inc., New York
5. **R. Paul Kors,** Kors Montgomery International, Houston
6. **Russell S. Reynolds, Jr.,** Russell Reynolds Associates, New York
7. **Durant A. Hunter,** Gardiner Stone Hunter International, Boston
8. **Jeffrey G. Bell,** Norman Broadbent International, New York
9. **Dayton Ogden,** SpencerStuart, Stamford, CT
10. **Windle B. Priem,** Korn/Ferry International, New York

Lynn Tendler Bignell, Gilbert Tweed Associates, Inc., New York
John H. Callen, Jr., Ward Howell International, New York
William B. Clemens, Jr., Norman Broadbent International, New York
Richard J. Cronin, Hodge-Cronin & Associates, Inc., Rosemont, IL
Ralph Dieckmann, Dieckmann & Associates, Chicago
Leon A. Farley, Leon A. Farley Associates, San Francisco
Dulany Foster, Jr., Korn/Ferry International, Stamford, CT
A.D. Hart, Jr., Russell Reynolds Associates, New York
David Hoffmann, DHR International, Chicago
Richard K. Ives, Wilkinson & Ives, San Francisco
David S. Joys, Higdon, Joys & Mingle, New York
Kai Lindholst, Egon Zehnder International, Chicago
Laurence R. Massé, Ward Howell International, Barrington, IL
Millington F. McCoy, Gould & McCoy, Inc., New York
Ferdinand Nadherny, Russell Reynolds Associates, Chicago
Larry Nein, Nordeman Grimm, Inc., Chicago
Frank Rico, Jr., J.R. Akin & Company, Fairfield, CT
Brenda L. Ruello, Heidrick & Struggles, Inc., New York
Charles W. Sweet, A.T. Kearney, Chicago
William H. Willis, Jr., William Willis Worldwide, Inc., Greenwich, CT

LEGAL

1. **W. Michael Danforth,** Hyde Danforth & Company, Dallas
2. **Bert H. Early,** Bert H. Early Associates Inc., Chicago (LE)
3. **David R. Peasback,** Canny, Bowen Inc., New York
4. **W. Jerry Hyde,** Hyde Danforth & Company, Dallas
5. **Leon A. Farley,** Leon A. Farley Associates, San Francisco
6. **E. Pendleton James,** Pendleton James & Associates, New York
7. **Barbara L. Provus,** Shepherd, Bueschel & Provus, Inc., Chicago
8. **Gary Kreutz,** Kreutz Consulting, Lake Forest, IL
9. **Jeffrey G. Bell,** Norman Broadbent International, New York
10. **Fred Siegel,** Conex, Inc., New York

Otis H. Bowden II, Bowden & Company, Inc., Cleveland
Jack R. Clarey, Jack Clarey Associates, Inc., Northbrook, IL
W. Hoyt Colton, W. Hoyt Colton Associates Inc., New York
David M. DeWilde, Chartwell Partners, San Francisco
Robert W. Dingman, Robert W. Dingman Co., Inc., Westlake Village, CA
Ronald G. Goerss, Smith, Goerss & Ferneborg, Inc., San Francisco
A.D. Hart, Jr., Russell Reynolds Associates, New York
Henry G. Higdon, Higdon, Joys & Mingle, New York
Durant A. Hunter, Gardiner Stone Hunter International, Boston
David S. Joys, Higdon, Joys & Mingle, New York

Richard Kinser, Kinser & Associates, New York
William H. Marumoto, The Interface Group, Ltd., Washington, DC
Jonathan E. McBride, McBride Associates, Inc., Washington, DC
Millington F. McCoy, Gould & McCoy, Inc., New York
Paul R. Ray, Jr., Paul Ray & Carré Orban International, Fort Worth
Norman C. Roberts, Norman Roberts & Associates, Inc., Los Angeles
John H. Robison, Robison & McAulay, Charlotte, NC
Mary E. Shourds, Houze, Shourds & Montgomery Inc., Long Beach, CA
Max M. Ulrich, Ward Howell International, New York
William R. Wilkinson, Wilkinson & Ives, San Francisco

MANUFACTURING/PRODUCTION/OPERATIONS

1. **Leon A. Farley,** Leon A. Farley Associates, San Francisco
2. **Richard J. Cronin,** Hodge-Cronin & Associates, Inc., Rosemont, IL
3. **Mike Jacobs,** Thorne, Brieger Associates, Inc., New York
4. **William R. Wilkinson,** Wilkinson & Ives, San Francisco
5. **John P. DiVenuto,** Deven Associates International, Verona, NJ
6. **David Hoffmann,** DHR International, Chicago
7. **Robert D. Spriggs,** Spriggs & Company Inc., Glenview, IL
8. **Russell S. Reynolds, Jr.,** Russell Reynolds Associates, New York
9. **Frank Rico, Jr.,** J.R. Akin & Company, Fairfield, CT
10. **Clarence E. McFeely,** McFeely Wackerle Shulman, Chicago

Robert M. Bryza, Robert Lowell International, Dallas
John H. Callen, Jr., Ward Howell International, New York
Jack R. Clarey, Jack Clarey Associates, Inc., Northbrook, IL
W. Michael Danforth, Hyde Danforth & Company, Dallas
Robert W. Dingman, Robert W. Dingman Co., Inc., Westlake Village, CA
William E. Gould, Gould & McCoy, Inc., New York
Robert L. Heidrick, The Heidrick Partners, Inc., Chicago
George W. Henn, Jr., G.W. Henn & Company, Columbus, OH
William C. Houze, William C. Houze & Co., La Quinta, CA
Richard K. Ives, Wilkinson & Ives, San Francisco
John F. Johnson, Lamalie Associates, Cleveland
Theodore E. Lusk, Nadzam, Lusk & Associates, Santa Clara, CA
James Masciarelli, Fenwick Partners, Lexington, MA
Herbert Mines, Herbert Mines Associates, Inc., New York
P. John Mirtz, Mirtz Morice Inc., Stamford, CT
George W. Ott, Ott & Hansen Inc., Pasadena, CA
Daniel M. Shepherd, Shepherd, Bueschel & Provus, Inc., Chicago
Mary E. Shourds, Houze, Shourds & Montgomery Inc., Long Beach, CA
Judith M. VonSeldeneck, The Diversified Search Companies, Philadelphia
Thomas C. Zay, Zay & Company, Atlanta

MARKETING/SALES—CONSUMER

1. **Thomas J. Neff,** SpencerStuart, New York
2. **Roger M. Kenny,** Kenny, Kindler, Hunt & Howe, New York
3. **Leon A. Farley,** Leon A. Farley Associates, San Francisco
4. **Robert W. Dingman,** Robert W. Dingman Co., Inc., Westlake Village, CA
5. **William E. Gould,** Gould & McCoy, Inc., New York

6.   **Windle B. Priem,** Korn/Ferry International, New York
7.   **John P. DiVenuto,** Deven Associates International, Verona, NJ
8.   **William R. Wilkinson,** Wilkinson & Ives, San Francisco
9.   **Clarence E. McFeely,** McFeely Wackerle Shulman, Chicago
10.   **Thomas C. Zay,** Zay & Company, Atlanta

John H. Callen, Jr., Ward Howell International, New York
Peter G. Grimm, Nordeman Grimm, Inc., New York
A.D. Hart, Jr., Russell Reynolds Associates, New York
Robert L. Heidrick, The Heidrick Partners, Inc., Chicago
William G. Hetzel, William Hetzel Associates, Inc., Schaumburg, IL
David Hoffmann, DHR International, Chicago
D. John Ingram, Ingram, Inc., New York
Mike Jacobs, Thorne, Brieger Associates, Inc., New York
David S. Joys, Higdon, Joys & Mingle, New York
John Lucht, The John Lucht Consultancy, New York
Jonathan E. McBride, McBride Associates, Inc., Washington, DC
Millington F. McCoy, Gould & McCoy, Inc., New York
Carl W. Menk, Canny, Bowen Inc., New York
Herbert Mines, Herbert Mines Associates, Inc., New York
Barbara L. Provus, Shepherd, Bueschel & Provus, Inc., Chicago
Paul R. Ray, Sr., Paul Ray & Carré Orban International, Ft. Worth
Frank Rico, Jr., J.R. Akin & Company, Fairfield, CT
Robert D. Spriggs, Spriggs & Company Inc., Glenview, IL
J. Alvin Wakefield, Gilbert Tweed Associates, Inc., Pittsford, VT
William H. Willis, Jr., William Willis Worldwide, Inc., Greenwich, CT

MARKETING/SALES—INDUSTRIAL

1.   **Leon A. Farley,** Leon A. Farley Associates, San Francisco
2.   **Clarence E. McFeely,** McFeely Wackerle Shulman, Chicago
3.   **J. Gerald Simmons,** Handy Associates, New York
4.   **Robert W. Dingman,** Robert W. Dingman Co., Inc., Westlake Village, CA
5.   **Roger M. Kenny,** Kenny, Kindler, Hunt & Howe, New York
6.   **John P. DiVenuto,** Deven Associates International, Verona, NJ
7.   **William R. Wilkinson,** Wilkinson & Ives, San Francisco
8.   **D. John Ingram,** Ingram, Inc., New York
9.   **Barbara L. Provus,** Shepherd, Bueschel & Provus, Inc., Chicago
10.   **Robert L. Heidrick,** The Heidrick Partners, Inc., Chicago

Robert M. Bryza, Robert Lowell International, Dallas
John H. Callen, Jr., Ward Howell International, New York
Richard J. Cronin, Hodge-Cronin & Associates, Inc., Rosemont, IL
William E. Gould, Gould & McCoy, Inc., New York
Peter G. Grimm, Nordeman Grimm, Inc., New York
A.D. Hart, Jr., Russell Reynolds Associates, New York
William G. Hetzel, William Hetzel Associates, Inc., Schaumburg, IL
David Hoffmann, DHR International, Chicago
William C. Houze, William C. Houze & Co., La Quinta, CA
Durant A. Hunter, Gardiner Stone Hunter International, Boston
Richard K. Ives, Wilkinson & Ives, San Francisco

Mike Jacobs, Thorne, Brieger Associates, Inc., New York
David S. Joys, Higdon, Joys & Mingle, New York
Gary Kreutz, Kreutz Consulting, Lake Forest, IL
Kai Lindholst, Egon Zehnder International, Chicago
Jonathan E. McBride, McBride Associates, Inc., Washington, DC
Millington F. McCoy, Gould & McCoy, Inc., New York
Richard Sbarbaro, Lauer, Sbarbaro Associates, Chicago
Robert Slater, Slater & Associates, Dallas
Robert D. Spriggs, Spriggs & Company Inc., Glenview, IL

MERCHANDISING

1. **Herbert Mines,** Herbert Mines Associates, Inc., New York
2. **Jack Seitchik,** Seitchik, Corwin & Seitchik, San Francisco
3. **Brenda L. Ruello,** Heidrick & Struggles, Inc., New York
4. **John H. Callen, Jr.,** Ward Howell International, New York
5. **Barbara L. Provus,** Shepherd, Bueschel & Provus, Inc., Chicago
6. **Henry G. Higdon,** Higdon, Joys & Mingle, New York
7. **J. Alvin Wakefield,** Gilbert Tweed Associates, Inc., Pittsford, VT
8. **Thomas C. Zay,** Zay & Company, Atlanta
9. **Mike Jacobs,** Thorne, Brieger Associates, Inc., New York
10. **George W. Ott,** Ott & Hansen Inc., Pasadena, CA

MIS/COMPUTER OPERATIONS

1. **Jay Gaines,** Jay Gaines & Company, New York
2. **Mary E. Shourds,** Houze, Shourds & Montgomery Inc., Long Beach, CA
3. **George W. Henn, Jr.,** G.W. Henn & Company, Columbus, OH
4. **Ronald G. Goerss,** Smith, Goerss & Ferneborg, Inc., San Francisco
5. **David M. DeWilde,** Chartwell Partners, San Francisco
6. **James Morice,** Mirtz Morice Inc., Stamford, CT
7. **Robert Slater,** Slater & Associates, Dallas
8. **David Hoffmann,** DHR International, Chicago
9. **George W. Ott,** Ott & Hansen Inc., Pasadena, CA
10. **Norman C. Roberts,** Norman Roberts & Associates, Inc., Los Angeles

Robert M. Bryza, Robert Lowell International, Dallas
Jack R. Clarey, Jack Clarey Associates, Inc., Northbrook, IL
Robert W. Dingman, Robert W. Dingman Co., Inc., Westlake Village, CA
Michael S. Dunford, Michael S. Dunford, Inc., Glen Ellyn, IL
Leon A. Farley, Leon A. Farley Associates, San Francisco
Dulany Foster, Jr., Korn/Ferry International, Stamford, CT
Joseph E. Griesedieck, Jr., SpencerStuart, San Francisco
Peter G. Grimm, Nordeman Grimm, Inc., New York
Michael J. Hoevel, Poirier, Hoevel & Company, Los Angeles
Louis A. Hoyda, Thorndike Deland Associates, New York
David Kettwig, A.T. Kearney, Chicago
R. Paul Kors, Kors Montgomery International, Houston
P. John Mirtz, Mirtz Morice Inc., Stamford, CT
Jacques C. Nordeman, Nordeman Grimm, Inc., New York
David Powell, David Powell, Inc., Woodside, CA
Norman C. Roberts, Norman Roberts & Associates, Inc., Los Angeles

Brenda L. Ruello, Heidrick & Struggles, Inc., New York
William K. Sur, Canny, Bowen Inc., New York
Judith M. VonSeldeneck, The Diversified Search Companies, Philadelphia
Thomas C. Zay, Zay & Company, Atlanta

PLANNING

1. **Windle B. Priem,** Korn/Ferry International, New York
2. **Jay Gaines,** Jay Gaines & Company, New York
3. **Jeffrey G. Bell,** Norman Broadbent International, New York
4. **William B. Clemens, Jr.,** Norman Broadbent International, New York
5. **Claudia Lacy Kelly,** Norman Broadbent International, New York
6. **Peter G. Grimm,** Nordeman Grimm, Inc., New York
7. **E. Pendleton James,** Pendleton James & Associates, New York
8. **John F. Johnson,** Lamalie Associates, Cleveland
9. **James Heuerman,** Korn/Ferry International, San Francisco (HE)
10. **Fred Siegel,** Conex, Inc., New York

Robert M. Callan, Callan & Associates, Oak Brook, IL
David M. DeWilde, Chartwell Partners, San Francisco
Ralph Dieckmann, Dieckmann & Associates, Chicago
James J. Drury III, SpencerStuart, Chicago
Michael S. Dunford, Michael S. Dunford, Inc., Glen Ellyn, IL
John T. Gardner, Lamalie Associates, Chicago
William E. Gould, Gould & McCoy, Inc., New York
William G. Hetzel, William Hetzel Associates, Inc., Schaumburg, IL
Durant A. Hunter, Gardiner Stone Hunter International, Boston
Richard K. Ives, Wilkinson & Ives, San Francisco
David S. Joys, Higdon, Joys & Mingle, New York
Gary Kreutz, Kreutz Consulting, Lake Forest, IL
Millington F. McCoy, Gould & McCoy, Inc., New York
Ferdinand Nadherny, Russell Reynolds Associates, Chicago
Jacques C. Nordeman, Nordeman Grimm, Inc., New York
Eleanor H. Raynolds, Ward Howell International, New York
Robert L. Smith, Robert L. Smith & Company, New York
Gail Hamity Vergara, SpencerStuart, Chicago (HE)
William R. Wilkinson, Wilkinson & Ives, San Francisco
William H. Willis, Jr., William Willis Worldwide, Inc., Greenwich, CT

PUBLIC RELATIONS/GOVERNMENT AFFAIRS

1. **Jonathan E. McBride,** McBride Associates, Inc., Washington, DC
2. **Carl W. Menk,** Canny, Bowen Inc., New York
3. **E. Pendleton James,** Pendleton James & Associates, New York
4. **William H. Marumoto,** The Interface Group, Ltd., Washington, DC
5. **Barbara L. Provus,** Shepherd, Bueschel & Provus, Inc., Chicago
6. **Charles M. Meng,** Meng, Finseth & Associates, Torrance, CA
7. **Gary J. Posner,** George Kaludis Associates, Nashville (ED)
8. **Richard Kinser,** Kinser & Associates, New York
9. **Gail Hamity Vergara,** SpencerStuart, Chicago (HE)
10. **Laurence R. Massé,** Ward Howell International, Barrington, IL

Otis H. Bowden II, Bowden & Company, Inc., Cleveland
Dulany Foster, Jr., Korn/Ferry International, Stamford, CT

Frank A. Garofolo, Garofolo, Curtiss, Lambert & MacLean, Ardmore, PA
Peter G. Grimm, Nordeman Grimm, Inc., New York
James Heuerman, Korn/Ferry International, San Francisco (HE)
Louis A. Hoyda, Thorndike Deland Associates, New York
W. Jerry Hyde, Hyde Danforth & Company, Dallas
John F. Johnson, Lamalie Associates, Cleveland
Millington F. McCoy, Gould & McCoy, Inc., New York
Richard M. McFarland, Brissenden, McFarland, Wagoner & Fuccella, Inc.,
    Stamford, CT
Ferdinand Nadherny, Russell Reynolds Associates, Chicago
Thomas H. Ogdon, The Ogdon Partnership, New York
Norman C. Roberts, Norman Roberts & Associates, Inc., Los Angeles
John H. Robison, Robison & McAulay, Charlotte, NC
Steven A. Seiden, Seiden Associates, New York
Fred Siegel, Conex, Inc., New York
Robert D. Spriggs, Spriggs & Company Inc., Glenview, IL
J. Alvin Wakefield, Gilbert Tweed Associates, Inc., New York
Putney Westerfield, Boyden International, San Francisco
William H. Willis, Jr., William Willis Worldwide, Inc., Greenwich, CT

PURCHASING/MATERIALS

1. Martin H. Bauman, Martin Bauman Associates, Inc., New York
2. David R. Peasback, Canny, Bowen Inc., New York
3. John R. Akin, J.R. Akin & Company, Fairfield, CT
4. James Montgomery, Houze, Shourds & Montgomery Inc., Long Beach,
    CA
5. William G. Hetzel, William Hetzel Associates, Inc., Schaumburg, IL
6. Lynn Tendler Bignell, Gilbert Tweed Associates, Inc., New York
7. Michael J. Hoevel, Poirier, Hoevel & Company, Los Angeles
8. Judith M. VonSeldeneck, The Diversified Search Companies, Philadelphia
9. William B. Clemens, Jr., Norman Broadbent International, New York
10. O. William Battalia, Battalia, Winston International, New York

Robert M. Callan, Callan & Associates, Oak Brook, IL
David H. Charlson, Chestnut Hill Partners, Ltd., Deerfield, IL
W. Michael Danforth, Hyde Danforth & Company, Dallas
Mike Jacobs, Thorne, Brieger Associates, Inc., New York
Theodore E. Lusk, Nadzam, Lusk & Associates, Santa Clara, CA
Laurence R. Massé, Ward Howell International, Barrington, IL
George W. Ott, Ott & Hansen Inc., Pasadena, CA
Jack Seitchik, Seitchik, Corwin & Seitchik, San Francisco

RESEARCH AND DEVELOPMENT

1. William E. Gould, Gould & McCoy, Inc., New York
2. Richard M. McFarland, Brissenden, McFarland, Wagoner & Fuccella, Inc.,
    Stamford, CT
3. Richard K. Ives, Wilkinson & Ives, San Francisco
4. David H. Charlson, Chestnut Hill Partners, Ltd., Deerfield, IL
5. Kai Lindholst, Egon Zehnder International, Chicago
6. Donald T. Allerton, Allerton, Heneghan & O'Neill, Chicago
7. William H. Willis, Jr., William Willis Worldwide, Inc., Greenwich, CT

8.   **William K. Sur,** Canny, Bowen Inc., New York
9.   **Richard J. Cronin,** Hodge-Cronin & Associates, Inc., Rosemont, IL
10. **John P. DiVenuto,** Deven Associates International, Verona, NJ

O. William Battalia, Battalia, Winston International, New York
Skott B. Burkland, Skott/Edwards, Rutherford, NJ
Peter Crist, Russell Reynolds Associates, Chicago
W. Michael Danforth, Hyde Danforth & Company, Dallas
A.D. Hart, Jr., Russell Reynolds Associates, New York
Robert L. Heidrick, The Heidrick Partners, Inc., Chicago
George W. Henn, Jr., G.W. Henn & Company, Columbus, OH
William A. Hertan, Executive Manning Corp., Ft. Lauderdale, FL
Mike Jacobs, Thorne, Brieger Associates, Inc., New York
R. Paul Kors, Kors Montgomery International, Houston
Theodore E. Lusk, Nadzam, Lusk & Associates, Santa Clara, CA
James Masciarelli, Fenwick Partners, Lexington, MA
Jonathan E. McBride, McBride Associates, Inc., Washington, DC
Frank Rico, Jr., J.R. Akin & Company, Fairfield, CT
Andrew Sherwood, Goodrich & Sherwood Company, New York
Robert D. Spriggs, Spriggs & Company Inc., Glenview, IL
Charles W. Sweet, A.T. Kearney, Chicago
Max M. Ulrich, Ward Howell International, New York
William R. Wilkinson, Wilkinson & Ives, San Francisco
Janis M. Zivic, The Zivic Group, Inc., San Francisco

WOMEN, HANDICAPPED, MINORITIES

1.   **J. Alvin Wakefield,** Gilbert Tweed Associates, Inc., New York
2.   **William H. Marumoto,** The Interface Group, Ltd., Washington, DC
3.   **Donald T. Allerton,** Allerton, Heneghan & O'Neill, Chicago
4.   **Claudia Lacy Kelly,** Norman Broadbent International, New York
5.   **Gary J. Posner,** George Kaludis Associates, Nashville (ED)
6.   **John P. DiVenuto,** Deven Associates International, Verona, NJ
7.   **Norman C. Roberts,** Norman Roberts & Associates, Inc., Los Angeles
8.   **Gail Hamity Vergara,** SpencerStuart, Chicago (HE)
9.   **John R. Akin,** J.R. Akin & Company, Fairfield, CT
10. **William A. Hertan,** Executive Manning Corp., Fort Lauderdale, FL

ORGANIZATIONAL OR INDUSTRY SPECIALIZATION

Categories

Aerospace	Government agencies/municipalities
Agriculture/forestry/fishing	Health services/hospitals
Associations/societies/nonprofit organizations	Holding companies
Banks and S&Ls	Hotels, resorts, private clubs
Chemicals and allied products	Insurance
Communications/telecommunications	Investment banking
Computer software	Law, accounting, and consulting firms
Construction	Machinery, except electrical
Electrical and electronic machinery	Measuring, analyzing, controlling and
Energy	photographic instruments
Fabricated metal products	Mining
Food and kindred products	Packaging

Categories (cont.)

Office machinery and computers
Paper and allied products
Perfume, cosmetics, and toilet goods
Pharmaceutical/medical products
Primary metal industries
Publishing and printing
Radio and television broadcasting
Real estate
Retail
Rubber and plastic products

Security and commodity brokers, dealers,
 and exchanges
Textiles
Tobacco and liquor
Transportation by air, rail, truck, or water
Transportation equipment
Universities, colleges, schools
Venture capital
Wholesale trade

AEROSPACE

1. **Gerard R. Roche,** Heidrick & Struggles, Inc., New York
2. **Frederick W. Wackerle,** McFeely Wackerle Shulman, Chicago
3. **Leon A. Farley,** Leon A. Farley Associates, San Francisco
4. **Paul R. Ray, Sr.,** Paul Ray & Carré Orban International, Fort Worth, TX
5. **Frank Rico, Jr.,** J.R. Akin & Company, Fairfield, CT
6. **Ferdinand Nadherny,** Russell Reynolds Associates, Chicago
7. **Richard M. Ferry,** Korn/Ferry International, Los Angeles
8. **William C. Houze,** William C. Houze & Company, La Quinta, CA
9. **William A. Hertan,** Executive Manning Corporation, Fort Lauderdale, FL
10. **Michael J. Hoevel,** Poirier, Hoevel & Company, Los Angeles

John R. Akin, J.R. Akin & Company, Fairfield, CT
Otis H. Bowden, II, Bowden & Company, Inc., Cleveland
Robert M. Bryza, Robert Lowell International, Dallas
O.D. Cruse, SpencerStuart, Dallas
Robert W. Dingman, Robert W. Dingman Co., Inc., Westlake Village, CA
Bert H. Early, Bert H. Early Associates, Inc., Chicago
A.D. Hart, Jr., Russell Reynolds Associates, New York
William G. Hetzel, William Hetzel Associates, Inc., Schaumburg, IL
W. Jerry Hyde, Hyde Danforth & Company, Dallas
E. Pendleton James, Pendleton James & Associates, New York
Theodore E. Lusk, Nadzam, Lusk & Associates, Santa Clara, CA
William H. Marumoto, The Interface Group, Ltd., Washington, DC
Richard M. McFarland, Brissenden, McFarland, Wagoner & Fuccella, Inc.
   Stamford, CT
Charles M. Meng, Meng, Finseth & Associates, Torrance, CA
Carl W. Menk, Canny, Bowen Inc., New York
James Montgomery, Houze, Shourds & Montgomery Inc., Long Beach,
   CA
Larry Nein, Nordeman Grimm, Inc., Chicago
George W. Ott, Ott & Hansen Inc., Pasadena, CA
Fred Siegel, Conex, Inc., New York
Richard C. Slayton, Slayton International Inc., Chicago

AGRICULTURE/FORESTRY/FISHING

1. **William R. Wilkinson,** Wilkinson & Ives, San Francisco
2. **Robert W. Dingman,** Robert W. Dingman Co., Westlake Village, CA
3. **Peter Crist,** Russell Reynolds Associates, Chicago
4. **Charles W. Sweet,** A.T. Kearney, Chicago
5. **Michael Boxberger,** Korn/Ferry International, Chicago

ASSOCIATIONS/SOCIETIES/NONPROFIT ORGANIZATIONS

1. **Robert W. Dingman,** Robert W. Dingman Co., Westlake Village, CA
2. **John S. Lloyd,** Witt Associates, Oak Brook, IL
3. **William J. Bowen,** Heidrick & Struggles, Inc., Chicago
4. **Jonathan E. McBride,** McBride Associates, Inc., Washington, DC
5. **Ira W. Krinsky,** Ira W. Krinsky & Associates, Pasadena, CA
6. **William H. Marumoto,** The Interface Group, Ltd., Washington, DC
7. **Janis M. Zivic,** The Zivic Group, Inc., San Francisco
8. **John H. Callen, Jr.,** Ward Howell International Inc., New York
9. **E. Pendleton James,** Pendleton James & Associates, New York
10. **Gail Hamity Vergara,** SpencerStuart, Chicago

Michael D. Caver, Heidrick & Struggles, Inc., Chicago
W. Hoyt Colton, W. Hoyt Colton Associates Inc., New York
John P. DiVenuto, Deven Associates International, Verona, NJ
Robert M. Flanagan, Robert Flanagan Associates Inc., N. Salem, NY
John W. Franklin, Jr., Russell Reynolds Associates, Washington, DC
Frank A. Garofolo, Garofolo, Curtiss, Lambert & MacLean, Ardmore, PA
Gary Kreutz, Kreutz Consulting, Lake Forest, IL
John Lucht, The John Lucht Consultancy, New York
Millington F. McCoy, Gould & McCoy, Inc., New York
Richard M. McFarland, Brissenden, McFarland, Wagoner & Fuccella, Inc., Stamford, CT
Charles M. Meng, Meng, Finseth & Associates, Torrance, CA
Jacques C. Nordeman, Nordeman Grimm, Inc., New York
Paul R. Ray, Jr., Paul Ray & Carré Orban International, Fort Worth, TX
Eleanor H. Raynolds, Ward Howell International, New York
Norman C. Roberts, Norman Roberts & Associates, Inc., Los Angeles
Richard Sbarbaro, Lauer, Sbarbaro Associates, Chicago
Fred Siegel, Conex, Inc., New York
Judith M. VonSeldeneck, The Diversified Search Companies, Philadelphia
J. Alvin Wakefield, Gilbert Tweed Associates, Inc., Pittsford, VT
William H. Willis, Jr., William Willis Worldwide, Inc., Greenwich, CT

BANKS AND S&Ls

1. **Gerard R. Roche,** Heidrick & Struggles, Inc., New York
2. **Thomas J. Neff,** SpencerStuart, New York
3. **Leon A. Farley,** Leon A. Farley Associates, San Francisco
4. **Windle B. Priem,** Korn/Ferry International, New York
5. **Jay Gaines,** Jay Gaines & Company, New York
6. **Peter G. Grimm,** Nordeman Grimm, Inc., New York
7. **D. John Ingram,** Ingram, Inc., New York
8. **Russell S. Reynolds, Jr.,** Russell Reynolds Associates, New York
9. **David Hoffmann,** DHR International, Chicago
10. **Judith M. VonSeldeneck,** The Diversified Search Companies, Philadelphia

Jeffrey G. Bell, Norman Broadbent International, New York
William B. Clemens, Jr., Norman Broadbent International, New York
David M. DeWilde, Chartwell Partners, San Francisco
John P. DiVenuto, Deven Associates International, Verona, NJ
Richard M. Ferry, Korn/Ferry International, Los Angeles

William E. Gould, Gould & McCoy, Inc., New York
Robert L. Heidrick, The Heidrick Partners, Inc., Chicago
George W. Henn, Jr., G.W. Henn & Company, Columbus, OH
Richard K. Ives, Wilkinson & Ives, San Francisco
Mike Jacobs, Thorne, Brieger Associates, Inc., New York
David S. Joys, Higdon, Joys & Mingle, New York
Millington F. McCoy, Gould & McCoy, Inc., New York
Clarence E. McFeely, McFeely Wackerle Shulman, Chicago
Ferdinand Nadherny, Russell Reynolds Associates, Chicago
Dayton Ogden, SpencerStuart, Stamford, CT
Steven A. Seiden, Seiden Associates, New York
Fred Siegel, Conex, Inc., New York
Robert Slater, Slater & Associates, Dallas
William H. Willis, Jr., William Willis Worldwide, Inc., Greenwich, CT
Thomas C. Zay, Zay & Company, Atlanta

CHEMICALS AND ALLIED PRODUCTS

1. **Gerard R. Roche,** Heidrick & Struggles, Inc., New York
2. **Frederick W. Wackerle,** McFeely Wackerle Shulman, Chicago
3. **William E. Gould,** Gould & McCoy, New York
4. **Robert D. Spriggs,** Spriggs & Company, Inc., Glenview, IL
5. **Lynn Tendler Bignell,** Gilbert Tweed Associates, Inc., New York
6. **Richard J. Cronin,** Hodge-Cronin & Associates, Inc., Rosemont, IL
7. **R. Paul Kors,** Kors Montgomery International, Houston
8. **David Hoffmann,** DHR International, Chicago
9. **Robert L. Heidrick,** The Heidrick Partners, Inc., Chicago
10. **William G. Hetzel,** William Hetzel Associates, Inc., Schaumburg, IL

Martin H. Bauman, Martin H. Bauman Associates, Inc., New York
Michael Boxberger, Korn/Ferry International, Chicago
Robert M. Callan, Callan & Associates, Oak Brook, IL
David H. Charlson, Chestnut Hill Partners, Ltd., Deerfield, IL
Peter Crist, Russell Reynolds Associates, New York
Robert W. Dingman, Robert W. Dingman Co., Inc., Westlake Village, CA
John P. DiVenuto, Deven Associates International, Verona, NJ
A.D. Hart, Jr., Russell Reynolds Associates, New York
Kai Lindholst, Egon Zehnder International, Chicago
Richard M. McFarland, Brissenden, McFarland, Wagoner & Fuccella, Inc.,
    Stamford, CT
Clarence E. McFeely, McFeely Wackerle Shulman, Chicago
James Morice, Mirtz Morice Inc., Stamford, CT
Ferdinand Nadherny, Russell Reynolds Associates, Chicago
Larry Nein, Nordeman Grimm, Inc., Chicago
David R. Peasback, Canny, Bowen Inc., New York
Daniel M. Shepherd, Shepherd, Bueschel & Provus, Inc., Chicago
William K. Sur, Canny, Bowen Inc., New York
Max M. Ulrich, Ward Howell International, New York
Jack H. Vernon, Russell Reynolds Associates, Boston
William H. Willis, Jr., William Willis Worldwide, Inc., Greenwich, CT

COMMUNICATIONS/TELECOMMUNICATIONS

1. **Leon A. Farley,** Leon A. Farley Associates, San Francisco
2. **Gerard R. Roche,** Heidrick & Struggles, Inc., New York
3. **Thomas C. Zay,** Zay & Company, Atlanta
4. **John P. DiVenuto,** Deven Associates International, Verona, NJ
5. **Roger M. Kenny,** Kenny, Kindler, Hunt & Howe, New York
6. **Richard K. Ives,** Wilkinson & Ives, San Francisco
7. **Jonathan S. Holman,** The Holman Group, Inc., San Francisco
8. **Richard Sbarbaro,** Lauer, Sbarbaro Associates, Chicago
9. **Clarence E. McFeely,** McFeely Wackerle Shulman, Chicago
10. **E. Pendleton James,** Pendleton James & Associates, New York

Donald T. Allerton, Allerton, Heneghan & O'Neill, Chicago
Jeffrey G. Bell, Norman Broadbent International, New York
William B. Clemens, Jr., Norman Broadbent International, New York
Richard J. Cronin, Hodge-Cronin & Associates, Inc., Rosemont, IL
W. Michael Danforth, Hyde Danforth & Company, Dallas
James J. Drury III, SpencerStuart, Chicago
David Hoffmann, DHR International, Chicago
Theodore N. Jadick, Heidrick & Struggles, Inc., New York
Richard Kinser, Kinser & Associates, New York
Gary Kreutz, Kreutz Consulting, Lake Forest, IL
Theodore E. Lusk, Nadzam, Lusk & Associates, Santa Clara, CA
William H. Marumoto, The Interface Group, Ltd., Washington, DC
James Masciarelli, Fenwick Partners, Lexington, MA
Carl W. Menk, Canny, Bowen Inc., New York
Jacques C. Nordeman, Nordeman Grimm, Inc., New York
Thomas H. Ogdon, The Ogdon Partnership, New York
David R. Peasback, Canny, Bowen Inc., New York
David Powell, David Powell, Inc., Woodside, CA
William K. Sur, Canny, Bowen Inc., New York
William R. Wilkinson, Wilkinson & Ives, San Francisco

COMPUTER SOFTWARE

1. **Richard K. Ives,** Wilkinson & Ives, San Francisco
2. **Peter G. Grimm,** Nordeman Grimm, Inc., New York
3. **James Masciarelli,** Fenwick Partners, Lexington, MA
4. **Mary E. Shourds,** Houze, Shourds & Montgomery, Long Beach, CA
5. **Robert Slater,** Slater & Associates, Dallas
6. **Michael S. Dunford,** Michael S. Dunford, Inc., Glen Ellyn, IL
7. **William R. Wilkinson,** Wilkinson & Ives, San Francisco
8. **Jonathan E. McBride,** McBride Associates, Inc., Washington, DC
9. **Larry Nein,** Nordeman Grimm, Inc., Chicago
10. **Judith M. VonSeldeneck,** The Diversified Search Companies, Philadelphia

Skott B. Burkland, Skott/Edwards Consultants, Rutherford, NJ
O.D. Cruse, SpencerStuart, Dallas
Ralph Dieckmann, Dieckmann & Associates, Chicago
Robert W. Dingman, Robert W. Dingman Co., Inc., Westlake Village, CA
George W. Henn, Jr., G.W. Henn & Company, Columbus, OH
Jonathan S. Holman, The Holman Group, Inc., San Francisco
R. Paul Kors, Kors Montgomery International, Houston

Theodore E. Lusk, Nadzam, Lusk & Associates, Santa Clara, CA
James Montgomery, Houze, Shourds & Montgomery, Long Beach, CA
Robert L. Smith, Robert L. Smith & Company, New York

CONSTRUCTION

1. **Thomas C. Zay,** Zay & Company, Atlanta
2. **Carl W. Menk,** Canny, Bowen Inc., New York
3. **George W. Ott,** Ott & Hansen Inc., Pasadena, CA
4. **Ronald G. Goerss,** Smith, Goerss & Ferneborg, Inc., San Francisco
5. **Putney Westerfield,** Boyden International, San Francisco
6. **David R. Peasback,** Canny, Bowen Inc., New York
7. **Charles M. Meng,** Meng, Finseth & Associates, Torrance, CA
8. **Max M. Ulrich,** Ward Howell International, New York
9. **Robert M. Bryza,** Robert Lowell International, Dallas
10. **Richard J. Cronin,** Hodge-Cronin & Associates, Inc., Rosemont, IL

O. William Battalia, Battalia, Winston International, New York
Otis H. Bowden II, Bowden & Company, Inc., Cleveland
Bert H. Early, Bert H. Early Associates Inc., Chicago
Leon A. Farley, Leon A. Farley Associates, San Francisco
Richard M. Ferry, Korn/Ferry International, Los Angeles
Lawrence W. Hill, Russell Reynolds Associates, Houston
W. Jerry Hyde, Hyde Danforth & Company, Dallas
Richard K. Ives, Wilkinson & Ives, San Francisco
Theodore E. Lusk, Nadzam, Lusk & Associates, Santa Clara, CA
Norman C. Roberts, Norman Roberts & Associates, Inc., Los Angeles

ELECTRICAL AND ELECTRONIC MACHINERY

1. **Gerard R. Roche,** Heidrick & Struggles, Inc., New York
2. **Frederick W. Wackerle,** McFeely Wackerle Shulman, Chicago
3. **Leon A. Farley,** Leon A. Farley Associates, San Francisco
4. **E. Pendleton James,** Pendleton James & Associates, New York
5. **David Powell,** David Powell, Inc., Woodside, CA
6. **Donald T. Allerton,** Allerton, Heneghan & O'Neill, Chicago
7. **George W. Henn, Jr.,** G.W. Henn & Co., Columbus, OH
8. **William C. Houze,** William C. Houze & Co., La Quinta, CA
9. **William E. Gould,** Gould & McCoy, New York
10. **Mike Jacobs,** Thorne, Brieger Associates, Inc., New York

O. William Battalia, Battalia, Winston International, New York
Robert M. Bryza, Robert Lowell International, Dallas
Robert M. Callan, Callan & Associates, Oak Brook, IL
Richard J. Cronin, Hodge-Cronin & Associates, Inc., Rosemont, IL
Robert W. Dingman, Robert W. Dingman Co., Inc., Westlake Village, CA
Robert M. Flanagan, Robert Flanagan Associates Inc., N. Salem, NY
John T. Gardner, Lamalie Associates, Chicago
Joseph E. Griesedieck, Jr., SpencerStuart, San Francisco
William G. Hetzel, William Hetzel Associates, Inc., Schaumburg, IL
Jonathan S. Holman, The Holman Group, Inc., San Francisco
John F. Johnson, Lamalie Associates, Cleveland
David S. Joys, Hidgon, Joys & Mingle, New York

R. **Paul Kors,** Kors Montgomery International, Houston
Kai Lindholst, Egon Zehnder International, Chicago
Theodore E. Lusk, Nadzam, Lusk & Associates, Santa Clara, CA
James Masciarelli, Fenwick Partners, Lexington, MA
Clarence E. McFeely, McFeely Wackerle Shulman, Chicago
Paul R. Ray, Sr., Paul Ray & Carré Orban International, Fort Worth, TX
Charles W. Sweet, A.T. Kearney, Chicago
William R. Wilkinson, Wilkinson & Ives, San Francisco

ENERGY

1. **E. Pendleton James,** Pendleton James & Associates, New York
2. **Robert Slater,** Slater & Associates, Dallas
3. **R. Paul Kors,** Kors Montgomery International, Houston
4. **Charles M. Meng,** Meng, Finseth & Associates, Torrance, CA
5. **Richard M. McFarland,** Brissenden, McFarland, Wagoner & Fuccella, Inc., Stamford, CT
6. **Robert L. Heidrick,** The Heidrick Partners, Inc., Chicago
7. **John H. Robison,** Robison & McAulay, Charlotte, NC
8. **Max M. Ulrich,** Ward Howell International, New York
9. **W. Michael Danforth,** Hyde Danforth & Company, Dallas
10. **Leon A. Farley,** Leon A. Farley Associates, San Francisco

Jeffrey G. Bell, Norman Broadbent International, New York
Lynn Tendler Bignell, Gilbert Tweed Associates, Inc., New York
Michael Boxberger, Korn/Ferry International, Chicago
Robert M. Bryza, Robert Lowell International, Dallas
David E. Chambers, David Chambers & Associates, Inc., New York
Bert H. Early, Bert H. Early Associates Inc., Chicago
Richard M. Ferry, Korn/Ferry International, Los Angeles
David O. Harbert, Sweeney, Harbert & Mummert Inc., Tampa, FL
Henry G. Higdon, Hidgon, Joys & Mingle, New York
Lawrence W. Hill, Russell Reynolds Associates, Houston
W. Jerry Hyde, Hyde Danforth & Company, Dallas
Theodore E. Lusk, Nadzam, Lusk & Associates, Santa Clara, CA
Ferdinand Nadherny, Russell Reynolds Associates, Chicago
David R. Peasback, Canny, Bowen Inc., New York

FABRICATED METAL PRODUCTS

1. **Robert L. Heidrick,** The Heidrick Partners, Inc., Chicago
2. **Mike Jacobs,** Thorne, Brieger Associates, Inc., New York
3. **John F. Johnson,** Lamalie Associates, Cleveland
4. **Ferdinand Nadherny,** Russell Reynolds Associates, Chicago
5. **George W. Ott,** Ott & Hansen Inc., Pasadena, CA
6. **Robert M. Callan,** Callan & Associates, Oak Brook, IL
7. **Robert M. Bryza,** Robert Lowell International, Dallas
8. **Frank Rico, Jr.,** J.R. Akin & Company, Fairfield, CT
9. **Steven A. Seiden,** Seiden Associates, New York
10. **Laurence R. Massé,** Ward Howell International, Barrington, IL

Martin H. Bauman, Martin Bauman Associates, Inc., New York
Lynn Tendler Bignell, Gilbert Tweed Associates, Inc., New York

Peter Crist, Russell Reynolds Associates, Chicago
Richard J. Cronin, Hodge-Cronin & Associates, Inc., Rosemont, IL
W. Michael Danforth, Hyde Danforth & Company, Dallas
Ralph Dieckmann, Dieckmann & Associates, Chicago
Robert W. Dingman, Robert W. Dingman Co., Inc., Westlake Village, CA
Dulany Foster, Jr., Korn/Ferry International, Stamford, CT
John T. Gardner, Lamalie Associates, Chicago
George W. Henn, Jr., G.W. Henn & Company, Columbus, OH
William A. Hertan, Executive Manning Corporation, Fort Lauderdale, FL
William G. Hetzel, William Hetzel Associates, Inc., Schaumburg, IL
Kai Lindholst, Egon Zehnder International, Chicago
Theodore E. Lusk, Nadzam, Lusk & Associates, Santa Clara, CA
P. John Mirtz, Mirtz Morice Inc., Stamford, CT
Richard C. Slayton, Slayton International Inc., Chicago
Charles W. Sweet, A.T. Kearney, Chicago
Jack H. Vernon, Russell Reynolds Associates, Boston
Frederick W. Wackerle, McFeely Wackerle Shulman, Chicago
Thomas C. Zay, Zay & Company, Atlanta

FOOD AND KINDRED PRODUCTS

1. **Thomas J. Neff,** SpencerStuart, New York
2. **William E. Gould,** Gould & McCoy, New York
3. **Roger M. Kenny,** Kenny, Kindler, Hunt & Howe, New York
4. **William R. Wilkinson,** Wilkinson & Ives, San Francisco
5. **Jack R. Clarey,** Jack Clarey Associates, Inc., Northbrook, IL
6. **Paul R. Ray, Sr.,** Paul Ray & Carré Orban International, Fort Worth
7. **Robert W. Dingman,** Robert W. Dingman Co., Inc., Westlake Village, CA
8. **Barbara L. Provus,** Shepherd, Bueschel & Provus, Inc., Chicago
9. **Thomas C. Zay,** Zay & Company, Atlanta
10. **Robert D. Spriggs,** Spriggs & Company, Inc., Glenview, IL

O. William Battalia, Battalia, Winston International, New York
Richard J. Cronin, Hodge-Cronin & Associates, Inc., Rosemont, IL
James J. Drury III, SpencerStuart, Chicago
Ronald G. Goerss, Smith, Goerss & Ferneborg, Inc., San Francisco
Peter G. Grimm, Nordeman Grimm, Inc., New York
A.D. Hart, Jr., Russell Reynolds Associates, New York
David Hoffmann, DHR International, Chicago
Louis A. Hoyda, Thorndike Deland Associates, New York
D. John Ingram, Ingram, Inc., New York
John F. Johnson, Lamalie Associates, Cleveland
David S. Joys, Higdon, Joys & Mingle, New York
Richard Kinser, Kinser & Associates, New York
Gary Kreutz, Kreutz Consulting, Lake Forest, IL
Kai Lindholst, Egon Zehnder International, Chicago
John Lucht, The John Lucht Consultancy, New York
Carl W. Menk, Canny, Bowen Inc., New York
P. John Mirtz, Mirtz, Morice Inc., Stamford, CT
Gerard R. Roche, Heidrick & Struggles, Inc., New York
Fred Siegel, Conex, Inc., New York
William K. Sur, Canny, Bowen Inc., New York

GOVERNMENT AGENCIES/MUNICIPALITIES

1. **Norman C. Roberts,** Norman Roberts & Associates, Inc., Los Angeles
2. **Ira W. Krinsky,** Ira W. Krinsky & Associates, Pasadena, CA
3. **Charles M. Meng,** Meng, Finseth & Associates, Torrance, CA
4. **Paul R. Ray, Jr.,** Paul Ray & Carré Orban International, Fort Worth
5. **Janis M. Zivic,** The Zivic Group, Inc., San Francisco
6. **John H. Robison,** Robison & McAulay, Charlotte, NC
7. **William H. Marumoto,** The Interface Group, Ltd., Washington, DC

HEALTH SERVICES/HOSPITALS

1. **Robert W. Dingman,** Robert W. Dingman Co., Inc., Westlake Village, CA
2. **John S. Lloyd,** Witt Associates, Oak Brook, IL
3. **Judith M. VonSeldeneck,** The Diversified Search Companies, Philadelphia
4. **James Heuerman,** Korn/Ferry International, San Francisco
5. **Michael Kieffer,** Kieffer, Ford & Hadelman, Oak Brook, IL
6. **Gail Hamity Vergara,** SpencerStuart, Chicago
7. **Janis M. Zivic,** The Zivic Group, Inc., San Francisco
8. **Michael D. Caver,** Heidrick & Struggles, Inc., Chicago
9. **Neal L. Maslan,** Ward Howell International, Encino, CA
10. **Theodore N. Jadick,** Heidrick & Struggles, Inc., New York

John R. Akin, J.R. Akin & Company, Fairfield, CT
William J. Bowen, Heidrick & Struggles, Inc., Chicago
David H. Charlson, Chestnut Hill Partners, Ltd., Deerfield, IL
W. Hoyt Colton, W. Hoyt Colton Associates Inc.
Frank A. Garofolo, Garofolo, Curtiss, Lambert & MacLean, Ardmore, PA
Robert L. Heidrick, The Heidrick Partners, Inc., Chicago
William A. Hertan, Executive Manning Corp., Fort Lauderdale, FL
Henry G. Higdon, Higdon, Joys & Mingle, New York
David Hoffmann, DHR International, Chicago
William C. Houze, William C. Houze & Co., La Quinta, CA
Louis A. Hoyda, Thorndike Deland Associates, New York
W. Jerry Hyde, Hyde Danforth & Company, Dallas
Charles M. Meng, Meng, Finseth & Associates, Torrance, CA
James Morice, Mirtz Morice Inc., Stamford, CT
Frank Rico, Jr., J.R. Akin & Company, Fairfield, CT
Norman C. Roberts, Norman Roberts & Associates, Inc., Los Angeles
Richard Sbarbaro, Lauer, Sbarbaro Associates, Chicago
Robert L. Smith, Robert L. Smith & Company, New York
Max M. Ulrich, Ward Howell International, New York
Jack H. Vernon, Russell Reynolds Associates, Boston

HOLDING COMPANIES

1. **Thomas J. Neff,** SpencerStuart, New York
2. **Frederick W. Wackerle,** McFeely Wackerle Shulman, Chicago
3. **Clarence E. McFeely,** McFeely Wackerle Shulman, Chicago
4. **Peter G. Grimm,** Nordeman Grimm, Inc., New York
5. **Richard M. Ferry,** Korn/Ferry International, Los Angeles
6. **Steven A. Seiden,** Seiden Associates, New York
7. **David Hoffmann,** DHR International, Chicago

8. **Robert D. Spriggs,** Spriggs & Company, Inc., Glenview, IL
9. **Russell S. Reynolds, Jr.,** Russell Reynolds Associates, New York
10. **Jack R. Clarey,** Jack Clarey Associates, Inc., Northbrook, IL

David H. Charlson, Chestnut Hill Partners, Ltd., Deerfield, IL
William B. Clemens, Jr., Norman Broadbent International, New York
David M. DeWilde, Chartwell Partners, San Francisco
Ralph Dieckmann, Dieckmann & Associates, Chicago
Dulany Foster, Jr., Korn/Ferry International, Stamford, CT
Henry G. Higdon, Higdon, Joys & Mingle, New York
Michael J. Hoevel, Poirier, Hoevel & Company, Los Angeles
Richard K. Ives, Wilkinson & Ives, San Francisco
Claudia Lacy Kelly, Norman Broadbent International, New York
David Kettwig, A.T. Kearney, Chicago
Richard Kinser, Kinser & Associates, New York
Charles M. Meng, Meng, Finseth & Associates, Torrance, CA
P. John Mirtz, Mirtz Morice, Inc., Stamford, CT
James Morice, Mirtz Morice, Inc., Stamford, CT
Jacques C. Nordeman, Nordeman Grimm, Inc., New York
George W. Ott, Ott & Hansen Inc., Pasadena, CA
David R. Peasback, Canny, Bowen Inc., New York
Brenda L. Ruello, Heidrick & Struggles, Inc., New York
Richard Sbarbaro, Lauer, Sbarbaro Associates, Chicago
Robert L. Smith, Robert L. Smith & Company, New York

HOTELS, RESORTS, PRIVATE CLUBS

1. **Carol S. Jeffers,** John Sibbald Associates, Inc., Chicago
2. **W. Michael Danforth,** Hyde Danforth & Company, Dallas
3. **John W. Franklin, Jr.,** Russell Reynolds Associates, Washington, DC
4. **Robert Slater,** Slater & Associates, Dallas
5. **Fred Siegel,** Conex, Inc., New York
6. **Eleanor H. Raynolds,** Ward Howell International, New York
7. **Judith M. VonSeldeneck,** The Diversified Search Companies, Philadelphia
8. **Janis M. Zivic,** The Zivic Group, Inc., San Francisco
9. **W. Jerry Hyde,** Hyde Danforth & Company, Dallas
10. **Donald T. Allerton,** Allerton, Heneghan & O'Neill, Chicago

Michael S. Dunford, Michael S. Dunford, Inc., Glen Ellyn, IL
Robert M. Flanagan, Robert Flanagan Associates Inc., N. Salem, NY
Robert L. Heidrick, The Heidrick Partners, Inc., Chicago
Henry G. Higdon, Higdon, Joys & Mingle, Chicago
Claudia Lacy Kelly, Norman Broadbent International, New York
Jonathan E. McBride, McBride Associates, Inc., Washington, DC
David R. Peasback, Canny, Bowen Inc., New York
Mary E. Shourds, Houze, Shourds & Montgomery, Long Beach, CA
Steven A. Seiden, Seiden Associates, New York

INSURANCE

1. **Windle B. Priem,** Korn/Ferry International, New York
2. **D. John Ingram,** Ingram, Inc., New York
3. **A.D. Hart, Jr.,** Russell Reynolds Associates, New York

4. **William B. Clemens, Jr.,** Norman Broadbent International, New York
5. **John Lucht,** The John Lucht Consultancy, New York
6. **Jonathan E. McBride,** McBride Associates, Inc., Washington, DC
7. **Richard K. Ives,** Wilkinson & Ives, San Francisco
8. **Jeffrey G. Bell,** Norman Broadbent International, New York
9. **Ralph Dieckmann,** Dieckmann & Associates, Chicago
10. **James Morice,** Mirtz Morice Inc., Stamford, CT

David H. Charlson, Chestnut Hill Partners, Ltd., Deerfield, IL
Jack R. Clarey, Jack Clarey Associates, Inc., Northbrook, IL
W. Hoyt Colton, W. Hoyt Colton Associates, Inc., New York
David M. DeWilde, Chartwell Partners, San Francisco
Michael S. Dunford, Michael S. Dunford, Inc., Glen Ellyn, IL
Richard M. Ferry, Korn/Ferry International, Los Angeles
Peter G. Grimm, Nordeman Grimm, Inc., New York
Robert L. Heidrick, The Heidrick Partners, Inc., Chicago
George W. Henn, Jr., G.W. Henn & Company, Columbus, OH
Louis A. Hoyda, Thorndike Deland Associates, New York
Durant A. Hunter, Gardiner Stone Hunter International, Boston
Claudia Lacy Kelly, Norman Broadbent International, New York
David Kettwig, A.T. Kearney, Chicago
Richard Kinser, Kinser & Associates, New York
John S. Lloyd, Witt Associates, Oak Brook, IL
Carl W. Menk, Canny, Bowen Inc., New York
Dayton Ogden, SpencerStuart, New York
Richard Sbarbaro, Lauer, Sbarbaro Associates, Chicago
Steven A. Seiden, Seiden Associates, New York
William H. Willis, Jr., William Willis Worldwide, Inc., Greenwich, CT

INVESTMENT BANKING

1. **Thomas J. Neff,** SpencerStuart, New York
2. **Windle B. Priem,** Korn/Ferry International, New York
3. **Jay Gaines,** Jay Gaines & Company, New York
4. **Jeffrey G. Bell,** Norman Broadbent International, New York
5. **Dayton Ogden,** SpencerStuart, New York
6. **Russell S. Reynolds, Jr.,** Russell Reynolds Associates, New York
7. **David S. Joys,** Higdon, Joys & Mingle, New York
8. **Durant A. Hunter,** Gardiner Stone Hunter International, Boston
9. **Peter Crist,** Russell Reynolds Associates, Chicago
10. **Claudia Lacy Kelly,** Norman Broadbent International, New York

O. William Battalia, Battalia, Winston International, New York
Martin H. Bauman, Martin Bauman Associates, Inc., New York
Michael Boxberger, Korn/Ferry International, Chicago
William B. Clemens, Jr., Norman Broadbent International, New York
W. Hoyt Colton, W. Hoyt Colton Associates Inc., New York
David M. DeWilde, Chartwell Partners, San Francisco
John P. Divenuto, Deven Associates International, Verona, NJ
Frank A. Garofolo, Garofolo, Curtiss, Lambert & MacLean, Ardmore, PA
David Kettwig, A.T. Kearney, Chicago
Jonathan E. McBride, McBride Associates, Inc., Washington, DC
Clarence E. McFeely, McFeely Wackerle Shulman, Chicago
Larry Nein, Nordeman Grimm, Inc., Chicago

Paul R. Ray, Sr., Paul Ray & Carré Orban International, Fort Worth
Steven A. Seiden, Seiden Associates, New York
Fred Siegel, Conex, Inc., New York
William R. Wilkinson, Wilkinson & Ives, San Francisco

LAW, ACCOUNTING, AND CONSULTING FIRMS

1. **Clarence E. McFeely,** McFeely Wackerle Shulman, Chicago
2. **W. Michael Danforth,** Hyde Danforth & Company, Dallas
3. **William B. Clemens, Jr.,** Norman Broadbent International, New York
4. **John H. Callen, Jr.,** Ward Howell International, Inc., New York
5. **Millington F. McCoy,** Gould & McCoy, New York
6. **Fred Siegel,** Conex, Inc., New York
7. **W. Jerry Hyde,** Hyde Danforth & Company, Dallas
8. **Bert H. Early,** Bert H. Early Associates, Inc., Chicago
9. **Claudia Lacy Kelly,** Norman Broadbent International, New York
10. **Leon A. Farley,** Leon A. Farley Associates, San Francisco

Jack R. Clarey, Jack Clarey Associates, Inc., Northbrook, IL
David M. DeWilde, Chartwell Partners, San Francisco
Ralph Dieckmann, Dieckmann & Associates, Chicago
John P. DiVenuto, Deven Associates International, Verona, NJ
Dulany Foster, Jr., Korn/Ferry International, Stamford, CT
Jay Gaines, Jay Gaines & Company, New York
John T. Gardner, Lamalie Associates, Chicago
William A. Hertan, Executive Manning Corp., Ft. Lauderdale, FL
Mike Jacobs, Thorne, Brieger Associates, Inc., New York
Theodore N. Jadick, Heidrick & Struggles, Inc., New York
David Kettwig, A.T. Kearney, Chicago
Richard Kinser, Kinser & Associates, New York
R. Paul Kors, Kors, Montgomery International, Houston
William H. Marumoto, The Interface Group, Ltd., Washington, DC
Jonathan E. McBride, McBride Associates, Inc., Washington, DC
Jacques C. Nordeman, Nordeman Grimm, Inc., New York
Norman C. Roberts, Norman Roberts & Associates, Inc., Los Angeles
Brenda L. Ruello, Heidrick & Struggles, Inc., New York
Robert L. Smith, Robert L. Smith & Company, New York
Janis M. Zivic, The Zivic Group, Inc., San Francisco

MACHINERY, EXCEPT ELECTRICAL

1. **Frederick W. Wackerle,** McFeely Wackerle Shulman, Chicago
2. **Jack R. Clarey,** Jack Clarey Associates, Inc., Northbrook, IL
3. **Robert M. Bryza,** Robert Lowell International, Dallas
4. **Robert L. Heidrick,** The Heidrick Partners, Inc., Chicago
5. **Robert M. Callan,** Callan & Associates, Oak Brook, IL
6. **John T. Gardner,** Lamalie Associates, Chicago
7. **Robert D. Spriggs,** Spriggs & Company Inc., Glenview, IL
8. **Kai Lindholst,** Egon Zehnder International, Chicago
9. **John R. Akin,** J.R. Akin & Company, Stamford, CT
10. **Lynn Tendler Bignell,** Gilbert Tweed Associates, Inc., New York

Peter Crist, Russell Reynolds Associates, Chicago
Ralph Dieckmann, Dieckmann & Associates, Chicago

William C. Houze, William C. Houze & Co., La Quinta, CA
Mike Jacobs, Thorne, Brieger Associates, Inc., New York
John F. Johnson, Lamalie Associates, Cleveland
James Masciarelli, Fenwick Partners, Lexington, MA
Laurence R. Massé, Ward Howell International, Barrington, IL
Clarence E. McFeely, McFeely Wackerle Shulman, Chicago
Frank Rico, Jr., J.R. Akin & Company, Fairfield, CT
Richard C. Slayton, Slayton International Inc., Chicago
J. Alvin Wakefield, Gilbert Tweed Associates, Inc., Pittsford, VT

MEASURING, ANALYZING, CONTROLLING, AND PHOTOGRAPHIC INSTRUMENTS

1. **George W. Henn, Jr.,** G.W. Henn & Company, Columbus, OH
2. **Lynn Tendler Bignell,** Gilbert Tweed Associates, Inc., New York
3. **Millington F. McCoy,** Gould & McCoy, New York
4. **Jack H. Vernon,** Russell Reynolds Associates, Boston
5. **O.D. Cruse,** SpencerStuart, Dallas
6. **James Masciarelli,** Fenwick Partners, Lexington, MA
7. **Theodore E. Lusk,** Nadzam, Lusk & Associates, Santa Clara, CA
8. **Jonathan S. Holman,** The Holman Group, Inc., San Francisco
9. **William G. Hetzel,** William Hetzel Associates, Inc., Schaumburg, IL
10. **R. Paul Kors,** Kors Montgomery International, Houston

Robert M. Callan, Callan & Associates, Oak Brook, IL
David S. Joys, Hidgon, Joys & Mingle, New York
Kai Lindholst, Egon Zehnder International, Chicago
George W. Ott, Ott & Hansen Inc., Pasadena, CA
Richard C. Slayton, Slayton International Inc., Chicago

MINING

1. **David Powell,** David Powell, Inc., Woodside, CA
2. **John T. Gardner,** Lamalie Associates, Chicago
3. **R. Paul Kors,** Kors Montgomery International, Houston
4. **Robert D. Spriggs,** Spriggs & Company Inc., Glenview, IL
5. **Lawrence W. Hill,** Russell Reynolds Associates, Houston
6. **O. William Battalia,** Battalia, Winston International, New York
7. **John F. Johnson,** Lamalie Associates, Cleveland

OFFICE MACHINERY AND COMPUTERS

1. **Gerard R. Roche,** Heidrick & Struggles, Inc., New York
2. **Richard K. Ives,** Wilkinson & Ives, San Francisco
3. **Thomas J. Neff,** SpencerStuart, New York
4. **Leon A. Farley,** Leon A. Farley Associates, San Francisco
5. **Jonathan E. McBride,** McBride & Associates, Washington, DC
6. **James Masciarelli,** Fenwick Partners, Lexington, MA
7. **Mary E. Shourds,** Houze, Shourds & Montgomery, Long Beach, CA
8. **Theodore E. Lusk,** Nadzam, Lusk & Associates, Santa Clara, CA
9. **James Montgomery,** Houze, Shourds & Montgomery, Long Beach, CA
10. **John R. Akin,** J.R. Akin & Company, Fairfield, CT

Donald T. Allerton, Allerton, Heneghan & O'Neill, Chicago
O. William Battalia, Battalia, Winston International, New York

John P. DiVenuto, Deven Associates International, Verona, NJ
Michael S. Dunford, Michael S. Dunford, Inc., Glen Ellyn, IL
Dulany Foster, Jr., Korn/Ferry International, Stamford, CT
Ronald G. Goerss, Smith, Goerss & Ferneborg, Inc., San Francisco
William G. Hetzel, William Hetzel Associates, Inc., Schaumburg, IL
David Hoffmann, DHR International, Chicago
Jonathan S. Holman, The Holman Group, Inc., San Francisco
W. Jerry Hyde, Hyde Danforth & Company, Dallas
Mike Jacobs, Thorne, Brieger & Associates, Inc., New York
John F. Johnson, Lamalie Associates, Cleveland
R. Paul Kors, Kors Montgomery International, Houston
Laurence R. Massé, Ward Howell International, Barrington, IL
George W. Ott, Ott & Hansen Inc., Pasadena, CA
Barbara L. Provus, Shepherd, Bueschel & Provus, Inc., Chicago
J. Gerald Simmons, Handy Associates, New York
Robert L. Smith, Robert L. Smith & Company, New York
William K. Sur, Canny, Bowen Inc., New York
William H. Willis, Jr., William Willis Worldwide, Inc., Greenwich, CT

PACKAGING

1. **Michael Boxberger,** Korn/Ferry International, Chicago
2. **William H. Marumoto,** The Interface Group, Ltd., Washington, DC
3. **Robert M. Callan,** Callan & Associates, Oak Brook, IL
4. **David Hoffmann,** DHR International, Chicago
5. **Kai Lindholst,** Egon Zehnder International, Chicago
6. **Richard J. Cronin,** Hodge-Cronin & Associates, Inc., Rosemont, IL
7. **Fred Siegel,** Conex, Inc., New York
8. **Andrew Sherwood,** Goodrich & Sherwood Company, New York
9. **Henry G. Higdon,** Higdon, Joys & Mingle, New York
10. **Peter G. Grimm,** Nordeman Grimm, Inc., New York

   Carl W. Menk, Canny, Bowen Inc., New York
   David R. Peasback, Canny, Bowen Inc., New York
   J. Alvin Wakefield, Gilbert Tweed Associates, Inc., Pittsford, VT
   William H. Willis, Jr., William Willis Worldwide, Inc., Greenwich, CT
   Thomas C. Zay, Zay & Company, Atlanta

PAPER AND ALLIED PRODUCTS

1. **John F. Johnson,** Lamalie Associates, Cleveland
2. **William G. Hetzel,** William Hetzel Associates, Inc., Schaumburg, IL
3. **David R. Peasback,** Canny, Bowen Inc., New York
4. **O. William Battalia,** Battalia, Winston International, New York
5. **Richard M. McFarland,** Brissenden, McFarland, Wagoner & Fuccella, Inc., Stamford, CT
6. **Millington F. McCoy,** Gould & McCoy, New York
7. **William K. Sur,** Canny, Bowen Inc., New York
8. **P. John Mirtz,** Mirtz Morice Inc., Stamford, Ct
9. **Robert D. Spriggs,** Spriggs & Company Inc., Glenview, IL
10. **William A. Hertan,** Executive Manning Corp., Fort Lauderdale, FL

   Robert M. Callan, Callan & Associates, Oak Brook, IL
   David E. Chambers, David Chambers & Associates, Inc., New York

Richard J. Cronin, Hodge-Cronin & Associates, Inc., Rosemont, IL
Bert H. Early, Bert H. Early Associates Inc., Chicago
Ronald G. Goerss, Smith, Goerss & Ferneborg, Inc., San Francisco
Peter G. Grimm, Nordeman Grimm, Inc., New York
A.D. Hart, Jr., Russell Reynolds Associates, New York
George W. Henn, Jr., G.W. Henn & Company, Columbus, OH
Richard Kinser, Kinser & Associates, New York
Steven A. Seiden, Seiden Associates, New York
Putney Westerfield, Boyden International, San Francisco

PERFUME, COSMETICS, AND TOILET GOODS

1. **William E. Gould,** Gould & McCoy, New York
2. **P. John Mirtz,** Mirtz Morice Inc., Stamford, CT
3. **Frank Rico, Jr.,** J.R. Akin & Company, Fairfield, CT
4. **J. Alvin Wakefield,** Gilbert Tweed Associates, Inc., Pittsford, VT
5. **William K. Sur,** Canny, Bowen Inc., New York
6. **Theodore N. Jadick,** Heidrick & Struggles, Inc., New York
7. **Paul R. Ray, Sr.,** Paul Ray & Carré Orban International, Fort Worth
8. **Skott B. Burkland,** Skott/Edwards, Rutherford, NJ
9. **D. John Ingram,** Ingram, Inc., New York
10. **Dulany Foster, Jr.,** Korn/Ferry International, Stamford, CT

Martin H. Bauman, Martin Bauman Associates, Inc., New York
David E. Chambers, David Chambers & Associates, Inc., New York
David H. Charlson, Chestnut Hill Partners, Ltd., Deerfield, IL
James J. Drury III, SpencerStuart, Chicago
David S. Joys, Higdon, Joys & Mingle, New York
John Lucht, The John Lucht Consultancy, New York
Paul R. Ray, Jr., Paul Ray & Carré Orban International, Fort Worth
Andrew Sherwood, Goodrich & Sherwood Company, New York
Putney Westerfield, Boyden International, San Francisco

PHARMACEUTICAL/MEDICAL PRODUCTS

1. **William E. Gould,** Gould & McCoy, New York
2. **Roger M. Kenny,** Kenny, Kindler, Hunt & Howe, New York
3. **Frederick W. Wackerle,** McFeely Wackerle Shulman, Chicago
4. **A.D. Hart, Jr.,** Russell Reynolds Associates, New York
5. **Carl W. Menk,** Canny, Bowen Inc., New York
6. **Jonathan E. McBride,** McBride & Associates, Inc., Washington, DC
7. **Barbara L. Provus,** Shepherd, Bueschel & Provus, Inc., Chicago
8. **Kai Lindholst,** Egon Zehnder International, Chicago
9. **Donald T. Allerton,** Allerton, Heneghan & O'Neill, Chicago
10. **David H. Charlson,** Chestnut Hill Partners, Ltd., Deerfield, IL

O. William Battalia, Battalia, Winston International, New York
Jack R. Clarey, Jack Clarey Associates, Inc., Northbrook, IL
John P. DiVenuto, Deven Associates International, Verona, NJ
Dulany Foster, Jr., Korn/Ferry International, Stamford, CT
Ronald G. Goerss, Smith, Goerss & Ferneborg, Inc., San Francisco
Peter G. Grimm, Nordeman Grimm, Inc., New York

Mike Jacobs, Thorne, Brieger Associates, Inc., New York
E. Pendleton James, Pendleton James & Associates, New York
John Lucht, The John Lucht Consultancy, New York
Millington F. McCoy, Gould & McCoy, New York
Clarence E. McFeely, McFeely Wackerle Shulman, Chicago
George W. Ott, Ott & Hansen Inc., Pasadena, CA
David Powell, David Powell, Inc., Woodside, CA
Frank Rico, Jr., J.R. Akin & Company, Fairfield, CT
Daniel M. Shepherd, Shepherd, Bueschel & Provus, Inc., Chicago
William K. Sur, Canny, Bowen Inc., New York
Judith M. VonSeldeneck, The Diversified Search Companies, Philadelphia
J. Alvin Wakefield, Gilbert Tweed Associates, Inc., Pittsford, VT
William R. Wilkinson, Wilkinson & Ives, San Francisco
William H. Willis, Jr., William Willis Worldwide, Inc., Greenwich, CT

PRIMARY METAL INDUSTRIES

1. **David O. Harbert,** Sweeney, Harbert & Mummert Inc., Tampa, FL
2. **George W. Henn, Jr.,** G.W. Henn & Company, Columbus, OH
3. **Richard C. Slayton,** Slayton International Inc., Chicago
4. **W. Michael Danforth,** Hyde Danforth & Company, Dallas
5. **Michael S. Dunford,** Michael S. Dunford, Inc., Glen Ellyn, IL
6. **William A. Hertan,** Executive Manning Corp., Fort Lauderdale, FL

PUBLISHING AND PRINTING

1. **John Lucht,** The John Lucht Consultancy, New York
2. **Daniel M. Shepherd,** Shepherd, Bueschel & Provus, Inc., Chicago
3. **J. Gerald Simmons,** Handy Associates, New York
4. **Frederick W. Wackerle,** McFeely Wackerle Shulman, Chicago
5. **Louis A. Hoyda,** Thorndike Deland Associates, New York
6. **Putney Westerfield,** Boyden International, San Francisco
7. **John H. Robison,** Robison & McAulay, Charlotte, NC
8. **Janis M. Zivic,** The Zivic Group, Inc., San Francisco
9. **Thomas H. Ogdon,** The Ogdon Partnership, New York
10. **Kai Lindholst,** Egon Zehnder International, Chicago

David E. Chambers, David Chambers Associates, Inc., New York
Richard J. Cronin, Hodge-Cronin & Associates, Inc., Rosemont, IL
Ralph Dieckmann, Dieckmann & Associates, Chicago
John T. Gardner, Lamalie Associates, Chicago
A.D. Hart, Jr., Russell Reynolds Associates, New York
William H. Marumoto, The Interface Group, Ltd., Washington, DC
Robert D. Spriggs, Spriggs & Company Inc., Glenview, IL

RADIO AND TELEVISION BROADCASTING

1. **Gerard R. Roche,** Heidrick & Struggles, Inc., New York
2. **John Lucht,** The John Lucht Consultancy, New York
3. **Joseph E. Griesedieck, Jr.,** SpencerStuart, San Francisco

4.   **Michael J. Hoevel,** Poirier, Hoevel & Company, Los Angeles
5.   **Carl W. Menk,** Canny, Bowen Inc., New York
6.   **Clarence E. McFeely,** McFeely Wackerle Shulman, Chicago

REAL ESTATE

1.   **Dayton Ogden,** SpencerStuart, New York,
2.   **William E. Gould,** Gould & McCoy, New York
3.   **Roger M. Kenny,** Kenny, Kindler, Hunt & Howe, New York
4.   **Windle B. Priem,** Korn/Ferry International, New York
5.   **David M. DeWilde,** Chartwell Partners, San Francisco
6.   **John W. Franklin, Jr.,** Russell Reynolds Associates, Washington, DC
7.   **Thomas H. Ogdon,** The Ogdon Partnership, New York
8.   **Brenda L. Ruello,** Heidrick & Struggles, Inc., New York
9.   **Charles M. Meng,** Meng, Finseth & Associates, Torrance, CA
10.   **Richard M. Ferry,** Korn/Ferry International, Los Angeles

Martin H. Bauman, Martin Bauman Associates, Inc., New York
W. Hoyt Colton, W. Hoyt Colton Associates Inc., New York
W. Michael Danforth, Hyde Danforth & Company, Dallas
Leon A. Farley, Leon A. Farley Associates, San Francisco
Robert M. Flanagan, Robert Flanagan Associates Inc., N. Salem, NY
David Hoffmann, DHR International, Chicago
David S. Joys, Higdon, Joys & Mingle, New York
Claudia Lacy Kelly, Norman Broadbent International, New York
David Kettwig, A.T. Kearney, Chicago
Ferdinand Nadherny, Russell Reynolds Associates, Chicago
Larry Nein, Nordeman Grimm, Inc., Chicago
Jacques C. Nordeman, Nordeman Grimm, Inc., New York
George W. Ott, Ott & Hansen Inc., Pasadena, CA
John H. Robison, Robison & McAulay, Charlotte, NC
William H. Willis, Jr., William Willis Worldwide, Inc., Greenwich, CT

RETAIL

1.   **Herbert Mines,** Herbert Mines Associates Inc., New York
2.   **A.D. Hart, Jr.,** Russell Reynolds Associates, New York
3.   **Brenda L. Ruello,** Heidrick & Struggles, Inc., New York
4.   **James J. Drury III,** SpencerStuart, Chicago
5.   **Barbara L. Provus,** Shepherd, Bueschel & Provus, Inc., Chicago
6.   **Thomas J. Neff,** SpencerStuart, New York
7.   **Paul R. Ray, Sr.,** Paul Ray & Carré Orban International, Fort Worth
8.   **Roger M. Kenny,** Kenny, Kindler, Hunt & Howe, New York
9.   **Peter G. Grimm,** Nordeman Grimm, Inc., New York
10.   **Thomas C. Zay,** Zay & Company, Atlanta

Martin H. Bauman, Martin Bauman Associates, Inc., New York
Robert M. Callan, Callan & Associates, Oak Brook
Bert H. Early, Bert H. Early Associates Inc., Chicago
Richard M. Ferry, Korn/Ferry International, Los Angeles
John T. Gardner, Lamalie Associates, Chicago
Ronald G. Goerss, Smith, Goerss & Ferneborg, Inc., San Francisco

Joseph E. Griesedieck, Jr., SpencerStuart, San Francisco
Michael J. Hoevel, Poirier, Hoevel & Company, Los Angeles
David Hoffmann, DHR International, Chicago
Mike Jacobs, Thorne, Brieger Associates, Inc., New York
E. Pendleton James, Pendleton James & Associates, New York
Claudia Lacy Kelly, Norman Broadbent International, New York
John Lucht, The John Lucht Consultancy, New York
Larry Nein, Nordeman Grimm, Inc., Chicago
Frank Rico, Jr., J.R. Akin & Company, Fairfield, CT
Norman C. Roberts, Norman Roberts & Associates, Inc., Los Angeles
Jack Seitchik, Seitchik, Corwin & Seitchik Inc., San Francisco
Fred Siegel, Conex, Inc., New York
William K. Sur, Canny, Bowen Inc., New York
Putney Westerfield, Boyden International, San Francisco

RUBBER AND PLASTIC PRODUCTS

1. **John F. Johnson,** Lamalie Associates, Cleveland
2. **Mike Jacobs,** Thorne, Brieger Associates, Inc., New York
3. **William G. Hetzel,** William Hetzel Associates, Inc., Schaumburg, IL
4. **George W. Henn, Jr.,** G.W. Henn & Company, Columbus, OH
5. **Robert M. Bryza,** Robert Lowell International, Dallas
6. **Richard M. McFarland,** Brissenden, McFarland, Wagoner & Fuccella, Inc., Stamford, CT
7. **Ferdinand Nadherny,** Russell Reynolds Associates, New York
8. **Richard J. Cronin,** Hodge-Cronin & Associates, Inc., Rosemont, IL
9. **Daniel M. Shepherd,** Shepherd, Bueschel & Provus, Inc., Chicago
10. **Richard C. Slayton,** Slayton International Inc., Chicago

   Otis H. Bowden II, Bowden & Company, Inc., Cleveland
   P. John Mirtz, Mirtz Morice Inc., Stamford, CT
   Norman C. Roberts, Norman Roberts & Associates, Inc., Los Angeles
   Andrew Sherwood, Goodrich & Sherwood Company, New York

SECURITY AND COMMODITY BROKERS, DEALERS, AND EXCHANGES

1. **Thomas J. Neff,** SpencerStuart, New York
2. **Jay Gaines,** Jay Gaines & Company, New York
3. **Windle B. Priem,** Korn/Ferry International, New York
4. **Jeffrey G. Bell,** Norman Broadbent International, New York
5. **Russell S. Reynolds, Jr.,** Russell Reynolds Associates, New York
6. **Durant A. Hunter,** Gardiner Stone Hunter International, Boston
7. **Henry G. Higdon,** Higdon, Joys & Mingle, New York
8. **Jacques C. Nordeman,** Nordeman Grimm, Inc., New York
9. **Ferdinand Nadherny,** Russell Reynolds Associates, Chicago
10. **W. Hoyt Colton,** W. Hoyt Colton Associates Inc., New York

   Robert M. Flanagan, Robert Flanagan Associates Inc., N. Salem, NY
   Richard K. Ives, Wilkinson & Ives, San Francisco
   Claudia Lacy Kelly, Norman Broadbent International, New York
   David Kettwig, A.T. Kearney, Chicago

Eleanor H. Raynolds, Ward Howell International, New York
Richard Sbarbaro, Lauer, Sbarbaro Associates, Chicago
Mary E. Shourds, Houze, Shourds & Montgomery Inc., Long Beach, CA

TEXTILES

1. **John H. Callen, Jr.,** Ward Howell International Inc., New York
2. **Thomas C. Zay,** Zay & Company, Atlanta
3. **Herbert Mines,** Herbert Mines Associates, Inc., New York
4. **John H. Robison,** Robison & McAulay, Charlotte, NC
5. **Jack Seitchik,** Seitchik, Corwin & Seitchik Inc., San Francisco
6. **A.D. Hart, Jr.,** Russell Reynolds Associates, New York
7. **William K. Sur,** Canny, Bowen Inc., New York

TOBACCO AND LIQUOR

1. **James Morice,** Mirtz Morice Inc., Stamford, CT
2. **Andrew Sherwood,** Goodrich & Sherwood Company, New York
3. **Gerard R. Roche,** Heidrick & Struggles, Inc., New York
4. **David S. Joys,** Higdon, Joys & Mingle, New York
5. **James J. Drury III,** SpencerStuart, Chicago
6. **William H. Marumoto,** The Interface Group, Ltd., Washington, DC
7. **John F. Johnson,** Lamalie Associates, Cleveland
8. **Laurence R. Massé,** Ward Howell International, Barrington, IL
9. **Kai Lindholst,** Egon Zehnder International, Chicago

TRANSPORTATION BY AIR, RAIL, TRUCK, OR WATER

1. **Gerard R. Roche,** Heidrick & Struggles, Inc., New York
2. **Robert Slater,** Slater & Associates, Dallas
3. **John P. DiVenuto,** Deven Associates International, Verona, NJ
4. **Robert W. Dingman,** Robert W. Dingman Co., Inc., Westlake Village, CA
5. **Martin H. Bauman,** Martin Bauman Associates, Inc., New York
6. **William C. Houze,** William C. Houze & Co., La Quinta, CA
7. **D. John Ingram,** Ingram, Inc., New York
8. **Dayton Ogden,** SpencerStuart, Stamford, CT
9. **David R. Peasback,** Canny, Bowen Inc., New York
10. **Norman C. Roberts,** Norman Roberts & Associates, Inc., Los Angeles

Peter Crist, Russell Reynolds Associates, Chicago
James J. Drury III, SpencerStuart, Chicago
Leon A. Farley, Leon A. Farley Associates, San Francisco
Robert M. Flanagan, Robert Flanagan Associates Inc., N. Salem, NY
John W. Franklin, Jr., Russell Reynolds Associates, Washington, DC
Ronald G. Goerss, Smith, Goerss & Ferneborg, Inc., San Francisco
Henry G. Higdon, Higdon, Joys & Mingle, New York
E. Pendleton James, Pendleton James & Associates, New York
David S. Joys, Higdon, Joys & Mingle, New York
R. Paul Kors, Kors Montgomery International, Houston
Carl W. Menk, Canny, Bowen Inc., New York
Russell S. Reynolds, Jr., Russell Reynolds Associates, New York
John H. Robison, Robison & McAulay, Charlotte, NC
Steven A. Seiden, Seiden Associates, New York

Richard C. Slayton, Slayton International Inc., Chicago
Robert L. Smith, Robert L. Smith & Company, New York
Robert D. Spriggs, Spriggs & Company Inc., Glenview, IL
J. Alvin Wakefield, Gilbert Tweed Associates, Inc., Pittsford, VT
William R. Wilkinson, Wilkinson & Ives, San Francisco

TRANSPORTATION EQUIPMENT

1. **John F. Johnson,** Lamalie Associates, Cleveland
2. **Otis H. Bowden II,** Bowden & Company, Inc., Cleveland
3. **Laurence R. Massé,** Ward Howell International, Barrington, IL
4. **Mary E. Shourds,** Houze, Shourds & Montgomery, Inc., Long Beach, CA
5. **James Morice,** Mirtz Morice Inc., Stamford, CT
6. **Gary Kreutz,** Kreutz Consulting, Lake Forest, IL
7. **William G. Hetzel,** William Hetzel Associates, Inc., Schaumburg, IL
8. **Frederick W. Wackerle,** McFeely Wackerle Shulman, Chicago
9. **John T. Gardner,** Lamalie Associates, Chicago
10. **Robert M. Bryza,** Robert Lowell International, Dallas

UNIVERSITIES, COLLEGES, SCHOOLS

1. **William J. Bowen,** Heidrick & Struggles, Inc., Chicago
2. **Ira W. Krinsky,** Ira W. Krinsky & Associates, Pasadena, CA
3. **Gary J. Posner,** George Kaludis Associates, Nashville
4. **John Lucht,** The John Lucht Consultancy, New York
5. **Janis M. Zivic,** The Zivic Group, Inc., San Francisco
6. **Judith M. VonSeldeneck,** The Diversified Search Companies, Philadelphia
7. **W. Michael Danforth,** Hyde Danforth & Company, Dallas
8. **Michael D. Caver,** Heidrick & Struggles, Inc., Chicago
9. **Frank Rico, Jr.,** J.R. Akin & Company, Fairfield, CT
10. **William E. Gould,** Gould & McCoy, New York

W. Hoyt Colton, W. Hoyt Colton Associates Inc., New York
David M. DeWilde, Chartwell Partners, San Francisco
Frank A. Garofolo, Garofolo, Curtiss, Lambert & MacLean, Ardmore, PA
Laurence R. Massé, Ward Howell International, Barrington, IL
Millington F. McCoy, Gould & McCoy, New York
William C. Houze, William C. Houze & Co., La Quinta, CA
Charles M. Meng, Meng, Finseth & Associates, Torrance, CA
Eleanor H. Raynolds, Ward Howell International, New York
Norman C. Roberts, Norman Roberts & Associates, Inc., Los Angeles
John H. Robison, Robison & McAulay, Charlotte, NC
Richard Sbarbaro, Lauer, Sbarbaro Associates, Chicago
Jack H. Vernon, Russell Reynolds Associates, Boston
J. Alvin Wakefield, Gilbert Tweed Associates, Inc., Pittsford, VT

VENTURE CAPITAL

1. **William R. Wilkinson,** Wilkinson & Ives, San Francisco
2. **Michael Boxberger,** Korn/Ferry International, Chicago
3. **Jonathan S. Holman,** The Holman Group, Inc., San Francisco
4. **Martin H. Bauman,** Martin Bauman Associates, Inc., New York
5. **David M. DeWilde,** Chartwell Partners, San Francisco

6. **Skott B. Burkland,** Skott/Edwards, Rutherford, NJ
7. **Neal L. Maslan,** Ward Howell International, Encino, CA
8. **Herbert Mines,** Herbert Mines Associates, Inc., New York
9. **Durant A. Hunter,** Gardiner Stone Hunter International, Boston
10. **Jeffrey G. Bell,** Norman Broadbent International, New York

O. William Battalia, Battalia, Winston International, New York
William B. Clemens, Jr., Norman Broadbent International, New York
W. Hoyt Colton, W. Hoyt Colton Associates Inc., New York
W. Michael Danforth, Hyde Danforth & Company, Dallas
John P. DiVenuto, Deven Associates International, Verona, NJ
James J. Drury III, SpencerStuart, Chicago
Louis A. Hoyda, Thorndike Deland Associates, New York
Richard K. Ives, Wilkinson & Ives, San Francisco
David S. Joys, Higdon, Joys & Mingle, New York
Richard Kinser, Kinser & Associates, New York
Gary Kreutz, Kreutz Consulting, Lake Forest, IL
James Masciarelli, Fenwick Partners, Lexington, MA
Jonathan E. McBride, McBride Associates, Inc., Washington, DC
Richard M. McFarland, Brissenden, McFarland, Wagoner & Fuccella, Inc., Stamford, CT
Russell S. Reynolds, Jr., Russell Reynolds Associates, New York
Brenda L. Ruello, Heidrick & Struggles, Inc., New York
Robert D. Spriggs, Spriggs & Company Inc., Glenview, IL
Jack H. Vernon, Russell Reynolds Associates, Boston
Judith M. VonSeldeneck, The Diversified Search Companies, Philadelphia
William H. Willis, Jr., William Willis Worldwide, Inc., Greenwich, CT

WHOLESALE TRADE

1. **John H. Callen, Jr.,** Ward Howell International, New York
2. **Herbert Mines,** Herbert Mines Associates, Inc., New York
3. **Martin H. Bauman,** Martin Bauman Associates, Inc., New York
4. **David O. Harbert,** Sweeney, Harbert & Mummert Inc., Tampa, FL
5. **Robert M. Flanagan,** Robert Flanagan Associates Inc., N. Salem, NY
6. **Joseph E. Griesedieck, Jr.,** SpencerStuart, San Francisco
7. **Mike Jacobs,** Thorne, Brieger Associates, Inc., New York
8. **Michael J. Hoevel,** Poirier, Hoevel & Company, Los Angeles
9. **Steven A. Seiden,** Seiden Associates, New York

THE TOP EXECUTIVE RECRUITERS IN CANADA AND MEXICO

These recruiters are ranked on the basis of nominations from client organizations and recruiting peers. Recruiting specialities are listed in order provided by the recruiter.

CANADA

1. **GEORGE R. ENNS,** George Enns Partners Inc., Toronto

Industries/Organizations	*Functions*
Food and kindred products	General management
Communications/telecommunications	Marketing/sales — consumer
Publishing and printing	Finance and accounting
Banks	Human resources/personnel
Retail trade	Marketing/sales — industrial
Holding companies	Operations
Electrical and electronic machinery	Merchandising

2. **ANNE M. FAWCETT,** The Caldwell Partners Int'l., Toronto

Industries/Organizations	*Functions*
Holding companies	General management
Financial services	Marketing/sales — consumer
Telecommunications	Marketing/sales — industrial
Pharmaceutical/scientific	Finance and accounting
Not-for-profit organizations	Human resources/personnel
Marketing/sales — consumer	MIS/computer operations
Secondary manufacturing	
Office machinery and computers	

3. **SIDNEY A. HUMPHREYS,** Korn/Ferry International, Toronto

Industries/Organizations	*Functions*
Office machinery and computers	General management
Insurance	International
Banks	Director recruitment
Investment banking	Finance and accounting
Manufacturing	Planning
Communications/telecommunications	Marketing/sales — industrial
Real estate	Marketing/sales — consumer
Mining	MIS/computer operations
Private clubs	Human resources/personnel

4. **C. DOUGLAS CALDWELL,** The Caldwell Partners Int'l., Toronto

Industries/Organizations	*Functions*
Holding companies	General management
Marketing organizations	Finance and accounting
Financial services	Marketing/sales—consumer
Communications/telecommunications	Marketing/sales—industrial
Pharmaceutical/medical products	Administration
Health services/hospitals	
Manufacturing	
Distribution	
Government agencies	
Energy	

5. **HUGH ILLSLEY,** Ward Howell Illsley & Partners, Toronto

Industries/Organizations	*Functions*
Holding companies	General management
Investment banking	Director recruitment
Banks	Finance and accounting
Retail trade	Human resources/personnel
Wholesale trade	International
Machinery, except electrical	
Pharmaceutical/medical products	
Chemicals and allied products	

6. **J. ROBERT SWIDLER,** Egon Zehnder International, Montreal

Industries/Organizations	*Functions*
Law, accounting, consulting firms	General management
Holding companies	Finance and accounting
Banks	Marketing/sales—consumer
Real estate	Human resources/personnel
Paper and allied products	Legal
Retail trade	Manufacturing/production/operations
Office machinery and computers	
Food and kindred products	
Communications/telecommunications	
Hotels, resorts, private clubs	

7. **GERRY BAKER,** Baker Harris & Partners Ltd., Toronto

Industries/Organizations	*Functions*
Office machinery and computers	Marketing/sales—industrial
Computer software	General management
Electrical and electronic machinery	Advertising/promotion
Communications/telecommunications	Direct marketing
Venture capital firms	
Aerospace	

MEXICO

1. HORACIO J. McCOY, Korn/Ferry International, Mexico City

Industries/Organizations	Functions
Food and kindred products	General management
Banks	International
Holding companies	Marketing/sales—consumer
Perfume, cosmetics, toilet goods	Finance and accounting
Retail trade	Manufacturing/production/operations
Pharmaceutical/medical products	Planning
Investment banking	Human resources/personnel
Security brokers and exchanges	Public relations/government affairs

2. JOHN E. SMITH, JR., Smith Search, S.C., Mexico City

Industries/Organizations	Functions
Food and kindred products	General management
Chemical and allied products	Marketing/sales—consumer
Fabricated metal industries	Finance and accounting
Banks	Manufacturing/production/operations
Holding companies	

3. CRAIG J. DUDLEY, Conrey Interamericana, S.A. de C.V., Mexico City

Industries/Organizations	Functions
Food and kindred products	General management
Paper and allied products	Marketing/sales—consumer
Chemicals and allied products	Marketing/sales—industrial
Fabricated metal products	Direct marketing
Office machinery and computers	Finance and accounting
Transportation by air/rail/water	MIS/computer operations
Communications/telecommunications	International
Investment banking	Manufactruing/production/operations
Insurance	Human resources/personnel
Hotels, resorts, private clubs	Merchandising

4. MANUEL A. PAPAYANOPULOS T., Korn/Ferry International, Mexico City

Industries/Organizations	Functions
Pharmaceutical/medical products	General management
Food and kindred products	Human resources/personnel
Perfume, cosmetics, toilet goods	Marketing/sales—consumer
Office machinery and computers	Finance and accounting
Computer software	Manufacturing/production/operations
Chemicals and allied products	Marketing/sales—industrial
Packaging	MIS/computer operations
Transportation by air/rail/water	Purchasing/materials
Communications/telecommunications	Legal
Rubber and plastic products	Planning

7

THE ACADEMY COMPANIES

Poor Jack Welch. He and his able predecessors at General Electric have attempted for decades to guard borders more violated than the Rio Grande at low-water time.

When it comes to the development of managerial talent, General Electric is in a league of its own—or at least that's what North America's top executive recruiters say. And who could argue that they would not be the best possible determiners? From the very inception of the executive search business almost seventy years ago, recruiters have made their livings and built their reputations on the premise that they can not only assess talent when they see it but know precisely which organizations they must penetrate to find it. Industry by industry, function by function, year in and year out, recruiters have evolved their own empirically derived map to the pools of talent most likely to contain their perfect placements.

Of course, this doesn't mean that the recruiter is always successful in finding his or her placement in the most likely academy companies, but a recruiter who does not probe such companies is like a trout fisherman casting a line in the Louisiana bayous. That isn't to say that there might not be a trout in the bayous, but if there is, there are certainly some significant questions—like how the poor creature got there in the first place, who taught it what it knows, and where is it going in a swamp?

Through their years of searching, the best executive recruiters have discovered those companies particularly worth investigating for candidates with especially good training and experience in their specific areas of interest. Many times, too, an academy company's "alumni" are as desirable to a new employer as those still employed at the company. Therefore, for any professional—and every recent graduate who aspires to career progress and leadership—it is especially savvy to be currently employed by, or to have worked with in the past, an academy company. They are as much career makers as the recruiters themselves. Not only are these companies the standouts in their respective industries or functions in *developing* talent, but as a consequence they are the ones *most heavily hunted by the headhunters.*

In the pages that follow, America's academy companies are identified for the very first time. (For the process by which they were selected, see pages 12–13.) The top 50 are ranked on the basis of the actual points they achieved from the 356 executive recruiters who offered their opinions. Following this are the rankings of the leading companies in 16 prominent industries and 9 major business functions. There are ten academy companies listed in each category, except in those instances where fewer were found to be relatively far ahead of all others in that category.

Industries and functions represented in the rankings of recruiters in the previous chapter, but not included in the academy company section, have been omitted either because no single company or group of companies stood out or because the number of nominations received in that industry or function was considered statistically insignificant.

Now one last word to Jack Welch about his plight at General Electric. Notwithstanding all the probing and raiding from headhunters the world over, or the intrusions of competitors recruiting on their own, you must still take a great deal of satisfaction, Mr. Welch, in seeing how overwhelming the real-world evidence is that G.E. stands apart as the greatest developer of professional and managerial talent that twentieth-century enterprise has known. Bar none. Our hats are off to you in particular but also to those other chief executive officers who lead the class in the rest of America's academy companies.

AMERICA'S TOP 50 ACADEMY COMPANIES

	Company/Headquarters	Description of Business	Nomination Points
1.	General Electric Company Fairfield, CT	Diversified manufacturer, high-tech products; services	658
2.	PepsiCo, Inc. Purchase, NY	Consumer beverages, snacks, and restaurants	274
3.	International Business Machines Armonk, NY	Computer hardware and software manufacturer and marketer	265
4.	The Procter & Gamble Company Cincinnati, OH	Consumer health, beauty aid, food, and household products	245
5.	Citibank[a] New York, NY	Commercial banking services	153
6.	Ford Motor Company Dearborn, MI	Manufacturer of automobiles, trucks, and parts; services	136
7.	Merck & Company, Inc. Rahway, NJ	Drugs, animal health products, and specialty chemicals	132
8.	Kraft/General Foods[b] Glenview, IL	Prepared consumer food products	131
9.	Hewlett-Packard Company Palo Alto, CA	Electronic equipment, office and factory automation; software	120
10.	Xerox Corporation Stamford, CT	Copiers and duplicating equipment	94
11.	Emerson Electric Co. St. Louis, MO	Manufacturers of electrical and electronic products	82
12.	Rockwell International Corp. El Segundo, CA	Defense electronics, industrial automation, telecommunications	68
13.	McKinsey & Co. New York, NY	General management consulting	67
14.	Bankers Trust Co.[c] New York, NY	Commercial banking	60
15.	Johnson & Johnson New Brunswick, NJ	Consumer health products, diagnostic and medical equipment	60
16.	Baxter International Inc. Deerfield, IL	Manufacturer and distributor of health care products and services	59
17.	General Mills, Inc. Minneapolis, MN	Prepared consumer food products and specialty restaurants	55
18.	Abbott Laboratories Abbott Park, IL	Drugs, hospital products, nutritionals and diagnostic products	54
19.	American Telephone & Telegraph New York, NY	Telecommunications worldwide; computers	52
20.	ITT Corporation New York, NY	Electronic and electromechanical products and systems; services	51
21.	Monsanto Company St. Louis, MO	Industrial and agricultural chemicals, drugs, sweeteners	50
22.	Bristol-Myers Squibb Company New York, NY	Drugs, household products, implants, and nutritionals	49

AMERICA'S TOP 50 ACADEMY COMPANIES (continued)

Company/Headquarters	Description of Business	Nomination Points
23. Morgan Guaranty Trust Co. NY[d] New York, NY	Commercial banking	48
24. Morgan Stanley Group Inc. New York, NY	Investment banking, securities trading worldwide	48
25. Motorola, Inc. Schaumburg, IL	Semiconductors, mobile radios, electronic hardware and systems	48
26. American Airlines, Inc.[e] Fort Worth, TX	Air transportation and related services	47
27. The Goldman Sachs Group, LP New York, NY	Investment banking and related financial services	46
28. The Coca-Cola Company Atlanta, Georgia	Consumer beverages	45
29. American Express Company New York, NY	Diversified financial services; direct marketing	45
30. E.I. duPont de Nemours & Company Wilmington, DE	Chemicals, fibers, coal, natural gas, diversified business products	45
31. The Boeing Company Seattle, WA	Commercial and military aircraft and aerospace manufacturer	44
32. Arthur Andersen & Co. Chicago, IL	Public accounting and related business consulting services	42
33. Avon Products, Inc. New York, NY	Direct marketers of cosmetics and gift items	41
34. The Dow Chemical Company Midland, MI	Chemicals and plastics worldwide; consumer health care products	40
35. Amoco Corporation Chicago, IL	Petroleum refining and marketing, chemicals and automobile products	39
36. Microsoft Corporation Redmond, WA	Developer of PC systems and applications software	39
37. Wells Fargo Bank[f] San Francisco, CA	Commercial banking	38
38. Colgate-Palmolive Company New York, NY	Consumer personal care, laundry, and household products	37
39. Time Warner Inc. New York, NY	Magazine and book publishing, cable TV, related media, and entertainment	36
40. Exxon Corporation New York, NY	Petroleum, natural gas, petrochemicals, and coal producer	36
41. Electronic Data Systems Corp.[g] Dallas, TX	Electronic data processing services and systems	36
42. The Limited, Inc. Columbus, OH	Retail clothing stores and apparel contract manufacturing	35
43. Minnesota Mining & Manufacturing St. Paul, MN	Industrial, consumer, electronic, imaging, and life science products	34
44. RJR Nabisco, Inc. New York, NY	Tobacco, confectionery, and other consumer food products	32

AMERICA'S TOP 50 ACADEMY COMPANIES (continued)

	Company/Headquarters	Description of Business	Nomination Points
45.	Chubb & Son, Inc.[h] Warren, NJ	Property and casualty insurer	32
46.	The May Department Stores Co. St. Louis, MO	Operator of conventional department stores; discount shoes	32
47.	Union Pacific Corporation Bethlehem, PA	Rail transportation, trucking, natural resources, waste management	32
48.	Philip Morris U.S.A.[i] New York, NY	Tobacco products manufacturing and marketing	31
49.	General Motors Corporation Detroit, MI	Automobiles, trucks, parts, locomotives; defense products; services	30
50.	CIGNA Corporation Philadelphia, PA	Property and casualty insurance and diversified financial services	30

Note: Companies tied on the basis of total points from recruiters are ranked according to the number of first-place nominations.

[a] Subsidiary of Citicorp.

[b] Subsidiary of Philip Morris Companies, Inc.

[c] Subsidiary of Bankers Trust New York Corporation.

[d] Subsidiary of J.P. Morgan & Co., Inc.

[e] Subsidiary of AMR Corporation.

[f] Subsidiary of Wells Fargo & Company.

[g] Subsidiary of General Motors Corporation.

[h] Subsidiary of Chubb Corp.

[i] An operating company of Philip Morris Companies, Inc.

ACADEMY COMPANIES' INDUSTRY RANKINGS

AEROSPACE

1. **General Electric Company**, Fairfield, CT
2. **The Boeing Company**, Seattle, WA
3. **Rockwell International Corp.**, El Segundo, CA
4. **Hughes Aircraft Company**, Los Angeles, CA
5. **TRW Inc.**, Cleveland, OH
6. **General Dynamics Corporation**, St. Louis, MO
7. **Martin Marietta Corporation**, Bethesda, MD
8. **Litton Industries, Inc.**, Beverly Hills, CA
9. **Textron, Inc.**, Providence, RI
10. **Raytheon Company**, Lexington, MA

BANKING

1. **Citibank**, New York, NY
2. **Bankers Trust Co.**, New York, NY
3. **Morgan Guaranty Trust Co. NY**, New York, NY

4. **Wells Fargo Bank**, San Francisco, CA
5. **Chase Manhattan Bank**, New York, NY
6. **Bank of America**, San Francisco, CA
7. **NCNB Corporation**, Charlotte, NC
8. **Wachovia Bank & Trust Company**, Winston-Salem, NC
9. **First Interstate Bancorp**, Los Angeles, CA
10. **Northern Trust Company**, Chicago, IL

CHEMICAL AND ALLIED PRODUCTS

1. **Monsanto Company**, St. Louis, MO
2. **The Dow Chemical Company**, Midland, MI
3. **General Electric Plastics Group**, Pittsfield, MA
4. **E.I. duPont de Nemours & Company**, Wilmington, DE
5. **Union Carbide Corporation**, Danbury, CT
6. **NALCO Chemical Co.**, Naperville, IL
7. **B.F. Goodrich Co.**, Akron, OH
8. **Hoechst-Celanese**, Somerville, NJ
9. **Eastman Chemical Products Inc.**, Kingsport, TN
10. **Minnesota Mining & Manufacturing**, St. Paul, MN

COMMUNICATIONS AND TELECOMMUNICATIONS

1. **American Telephone & Telegraph**, New York, NY
2. **Federal Express Corporation**, Memphis, TN
3. **MCI Communications Corp.**, Washington, DC
4. **GTE Corporation**, Stamford, CT
5. **Northern Telecom Inc.**, Nashville, TN
6. **Scientific-Atlanta Inc.**, Atlanta, GA
7. **Bell Labs**, New York, NY
8. **U.S. West, Inc.**, Englewood, CO
9. **Pacific Telesis Group**, San Francisco, CA
10. **Communications Satellite Corp. (Comsat)**, Washington, DC

CONSULTING AND ACCOUNTING FIRMS

1. **McKinsey & Co.**, New York, NY
2. **Booz, Allen & Hamilton**, New York, NY
3. **Boston Consulting Group**, Boston, MA
4. **Arthur Andersen & Co.**, Chicago, IL
5. **Price Waterhouse & Co.**, New York, NY

ELECTRICAL AND ELECTRONIC MACHINERY

1. **General Electric Company**, Fairfield, CT
2. **International Business Machines**, Armonk, NY
3. **Hewlett-Packard Company**, Palo Alto, CA
4. **Motorola, Inc.**, Schaumburg, IL
5. **NCR Corporation**, Dayton, OH
6. **Nordson Corp.**, Cleveland, OH
7. **Asea Brown Boveri**, Stamford, CT
8. **Xerox Corporation**, Stamford, CT

9. **Emerson Electric Co.**, St. Louis, MO
10. **Teradyne Inc.**, Boston, MA

FOOD AND KINDRED PRODUCTS

1. **Kraft/General Foods**, Glenview, IL
2. **PepsiCo, Inc.**, Purchase, NY
3. **The Procter & Gamble Company**, Cincinnati, OH
4. **General Mills, Inc.**, Minneapolis, MN
5. **The Coca-Cola Company**, Atlanta, GA
6. **RJR Nabisco, Inc.**, New York, NY
7. **The Pillsbury Company**, Minneapolis, MN
8. **H.J. Heinz Company**, Pittsburgh, PA
9. **Nestle Foods Corp.**, New York, NY
10. **The Quaker Oats Company**, Chicago, IL

INSURANCE

1. **CIGNA Corporation**, Philadelphia, PA
2. **Chubb & Son, Inc.**, Warren, NJ
3. **The Prudential Insurance Co. of America**, Newark, NJ
4. **Aetna Life & Casualty Co.**, Hartford, CT
5. **Capital Holding Corp.**, Louisville, KY
6. **Nationwide Mutual Insurance Company**, Columbus, OH
7. **American General Corp.**, Houston, TX
8. **Northwestern Mutual**, Milwaukee, WI
9. **State Farm**, Bloomington, IL
10. **The Hartford Insurance Group**, Hartford, CT
11. **Allstate Insurance Companies**, Northbrook, IL

INVESTMENT BANKING

1. **Morgan Stanley Group, Inc.**, New York, NY
2. **The Goldman Sachs Group, LP**, New York, NY
3. **Merrill Lynch & Co., Inc.**, New York, NY
4. **The First Boston Corporation**, New York, NY
5. **S.G. Warburg & Co. Inc.**, New York, NY

OFFICE MACHINERY AND COMPUTERS

1. **International Business Machines**, Armonk, NY
2. **Hewlett-Packard Company**, Palo Alto, CA
3. **Xerox Corporation**, Stamford, CT
4. **Pitney Bowes, Inc.**, Stamford, CT
5. **Digital Equipment Corporation**, Maynard, MA

PAPER AND ALLIED PRODUCTS

1. **International Paper Company**, Purchase, NY
2. **James River Corporation**, Richmond, VA
3. **Georgia-Pacific Corporation**, Atlanta, GA
4. **Weyerhauser Company**, Tacoma, WA
5. **Union Camp Corporation**, Wayne, NJ

PERFUME, COSMETICS, AND TOILET GOODS

1. **The Procter & Gamble Company**, Cincinnati, OH
2. **Avon Products, Inc.**, New York, NY
3. **Colgate-Palmolive Company**, New York, NY
4. **Estee Lauder Inc.**, New York, NY
5. **The Gillette Company**, Boston, MA

PHARMACEUTICAL AND MEDICAL PRODUCTS

1. **Merck & Company, Inc.**, Rahway, NJ
2. **Abbott Laboratories**, Abbott Park, IL
3. **Baxter International, Inc.**, Deerfield, IL
4. **Johnson & Johnson**, New Brunswick, NJ
5. **Pfizer, Inc.**, New York, NY
6. **Bristol-Meyers Squibb Company**, New York, NY
7. **SmithKline Beecham PLC**, Philadelphia, PA
8. **Hoffmann-LaRoche Inc.**, Nutley, NJ
9. **Ciba-Geigy Corp.**, Ardsley, NY
10. **C.R. Bard, Inc.**, Murray Hill, NJ

PUBLISHING AND PRINTING

1. **Time Warner Inc.**, New York, NY
2. **Simon & Schuster Inc.**, New York, NY
3. **Dow Jones & Company, Inc.**, New York, NY
4. **Knight-Ridder, Inc.**, Miami, FL
5. **R.R. Donnelly & Sons Company**, Chicago, IL

RETAIL

1. **The May Department Stores Company**, St. Louis, MO
2. **The Limited, Inc.**, Columbus, OH
3. **Federated Department Stores**, Cincinnati, OH
4. **Dayton Hudson Corporation**, Minneapolis, MN
5. **R.H. Macy & Co., Inc.**, New York, NY
6. **The Gap, Inc.**, San Bruno, CA
7. **Wal-Mart Stores, Inc.**, Bentonville, AR

TRANSPORTATION

1. **American Airlines, Inc.**, Ft. Worth, TX
2. **Union Pacific Corporation**, Bethlehem, PA
3. **Delta Air Lines, Inc.**, Atlanta, GA
4. **United Airlines**, Chicago, IL
5. **USAir Group, Inc.**, Arlington, VA

ACADEMY COMPANIES' FUNCTIONAL RANKINGS

GENERAL MANAGEMENT

1. **General Electric Company**, Fairfield, CT
2. **International Business Machines**, Armonk, NY
3. **Emerson Electric Co.**, St. Louis, MO

4. **Hewlett-Packard Company**, Palo Alto, CA
5. **PepsiCo, Inc.**, Purchase, NY
6. **The Procter & Gamble Company**, Cincinnati, OH
7. **Kraft/General Foods**, Glenview, IL
8. **Johnson & Johnson**, New Brunswick, NJ
9. **ITT Corporation**, New York, NY
10. **Xerox Corporation**, Stamford, CT
11. **Minnesota Mining and Manufacturing**, St. Paul, MN
12. **Motorola, Inc.**, Schaumburg, IL
13. **Rubbermaid Inc.**, Wooster, OH
14. **Bristol-Meyers Squibb Company**, New York, NY
15. **Honeywell Inc.**, Minneapolis, MN
16. **RJR Nabisco, Inc.**, New York, NY
17. **American Express Corporation**, New York, NY
18. **United Technologies Corporation**, Hartford, CT
19. **Merck & Company, Inc.**, Rahway, NJ
20. **Colgate Palmolive Company**, New York, NY

FINANCE AND ACCOUNTING

1. **Ford Motor Company**, Dearborn, MI
2. **General Electric Company**, Fairfield, CT
3. **ITT Corporation**, New York, NY
4. **PepsiCo, Inc.**, Purchase, NY
5. **Emerson Electric Co.**, St. Louis, MO
6. **Rockwell International Corp.**, El Segundo, CA
7. **Arthur Andersen & Co.**, Chicago, IL
8. **Monsanto Company**, St. Louis, MO
9. **Merrill Lynch & Co., Inc.**, New York, NY
10. **Xerox Corporation**, Stamford, CT

HUMAN RESOURCES/PERSONNEL

1. **PepsiCo, Inc.**, Purchase, NY
2. **General Electric Company**, Fairfield, CT
3. **International Business Machines**, Armonk, NY
4. **Xerox Corporation**, Stamford, CT
5. **American Express Company**, New York, NY
6. **Johnson & Johnson**, New Brunswick, NJ
7. **Citicorp**, New York, NY
8. **Motorola, Inc.**, Schaumburg, IL
9. **Dresser Industries, Inc.**, Dallas, TX
10. **Merck & Company Inc.**, Rahway, NJ

INTERNATIONAL

1. **PepsiCo, Inc.**, Purchase, NY
2. **International Business Machines**, Armonk, NY
3. **The Coca-Cola Company**, Atlanta, GA
4. **ABB Asea Brown Boveri, Ltd.**, Stamford, CT
5. **Philip Morris Companies, Inc.**, New York, NY
6. **Honeywell Inc.**, Minneapolis, MN
7. **SmithKline Beecham, PLC**, Philadelphia, PA

8. **Ford Motor Company**, Dearborn, MI
9. **CPC International**, Englewood Cliffs, NJ
10. **Nestlé Foods Corp.**, New York, NY

MANUFACTURING/PRODUCTION/OPERATIONS

1. **General Electric Company**, Fairfield, CT
2. **Hewlett-Packard Company**, Palo Alto, CA
3. **The Procter & Gamble Company**, Cincinnati, OH
4. **Ford Motor Company**, Dearborn, MI
5. **Emerson Electric Co.**, St. Louis, MO
6. **General Motors Corporation**, Detroit, MI
7. **Motorola, Inc.**, Schaumburg, IL
8. **Rockwell International Corp.**, El Segundo, CA
9. **Texas Instruments Inc.**, Dallas, TX
10. **The Boeing Company**, Seattle, WA

MARKETING/SALES—CONSUMER

1. **The Procter & Gamble Company**, Cincinnati, OH
2. **PepsiCo, Inc.**, Purchase, NY
3. **Kraft/General Foods**, Glenview, IL
4. **General Mills, Inc.**, Minneapolis, MN
5. **Philip Morris USA**, New York, NY
6. **American Express Company**, New York, NY
7. **Unilever United States, Inc.**, New York, NY
8. **Bristol-Meyers Squibb Company**, New York, NY
9. **General Electric Company**, Fairfield, CT
10. **Sara Lee Corporation**, Chicago, IL

MARKETING/SALES—INDUSTRIAL

1. **International Business Machines**, Armonk, NY
2. **Xerox Corporation**, Stamford, CT
3. **Hewlett-Packard Company**, Palo Alto, CA
4. **General Electric Company**, Fairfield, CT
5. **Rockwell International Corp.**, El Segundo, CA

MIS/COMPUTER OPERATIONS

1. **International Business Machines**, Armonk, NY
2. **Electronic Data Systems Corp.**, Dallas, TX
3. **Arthur Andersen & Co.**, Chicago, IL
4. **General Motors Corporation**, Detroit, MI
5. **Citibank**, New York, NY
6. **Bankers Trust Co.**, New York, NY
7. **Delta Air Lines Inc.**, Atlanta, GA
8. **American Express Company**, New York, NY
9. **American Airlines, Inc.**, Ft. Worth, TX
10. **Charles Schwab & Co. Inc.**, San Francisco, CA

RESEARCH AND DEVELOPMENT

1. **Merck & Company, Inc.**, Rahway, NJ
2. **International Business Machines**, Armonk, NY
3. **General Electric Company**, Fairfield, CT
4. **Eli Lilly & Co.**, Indianapolis, IN
5. **Xerox Corporation**, Stamford, CT
6. **Monsanto Company**, St. Louis, MO
7. **American Telephone & Telegraph**, New York, NY
8. **The Procter & Gamble Company**, Cincinnati, OH
9. **E.I. duPont de Nemours & Company**, Wilmington, DE
10. **Battelle Memorial Institute**, Columbus, OH

ABOUT THE AUTHOR

John Sibbald, President of John Sibbald Associates, Inc. a Chicago-based executive search firm, has managed over 500 search assignments, both domestic and international, in virtually every industry and in every functional area. Until starting his firm in 1975, he was the Vice President and Partner in charge of the Executive Personnel Division of Booz, Allen & Hamilton in Chicago, and for over three years prior to this he was associated with the same division in Booz, Allen's New York office. Prior to Booz, Allen, Mr. Sibbald was President and Chief Executive Officer of ReCon Systems Corp., a publicly traded computer systems firm. In addition, he has worked for Pfizer, Inc. and Hewitt Associates. He received his B.A. from the University of Nevada and his M.A. from the University of Illinois.